Parties, Interest Groups, and Political Campaigns

Parties, Interest Groups, and Political Campaigns

Matthew J. Burbank
Ronald J. Hrebenar
Robert C. Benedict
University of Utah

Paradigm Publishers
Boulder • London

Published in the United States by Paradigm Publishers,
3360 Mitchell Lane, Suite E, Boulder, CO 80301 USA.

Paradigm Publishers is the trade name of Birkenkamp & Company, LLC,
Dean Birkenkamp, president and publisher.

Library of Congress Cataloging-in-Publication Data
    Burbank, Matthew.
    Parties, interest groups, and political campaigns /
    Matthew J. Burbank, Ronald J. Hrebenar, Robert C. Benedict.
        p.   cm.
    Includes bibliographical references and index.
    ISBN 978-1-59451-319-0 (alk. paper)
    1. Political parties—United States.   2. Pressure groups—United States.
    3. Political campaigns—United States.   I. Hrebenar, Ronald J., 1945–
    II. Benedict, Robert C.   III. Title.
JK2261.H87 2008
324.70973—dc22   2007039535

Printed and bound in the United States of America on acid-free paper that meets the standards of the American National Standard for Permanence of Paper for Printed Library Materials.

11   10   09   08   07 / 1 2 3 4 5

To Mary, Michiko, and Judy

Contents

List of Tables, Figures, and Boxes

Tables

Figures

Boxes

Preface

This book is about political parties, interest groups, and campaigns. Our central theme is the greater interaction of interest groups and political parties in political campaigns of all types. We tried to synthesize materials about the role that parties and interest groups play in American political campaigns. Then we placed our analysis into a historical framework and tried to explain how the once-dominant parties have now joined with interest groups to use modern political campaigning techniques in both candidate- and issue-centered campaigns.

Most college textbooks for the courses we are targeting focus on only one of the three areas we cover. A goal of this text is to provide "one-stop shopping" for both professors and students while at the same time communicating the important trends linking parties, campaigns, and interest groups in the contemporary political arena.

Features of Our Text

- Integrated coverage of political parties, campaigns, and interest groups in a single text— affordably priced and engagingly presented.

- Concise, clear presentation of important topics such as

  - campaign finance laws,

  - the rise of 527 groups,

  - campaign organization and strategy,

  - the presidential nomination process,

  - the workings of the electoral college,

  - political participation and voting behavior,

  - the role of interest groups in advocacy campaigns,

  - the lobbying process,

  - the "K Street strategy,"

  - and the Abramoff lobbying scandal.

- Up-to-date information from the 2004 presidential elections, the 2006 congressional elections, and looking ahead to the 2008 elections.

- A variety of boxed features, tables, figures, and photos adding visual interest.

- A glossary of key terms, highlighted throughout the text and defined in a concise compendium at the end of the text.

Acknowledgments

We wish to thank Jennifer Knerr, the political science editor at Paradigm Publishers, who encouraged us to pursue this book. This book benefited from helpful reviews by Professor Stephen Frantzich and Professor Darrell West, and we extend our thanks to these reviewers for their valuable comments. We also wish to thank Melissa Goldsmith for helpful comments on several chapters, Carrie Humphreys for excellent research assistance, and Lori Hobkirk for her skillful copyediting. This book was jointly written, but the primary responsibility for writing each of the chapters is as follows: Matthew Burbank, Chapters 2, 3, 4, and 5; Robert Benedict, Chapters 6 and 7; and Ronald Hrebenar, Chapters 8, 9, and 10. Chapter 1 and the Conclusion were coauthored by Burbank and Hrebenar.

Matthew J. Burbank
Ronald J. Hrebenar
Robert C. Benedict
Salt Lake City

CHAPTER 1

An Introduction to Parties, Interest Groups, and Campaigns

Political parties, interest groups, and campaigns are an essential feature of contemporary American politics. Political parties were invented in the United States as presidential elections became competitive in the late 1790s, and parties have played a vital role in American politics ever since. As political scientist E. E. Schattschneider claimed, "Modern democracy is unthinkable save in terms of the parties" (1942, 1). In the early decades of the republic, interest groups were subordinated to the much more powerful parties. But as the country grew, the economy became more industrial and the range of government activities gradually expanded; more interest groups developed, and these groups paid more attention to politics. By the end of the nineteenth century, the nation's capital had become a major arena for **lobbying**. However, the real power of "pressure group" politics was on the state level as various lobbies came to dominate state capitals. As one commentator noted, "Standard Oil did everything to the Pennsylvania legislature except refine it" (Thayer 1973, 37). In 1908, political scientist Arthur F. Bentley called interest groups the core unit for understanding politics, and that observation is still true today.

In contemporary American politics, interest groups have so extended their range of activities that they are now challenging political parties in the latter's traditional campaign lair. Campaigns now provide a common arena for both political parties and interest groups. Of course, there have been interest groups in campaigns throughout our political history. The rapid growth of the new Republican party in the 1850s, for example, was largely driven by various abolitionist groups that used the party as a vehicle to pursue their policy goal of ending slavery. Similarly, the great increase in Democratic party power in the 1930s was, in part, a reflection of the increased political power of labor unions and their support of Democratic party campaigns. Although interest groups and political parties have long been key players, the role they have played in the drama of American politics has changed considerably over the past few decades.

Our theme in this book, then, is that as the role of political parties and interest groups in American politics has changed, campaigns have become the modern battleground. Candidates, parties, and interest groups all seek to dominate the media and influence skeptical voters in order to gain a hold on what has become an increasingly volatile issue agenda. We define the concept of campaigns broadly to include both candidate and issue campaigns that occur in one of three arenas—electoral, governmental, or public opinion. The changes that have produced a new style of American political campaigns have, in some ways, changed the nature of our democratic process. Clearly, contemporary American political campaigns, whether designed to elect a candidate to public office or sell a policy preference to the public, have changed along with the relationship between political parties and interest groups. This book explains how political organizations and political processes have come to this point.

The Changing Nature of American Political Campaigns

From the time strong party organizations emerged in the 1840s until the 1950s, political parties were the dominant organizations when it came to elections. While interest groups were certainly present, the major political parties had few rivals in terms of the conduct of political campaigns during this period. Parties began to lose control over electoral politics as party organizations began to weaken in the wake of Progressive-era reforms intended to end the tradition of patronage politics in local, state, and national governments. By the 1950s, there were indications that candidates rather than political parties were becoming central to a new style of campaigning. In the decades that followed, it became clear that presidential candidates could organize and fund their own campaigns using new technologies such as television and mass mailings. In these candidate-centered campaigns, candidates relied on hired political consultants rather than party workers to conduct opinion polls, design advertising strategies, and research issue positions. Candidate image management became the centerpiece of campaigns. Candidates have their images created, maintained, or shifted via the mass media—particularly television. The first successful use of television advertising in a national political campaign occurred in Dwight D. Eisenhower's 1952 presidential campaign. Candidate-centered campaigns were first evident in presidential election contests, but this new style of campaigning gradually spread to elections for

Congress, governors, and even some state and local offices.

Not only did contemporary campaigns become more candidate-centered, they also lasted longer and cost more. Once, presidential general election campaigns were relatively short-lived events, designed to mobilize core groups of party supporters to vote. Two months of active campaigning, from Labor Day to the first week of November, were sufficient to awaken voters and herd them to the polls in most election years. The process of nominating presidential candidates largely occurred within the political parties and with only limited involvement of voters. Thus, there was little need for candidates to launch their campaigns in advance of the presidential nominating conventions. After 1968, however, changes in the presidential nominating process led to an increasing importance of presidential primaries. This change meant that more citizens were involved, but it also meant that the presidential election process started before the first primary elections and lasted until after the general election.

Extended campaigns that relied heavily on media advertising and the use of professional consultants proved to be very expensive. To be competitive, candidates needed to raise enormous amounts of money. The need for larger amounts of money to run campaigns provided the opportunity for the political parties to reinvent themselves, and it provided the opportunity for an array of interest groups to take a more active part in presidential, congressional, and state-level campaigns. The major political parties adapted to the new realities by offering services such as campaign seminars, advice on advertising, and help with fund-raising to their candidates, especially those candidates for offices below the high-profile presidential level. But in order to provide these services, political parties, too, had to raise money. In the 1980s and 1990s, the major political parties became heavily reliant on **soft money**. These soft money contributions were typically large amounts that under federal law could be given to the political parties but not to individual candidates. Soft money contributions were not supposed to be used to support campaign activity, but by the 1996 presidential election it was clear that this restriction had completely broken down. The **Bipartisan Campaign Reform Act of 2002**, often referred to as the "McCain-Feingold" law after its legislative sponsors, prohibited political parties from accepting soft money contributions.

As this new style of campaigning developed, interest groups continued to proliferate in American politics, and these groups found ways to become active participants in political campaigns. For many groups, this meant creating **political action committees (PAC)** to raise money that could then be contributed to candidates. Contributions by PACs have become especially important for congressional candidates because interest groups are keen to help candidates get elected to Congress and then be in a position to influence federal legislation. In addition to the indirect role of using PACs to provide campaign contributions, some interest groups have also become more directly involved by conducting what are called advocacy campaigns. Advocacy campaigns are campaigns conducted by interest groups to influence public opinion on an issue using the same techniques developed to market candidates including opinion polling and advertising. In short, interest groups have become routinely involved in activities ranging from contributing to candidates to conducting their own advertising campaigns in order to influence public opinion. A survey of interest groups found that at the state level, 73 percent of interest groups reported that they had contributed money to candidates, nearly 50 percent indicated that they contributed money to political parties, nearly 50 percent said they had helped to recruit candidates to run for office, and 24 percent indicated that they had done their own issue advertising (Hogan 2005, 897).

The relationship among parties, interest groups, and campaigns is a dynamic one. But, the overlapping activity of political parties

and interest groups in recent campaigns has become especially prominent. The 2004 presidential contest between the incumbent, President George W. Bush, and his challenger, Senator John Kerry, illustrates this point.

Early in the race, the Bush campaign launched a $40 million advertising blitz intended to portray Kerry as a "flip-flopper." Because these ads were being run prior to the Democratic National Convention when Senator Kerry would formally become his party's nominee, the Kerry campaign lacked the resources to answer with its own advertising. A separate organization called the Media Fund, however, responded to the Bush campaign's ads with a $50 million advertising campaign against Bush (Chaddock 2004). The Media Fund was an example of an organization known as a **527 group**, after the section number of the tax code that defines these groups. While formally independent of the Kerry campaign, this organization was created by a longtime Democratic party activist for the purpose of helping John Kerry get elected (Grimaldi and Edsall 2004). The Republican side, too, used 527 organizations to their advantage. Indeed, it was a 527 group called Swift Boat Veterans for Truth that created and aired a series of television ads intended to raise doubts about Kerry's service in Vietnam. In short, not only did the traditional actors—political parties and candidates—attempt to influence voters in the 2004 presidential elections, so did a variety of groups created and funded by outside individuals and interests. Nor were the activities of outside groups limited to advertising. In the 2004 campaign, independent groups were also heavily involved in "get out the vote" efforts that have traditionally been conducted by political parties and candidates.

The changing nature of American political campaigns is illustrated in figure 1.1. This figure shows both the old style, with limited overlap between the activities of parties and interest groups, and the new style of campaigns where there is substantial overlap. As the figure suggests, campaigns are the linkage

FIGURE 1.1 The Old Style and the New Style of Campaign Activities

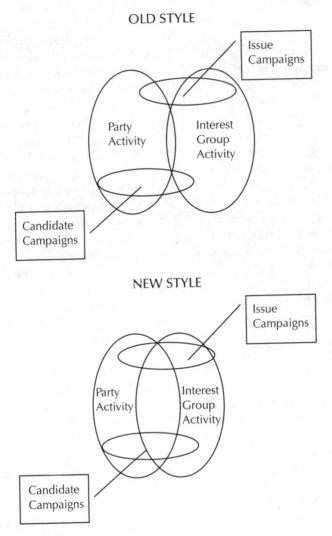

Source: Created by authors.

between political parties and interest groups, and the nature of that linkage has changed. More and more, the activities of parties and interest groups overlap in the various arenas of American politics. Those arenas include the various legislatures from Congress to the councils and commissions in the nation's cities and counties, executives and bureaucracies from the federal government down to the local library special districts, and judicial chambers from the Supreme Court to city or district courts in the fifty states. Increasingly, the thousands of elections that are periodically contested witness the activities of both parties and interest groups. Previously, interest groups were more interested in issue campaigns conducted in initiatives and referenda, but now they are often important participants in party and candidate campaigns.

At one time, parties dominated American political campaigns and government. That is not the case in today's politics and government.

In many places, interest groups are as important, if not more important, than their party rivals. This is the new style of American politics: parties, interest groups, and campaigns.

Returning to the "good old days" when the parties ruled the political scene, or even to the days of candidate-dominated elections, is not a realistic option. We have entered a new political era in which parties and interest groups are both deeply involved in political campaigns. As James Reichley (1996, 12) has concluded,

> We are not going back to the times in the late nineteenth and early twentieth centuries when the major parties were like great popular armies, almost churches, which fought in well-drilled and enthusiastic ranks in each campaign. Other forces—the media, interest groups, citizen watchdog organizations, professional campaign consultants—will continue to rival the parties for influence in our politics.

The Study of Parties, Interest Groups, and Campaigns

This book organizes the study of political organizations and modern campaigns into three main areas. We begin by examining political parties and their role in American politics. Chapter 2 introduces political parties and describes their development over the course of American political history. Chapter 3 discusses the organization of the contemporary political parties from the party activists to the national parties. And Chapter 4 locates the parties within the context of American elections by describing the features of the American electoral system.

In Chapter 5, we begin focusing on campaigns by looking at citizens and the nature of political participation and especially voting in America. Chapter 6 examines contemporary political finance and the problems associated with "political money." Chapter 7 relates how American campaigns have changed and how parties, candidates, and groups have adjusted to the modern realities of campaigning in the information age.

Our focus on interest groups begins in Chapter 8 with an analysis of the internal aspects of interest groups and describes how they relate to the participation of interest groups in political campaigns of all types. Chapter 9 examines the role of interest groups in candidate and advocacy campaigns. The section on interest groups concludes, in Chapter 10, with a discussion of the nature of lobbying in contemporary American politics.

CHAPTER 2

The Development of
Political Parties in America

The history of political parties in the United States is colorful and complex. Over the course of more than two hundred years of American elections, numerous political parties have competed for votes. Some parties, such as the contemporary Democratic and Republican parties, have existed as continuous organizations for extended periods of time. Other parties, such as the Prohibition party or the Socialist party, fielded presidential candidates for years but with little success. Other parties existed for only an election or two, or competed in only a few states.

In this chapter, we focus on changes that have occurred in the major political parties over the course of electoral competition in the United States. As table 2.1 shows, we identify four distinct periods of party organization. American parties have changed over time in response to new political and social conditions. The first parties to emerge in this nation were composed almost entirely of elite national politicians. In organizational terms, political parties were elite caucuses that helped unite politicians and allowed them to advance their common policies. These early parties also became a means for politicians to seek support among the small number of voters in various states. As the electorate grew in the 1820s and 1830s, parties became more organizationally sophisticated in order to mobilize large numbers of voters. The period

of mass party organizations saw the development of elaborate national conventions, party platforms, mass rallies with partisan speakers, and highly effective techniques for mobilizing voters. By the dawn of the twentieth century, however, strong party organizations were under attack. Changing social conditions and Progressive legislation led to a decline in party organization. The existing parties did not disappear, but these newly "reformed" parties had to adapt to the new political rules laid down by state governments. Beginning in the 1950s and 1960s, however, conditions again changed, particularly with the advent of television and political polling. In the present era of "candidate-centered" elections, parties have become organizations dedicated to providing the technology and services that candidates need to get elected. In short, the political parties of today differ from the organizations that existed in the 1940s or the 1890s—their structure and activities having changed to adapt to new political circumstances.

The history of political parties has often been described in terms of **realignment theory** (see box 2.1). Although realignment theory has many strengths, it also has an important weakness: it implicitly assumes that parties have remained essentially the same over the course of American history. Consequently, realignment theory does not provide a clear understanding of the role of political

6

TABLE 2.1 Organizational Change and the Major American Parties

Years	Organization	Major Parties	Defining Elections
1796–1828	Elite caucuses	Federalist Jeffersonian-Republicans	1800, 1824
1830–1900	Mass organizations	Democrats Whigs Republicans	1840, 1860, 1896
1900–1960	Reformed parties	Democrats Republicans	1912, 1932, 1952
1960–present	Service parties	Democrats Republicans	1960, 1968, 1980, 2000

Source: Created by authors.

parties in contemporary electoral politics. As historian Joel H. Silbey states, realignment theory "has not been able to account for what has happened over the past generation of American politics, despite the often frustrating search by scholars to locate the electoral realignment that was due in 1964, 1968, or thereabout" (1991a, 3). Silbey (1991a; 1991b) argues that realignment theory is a viable explanation for electoral change only for the period of American history, roughly 1830 to 1930, in which political parties had the ability to mobilize large numbers of voters. Political scientist David Mayhew goes further, arguing that "the realignment way of thinking adds little or no illumination" and ought to be abandoned as a theoretical "dead end" (2002, 165). Since our purpose in this book is to explain the role of political parties, interest groups, and campaigns in contemporary American politics, we have chosen to emphasize how American political parties have changed over time. We believe that an examination of the partisan and organizational changes that have occurred in the United States will help to provide a more complete understanding of contemporary political parties in American politics.

The First Parties

Ratification of the Constitution and establishment of a new national government created the conditions for the emergence of national political parties in the United States. For the first time, there was a national government that could exercise power apart from the state governments. These new federal institutions transcended the local political groups and notable families, which provided cohesion for politics in the states. Still, there was no rush to organize national political parties after the Constitution was ratified in 1788.

National Politics in an Antiparty Era

Political parties were not formed in the earliest days of the republic because they were regarded as, at worst, an outright threat to the operation of republican government or, at best, a necessary evil (Hofstadter 1969, 16–28). Nearly all the leading figures of the constitutional period regarded political parties as detrimental to the "public good." As practical politicians, these leaders recognized that people have differing interests and opinions.

BOX 2.1 Realignment Theory

Beginning in 1896, the Republican party won seven of the nine presidential elections leading up to 1932. Starting in 1932, the Democrats went on to win the next five presidential elections in a row. Clearly, something changed in 1932. The purpose of realignment theory is to offer an explanation for the periods of stability and change in national electoral competition.

There are two fundamental concepts associated with realignment theory. The first is the concept of a **party system** (Burnham 1970). A party system is a period of time in which there is stable competition between two major political parties. A party system may be a period of relative equality between the major parties, so that election contests are highly competitive. More commonly, however, a party system is characterized as a period in which one party is dominant. Under normal circumstances, the dominant party is expected to win presidential elections and control Congress as well.

The second fundamental concept is **realignment**. Realignment is the process by which party systems change. Political scientist V. O. Key (1955; 1959) described two types of realignment: critical elections and secular realignment. A critical election is a single election that marks the end of an existing party system and the beginning of a new party system. The election of 1932, which ended Republican dominance and ushered in a new period of Democratic dominance, is often identified as a critical election. A true critical election, according to Key (1955), should exhibit a sharp break from past election results and should be durable. In contrast to a critical election, realignment may occur over a series of elections. Change that occurs over a series of elections is called a "secular realignment." Although secular realignments do not show a sharp break with past voting patterns, they result in durable new alignments. The elections between 1856 and 1860, which led to the demise of the Whig party, the split of the Democratic party, and the emergence of the Republican party, are often cited as an example of a secular realignment. A period in which the previously stable alignment of a party system begins to break down but has not been replaced by a new alignment is referred to as "dealignment" (Beck 1979). Thus, an existing party system may change as a result of a critical election or a process of secular realignment; it may also experience dealignment.

Scholars generally agree that realignment theory identifies five distinct party systems with the following approximate dates and major parties:

1. 1796–1816, First Party System: Jeffersonian Republicans and Federalists
2. 1840–1856, Second Party System: Democrats and Whigs
3. 1860–1896, Third Party System: Republicans and Democrats
4. 1896–1932, Fourth Party System: Republicans and Democrats
5. 1932–?, Fifth Party System: Democrats and Republicans

There is a good deal of debate among scholars as to why and how realignment occurs. The conventional view is that a party system reflects the enduring appeal of the dominant political party to a coalition of social groups in the electorate. A realignment, then, comes about when changing political circumstances, such as economic hardship or the emergence of a new political issue, alter the appeal of a party to members of the electorate (Sundquist 1983). The question mark in place of a date at the end of the fifth party system indicates that there is no scholarly consensus on which election, if any, marks the end of that party system. Indeed, much of the dissatisfaction with realignment theory has stemmed from the debate over how to describe electoral politics from the 1960s to the present in terms of party alignments.

A number of scholars have raised serious questions about whether realignment theory offers a convincing explanation for electoral change in the United States (e.g., Ladd 1991; Mayhew 2002; Silbey 1991a). Yet, other scholars continue to use realignment theory and argue that it provides a useful way to think about American electoral politics (Paulson 2000; Rosenof 2003; Stonecash 2006). The debate is far from over, but important questions have been raised about how to best understand both the long-term patterns as well as contemporary electoral politics.

But they believed that political competition based on organized groups—what James Madison called "factions"—would lead to disorder and disharmony. Indeed, one of the strongest justifications for the Constitution was that it created a new government with enough power to solve practical problems but made the exercise of power diffuse enough to discourage dominance by any one group. As Madison wrote in *The Federalist Papers,* no. 10, "Among the numerous advantages promised by a well constructed Union, none deserves to be more accurately developed than its tendency to break and control the violence of faction." Years later, as he prepared to leave the presidency, George Washington warned that the formation of parties "agitates the Community with ill-founded jealousies and false alarms, kindles the animosity of one part against another, foments occasional riot and insurrection." The ideas expressed by Madison and Washington reflected a common antiparty sentiment based on the sense that parties would only make it more difficult to reach agreement on the actions needed to promote the public good.

Early on, political parties were simply not necessary. The conduct of politics at both the state and the national level was largely an elite affair with participation in public office dominated by a few people from powerful families. The number of people eligible to vote was small, as most states limited eligibility to property-owning men. Opportunities for public debate were limited by the difficulty of communication in a predominantly agrarian society. As a result, there was little need for organizations designed to mobilize citizens to vote or to provide a vehicle for politicians to communicate their views to members of the electorate.

Thus, when the Constitution was established, there was little practical need for organized political parties, and a widespread view among leading members of the new government was that organized factions would be harmful. With President Washington in office, it was possible for a short time to operate the new national government without political parties. Yet, ironically, it was a series of disputes over political issues during Washington's administration that led to the formation of the first American political parties.

The Emergence of American Political Parties

The Federalist and Jeffersonian Republican parties came into existence in the late 1790s as a result of policy differences between two members of Washington's administration, Thomas Jefferson and Alexander Hamilton. The debate centered on what role the federal government should play in economic activity (Beeman 1994). Treasury secretary Hamilton pressed for the national government to assume responsibility for paying the debt that individual states had incurred during the Revolutionary War. Later, Hamilton pushed for the creation of a national bank to carry out the economic policies of the central government. Hamilton's plans were opposed by many who had been against the creation of a federal government in the first place, the Anti-Federalists, and even by some political leaders who had supported ratification of the Constitution.

Hamilton's economic policies were opposed from within the Washington administration by Thomas Jefferson. The differences between the two men were exacerbated by their sharply different views over matters of foreign policy. In 1793, as a result of the French Revolution, the new government in France declared war on Great Britain and called upon the United States for assistance. Jefferson, though anxious to keep America out of war, sided with the French. Hamilton, concerned that American merchants would lose valuable trade with Britain, argued that the change in government resulting from the French Revolution made French claims to American assistance invalid. The debate was resolved by President Washington's declaration of American neutrality in the war between France and Britain.

Maintaining a neutral position was not easy, however. Disagreements about American policy arose between supporters of France and supporters of Britain in the United States. Further, a series of disputes arose between the United States and Britain over shipping. These disputes were resolved by a treaty with Britain negotiated by John Jay. The Jay Treaty was ratified by the Senate in the summer of 1795 by a close vote. When the provisions of the Jay Treaty became public, opponents raised highly charged objections to provisions that they regarded as favoring merchants and others with interests in trade with Britain.

Although ratified by the Senate, opponents of the Jay Treaty tried to block implementation of the treaty by voting down funds in the House of Representatives. This effort, led by none other than James Madison, was a key development in the organization of the first American political party. Treaty opponents were narrowly defeated, but the House debate "marked one of the first organized attempts by an opposition group to defeat an important administration proposal" (Hoadley 1986, 137).

The debate over the Jay Treaty was a turning point for several reasons. First, the series of votes in the House related to the question of funding the Jay Treaty showed solid evidence of consistent partisan voting by members of the House (Hoadley 1986, 135–139). Though the divisions were not sufficiently strong to argue that party organization had been established in Congress, they do provide evidence of an emerging opposition to the policies of the president's administration. A second significant development was that after losing in Congress, treaty opponents attempted to make their case among the electorate. Opponents of the Jay Treaty organized a series of mass protest meetings held in towns from Georgia to New Hampshire (Charles 1956, 83). Here, for the first time, was evidence of popularly supported political parties on a national level.

Supporters of the Washington administration's policy were alarmed by the actions of its opponents. Though each group believed that its members were the true supporters of "republican principles," it was increasingly clear that there were marked differences in the domestic and foreign policies of each side. With these policy differences in mind, supporters of the administration promoted the candidacy of John Adams for president and Thomas Pinckney for vice president in the upcoming election in 1796. Through private correspondence, those opposed to the administration's policies supported Thomas Jefferson for president and Aaron Burr for vice president.

Debate over the Jay Treaty and the direction of relations with France and Britain were important matters dividing the two sides. Despite the policy differences, there is little evidence of party organization or party labels being used in the presidential or congressional elections of 1796. Indeed, because the election was conducted according to the original Constitutional provisions, John Adams was elected president by the electoral college and Thomas Jefferson was elected vice president since he had the second highest number of electoral votes, even though Jefferson was Adams's opponent in the election.

Actions taken during President Adams's time in office, including passage of the Alien and Sedition Acts, spurred the creation of party organization. Supporters of Adams, commonly identified by this point as Federalists, won a strong majority in the congressional elections of 1798. By the time of the presidential election of 1800, however, the superior organizational efforts of the Jeffersonian Republicans and divisions among the Federalists resulted in a victory for Thomas Jefferson.

The election of 1800 marked an important milestone in the organizational development of political parties, the selection of candidates by congressional caucus. In 1800, members of Congress organized themselves into competing Republican and Federalist party caucuses to nominate candidates for the presidency. The Federalist members of Congress chose Adams for president and Charles Cotesworth Pinckney for vice president, whereas the Republican caucus nominated Jefferson and Burr. Though none of the candidates actively campaigned for office, preferring to leave such unseemly conduct to their supporters,

there was abundant evidence of strong partisan sentiment. "Electioneering was done by newspaper, pamphlet, and occasional public meetings. . . . Jefferson was accused of being a Jacobin, an atheist, and a French agent; Adams was asserted to be an autocrat and a slavish admirer of the British monarchy" (Morison 1965, 80).

The Republican candidates had a clear majority in the electoral college vote, but the election had to be decided in the House of Representatives because a tie had occurred between Jefferson and Burr. Federalists attempted to take advantage of the circumstance and maneuvered to get Burr, instead of Jefferson, elected president. After a great deal of political wrangling, Jefferson was elected president with Burr as vice president.

With the election of 1800, evidence of party competition had become clear. The Federalist party, associated with leaders such as John Adams and Alexander Hamilton, advocated the broad exercise of federal power to promote commerce and a policy of strong ties with Great Britain, the most important commercial and military nation of the day. The Republican party, led by James Madison and Thomas Jefferson, was wary of Britain, favored maintaining the American alliance with France, and did not favor the use of federal power to promote commerce.

Several important points should be emphasized about the creation of political parties. First, the political parties that developed in the 1790s can best be characterized as **elite caucuses**. The parties did not develop as organizational entities that existed outside of Congress; rather, the parties were predominantly groups of like-minded members of Congress who met to express their views and plan strategy. The true birthplace of the first political parties was Congress (Hoadley 1986). The newly created Jeffersonian Republican party, for example, first endorsed candidates for the presidency and Congress and only later became involved in state elections (Ladd 1970, 81). Indeed, winning national elections was so significant to the early political parties that the Constitution was changed to accommodate this new reality. As the election of 1800 demonstrated, the Constitution's original method of selection, which gave two votes to each elector to cast for two different candidates, was not well suited to the practice of having political parties select candidates for both positions. This difficulty resulted in the Twelfth Amendment, ratified in 1804, which required electors to cast one ballot for president and a second for vice president.

Second, political parties emerged in the United States for essentially pragmatic reasons. The politicians who founded the parties were not consciously seeking to do so. What these politicians wanted was support for their policies. To gain support, they sought to influence voters, win elections, and satisfy diverse group interests; consequently, parties were invented (Chambers 1967, 10). The pragmatic origin of political parties is significant because, as we noted above, the prevailing political views of the day were very much antiparty. Despite the antiparty culture, political parties came into being to promote the policies advocated by contending groups of elites. Ultimately, political parties came to be recognized not just as sources of divisiveness but as vehicles for the expression of contending political views. Accepting the legitimacy of political opposition within the constitutional framework was a significant step in the development of a truly democratic form of government.

Finally, from their origins in Congress, parties became a tool for engaging a broader range of citizens in the debates of national politicians. Leaders such as Madison, Jefferson, and Hamilton sought to organize support for their side by contacting local officials or influential citizens in the various states. One organizational technique of the day was the use of "committees of correspondence." These committees were composed of well-known state leaders who would write to like-minded citizens throughout the state and urge them to hold local meetings (Ladd 1970,

81). Of course, the extent of party organization varied widely from state to state. In Pennsylvania and New York, party organizations flourished, whereas other states did not experience the development of persistent party organizations and had only short-lived periods of party competition.

The Demise of the Federalists

Competition between the first parties lasted for only a short time. If we date the inception of organized parties from the election of 1800, it is clear that the competition is all but over by 1816. Deprived of national office by Jefferson's victory in 1800, the Federalists never regained their pre–1800 electoral strength and soon disappeared from the national political scene (Ladd 1970, 83). A crucial blow to the party's hopes for a comeback occurred when leaders called the Hartford Convention during the War of 1812 to discuss the future of New England. The convention discussed proposals for New England states to secede from the United States. As a result, "a stigma of unpatriotism, from which it never recovered, was attached to the Federalist party" (Morison 1965, 128). The last Federalist to run for the presidency was Rufus King of New York in 1816. King won only three states, and his weak showing further diminished the party's competitiveness.

Why did the Federalists disappear? One explanation is that when the War of 1812 ended, foreign policy ceased to be a strong basis of contention between the parties or in American society generally. Also, because party loyalties and party organization were quite uncertain at the time, it was relatively easy for aspiring politicians to shift to Republican ranks as that party came to dominate the national government. Finally, the various party leaders had no intention of creating parties as independent organizations. Political leaders of the time viewed politics as a duty rather than a profession; thus, there was little commitment to building long-lasting political organizations.

After Jefferson served two terms as president, his close ally James Madison was elected president in 1808 and reelected in 1812. During Madison's term in office, the Jeffersonian Republican party came to dominate national politics. By the time that James Monroe was elected president in 1816, the Republicans encountered no effective opposition. Without an opposing political party, whoever secured the Republican party's nomination in the congressional caucus was assured of winning the presidency. In the congressional caucus, James Monroe of Virginia narrowly defeated William Crawford of Georgia. The period after Monroe's election as president has since been known as the "era of good feelings" in recognition of the decline of partisanship. Still, this period from 1816 to 1824 was marked by the maneuvering of ambitious politicians within the dominant Republican party.

Transition to a New Party System

James Monroe was reelected in 1820 without opposition. Jefferson's party had truly come to dominate national politics. Yet, change was occurring. In particular, a generational shift was under way as leaders from the constitutional period—Washington, Jefferson, Madison, and Monroe—moved away from the political scene. A new generation of political leaders—including Henry Clay, John Calhoun, and Andrew Jackson—were becoming prominent. New political issues also emerged. The Missouri Compromise of 1820 had temporarily removed slavery as a divisive issue, but issues such as protective tariffs, the establishment of a national bank, and the need for internal improvements were hotly debated.

The election of 1824 marked an important transition. The election signaled the end of the "era of good feelings" as rivalry for the presidency intensified. The presidential election of 1824 was contested by four candidates, all Republicans. Competition to become the party's nominee revealed the organizational weakness of the Republican

party and, in particular, the weakness of the congressional caucus as a method for selecting the party's presidential nominee. William H. Crawford from Georgia, Treasury secretary in Monroe's administration, was selected by the congressional caucus as the party's nominee. Unfortunately for Crawford, the caucus was poorly attended. Only 66 of 212 Republican members participated. As a result, other candidates emerged to contest the nomination. Henry Clay, the Speaker of the House, was nominated by his home state legislature in Kentucky. Senator Andrew Jackson from Tennessee was also nominated by his home state legislature. Finally, several state legislatures chose to nominate John Quincy Adams of Massachusetts. John C. Calhoun of South Carolina, Monroe's secretary of war, was unable to garner sufficient support for his presidential aspirations and so consented to be nominated as the party's candidate for vice president.

After the campaign ended and the electoral votes were counted, however, no candidate had the necessary majority of 132 electoral votes. Andrew Jackson was the leading candidate with 99 electoral votes, but John Quincy Adams had 84, William Crawford had 41, and Henry Clay had 37. Because there was no majority in the electoral college, the House of Representatives decided the election. In the House, each state got one vote as stipulated in the Constitution. After striking a deal with Clay for the votes of his supporters, John Quincy Adams was elected president by the House on the first ballot, receiving the votes of thirteen out of the twenty-four states. Once sworn in as president, Adams named Clay to be his secretary of state.

Supporters of Andrew Jackson were outraged at having been outmaneuvered, and they denounced the deal between Adams and Clay as a "corrupt bargain." Jackson's supporters immediately began planning for the next election. The coalition of Jackson's supporters had little in common except their hope for a Jackson victory. Martin Van Buren led the remnants of the Crawford forces into

Jackson's camp, joining Vice President Calhoun and other politicians. Thus, as the election of 1828 approached, there was still only one dominant party, the Republicans, but two very clear factions: the Jackson-Calhoun coalition, strongest in the western and southern states, and the Adams-Clay supporters, who were strongest in New England.

The Mass Party Era

Though Andrew Jackson was defeated in his bid to be president in 1824, it was hardly the end of his political career. Indeed, the three presidential elections of 1824, 1828, and 1832 were largely defined in terms of support for (or opposition to) Andrew Jackson (Shade 1994, 48). Political parties as independent organizations with strong support in the popular electorate did not become fully evident until 1840. Still, the roots of these new political organizations were set in the Jacksonian period. In partisan terms, the key events of this period were the transformation of the party of Jefferson into the party of Jackson and the emergence of a new opposition party. In organizational terms, the key events were the demise of caucus-based parties and the growth of a mass electorate.

The Expanding Electorate and the Arrival of New Parties

The election of 1828 was the first since 1800 in which the leading candidate was not nominated by congressional caucus. Jackson was nominated by state legislatures, local mass meetings, and state conventions. In the election of 1828, Jackson won 56 percent of the popular vote and 178 electoral votes to defeat the incumbent, President John Quincy Adams.

The campaign between Adams and Jackson was not a high-minded debate featuring opposing philosophies of government. Rather, it was highly personal and negative, with supporters of Jackson charging President Adams with corruption and, in return, Adams's supporters raising questions about Jackson's personal conduct. More importantly, however, the 1828 campaign was perhaps the first truly popular presidential campaign. The campaign featured parades, speeches at mass meetings, and other public demonstrations of support to involve citizens in the process. As table 2.2 shows, between 1824 and 1828 there was a substantial increase in both the number of citizens casting ballots and the turnout rate; the number of voters participating in 1828 was more than triple the size of the active electorate in 1824.

As president, Jackson rewarded his supporters through patronage politics—the "spoils systems." Rewarding supporters with material benefits such as government jobs or government business was hardly new in American politics. Still, as historian Samuel Eliot Morison (1965, 165) put it,

> It is a fair statement that Jackson introduced the spoils system into the federal government, and that he never regretted it. His theory, stated in his first annual message, was that "the duties of all public offices" were so "plain and simple" that any man of average intelligence was qualified; and that more would be lost by continuing men in office than could be gained by experience.

During Jackson's first term in office, however, a key element of his coalition was altered when Jackson had a falling out with Vice President John Calhoun over personal and political differences. Martin Van Buren of New York, a supporter of Jackson's since the election of 1824, became the president's heir apparent. The election of 1832 thus featured Jackson running for reelection with Martin Van Buren as his vice-presidential candidate. The remnants of the old Adams-Clay faction, using the name National Republicans, nominated Henry Clay and John Sargeant. The election also included a prominent third party, the Anti-Masons, who ran William Wirt and Amos Ellmaker.

TABLE 2.2 Growth of the National Electorate: Votes and Turnout in Presidential Elections, 1824–1860

Election	Number of States	Total Votes Cast	Turnout (percent)
1824	18	365,833	26.7
1828	22	1,148,018	57.3
1832	23	1,293,973	56.7
1836	25	1,503,534	56.5
1840	25	2,411,808	80.3
1844	25	2,703,659	79.0
1848	29	2,879,184	72.8
1852	30	3,161,830	69.5
1856	30	4,054,647	79.4
1860	32	4,685,561	81.8

Sources: Total votes are from Congressional Quarterly (1985) and the estimates of percentage turnout are from Burnham (1987, 113).

The election of 1832 marked two important milestones in party organization. The first was the use of party conventions to nominate presidential candidates. The National Republicans used a convention to nominate Clay and Sargeant, as did the supporters of Jackson, who met in Baltimore to endorse Jackson and nominate Van Buren for vice president. But the first national party convention, held in 1831, was organized by the Anti-Masonic party.

The Anti-Masonic party itself was the second milestone. Not only was it the first significant third party in a presidential election, it was also the first "extra-legislative" party to nominate a presidential candidate. That is, the Anti-Masons were not organized around a congressional or an administrative faction but represented the views of ordinary citizens, in this case, citizens who were opposed to secret societies, such as the Masons. Although the Anti-Masonic party did not last long as a political force, the party is notable for its origins and its ability to nominate and run a presidential candidate.

Andrew Jackson was reelected in 1832 by a sizable margin. His second term, however, was filled with difficulties. Jackson's activities as president had created a diverse group of political opponents, who by 1834 were referring to themselves as "Whigs." The name was chosen because the Whigs had been the party of opposition to royal government during the American Revolution. It was intended to remind people of the highhanded ways of "King Andrew," as opponents called Jackson.

Though united in their opposition to Jackson's administration, the Whigs could not unite behind a single presidential candidate, in part because of the rudimentary nature of their party organization. In 1836, the Whigs ran three regional candidates: William Henry Harrison, who competed in fifteen states; Hugh Lawson White, who was the Whig candidate in many southern states; and Daniel Webster, who ran in his home state of Massachusetts. Martin Van Buren, Jackson's chosen successor, ran against these various regional candidates using "Democratic Republican" as his party label.

Van Buren won the election, but the Whigs had reason to be encouraged. The three Whig candidates, combined, received roughly 738,000 votes (49 percent) to 764,000 for Van Buren (51 percent). The Whigs also demonstrated an ability to compete in the southern states, which Andrew Jackson had previously dominated completely. Though the Whigs proved to be capable of attracting votes, the election of 1836 was not a simple contest between two political parties. No fewer than five presidential candidates and eight different tickets received votes in the electoral college balloting (Shade 1994, 45). And, for the only time in American history, the Senate was required to select the vice president in accordance with the Twelfth Amendment because no candidate had a majority of electoral votes. The Senate elected the Democratic Republican candidate, Richard Mentor Johnson.

Whigs Versus Democrats

The four presidential elections between 1840 and 1852 featured competition between two clearly defined and well-organized parties, the Whigs and the Democrats. Prior to 1840, candidates had competed under a variety of labels, and party organization was often rudimentary. After 1840, the parties consistently held national conventions to nominate candidates and began to write platforms, a mark of the increasing organizational sophistication of the political parties.

The election of 1840 was marked by an intense campaign that attracted enormous popular attention. As table 2.2 shows, nearly 2.5 million citizens voted in 1840, and the turnout rate was 80 percent. President Van Buren was nominated for reelection by his party, now calling itself the Democratic party. The Democrats drew up a detailed platform but could not agree on a vice-presidential candidate and so left that choice to the electors from each state. The Whig party held a convention in 1839 and nominated William Henry Harrison of Ohio, a folk hero from his military exploits at the Battle of Tippecanoe in 1811, and John Tyler of Virginia. The campaign of 1840 was long on symbolism and short on substance, exemplified by the Whig campaign slogan, "Tippecanoe and Tyler too!" The Whigs attempted to capitalize on Harrison's status as a war hero and contrasted Harrison's image as a plainspoken farmer with the allegedly aristocratic manners of Martin Van Buren. Historian Samuel Eliot Morison (1965, 200) summed up the election as follows:

> The reason why the 1840 campaign became the jolliest and most idiotic presidential contest in our history is that the Whigs beat the Democrats by their own methods. They adopted no platform, nominated a military hero, ignored real issues, and appealed to the emotions rather than the brains of voters. Expectations of profit

and patronage were employed to "get out the vote," and the people were given a big show.

Harrison defeated Van Buren but died after only a month in office and was replaced by the vice president, John Tyler. The Whig party also won control of Congress in 1840. Henry Clay, who had been passed over by the Whigs for the party's presidential nomination, served as leader of the Whigs in Congress. Tyler and Clay, both seeking to lead the Whig party, were soon at odds over the issue of reestablishing the Bank of the United States, and the first Whig administration ended in disarray.

Disputes within the Whig party helped the Democrats regain the presidency in 1844. The Democrats nominated James Polk, while the Whigs chose Henry Clay to carry their presidential standard. The election of 1844 featured a third party challenge from the Liberty party, an antislavery party that had grown out of the abolitionist movement. Though it won about 2 percent of the vote nationally, the Liberty party split the Whig vote in New York and helped Polk and the Democratic party carry New York's thirty-six electoral votes (Rosenstone, Behr, and Lazarus 1996, 50).

In 1848 the Whigs recaptured the White House by again nominating a military hero, Zachary Taylor. The Democrats chose Senator Lewis Cass from Michigan as their presidential candidate. Unfortunately for the Democrats, Cass's moderate position on the question of extending slavery into new territories satisfied neither the southern branch of the party nor the more antislavery elements of the northern party. In fact, some northern Democrats, especially a group of New Yorkers known as "Barnburners," backed the candidate of a new third party, the Free Soil party. The Free Soil party opposed the extension of slavery into the territory recently acquired from Mexico and chose as its candidate Martin Van Buren, the former president. Ultimately Taylor won the election but died after a brief time in office and was replaced by Vice President Millard Fillmore. Democrats regained the presidency in 1852, when Franklin Pierce defeated Whig candidate Winfield Scott. The remnants of the Free Soil party again contested the presidency in 1852, but the party was not as important as it had been in 1848.

The election of 1852 was the last to feature a contest between Whigs and Democrats. The collapse of the Whig party was due, in large part, to the nature of its electoral coalition. The Whigs were a truly national party that relied on the joint appeal of economic progressivism and social conservatism (Reichley 1992, 97–102). The political issues surrounding the question of slavery caused enormous disruption throughout American politics during the 1840s and 1850s. The reemergence of slavery as a political issue led to the demise of the Whigs as an organized party. The slavery issue also split the Democratic party into northern and southern wings, and it ultimately created the conditions for a new political party, the Republicans.

Both Whig and Democratic parties foundered on the issue of slavery. Yet, in terms of party organization, the changes that occurred during the 1840s were remarkable. By 1850, party organizations had greatly surpassed the rudimentary parties of the 1820s and had, indeed, become mass party organizations. Unlike the parties of the 1820s, the parties of the 1850s were truly national in scope. After 1840, "the nature of the presidential contest changed from one rooted in cohesive state interests to one structured by national parties that penetrated into the states" (Shade 1994, 49). The pursuit of national appeal led the major parties to "balance" their presidential and vice-presidential candidates in an effort to maximize their appeal to different parts of the nation. More importantly, party organizations of the 1850s were much more institutionalized than earlier parties. Party conventions, those national meetings of party supporters to nominate a presidential ticket, had become established

and the parties regularly issued platforms spelling out their positions. Finally, by the middle of the nineteenth century American political parties had become the primary connection between average citizens and government. As table 2.2 shows, the size of the eligible electorate had grown substantially, at least for white males, and parties were the vehicles for getting out the vote as well as rewarding supporters with the tangible benefits of office.

The Civil War and the Rise of the Republicans

The collapse of the Whig party and the split of the Democratic party in 1860 created an opportunity for a new political party. The Republican party, however, did not simply replace the Whigs (Gienapp 1987). In the early 1850s, the political party that seemed poised to take over from the Whigs was the American party. The American party grew out of an anti-immigrant and anti-Catholic movement organized into secret societies called the "Know-Nothings" because of members' pledges to say that they knew nothing of such organizations (Reichley 1992, 108–110). After Democrat Franklin Pierce was elected in 1852, the Know-Nothings began to organize politically and nominated candidates to run under the American party label. In 1854, the American party swept state elections in Massachusetts, winning the governorship and dominating the state legislature. The next year, the party won control of state legislatures in three New England states as well as Maryland and Kentucky.

By the mid–1850s, the American party appeared poised to become the next major political party. But then it, too, foundered on the slavery issue. In 1856, the American party's national convention ended in disarray due to differences between northern and southern delegates over the Kansas-Nebraska Act. The Kansas-Nebraska Act was legislation passed in May 1854 by Democrats in Congress that effectively repealed the

Compromise of 1820, banning slavery in northern territories. The American party adopted a platform supporting the Kansas-Nebraska Act and thus supporting slavery in the eyes of northern delegates, who promptly left the convention. The convention nominated former president Millard Fillmore as its candidate for president. While accepting the nomination, Fillmore disavowed the anti-Catholic views of the party. Thus, with Fillmore as the American party candidate and with an apparent proslavery plank in its platform, northern voters who were either anti-Catholic or antislavery had little reason to support the party.

Passage of the Kansas-Nebraska Act was also instrumental in the creation of the Republican party. Meetings were held in many cities and towns throughout the North in 1854 to oppose any action by Congress that allowed the expansion of slavery. At one such meeting held in Ripon, Wisconsin, participants called for the fusion of former Whigs, antislavery Democrats, supporters of the old Free Soil party, and dissatisfied Know-Nothings into a new Republican party. This new party struggled initially to compete against the American party for support in northern states (Gienapp 1987). American party candidates stressed the issues of temperance, anti-immigration, and anti-Catholicism, whereas the Republican party increasingly became defined by its opposition to the extension of slavery.

In 1856, the Republican party nominated celebrated western explorer John C. Frémont for president. The election of 1856 featured a three-way race between Frémont, Democrat James Buchanan, and American party candidate Millard Fillmore. Though Buchanan won the election narrowly, the Republican candidate did remarkably well, winning 33 percent of the national vote despite having no support in southern states. Perhaps most importantly, Frémont finished ahead of both Buchanan and Fillmore in most northern states, thus establishing the Republican party rather than the American party as the Demo-

crats' chief rival. "Defeating the Know-Nothings to become the dominant opposition party was the most important victory that the Republican party would ever win in its long and storied history" (Gienapp 1994, 72).

The election of 1860 confirmed the Republicans as the dominant party in the North and led to the splintering of the Democrats. The election was contested by four candidates: Abraham Lincoln of Illinois, the Republican candidate; Senator Steven A. Douglas of Illinois, Lincoln's old nemesis and the candidate of northern Democrats; Vice President John Breckinridge of Kentucky, the candidate of southern Democrats; and Senator John Bell of Tennessee, the nominee of the Constitutional Union party. Yet in most states, the contest boiled down to a two-party fight: Lincoln versus Douglas in the North and Bell versus Breckinridge in the South. The election attracted considerable popular attention and voter turnout rose to 82 percent.

While remaining an antislavery party, the Republicans added several economic issues to their campaign platform—such as support for western homesteading and a protective tariff—to attract a broader base of votes. Republican efforts paid off. Lincoln carried all of the free states of the North and West except New Jersey, whose electors were split between Lincoln and Douglas. Bell won Kentucky, Virginia, and Tennessee, while Douglas carried only Missouri and part of New Jersey. Breckinridge won nine states in the Deep South plus the border states of Maryland and Delaware. In electoral votes, Lincoln had 180, Breckinridge, 72, Bell, 39, and Douglas, 12. After 1860, the Republicans clearly replaced the Whigs and the American party in the northern states and became the dominant national party, since the Democratic party was divided into northern and southern wings.

Shortly after the election, several southern states left the Union and the Civil War began. In the North, many Democrats supported the war and took the name "War Democrats." Other Democrats, who became known as

"Copperheads," opposed the war and provided opposition to the Lincoln administration. Some scholars have argued that the beneficial effects of a functioning two-party system were a factor in the Union victory (McKitrick 1967). Strong political opposition forced the Lincoln administration to maintain party unity and seek support from others when possible. The Confederate government, on the other hand, was without a party system and thus had no outlet for organized opposition. The greatest source of opposition to Lincoln's war effort, however, came from within his own party. "Radical Republicans" in Congress wanted greater congressional guidance of the war effort, emancipation of the slaves, and political reconstruction of the South after the war.

In an attempt to reduce the influence of the Radical Republicans, Lincoln resorted to coalition politics and broadened the Republican party to include War Democrats. First in Ohio and later in other states, the new Republican party became the Union party. Although some Radical Republicans would have preferred another candidate in 1864, the Union party nominated Lincoln for reelection. Lincoln defeated George B. McClellan, the War Democrats' nominee and a former general in the Union Army.

Following the end of the war and the assassination of Lincoln, Vice President Andrew Johnson, a War Democrat, took over as president. As efforts to reintegrate the southern states into the Union progressed, Johnson and congressional Republicans crossed swords. In 1868, congressional Republicans had Johnson impeached by the House of Representatives and very nearly convicted in the Senate.

As the southern states reentered the Union, Democrats resumed the role of the main opposition party. In the summer of 1868, the Democratic party attempted to restore some of its political vitality by nominating Horatio Seymour, a moderately conservative governor of New York, as its candidate for president. The Republican party sought to overcome its own internal fissures by nominating a war

hero, Ulysses S. Grant, as its presidential candidate. Grant swept the election, winning most of the northern states and seven reconstructed southern states for a total of 214 electoral votes to 80 for Seymour. Grant's first administration was beset by difficulties, including opposition to his renomination from within his own party. Still, Grant was popular with voters, and he won reelection easily in 1872.

Despite the disruptions of the Civil War, the parties remained robust organizations. In large part, the need for strong organization was spurred by close competition between Republicans and Democrats from the mid–1870s to the 1890s. Republicans had a strong base of support in the North and Midwest and strong ties to business. Democrats moved to regain control of the southern states, with the easing of federal intervention, and continued to do well in many northern cities. The partisan balance of the period extended to both Congress and the presidency. In the five presidential elections between 1876 and 1892, Republicans won three. One of those Republican victories was the controversial election of 1876, when Republican Rutherford Hayes defeated Democrat Samuel Tilden in the electoral college, even though Tilden had more popular votes. Democrats managed to win the presidency in 1884 and 1892 with Grover Cleveland, former governor of New York and a strong supporter of business, as their candidate.

Party Machines

In the years following the Civil War, party organization reached its zenith in the political "machines" that dominated many American cities in the late nineteenth and early twentieth centuries. Party loyalty and concern with organization helped boost voter turnout to around 80 percent. As millions of people immigrated to the cities, mostly from European nations, they were quickly enrolled in the voting "armies" of the two parties.

Party machines existed primarily, though not exclusively, in urban locations with large populations of working people. As political scientist William Crotty (1994, 134–135) notes, party machines operated in a straightforward fashion:

> The machine and its leaders wanted political power. Political power led to personal wealth. To gain power, the machine needed to control public office by determining who the candidates were and by assuring them a loyal and predictable vote in elections. In return, the quid pro quo was that the machine provided services and tangible, material rewards on a personal basis for those who supported it.

Both Republican and Democratic party machines existed, although the Democratic party often had more appeal among urban immigrants because Republican leaders often supported political positions regarded as anti-immigrant, such as prohibition or English language laws (Reichley 1992, 141–143). Party machines were not, however, ideological in nature. They were fundamentally pragmatic organizations; their chief concern was to gain control of local government as a source of patronage and money.

One of the first and most enduring machines was Tammany Hall, established in New York City in 1787 (Allen 1993; Mushkat 1971). At the outset, Tammany was a nonpartisan benevolent society that entered politics to promote the presidential candidacy of Thomas Jefferson. Later, Tammany was run by William Marcy Tweed and the Tweed Ring. "Boss" Tweed used the Tammany organization to make money. "Under Tweed, Tammany changed from an organization primarily dedicated to winning elections to one brazenly employed for wholesale thievery" (Allen 1993, 81). After Tweed was jailed for corruption, "Honest John" Kelly took over the leadership of Tammany and turned it into an efficient vote mobilizer. "Kelly, it was said, 'found Tammany a horde and left it a political army'" (Reichley 1992, 143).

The financial (and at times political) corruption associated with machine politics undermined democracy in some cities to the point that elections became meaningless. If supporters of the party machine felt it was necessary to maintain control, they would have party workers stuff ballot boxes, hire "repeaters" to travel from poll to poll voting for the machine's candidates, or simply terrorize their opponents. Yet party machines also provided benefits by helping to acculturate immigrants and, in the days before the welfare state, provided working people with jobs and other tangible goods. As a result, party machines "fostered support for the governing system among the poor and the recently arrived by presenting a benign and supportive face to government bureaucracy" (Crotty 1994, 137).

Given their preoccupation with control of local government, the urban political machines were important to national parties primarily because they could supply votes for national candidates. Party machines existed in many cities across the United States from Boston, New York, and Philadelphia in the East to Cincinnati and Chicago in the Midwest to San Francisco in the West. Each organization was rooted in local politics and adapted to local conditions. Although some organizations, such as the Daley machine in Chicago, prospered into the 1950s and 1960s, for the most part the heyday of urban party machines occurred in the decades following the Civil War, years of unprecedented growth for American cities.

The Reform of Political Parties

The rise of party machines was tied to economic, social, and political conditions in a rapidly urbanizing nation. Conditions that helped create strong urban parties influenced national politics as well. America changed in the decades following the Civil War as it was transformed from an agricultural nation into an industrialized one.

A negative consequence of these changes was the feeling some Americans had that they and their communities no longer controlled their own fate. Farmers depended on commodities prices set in the world market; the speculations of financiers and wealthy industrialists affected economic conditions throughout the nation. Increasingly, the leaders of both major parties represented the views of leaders of business and industry and not of laborers or debtors. This situation bred frustration and tension, and when the first major industrial depression hit, the party system could no longer function as it had in preindustrial days.

Populism and the Decline of the Democrats

As America became more industrial and urban, farmers in the Midwest, South, and West lost much of the political influence they had traditionally enjoyed in a predominantly agricultural nation. Many farmers, believing that their interests were being ignored by both Democrats and Republicans, formed organizations dedicated to representing the interests of farmers. Between 1870 and 1896, a number of organizations emerged and experienced varying degrees of political success. For example, in 1873 the Granger movement had thousands of local Granges but by 1876 had come to an end politically. One political party, the Greenbacks, advocated printing paper money not backed by metal currency as a response to the economic problems of the day. The Greenbacks had close ties to the Granger movement and ran presidential candidates in 1876, 1880, and 1884. It was, however, the People's party, generally known as the Populists, that most directly threatened the continued dominance of the two major parties. In 1892, Populist candidate James Weaver received more than 8 percent of the national vote, won twenty-

two electoral votes, and carried the farming states of Kansas, Colorado, Idaho, North Dakota, and Nevada.

By the early 1890s, Democrats had restored themselves to prosperity in national politics. The Democrats won control of Congress and captured the White House with Grover Cleveland in 1892. Cleveland was a probusiness Democrat who was as conservative on economic questions as any Republican. Unfortunately for Democrats, even as President Cleveland was taking office in 1873, the economy was slipping into a financial "panic." Banks failed, businesses went bankrupt, industrial production slowed, and thousands of workers became unemployed.

Rather than adopt policy proposals favored by Populists and some Democrats—issuing currency backed by silver—President Cleveland worked hard to ensure the stability of the gold standard. Cleveland exercised his power over federal patronage as a way to encourage Congress to repeal laws promoting paper or silver-backed money. Cleveland also attempted, with less success, to reduce the rates of the Republican-supported tariff. The nation's economic difficulties were compounded by a wave of industrial strikes that stemmed, in part, from workers reacting to layoffs or wage cuts. Though pleasing to large businesses and the financial sector, Cleveland's policies did little to help farmers, small businesses, organized labor, or people looking for work, thus "fixing indelibly in the minds of many voters an association between the Democratic party and economic hard times that was to last for more than 30 years" (Reichley 1992, 167).

In the midterm elections of 1894, Republicans regained control of both houses of Congress. Democrats' poor showing in the midterm elections put them in a difficult position for the upcoming presidential election of 1896. Clearly, no Democratic candidate associated with President Cleveland would be in a strong position.

Blaming their political troubles on the "hard money" policies adopted by the

Cleveland administration, many Democrats supported a "free silver" plank in the party's platform. At the Democratic convention in the summer of 1896, the party selected William Jennings Bryan, a former member of the House of Representatives from Nebraska, as its presidential candidate. Bryan was a gifted speaker and evangelical Christian who won the nomination largely on the strength of his speech to the convention. Bryan closed his speech, favoring the "free silver" position, by evoking a brilliant rhetorical image: "We shall answer their demands for a gold standard by saying to them, you shall not press down upon the brow of labor this crown of thorns. You shall not crucify mankind upon a cross of gold."

Bryan's "Cross of Gold" speech secured the Democratic nomination and placed the Democratic party on the side of farmers and advocates of silver currency and against big business, the banks, and other supporters of the gold standard. The Populist party convention, meeting shortly after the Democrats, also chose Bryan as its presidential candidate. Bryan's presidential campaign was an attempt to bring together a coalition of evangelic Protestants and people from the predominantly rural western and southern states. Although Bryan made some efforts to attract urban working-class voters, he attacked not only big business and big money but big cities as well.

Republicans chose William McKinley, a former Congressman and governor of Ohio, as their presidential candidate. Under the direction of businessman Marcus Hanna, the Republicans ran an efficient campaign financed by the very businesses that Bryan attacked. The keys to the election, however, were that Republicans were successful in getting urban workers to identify their interests with the Republican party and that Bryan was largely unsuccessful in his appeal to Protestant voters of the North and Midwest (Kleppner 1987, 59–89). As James Sundquist(1983, 164) has noted, "Bryan's campaign polarized sentiment on what, for his purposes, was the wrong basis. He did not set class against class; he set rural against urban. When in his Cross of Gold speech he spoke of 'your cities' and 'our farms,' he cast out of his circle not just urban capital but urban labor too." Republicans appealed to urban workers by supporting an industrial tariff as a way to save jobs. Republicans also opposed silver currency and pointed out to urban workers that it would mean less money in their pockets if they were paid in inflated dollars.

McKinley won the election with 51 percent of the national vote, carrying all the large industrial states of the Northeast and Midwest plus California and Oregon. Bryan swept the southern states and won most of the sparsely populated western states but received only 176 electoral votes to McKinley's 271. The electoral coalition of business and northern urban workers that the Republicans established in 1896 proved to be quite durable. Republicans went on to win every presidential election from 1896 through 1928 with the exception of two, 1912 and 1916. Bryan ran twice more as a Democrat in 1900 and 1908, but he was defeated soundly by McKinley in 1900 and by William Howard Taft in 1908.

The election of 1896 was the end of the Populists as an electoral force. As the economy gradually recovered during McKinley's administration, the appeal of the Populist message diminished. Although a Populist candidate for president ran in the next three elections, the party got less than 1 percent of the national vote in each.

The Influence of the Progressives

During the first decade of the twentieth century, a new wave of reform demands swept the nation. The Progressive movement, as it was known, did not result from a single cause or seek a united goal; rather, it grew from a diverse set of roots (Reichley 1992, 186–193). Common among Progressives was a desire to improve the process of government. Progressives espoused many reforms that would eventually have an impact on the party system, including voter registration and ballot reform, referendum and citizen initiative, direct primaries, recall elections, nonpartisan elections, stronger civil service regulations to limit patronage, and expansion of the electorate particularly for women. In general, Progressive reformers were hostile to political bosses and the party machines that had come to dominate many city and state governments. Many of the reforms initiated during the Progressive era were intended to weaken party organizations.

Despite the antiparty tone, Republican leaders were able to adapt to many Progressive demands, and Theodore Roosevelt became identified as one of the Progressive leaders. Roosevelt was McKinley's vice president in 1900 and became president after McKinley was assassinated in 1901. Roosevelt went on to a sweeping victory in 1904, winning every state except the eleven states of the old Confederacy and the border states of Kentucky and Maryland.

The conservatism of William Howard Taft, Theodore Roosevelt's successor, left many Progressives feeling betrayed. After being denied the 1912 Republican nomination, Roosevelt formed a third party, the Progressive or "Bull Moose" party. Split into two camps, regular Republicans and Progressives, the Republican majority lost the presidency to Democrat Woodrow Wilson in 1912. Wilson won again in 1916 over Republican Charles Evans Hughes in an extremely close contest. The Bull Moose ticket polled enough votes in 1912 to put the regular Republican party into third place, but most of Roosevelt's supporters rejoined the Republican ranks after 1912. The Progressive party also ran a popular candidate, Robert LaFollette, in 1924. Although LaFollette got only 16.5 percent of the national vote, he carried his home state of Wisconsin and finished a strong second to Republican Calvin Coolidge in a number of northern and western states.

Whether as a separate party or a faction within existing parties, Progressives constituted an important political force. They were successful because they were able to get many of their reforms adopted by politicians in the major parties, even though they often worked against the interests of the party organizations. In short, Progressives were able to use the popular appeal of their proposals to implement change.

The Creation of the New Deal Coalition

Republican domination of the White House was restored in 1920. Though Republicans had a dominant coalition, party support was highly sectionalized: the South was solidly Democratic, whereas the Northeast and the Midwest were solidly Republican. Urban voters and rural Republicans continued to provide Republican majorities for Harding, Coolidge, and Hoover in 1920, 1924, and 1928. Indeed, in 1928, Republican Herbert Hoover won 58 percent of the popular vote and 444 electoral votes to Democrat Alfred Smith's 40 percent and 87 electoral votes.

When city voters shifted to the Republican side in 1896, it helped ensure almost solid Republican victories through 1928. But the shifting loyalties of urban voters in the North once again proved decisive in 1932. Actually, the loyalties of urban voters were in flux throughout the 1920s and began to shift toward the Democratic party during the 1928 candidacy of Alfred Smith (Key 1955). As governor of New York, Smith had become a spokesman for urban immigrants and their families and attracted a new class of voters to the Democratic party. Republicans began to lose their urban base early in the 1920s and reached rock bottom in 1936 with Roosevelt's second-term landslide.

The presidential election of 1932 marked a monumental shift in the political fortunes of the two major parties. In 1928 Republican Herbert Hoover carried all but eight states, six of which were in the South. By 1932, Hoover carried only six states; Democrat Franklin

Roosevelt won all the other states and amassed 472 out of 531 electoral votes. The shift to the Democrats in 1932 followed an economic crisis of unprecedented magnitude—the collapse of the stock market in 1929 followed by the Depression—resulting in high levels of unemployment and economic dislocation. The Hoover administration's response, in keeping with orthodox economic views of the day, was to keep the federal government's budget in balance and to let the business cycle run its course. Much as the panic of 1893 had earned the Democrats the label of the party of hard times, the economic collapse of the early 1930s had the same effect for Republicans.

Research on the voting patterns of the 1930s suggests that some of the Democratic gains came as a result of Republicans who converted to the Democratic party (Erikson and Tedin 1981; Sundquist 1983, 229–239). Other scholars, however, point out that millions of young people, many from immigrant families, reached voting age between 1924 and 1932 and argue that it was these new voters who flocked to the Democratic party in the early 1930s and helped to establish a new period of Democratic dominance (Anderson 1979). Whether through the conversion of previously Republican voters or through the mobilization of a new generation of voters, the political response to the trauma of the Depression created a preference for the Democratic party that was to last for many years.

Having campaigned on the rather vague promise of a "new deal," once in office Roosevelt moved quickly to use the powers of the federal government to tackle the country's economic problems. Although parts of Roosevelt's New Deal program would be declared unconstitutional by the Supreme Court and its effectiveness was uncertain, Roosevelt's actions were clearly endorsed by the electorate. Democrats won a huge majority of seats in both the House and the Senate in 1932 and increased those majorities in 1934. Following Roosevelt's win in 1932, the New Deal coalition was composed primarily of the solidly Democratic states of the Deep South and Border South, the Rocky Mountain states of the West, and working-class voters of the large northern cities. Roosevelt went on to win elections in 1936, 1940, and 1944; in each election Roosevelt got a clear majority of the popular vote and won more than four hundred electoral votes.

Although retaining its minority status, the Republican party improved its prospects in the latter years of the New Deal period. Democratic strength in Congress declined in 1938 and 1940. In 1942, Republicans won half of the nation's governorships, including New York and California. Republican performance in the 1940 and 1944 presidential elections showed some improvement over 1936, when Republican Alfred Landon of Kansas lost in a landslide. Landon carried only two states, Maine and Vermont. But in 1940, Wendell Wilkie carried ten states and by 1944 Thomas Dewey carried twelve states. The improvement in Republican electoral fortunes stemmed from increasing dissatisfaction with the Democrats, but Republicans had also taken steps in the "out" years to improve their party's organization. For example, in 1936 the Republicans named their party's general counsel, John Hamilton, full-time party chairman, the first time either party had a paid party chairman (Goldman 1990, 401).

Republicans were thus looking forward to campaigning against President Harry Truman in the 1948 election after four straight defeats at the hands of Franklin Roosevelt. Truman, the former senator from Missouri who was added to the Democratic ticket in 1944, became president in 1945 after Roosevelt's death. By 1948, Truman faced considerable opposition within the Democratic party as well as from Republicans. After a convention fight over a civil rights plank in the party's platform, anti-Truman southerners walked out of the convention. Southern "States' Rights" Democrats, commonly called "Dixiecrats," backed South Carolina governor Strom Thurmond as their presidential candidate. The goal of the Dixiecrats was to stop Truman's civil rights agenda by throwing the presidential contest into the House of Representatives, where the southern states hoped to exert greater leverage to strike a political deal. In addition to the Dixiecrat split, some liberal Democrats tried to push Henry Wallace to run as a "Progressive" candidate. Wallace had been vice president during Roosevelt's third term and a member of Truman's administration until his resignation. Wallace disagreed with Truman chiefly on the issue of relations with the Soviet Union in the postwar period.

With the Democratic coalition in disarray, it appeared that the Republican nominee, Governor Thomas Dewey of New York, would be the inevitable victor. Truman's campaign was underfinanced, poorly staffed, and not well supported by the party organization. Truman, however, proved himself to be a remarkable campaigner and conducted a thirty-thousand–mile railroad tour taking his message to the people. Given the disunity among the Democrats, Truman's campaign featured a populist attack on the "big money" Republicans represented by Thomas Dewey and the Republican Congress. Truman's attacks rallied a sufficient number of New Deal Democrats for him to pull off a surprise victory. Dewey got 45 percent of the national vote and won sixteen states, primarily in the Northeast and the plains states. Dixiecrat candidate Strom Thurmond won four Deep South states. Truman won the remaining twenty-eight states and received 303 electoral votes, despite winning only 49 percent of the national vote.

Decline of the Democrats

In hindsight, Truman's 1948 victory can be seen as the last election featuring a dominant New Deal coalition. The volatile nature of the Democratic coalition had become clear when Truman's reelection was challenged within his own party from both the left, over foreign policy, and the right, over civil rights.

Although elements of the New Deal coalition continued to influence Democratic electoral strategy into the 1960s and 1970s, the tensions apparent within the party in 1948 would ultimately lead to the dissolution of the New Deal coalition.

In 1952, Republicans selected a World War II military hero, Dwight D. Eisenhower, as their presidential nominee. Eisenhower was selected at the Republican convention over Senator Robert Taft of Ohio. His long service in office and his deep dedication to the party led to Taft's being known as "Mr. Republican." The selection of Eisenhower, a popular outsider, over Taft, a party stalwart, has led some commentators to argue that this choice was the first indication of a new era of candidate-centered politics (Broder 1972). Indeed, for both Democrats and Republicans, the 1950s were a low point for party organizational strength.

Eisenhower proved his appeal to voters by winning two national elections over Democratic candidate Adlai E. Stevenson. Eisenhower won more than 55 percent of the national vote in 1952, carrying all but nine states; in 1956 he won 57 percent of the popular vote, carrying all but seven states. Even the solidly Democratic South showed some signs of weakening as Eisenhower won Florida, Tennessee, and Virginia in 1952 and carried all three of those states plus Louisiana and Kentucky in 1956. In 1952, Republicans also obtained a narrow majority in both the House and Senate. Democrats regained the House in the 1954 midterm elections and would not relinquish control to the Republicans until 1994.

Party Organizations in the Modern Era

The postwar period witnessed several significant developments leading to changes in parties and campaigns. One was the rise of television. Television advertising for candidates was introduced during the Eisenhower-Stevenson presidential contests of the 1950s. As television ownership became widespread, this new technology transformed the conduct of campaigns. Newspapers had long been a staple of partisan communication, and politicians had used radio broadcasts since the 1930s. But television enabled candidates to communicate with potential voters in a more direct and personal fashion. Perhaps most significantly, television allowed candidates to bypass party organizations and party workers. In short, it contributed to a new era of "candidate-centered" rather than "party-centered" elections. Of course, television was not the only factor, but combined with other developments the spread of television changed the nature of modern campaigning.

Long-term organizational change was also under way. Party machines, so essential as vote mobilizers in the late nineteen and early twentieth centuries, were gradually dying. Changes in federal, state, and local laws extended civil service protection to government employees and weakened the ability of party politicians to control government jobs and dispense them as patronage to their supporters. Without patronage, party organizers found it more difficult to raise money and to command the votes of supporters. Other factors also contributed to the decline of party machines, such as the changing demographics of cities as the flow of immigrants slowed and city residents moved from urban neighborhoods to suburban areas. These changes weakened local party organizations, and the focus of party activities shifted from local to national parties. During the 1960s, the national committees of both major parties, the Republican National Committee (RNC) and the Democratic National Committee (DNC), began to play a more active role in efforts to promote the administration's policies when the party controlled the White House and shape policy positions for the parties. The national parties, especially the Republicans, increased the number of professional staff and improved fund-raising at the national level.

Party Competition and Candidate-Centered Elections

Democrats returned to the White House in 1960, when John F. Kennedy defeated Republican Richard Nixon in one of the closest contests in U.S. political history. Kennedy got 49.7 percent of the popular vote while Nixon received 49.6 percent; Kennedy won the election by 114,673 votes out of the 68 million votes cast. Despite his charismatic image, Kennedy's lack of a clear policy agenda made him vulnerable as the 1964 election approached. In an attempt to strengthen his support in the South and to patch up a quarrel between Texas Democrats, John Kennedy made a trip to Dallas in November 1963. It was on that trip that President Kennedy was assassinated. Vice President Lyndon Johnson assumed office and went on to lead the Democrats in the 1964 elections.

The contest for the 1964 Republican nomination pitted the conservative wing of the party, with its base of support in the West and the South, against the more liberal eastern wing of the party. The spirited nomination battle involved a number of candidates but came down to conservative favorite Senator Barry Goldwater of Arizona and New York's Nelson Rockefeller. In June, Goldwater edged out Rockefeller in a close contest in the California Republican primary. Goldwater's nomination marked a shift in the balance of power within the Republican party away from the Wall Street establishment toward conservative activists from the western states.

In the general election, Johnson won in a landslide over Goldwater, in part by playing on voters' fears that Goldwater was too conservative. Johnson won 61 percent of the popular vote and carried all but six states. Democrats increased their majority in the House and the Senate. The only good news for the Republicans was Goldwater won the electoral votes of five Deep South states plus his home state of Arizona. Johnson's strong showing allowed him to pursue his "Great Society" legislative agenda, which included federal support for education, the Voting Rights Act, and the Medicare program.

The Democratic triumph was short-lived. By 1968, the Democratic party was badly split over Johnson's Vietnam War policy. Southern Democrats were unhappy with Johnson and with northern Democrats over civil rights. Johnson's attempt to seek renomination faltered early in the process. Johnson won the preference vote in the Democratic party primary in New Hampshire in March 1968. But an antiwar candidate, Senator Eugene McCarthy, polled 42 percent of the vote. Johnson's weak showing encouraged not only the McCarthy campaign but other Democratic hopefuls as well. Robert Kennedy entered the race shortly after the New Hampshire primary. Although he may have been able to retain his party's nomination, President Johnson decided against seeking a second full term and withdrew from the nomination contest.

After Johnson withdrew, Vice President Hubert Humphrey joined the race. Although McCarthy and Kennedy were the leading candidates through the Democratic primary elections, Robert Kennedy was assassinated after the California primary, and only McCarthy and Humphrey were left as the Democratic convention approached. The regular Democratic organization backed Humphrey, who was nominated despite the fact that McCarthy went into the convention with the most pledged delegates.

The 1968 Democratic convention in Chicago was a disaster for the party. Antiwar protestors and police clashed during the convention, leading Senator Abraham Ribicoff of Connecticut to denounce the "Gestapo tactics" of the Chicago police during his televised speech. Ribicoff's speech drew a vehement protest from Chicago Mayor Richard Daley, who was on the convention floor at the time. In the general election, Democrats faced another challenge, this time from dissatisfied southern Democrats supporting the candidacy of George Wallace, segregationist governor from Alabama running on the American Independent party label.

On the Republican side, Richard Nixon was again selected as the party's nominee and chose Spiro Agnew of Maryland as his running mate. Nixon won a close victory over Humphrey in the general election with 43.4 percent of the popular vote, compared to 42.7 percent for Humphrey and 13.5 percent for Wallace. By 1972, however, Nixon used the advantages of incumbency skillfully and defeated Democratic nominee George McGovern in a landslide. Nixon won 61 percent of the popular vote and swept every state except Massachusetts (McGovern also won the three electoral votes of the District of Columbia). Nixon's victory in 1972, however, did not result in Republican dominance. Democrats maintained control of Congress, and Nixon's reputation was soon undermined by the Watergate scandal. Any hope of a new Republican majority based on Nixon's wins in 1968 and 1972 eroded with the resignations of first Agnew and then Nixon. The backlash against Republicans became evident in the 1974 midterm elections as a new crop of Democrats was elected to the House of Representatives.

After its 1968 convention debacle, the Democratic party embarked on a series of reform efforts that resulted in greater national party control over the presidential nomination process. In response to vocal complaints from party activists and others that Humphrey's selection at the 1968 convention was essentially undemocratic, the party convened a commission headed by George McGovern, senator from South Dakota, and Donald Fraser, congressman from Minnesota. The McGovern-Fraser commission made a series of far-reaching recommendations about delegate selection that were adopted by the DNC and put into place during the 1972 presidential nominating process. These reforms helped to increase participation within the party, but they further weakened the ability of state and local party organizations to control their delegates.

One of the first beneficiaries of the new rules was none other than George McGovern. McGovern was able to take advantage of the new rules, which opened up participation in the party, as he campaigned for the party's nomination against Senator Edmund Muskie of Maine. Although McGovern's nomination ended disastrously for the Democrats in the 1972, the Democratic party continued to "reform" party rules over the course of the next four general elections. One of the most important consequences of the reforms enacted by the Democratic party was the increased prominence of primary elections in the presidential nomination process (a topic covered in more detail in Chapter 4). The increased use of primary elections to select delegates for national party conventions affected Republicans as well as Democrats because states changed their laws in response to Democratic party reforms. The shift to primary elections in turn affected how candidates would compete for their party's nomination.

Shifting Party Fortunes in the Contemporary Era

Changes in the presidential nominating process became evident in 1976 when a dark horse candidate, Jimmy Carter, won the Democratic nomination. Carter, the former governor of Georgia, was virtually unknown on the national political stage at the beginning of 1976. But Carter was able to use a strong showing in early primaries to establish himself as a credible candidate and defeat his better-known rivals for the Democratic nomination. In the primaries and in the general election, Carter ran as a political "outsider" who was not a part of the Washington establishment.

Carter's opponent in the 1976 general election was Republican Gerald Ford, the incumbent president. Ford had been minority leader of the House but was appointed vice president by Richard Nixon after Spiro Agnew resigned. Ford became president in 1974 after Nixon resigned. Ford faced stiff competition for the Republican nomination from Ronald Reagan, whose candidacy was strongly supported by conservative activists. Ford managed to prevail in a close contest.

In the general election, Carter won a slim majority of the popular vote, 50.1 percent. Carter's victory, particularly his showing in southern states, led some Democrats to see the revival of the New Deal coalition. But political events during the Carter administration crushed any hope for a return of Democratic dominance. Although President Carter had some successes, economic problems at home and a foreign policy crisis put Democrats in a difficult situation leading into the 1980 elections. At home, the economy suffered from both high inflation and stagnant growth, a condition termed "stagflation." Abroad, the Soviets had invaded and occupied Afghanistan, reigniting Cold War worries about Soviet expansionism. Perhaps even more telling in the media age was the prolonged crisis of Americans held hostage in Iran. In short, Carter's campaign for a second term had significant obstacles to overcome. Among the first of these was a challenge within his own party during the Democratic primaries from Senator Edward Kennedy.

Republicans nominated Ronald Reagan as their candidate in 1980. One of Reagan's competitors for the nomination, John Anderson, was highly critical of Reagan's proposed economic policy and ultimately decided to run as an independent candidate in the general election. Reagan's nomination was partly a consequence of efforts to mobilize conservative activists within the party begun by Goldwater's supporters in 1964. Though Reagan was most strongly supported by Republican conservatives, his personal appeal as a candidate and his ability to communicate his message effectively cemented his support among Republicans and attracted other voters as well. Reagan, with running mate George Bush, won the 1980 election with a slight majority of the popular vote, 50.7 percent, but a commanding 489 electoral votes. Carter finished with 41 percent of the popular vote, and independent candidate John Anderson got 7 percent. Perhaps even more heartening for Republicans was that they picked up twelve seats in the Senate, giving them control, and thirty-five seats in the House. Although Democrats continued to maintain control of the House of Representatives, Republican fortunes had clearly improved since the Watergate scandal.

In 1984, President Reagan was easily reelected, with nearly 59 percent of the popular vote, over Democrat Walter Mondale. Reagan did well in all areas of the country and with virtually all social groups, with the exception of African American voters, Hispanic voters, and urban voters. Indicative of the era of candidate-centered elections, the coalition of supporters was more a "Reagan coalition" than a "Republican coalition." Despite the scope of Reagan's victory at the presidential level, Republican gains in Congress were modest. They gained fourteen seats in the House, though Democrats still held a substantial majority, and Republicans lost two seats in the Senate.

The results of the 1988 presidential election supported the view that 1984 was more of a Reagan coalition than a Republican one. In 1988, George H. W. Bush, who had served as Reagan's vice president for two terms, easily defeated Democrat Michael Dukakis. After a lackluster campaign, Bush won 54 percent of the popular vote to Dukakis's 46 percent. In comparison to Reagan's showing in 1984, however, Bush's support was several percentage points lower than Reagan's among nearly all social groups (Pomper 1989). Further, Democrats managed to maintain control over both houses of Congress (Democrats had regained control of the Senate in the 1986 midterm elections). Thus, despite three convincing wins at the presidential level, the Republican party could not demonstrate a dominant coalition because of its inability to control Congress. Instead, divided party government continued, with Republicans controlling the executive and Democrats controlling the legislative branch.

In 1992, it appeared that Democrats might have found a way out of the stalemate of divided party government. The 1992 election matched incumbent President George H. W. Bush against a little-known Democrat, Governor Bill Clinton of Arkansas. Bush had the advantage of his leadership in the Gulf crisis, which had pushed his presidential approval ratings to nearly 90 percent in March 1991, but the disadvantage of sluggish economic performance in the year preceding the election. Bush had faced a challenge from Patrick Buchanan in the Republican primaries. Although Buchanan's campaign was potentially divisive because of his appeal to social conservatives, President Bush was easily renominated. Among Democrats, Clinton emerged as the nominee only after a hard-fought battle with several other contenders.

Another factor in the 1992 election was a major independent candidate, H. Ross Perot, a billionaire Texas businessman. Perot got into the race, dropped out, and then reentered the race in September. Perot's candidacy made the outcome more unpredictable than usual. On election day, Bill Clinton was elected president with only 43 percent of the popular vote to George Bush's 37 percent and Ross Perot's 19 percent. Despite his small plurality in the popular vote, Clinton carried thirty-two states and the District of Columbia for a total of 370 electoral votes to Bush's 168. Perot failed to win any electoral votes but made a strong showing in a number of western states.

Coming out of the 1992 elections, the Democrats controlled the executive branch and both houses of Congress. Unfortunately for the Democratic party, President Clinton's first years in office were not highly successful and Republicans were able to take advantage. In the 1994 midterm elections, Republicans scored an important breakthrough, gaining fifty-two seats in the House and eight seats in the Senate to take control of both the House and Senate for the first time since 1952.

Going into the 1996 presidential election year, the scope of the Republican victory in 1994 should have put Republicans in a strong position. President Clinton, however, was able to use the circumstance to his political credit. With no challenge from within his party to his renomination, and with a strong economy, Clinton was able to position himself as a "new" Democrat. The Republican challenger, Senator Robert Dole from Kansas, had to survive a difficult primary challenge to win the nomination. The 1996 campaign included another challenge from Ross Perot, who had worked to create a new third party, the Reform party.

With the aid of a strong economy, Clinton and running mate Albert Gore won reelection handily. Clinton finished with 49 percent of the popular vote to Dole's 41 percent and Perot's 8 percent. Clinton won most of the states of the far West, the Midwest, and the Northeast, whereas Dole won most of the plains states and the southern states. In Congress, Republicans lost seats in the House but retained control and gained seats in the Senate to increase their majority. After the 1996 election, the era of divided party governed continued, but with Republicans controlling the House and Senate and Democrats, the White House.

The 2000 elections brought an end to divided party government, with Republicans winning the White House and controlling Congress, but only after the extraordinary events of the presidential contest. The 2000 presidential election featured a match-up between the Democratic incumbent vice president, Al Gore, and the Republican governor of Texas, George W. Bush, son of the former president, George H. W. Bush. Despite the political advantages of a strong national economy, Gore chose to emphasize a populist theme in the campaign and attempted to distance himself from the personal scandal that had embroiled President Clinton. On the other side, the Bush campaign combined an emphasis on traditional Republican issues such as tax cuts, with an effort to present a

more moderate image on social issues, with the candidate describing himself as a "compassionate conservative."

After a lackluster campaign, the 2000 presidential race produced a remarkable outcome: in a extremely close contest, Al Gore won a larger share of the popular vote with 48.4 percent to George W. Bush's 47.9 percent, but Bush was elected president because he won a majority of electoral college votes. Even more unusual was that Bush's victory was secured only when Florida's electoral votes were awarded to him after a hotly disputed vote recount process that produced numerous lawsuits and was ultimately settled more than a month after election day when the U.S. Supreme Court overturned a decision by the Florida Supreme Court, and Gore conceded the election.

The closeness and bitter partisanship of the 2000 presidential election was also evident in the 2004 presidential campaign in which the incumbent president, George W. Bush, was challenged by the Democrat's nominee, Senator John Kerry of Massachusetts. The 2004 presidential campaign was unusual because of the prominence of foreign policy as an issue, in particular the Bush administration's war on terrorism and its decision to invade Iraq in 2003. President Bush was reelected with 50.7 percent of the popular vote and 286 electoral college votes. The president's party also maintained control of the House and Senate giving the Republicans unified control in Washington despite the closeness of the national election results. Unified Republican control of the legislature and executive ended, however, after the 2006 midterm elections. In the second midterm election of George W. Bush's presidency, Democrats were able to gain control of both the House and Senate by winning an additional thirty-one seats in the House and six seats in the Senate (counting two independents elected to the Senate with the Democrats).

The broad pattern of national election results since World War II shows that neither party has been able to maintain a persistent electoral advantage. At the presidential level, and to a lesser extent at the congressional level, contemporary election outcomes appear to depend far more on the candidate and the campaign than on firmly established partisan coalitions.

Conclusion: The Changing Nature of American Political Parties

An examination of the history of American political parties from the ratification of the Constitution to the early twenty-first century reveals complexity and at times confusion. Still, some broad patterns are clearly discernible.

One pattern, and the central theme of this chapter, is that American political parties have changed enormously over time as they adapted to changing political circumstances. Perhaps the most important point to recognize is that successful political parties in the United States are highly pragmatic organizations. Although the political environment may change, political parties have maintained their goal of getting, or keeping, their supporters in power through elections. Even as political parties have changed, this aspect of political parties has remained constant.

When political parties first emerged in the 1790s, they were little more than a meeting place for elected officials who either opposed or supported the president's administration. The first parties provided a way of collecting elected national leaders into more or less cohesive groups that shared views on some of the important issues of the day. These parties existed primarily as a caucus—an organized meeting of political leaders. The first parties fulfilled the real need for an organized way for politicians to rally support for their policies.

As the United States grew, political parties became a means for organizing the expanding electorate. By the 1840s, political parties had developed into **mass party organizations** that incorporated their supporters into the process of choosing presidential nominees and developing the party's platform. Political parties existed as organizations outside of, and in addition to, the organizations that served members of Congress and the executive. Parties became the chief means for political leaders to communicate with supporters across the country. Indeed, some party leaders, both Democrats and Republicans, honed their organizations to become effective mobilizers of votes as they sought to control patronage jobs and government services. Although these party machines existed in states and counties across the nation, the most notorious were the ones that ran large cities such as New York, Boston, Chicago, Philadelphia, Kansas City, and San Francisco.

From the 1890s to the 1920s, a series of reforms were enacted that substantially reduced the power of political parties. These Progressive-era reforms directly undermined the control that parties could exert over their supporters. For instance, the introduction of the direct primary, in which voters, not party leaders, choose a party's nominee, reduced the power of political bosses. As these and other reforms were introduced, political corruption was reduced. There were, however, unintended consequences as well. For example, fewer people participated in elections when the link between parties and the tangible rewards of being a party supporter were broken.

As **reformed party organizations**, the parties did not wither away but increasingly became creatures of state government. New laws defining how candidates could get on the state's ballot or when primary elections would be held have enshrined the major political parties in the legal code. Political parties continued to provide a means for organizing legislative and executive business and, outside of government, continued to recruit candidates for office. But the heyday of strong party organizations that could mobilize large masses of voters was over.

One consequence of the decline of strong party organizations was the system of "candidate-centered" elections we see today in the United States. New technologies, such as television, telephone polls, and direct mail, have shifted the focus of elections onto the candidates and their personal campaign organizations (Wattenberg 1991). The parties adapted to these circumstances by becoming "service organizations" (Aldrich 1995). In response to the new style of campaigning, which emerged most forcefully in the 1960s and 1970s, contemporary parties have responded by providing the services that candidates seek. Parties organize workshops for potential candidates covering topics such as how to organize a campaign and how to dress for television. Parties also provide services such as polling, hosting candidate Internet sites, advice concerning campaign finance laws, policy papers on important issues, and telephone banks for voter registration or mobilization. Although a far cry from the old party machines, the shift to **service party organizations** appears to be a successful adaptation of contemporary political parties to the realities of electoral competition in the modern era.

CHAPTER 3

The Organization of Contemporary American Parties

In some ways, the contemporary Republican and Democratic parties resemble mid-sized corporations. They maintain permanent headquarters in Washington, have key executives who worry continually about the competition, and employ people who range from technical experts to receptionists. But to conclude that the major political parties operate like most corporations would seriously misread the nature of American parties.

The two major American political parties are not organized along strict hierarchical lines but are made up of several loosely connected organizations. The various organizations that comprise a modern party may be on the same team but are not necessarily part of a single command structure. At the center of each major party is its national committee, the Republican National Committee (RNC) or the Democratic National Committee (DNC), headed by a national chairperson. Yet the national chairperson is not the party's sole authority. Unlike a corporate chief executive officer, a party chair must work in conjunction with members of Congress and, if the party controls the White House, members of the president's administration. Not only must the party chairperson coordinate actions with elected officials in Washington, but he or she is not in a position to issue orders that will be carried out in Kansas or Idaho because each state has its own party organization subject to state law and is not a creature of the national party.

The important point is that the political parties are not the same as most modern, hierarchical organizations such as General Electric or Microsoft. Rather, each major party is a complex network of organizations with overlapping responsibilities and decentralized power. Why do the party organizations retain these loosely connected structures? Because American parties are a product of a complex political environment, a result of federalism and the separation of powers, and these structural features allow for maximum flexibility. Indeed, this flexibility has allowed the parties to adapt to the changing circumstances of American politics.

The adaptability of the parties to new political circumstances is well illustrated by changes that have occurred in the United States since World War II. The 1950s were, in many ways, the low point for American party organizations. The full force of Progressive reforms designed to weaken party machines and end political corruption had hit the state and local parties. The weakening of local parties hurt the national parties as well because the national parties had always relied on state and local organizations for resources. Even worse, just as the party organizations were in the doldrums, candidates were discovering that they could use new technologies, principally television, to appeal directly to voters. With this new technology and the resources to use it, candidates more than ever became the stars of the political show. The 1960s marked a transition to an era of "candidate-centered" elections (Wattenberg 1991).

Over the course of many years the parties adapted to these new circumstances by becoming "service" organizations. At the presidential level, campaign organizations have become self-contained entities complete with media consultants, pollsters, speech writers, state organizers, and the rest. Presidential candidates, in short, can largely conduct their operations without relying on a party organization. Most candidates, however, do not have that luxury. Thus, rather than try to revive the glory days of past political machines, modern political parties have moved to provide the services that candidates need. Both the national and state parties provide their candidates with a variety of services such as how to craft a message and communicate it to voters, how to deal with the press, the effective use of a campaign Web site, advice on raising money, and how to get the most out of paid advertising.

Our purpose in this chapter is to examine the complex structures of contemporary American parties in the era of parties as service organizations. We begin at the grass roots with the people who are the lifeblood of the party organizations, the party activists. Next, we examine the state and local parties and conclude with the national party organizations.

Party Activists

Comparing party organizations in different democratic nations allows us to identify two types of organizations: mass parties and cadre parties (Duverger 1963, 63–71). Mass political parties have a large number of dues-paying members who compose the bulk of the party organization. Mass parties are typically organized hierarchically with members participating, through local organizations, in the selection of party candidates and the party's positions on issues. An example of a mass political party is the British Labour party. Though its membership is down from its peak in the late 1970s, the Labour party still has roughly four million members, most of whom are affiliated to the party through membership in trade unions (Pelling and Reid 1996, 197–199).

Cadre parties, on the other hand, do not have many members. Instead, cadre parties are composed of small groups of activists who come together for a short period to get candidates elected to office. During an election, a cadre party may have a large number of activists working to promote the party's candidates; after the election, the party organization typically dwindles to a few officials. Because there is no base of members to organize, in practice the structure of a cadre party is rarely hierarchical. More often, a cadre party resembles a loose network of connections among candidates, officials, and a few dedicated activists (Schwartz 1990).

American parties are cadre parties. American political parties do not have large numbers of dues-paying members or strong hierarchical structures. Rather, American party organizations tend to be composed of a few party officials who maintain the party organization between elections. At election time, however, party activity increases and citizen activists pitch in to work for the party or its candidates.

The Social Basis of Party Activism

Who are these **party activists**? In general, we know that people who take an active role in the life of parties, whether as convention delegates, local party officials, or campaign volunteers, are not typical of other citizens. According to estimates from the American National Election Study surveys, about only 3 percent of the adult population reports having worked for a party or a candidate in recent election years. Party activists, as a group, are better educated, have higher incomes, and are more likely to have professional occupations than most citizens. As is true with other forms of political participation in the United States, there is a social distinction with regard to involvement in parties and campaigns: people with higher socioeconomic status are more likely to participate than people with lower socioeconomic status (Verba and Nie 1972, 129–133; Verba et al. 1993).

The socioeconomic distinctiveness of party activists is true of both Democrats and Republicans. As table 3.1 shows, people who serve as delegates to one of the major party's national conventions are generally better educated and have higher incomes than most American citizens. Although Democratic and Republican delegates are similar in socioeconomic terms, there are differences among party delegates as well. Democratic delegates are more likely to be ethnic or racial minorities, especially African-American, and are more likely to belong to a labor union than Republican delegates. Republican delegates are much more likely to identify themselves as "conservative" whereas Democratic delegates are more likely to call themselves "liberal." The characteristics of national convention delegates are broadly similar to descriptions of state and county party leaders (see Huckshorn 1976; Gibson et al. 1986).

In socioeconomic and ideological terms, party activists clearly differ from most citizens. What leads people to become party activists? As with political participation, generally, one factor associated with party activism is an exposure to partisan activity at a young age. People whose parents were involved in partisan activities are more likely to become activists as adults than people from politically inactive families (Jennings and Niemi 1981; Beck and Jennings 1982). A comparison between lifelong Democratic activists and activists who converted to the Republican party revealed that activists whose parents had been involved in politics were less likely to switch parties (Clark et al. 1991).

Thus involvement in political parties appears to be a function of both resources and learning. People with higher socioeconomic standing are more likely to take an active role in a party organization because they are more likely to have the necessary personal resources. Of course, not all party activists are people with high socioeconomic status, and certainly not all people of high socioeconomic status participate. Clearly, learning the value of participating in partisan activity from parents who engage in such actions can be a crucial motivation for individuals to become involved.

Incentives for Activism

Of course, people may get involved in party activities for different reasons. Studies of party activism have identified three types of incentives for organizational involvement: (1) material, (2) purposive, and (3) solidary (Clark and Wilson 1961; Wilson 1995, 30–55). Material incentives are tangible payoffs to the individual activist in return for participation. The tradition of party bosses providing government jobs to people who helped to get the party's candidates elected is an example of a material incentive for party activism. Purposive incentives, on the other hand, are less tangible rewards. A purposive incentive is a motivation based upon a sense of purpose. In other words, individuals become active in party activities in order to promote some cause such as the appeal of a particular candidate or a strongly held issue position. Individuals who get involved in party activities primarily because they believe in a particular issue or candidate are said to be motivated by purposive incentives. Finally, a solidary incentive is a motivation to become involved in party activity for social reasons such as friendship or group affiliation (see Crotty 1986). Campaign and party volunteers are often recruited to serve in the party by people they know.

The distinction between material and purposive incentives for party activists is a key difference between "professional" and "amateur" party activists. Professional activists (or "pragmatists" as they are sometimes called) are

TABLE 3.1 Characteristics of 2004 Party Convention Delegates and American Adults (in percent)

	Convention Delegates		All Adults
	Republican	Democrat	All Adults
Education			
Less than High School	0	0	9
High School Graduate	6	5	29
Some College	20	18	32
College Graduate	29	24	18
Postgraduate	44	53	11
Household Income			
Under $25,000	2	4	23
$25,000–50,000	6	11	22
$50,000–100,000	42	40	30
Over $100,000	42	42	13
Refused	8	6	12
Race/Ethnicity			
White	85	68	73
Black	6	18	15
Asian	2	3	3
Other	4	10	9
Labor Union Member			
Yes	3	25	9
No	97	75	91
Ideological Identification			
Very Liberal	1	22	14
Somewhat Liberal	1	19	14
Moderate	33	52	32
Somewhat Conservative	27	3	17
Very Conservative	33	0	23
Total n =	**1,200**	**1,085**	**1,212**

Note: Responses may not total to 100 percent due to rounding or because "don't know" responses have been excluded. For the all adult sample, two response categories differ from the delegate survey responses. On income, the top two categories are $50,000 to $105,000 and over $105,000. For ideological identification, the "very liberal" category was created by combining "extremely liberal" and "liberal" responses, and the "very conservative" category was created from the "extremely conservative" and "conservative" responses.

Sources: Convention delegate data compiled by the authors from *New York Times/CBS News* party delegate surveys available at www.nytimes.com. Raw data for the sample of all American adults are from the 2004 American National Election Study.

motivated primarily by material incentives. Although the days of vast numbers of patronage jobs are gone, involvement in a political party or candidate's campaign is often a stepping-stone to a job as a staff person, an appointment to an advisory board, or some other tangible reward. Professional activists are primarily concerned with winning elections because it is by winning that material rewards become available. In contrast, amateur activists (or "purists") are drawn to parties or campaigns by a desire to promote a particular issue position or a particular candidate. Thus, for amateurs, winning elections may not matter as much as supporting the "right" candidate or advocating the "correct" position on an issue, even if the candidate or position is not popular.

Both Democrats and Republicans have experienced tensions between amateur and professional activists within their ranks. In a classic study, political scientist James Q. Wilson (1962) studied amateur Democratic activists in three cities: Los Angeles, Chicago, and New York. These amateur activists were chiefly concerned with promoting various liberal policies within the Democratic party and attempted to make the party itself more open to citizen participation. These activists formed "Democratic clubs," organizations that existed separately from the party. For activists in these Democratic clubs, the opposition was less the Republican party than it was the local "regular" party organization controlled by materially oriented party professionals.

The differences between amateurs and professionals were starkly displayed in the Democratic party's presidential nomination process in 1968 (for an excellent summary, see Blum 1991, 287–310). In late 1967 and early 1968, a variety of amateur activists, especially college students, were drawn to the presidential campaign of Senator Eugene McCarthy because he opposed President Lyndon Johnson's Vietnam policy. Despite the passion of McCarthy's amateurs, professional activists led by Mayor Richard Daley of Chicago easily outmaneuvered McCarthy's supporters at the party's national convention in Chicago. Support from Daley and other party professionals was crucial in helping Vice President Hubert Humphrey to win the party's presidential nomination. Most professional activists considered Humphrey more electable than Senator McCarthy.

Although the professionals were able to control the nomination in 1968, dissatisfaction with the nomination process led many amateur activists to demand changes in the party's nomination procedures. Ultimately, these changes helped to weaken the control of

professionals such as Mayor Daley and, in 1972, helped the candidate of the party's liberal wing, Senator George McGovern, win the party's nomination for president. Amateur activists were also important to Jesse Jackson in his bids for the presidential nomination in 1984 and 1988. More recently, Howard Dean's strong showing early in the 2004 Democratic nomination contest can be attributed in part to his campaign's use of the Internet to attract liberal amateurs as a core base of supporters (Hindman 2005).

Republicans, too, have witnessed the struggle between professionals and amateurs. For example, many supporters of Arizona Senator Barry Goldwater's bid for the presidency in 1964 were amateur activists drawn to Goldwater more for his conservative views than his broad electoral appeal. As one Goldwater delegate at the 1964 Republican convention put it, "I'd rather stick by real principles this country was built on than win. Popularity isn't important; prestige isn't important; it's principles that matter" (quoted in Wildavsky 1965, 397). Though Goldwater was soundly defeated by Lyndon Johnson, conservative activists energized by his candidacy had a lasting impact on the Republican party. One of Goldwater's supporters was none other than Ronald Reagan who, at the urging of other Goldwater supporters, went on to run for governor of California (Reichley 1992, 333). Amateur activists within the Republican party have been prominent supporters of candidates Patrick Buchanan and Pat Robertson (Hertzke 1993, 157–171).

The contrast between amateur and professional activists captures an important element of party politics—the ongoing tension between principles and pragmatism. Though this tension surely exists in both the Democratic and Republican parties, there are good reasons not to exaggerate its importance. First, many people active in party politics are involved for a mixture of reasons, including policy and issue concerns, commitment to the party, and personal concerns (Miller and Jennings 1986, 91–96). Second, both of the major parties are relatively porous organizations that allow activists to flow in and out depending on the issues of the day and the selection of candidates. The influx of amateur activists into party politics during the 1960s raised concerns about possible negative consequences for party competition, but those negative effects never fully materialized (Herrera 1995; Miller and Jennings 1986). Amateur activists who are initially unsuccessful in changing the party may become disenchanted and drop out of party politics or may stay and adapt to the need for some degree of pragmatism (Dodson 1990). To underscore this point, a study of delegates to the 2000 Republican and Democratic national conventions found that states with more competitive elections and more professionalized state parties tended to send delegates who had more pragmatic views (Carsey, Green, Herrera, and Layman 2006). That is, delegates from states with highly competitive elections tended to reflect the importance of the pragmatic value of winning elections, while states with less electoral competition had delegates who tended to take a more purist orientation.

Although differences in motivation may allow us to classify party activists as professionals or amateurs, it is clear that both pragmatism and principle matter for individuals experienced in party politics. The authors of a study of state party activists concluded that "despite a strong tendency among our respondents to opt for ideological purity over electability in the abstract . . . Democratic and Republican activists were actually more concerned with electability than with ideology in choosing a party nominee" (Stone and Abramowitz 1983, 946).

State and Local Parties

Party activists are the lifeblood of the parties, but it is the state parties that have traditionally provided the organizational skeleton of American political parties. Although the nominating conventions provided a national focus, real power often rested with the state and local party officials who could deliver the votes. For most of American history, the national parties have served as umbrella organizations for a confederation of state parties. The national parties depended on state and local organizations for resources and votes. State and local parties are no longer dominant, however, because the national parties have become more structurally sound and professional in the post–World War II period. Still, state and local parties have not fallen by the wayside. State and local parties, too, have adapted to the changing circumstances of the American political scene.

State Parties and State Laws

Political parties are not discussed in the Constitution nor, for most of our history, have they been the subject of federal law. Instead, to the extent that political parties are provided for in the law, it is state law. The regulation of political parties differs markedly among states. Five states (Alaska, Delaware, Hawaii, Kentucky, and North Carolina) traditionally have had very limited regulations, whereas states such as Ohio, Illinois, Texas, and New Jersey have developed elaborate legal regulation of state parties (ACIR 1986, 128–143).

The regulation of political parties had its roots in the late 1880s and early 1890s, when states began to adopt the Australian ballot. Prior to this time, ballots were printed by the parties themselves and distributed to voters by party workers. When governments began to print official state ballots, all candidates were listed with their party affiliation. As party scholar Leon Epstein (1986, 165) has pointed out,

> The official ballot recognition of parties in 1888–90 provided the legal arguments for the most important regulation that followed. From its inception, official ballot recognition required that a party's nominations be certified by party officers to

government officials, and that only officers of certain parties—usually those polling a certain percentage of votes at the previous election—could thus certify.

Before the use of official state ballots, political parties were regarded as essentially private associations that were largely free from state regulation. After the adoption of the Australian ballot, which automatically provided positions on the ballot for state-recognized political parties, state governments had a greater interest in regulating the operation of political parties. It occurred over the course of several decades, but the switch to state-printed ballots was the beginning of the transition from political parties as strictly private associations to parties as "public utilities" (Epstein 1986). As public utilities, political parties gained legal recognition and, more importantly, their nominees gained routine access to the state's ballot. In return, the parties had to accept regulation by state government of their organizational structure and conduct of public business.

All states have laws governing election procedures and ballot access. As part of the regulation of the electoral process, states may have laws that define what constitutes a political party. State laws differ, however, on the extent to which they regulate the composition and internal working of political parties. In some states, the law may provide general guidelines as to how political parties are to be structured. For example, state law in Georgia (2006, 21–2–111), a state with a tradition of limited regulation, specifies that

Each political party shall establish and maintain a state executive committee exercising state-wide jurisdiction and control over party affairs and a county executive committee in each county in which it holds a primary, exercising county-wide jurisdiction and control over party affairs. . . . The state executive committee of each political party shall formulate, adopt, and promulgate rules and regulations, consistent with

law, governing the conduct of conventions and other party affairs. No such rule and regulation shall be effective until copies thereof, certified by the chairperson, have been filed with the Secretary of State.

Thus, Georgia law does require the existence of state and county executive committees, but it largely leaves the conduct of party affairs up to these party bodies. In contrast, states with a tradition of heavy regulation provide more extensive requirements about the structure of parties and the procedures they are to follow. For example, Ohio (2006) law distinguishes among major, intermediate, and minor parties, based on the percentage of votes received in gubernatorial or presidential elections. For major parties, it specifies the time when a state convention may be held, the composition of delegates to the state convention, and the membership and election procedures for the party's controlling committees. In sum, to a greater or lesser degree, states have come to regulate the structure and composition of parties as well as the rules and procedures by which parties are to operate.

Because regulation was intended to eliminate corrupt election practices, the power of state governments to regulate parties went unchallenged for many years. Several rulings by the Supreme Court, however, indicate that party organizations may have greater freedom from state regulation than state legislators have assumed. In *Tashjian v. Republican Party of Connecticut* (1986), the Supreme Court ruled that the state of Connecticut could not prevent the state Republican party from allowing registered independents to vote in its primary elections. Shortly afterward, the Court ruled in *Eu v. San Francisco County Democratic Central Committee* (1989) that certain California regulations were an unconstitutional burden on the First Amendment liberties of political parties. California had passed legislation that prevented party endorsements in primary elections, limited the length of time a person could serve as state party chair, and required the state party chair to rotate between residents of southern and northern California. The Court declared that California's regulations were unconstitutional because "a State cannot justify regulating a party's internal affairs without showing that such regulation is necessary to ensure an election that is orderly and fair" (*Eu v. San Francisco County Democratic Central Committee* 1989, 1025). In another important case from California, the U.S. Supreme Court ruled that an initiative passed by voters that required the state's political parties to change the way they conducted primary elections was a violation of any political party's constitutional freedom of association (*California Democratic Party v. Jones* 2000). The Supreme Court's ruling in this case reaffirmed that political parties, as organizations, enjoy the right not to have their candidate selection process determined by state government, even if that process is popular with voters.

These rulings raise questions about how extensively states can regulate party organizations and suggest that parties might be able to exercise more discretion in the conduct of their business. It is, however, unlikely that most state laws regulating parties will undergo extensive challenge any time soon. Many state regulations are not particularly burdensome, and most party activities are already in accordance with state law. If parties regard state regulation as intrusive, though, there is legal precedent for limiting state regulation unless the law is clearly necessary to promote the governmental interest in conducting free and fair elections.

State Party Organization

State parties are typically governed by a state central committee headed by a state party chairperson. The composition and duties of the state party central committees are determined by state law as well as the party's own rules. Most states have laws that specify how the party's central committee is to be composed, whereas other states simply leave it up to the parties themselves. In states that spec-

ify, there are generally two methods for selecting members. One method requires that members be elected in primary elections. Few states use this system and it is not favored by party officials because it limits their ability to influence the composition of their own central committee. More commonly, state laws require that central committee members be selected by state or county conventions. The convention method allows state party leaders more ability to influence the composition of the state central committee.

The duties of state central committees depend on state laws, party rules, and past practices. In some states, the party's central committee is directly responsible for selecting delegates to the national party convention or is charged with writing the state party's platform. For the most part, however, state central party committees are a mechanism for broadening the representation of the party and a means for shaping party policy. For example, if the state party chair wants to launch a new fund-raising campaign or organize a voter mobilization program in the state, working with central committee members would be a good way to gather support (whether or not it requires formal approval by the central committee).

A state central committee is the formal policymaking body, but party operations are usually handled by the state party chair. In most states, the state party chair is selected by the central committee, although other states require that the chair be elected by the delegates to the state party convention. State party chairs are generally chosen for a two-year term. State party chairs may remain for extended periods, but the more usual pattern is for the state chairperson to serve for only a short time. Two or three years is a common length of service for a state party chairperson (Aldrich 2000, 656; Huckshorn 1976, 46; Reichley 1992, 389). The job of a state party chair can be a demanding one. Formal duties differ from state to state, but the primary responsibility of a contemporary chairperson is to represent the state party organization both within the state and within the national party organization.

Within the state, the party chair must work to coordinate the efforts of various party constituencies. Political scientist Robert Huckshorn (1991, 1060) has identified four internal party responsibilities of a state chairperson: (1) to maintain a good working relationship with local party leaders and activists; (2) to maintain an effective relationship with the elected members of the state central committee; (3) to provide elected state officials, such as the governor or state legislators, with political help as necessary; and (4) to administer party headquarters and employ staff to carry out the goals of the party organization. Huckshorn's list provides a good sense of the various relationships within the state party that a chairperson has to cultivate. Of course, the job also involves developing relationships outside the party as well. For example, state party chairs should have good relations with a broad array of people outside the party organization such as potential campaign contributors, local businesspeople, union officials, and members of the media.

How well the state chairperson is able to carry out these duties depends on many factors in addition to personal ability, including the party's partisan performance and the status of the party organization. The party's partisan performance refers to how well the party has done in recent elections, in particular, whether the party controls the governorship or not. In a study of state party leaders, Huckshorn (1976, 69–95) identified three roles for state party chairs, depending on whether their party controls the governorship: (1) the political agent, (2) the in-party independent, and (3) the out-party independent. Political agents are state chairs selected by the incumbent governor and expected to serve as a partisan agent for the governor. In contrast, an in-party independent chairperson is usually selected without the support of the incumbent governor and so is regarded as being able to act on behalf of the party independently from the governor. Finally, when

the chairperson's party does not control the governorship, the state party chair is classified as an out-party independent, since selection as chair depends on the individual's standing within the party.

Another factor that affects the chairperson's job is the current strength of the state party organization. An important component of organizational strength is the extent of "bureaucratization" of the party, that is, the presence of professional leadership, paid staff, and regular sources of funds. As table 3.2 shows, nearly all state parties have a paid executive director, and a number of state parties have other paid staffers to run party operations. Table 3.2 also shows that nearly all state parties have held fund-raising events. Of course, some state party organizations will simply be less successful at raising money on a regular basis and maintaining a professional staff. Thus, it stands to reason that a state party chair who takes over an organization with a reliable source of funds and knowledgeable professional staff will be able to concentrate time and effort on recruiting candidates or developing strategy for an upcoming campaign. State chairs who inherit less proficient organizations will have to spend more time raising money, trying to fill party positions, and engaging in other routine activities.

State political parties differ in terms of their electoral success, the extent of regulation by state law, and their organizational strength. Yet all state parties share the goal of winning elections. The bottom line for political parties is to get their candidates into office, and much of what state parties actually do can be summarized in terms of this goal. In their study of state parties, Cotter et al. (1984, 19–26) identify state party activities as falling into two categories: institutional-support and candidate-directed activities. Institutional-support activities "enhance the capacity of the party organization to perform as a service bureau for a broad clientele and thus to generate broad support" (Cotter et al. 1984, 19). Party fund-raising, voter registration drives, analysis of issues, staffing party positions, and maintain-

TABLE 3.2 Attributes and Activities of State Party Organizations (in percent)

Party Employs	Republican	Democratic
Full-Time State Chair	50	56
Full-Time Executive Director	92	89
Public Relations Director	58	46
Research Staff	65	41
Field Staff	81	69
Party Activities		
Held Fund-Raising Event	100	97
Published Newsletter	92	89
Conducted Campaign Seminars	100	92
Operated Voter Identification Program	96	92
Conducted Public Opinion Surveys	96	66

Note: Figures are percentages of state party organizations based on a 1999 survey of state party chairs (26 Republican party chairs and 39 Democratic party chairs).

Source: Adapted from Aldrich (2000, 656–657).

ing the party's Internet site are examples of activities that maintain or enhance a party's institutional ability. Candidate-directed activities focus on getting candidates elected to office. Recruiting people to run for office, conducting campaign seminars, and providing assistance with campaign finance laws are examples of the candidate-directed services that state parties perform. As table 3.2 shows, nearly all state party organizations engage in these fundamental activities of raising money, publicizing the party and its activities, and assisting candidates.

Local Parties

The most basic operational unit of party organization in the United States is the county (or the equivalent unit in states such as Alaska and Louisiana). County party organizations may be composed of wards or precincts, but these units seldom have their own organizational structure. Most county parties have formal rules for their operation and are usually headed by a county chairperson. Unlike state organizations, however, county organizations are not very bureaucratic. A few county party organizations are highly organized, such as the Cook County Democratic party in Illinois or the Nassau County Republican party in New York, but most county organizations are run by volunteers with few resources. In sum, local party organizations are more personalized and less professional in their organizational structures than state parties. The more personalized leadership found at the county level has one notable benefit—less turnover in leadership. In contrast to state party chairs, county party chairs tend to remain in the same office for a longer period of time (Cotter et al. 1984, 44).

Although county parties do not have the resources of state parties, that should not be taken to mean they are inactive. In fact, research on local parties has demonstrated that they are far more organized and active than scholars had suspected (Cotter et al. 1984; Gibson et al. 1986). Table 3.3 lists a number of activities reported by local party leaders in a survey (Gibson, Frendreis, and Vertz 1989).

The list of activities undertaken by local parties during an election year suggests several things about the nature of local parties. First, the activities undertaken by local parties are similar for both Republicans and Democrats.

TABLE 3.3 Activities of Local Party Organizations (in percent)

Activity	Republican	Democrat
Distribute Campaign Literature	91	89
Organize Campaign Events	87	85
Distribute Posters and Signs	81	83
Arrange Fund-Raising Events	83	80
Hold Voter Registration Drives	78	79
Organize Telephone Campaigns	78	76
Prepare Press Releases	75	72
Contribute Money to Candidates	76	68
Send Mail to Voters	75	66
Conduct Door-to-Door Canvassing	69	67
Buy Newspaper Advertisements	66	61
Buy Radio/TV Advertisements	36	38
Use Public Opinion Surveys	26	22
Buy Billboard Space	10	10

Note: Figures are the percentage of local party organizations that reported engaging in the activity in the 1984 election.

Source: Adapted from Gibson, Frendreis, and Vertz (1989, 73–74).

Although Republican local parties report slightly higher levels of activities, the differences between the parties are surprisingly small. It appears that party organizations operate in a similar fashion at the local level regardless of partisanship. This conclusion fits with the finding that, in organizational terms, local parties tend to be quite similar. This does not hold true at the state level, however. State Republican parties are generally more sophisticated organizationally than state Democratic parties (Aldrich 2000; Cotter et al. 1984). At the local level, however, there are less notable differences between parties. "Generally, it is the larger, industrialized, and somewhat wealthier states which have the strongest local party organizations," both Democratic and Republican (Cotter et al. 1984, 51).

The activities in table 3.3, which are listed from most common to least common, suggest something else about the nature of local parties. The more common activities conducted by local parties tend to be those that involve mobilizing volunteers; the least common are those that require spending sizable amounts of money. Nearly all the local parties reported distributing literature, organizing campaign rallies, or distributing yard signs. Considerably fewer local parties reported conducting activities that required money, for example, buying advertisements on radio or television or renting billboards. The differences in these activities emphasize that local parties tend to thrive on people, whereas state and national parties thrive on money.

Changes in State and Local Parties

Over the past several decades, state parties have undergone a revitalization due, in large part, to their adaptation to the service party role. In contrast to the 1950s and 1960s, state parties have more money, are better organized, have more professional staff, and are engaged in a broad range of activities designed to help candidates and build party organization (Aldrich 2000; Cotter et al. 1984; Gibson, Frendreis, and Vertz 1989; Reichley 1992).

Of course, this change did not occur quickly, nor has it occurred uniformly across states. In general, the strengthening of party organization and greater activism of state and local parties have come about as a result of policies initiated by the national Republican party (Bibby 2002; Reichley 1992). The Republican party's persistent minority status nationally in the 1960s led the party to concentrate on improving its organizational capacity to assist candidates. As a result, Republicans began to provide cash and political expertise to help state Republican parties and, in doing so, established an organizational advantage over many state Democratic parties. Only later, in the mid–1980s, did the national Democratic party respond with similar programs to assist its state party organizations.

Another significant development has been the growth of legislative campaign committees in many states (Gierzynski 1992; Shea 1995). **Legislative campaign committees (LCCs)** are organizations that collect contributions from donors, usually interest groups, and distribute campaign contributions to candidates running for the state legislature. Much like their counterparts in Congress discussed later in this chapter, these organizations are structured by party (Democratic or Republican) and chamber (House or Senate). In New York, for example, four LCCs operate in the state: House Republicans, House Democrats, Senate Republicans, and Senate Democrats. Active LCCs exist in most states, but not all. New York, Wisconsin, Ohio, Indiana, Washington, and Illinois are all examples of states that have active LCCs capable of providing a range of services to legislative candidates in addition to making direct campaign contributions to candidates. In general, LCCs are most fully developed in states with professional legislatures and highly competitive state elections (Rosenthal 1995).

The development of LCCs suggests several important points. First, the emergence of LCCs has been fueled by the growing importance of money in state and local campaigns. It can be difficult for candidates in low-profile state elections to raise money, yet the cost of running for such offices has risen across the country. Thus, LCCs provide a mechanism for established state legislators to raise money from individuals and groups and use it to assist candidates from their party. The creation of LCCs is an extension of what has happened at the national level and reflects the efforts of state political leaders to adapt to contemporary circumstances.

Second, the spread of LCCs underscores the ambivalent nature of state party organizations. On the one hand, LCCs may strengthen party loyalties by funneling interest group money to legislators through a party-related organization. Newly elected legislators may feel an obligation to other members of their legislative party rather than to specific interest groups or wealthy donors. On the other hand, although organized along party lines, LCCs are organizationally separate from state parties. At times, an LCC may even compete with a state or local party organization. Daniel Shea (1995) describes a special legislative election in New York in which squabbling over campaign strategy between the local Democratic party and the Democratic Assembly Campaign Committee ended up hurting the Democratic candidate.

Finally, LCCs are not always used to pursue party goals. In addition to the "caucus" type of LCC created by Democrats or Republicans in the legislature, we have also seen the use of "leadership" LCCs (Gierzynski 1992, 39–43). A leadership campaign committee differs from a caucus LCC because it is controlled by a legislative leader. An extraordinary example of the use of a leadership LCC occurred when the Speaker of the California Assembly, Willie Brown, used his personal LCC to dole out $2.9 million in 1982 and $2.4 million to state legislative campaigns in 1984. Brown used his leadership committee rather than the Democratic party's LCC in order to maximize his personal control over the distribution of campaign contributions. Although the California example is an extreme case, some scholars point out that the use of leadership LCCs may encourage state legislators to be loyal to particular legislative leaders rather than political parties (Reichley 1992, 392; Rosenthal 1994).

The state party organizations of today have largely adapted to the role of service parties. State parties today are stronger and more professional organizations than they were in the 1950s and 1960s. Local parties are not the dominant party machines of the late nineteenth and early twentieth centuries, but they remain organized and active. The increased organizational strength of state and local parties raises a question: do the services supplied to candidates and the campaign activities conducted by the parties actually help candidates win elections? The answer to this question appears to be a qualified yes. There is evidence indicating that a state party that is organizationally stronger than its competitor has greater success in gubernatorial elections (Cotter et al. 1984, 101). The evidence for local parties is less clear-cut. Overall, there appears to be little relationship between local party strength and votes for the party's candidates. Local party strength does, however, appear to help with recruiting candidates to run for the state legislature and even for Congress (Frendreis, Gibson, and Vertz 1990). A survey of candidates who ran for the state legislature in seven states found that candidates rated the services provided by their political party as not being very helpful to their campaign (Hogan 2002). Still, these candidates saw local parties as being the most helpful with traditional grassroots activities, such as mobilizing voters on election day, while state party organizations and LCCs were seen as more helpful with activities such as fund-raising (Hogan 2002, 73–75).

State and local parties have, for the most part, adapted well to the new realities of candidate-centered elections. In most states, the political scene today is more complicated than it was forty years ago. In addition to political parties, states have seen a proliferation of political consultants, an increase in the number of interest groups and political action committees, and the emergence of new organizations such as the legislative campaign committees. The state parties, in particular, have responded by becoming more professional and active. But the demand for greater activity among state political parties may be coming at the cost of reduced autonomy as state parties have come to rely increasingly on resources provided by their national party organizations.

National Parties

It is common to refer to "the" Democratic party or "the" Republican party as if each party were a single national organization. The reality of party organization, of course, is more complex. Even at the national level, there is no single party organization. Rather, both major parties consist of several important organizations that together are what we think of as the Republican and Democratic parties. These various national organizations reflect the historical development of each party as well as features of the American political system.

The contemporary structures of both major parties today are similar. But each party has followed a different path with respect to adapting itself to the changing nature of politics. Change in the Democratic party has largely come about as party rules have been reformed to make the party more inclusive and representative. Change in the Republican party, in contrast, has largely been guided by efforts to improve the electoral performance of the party.

After the tumultuous convention of 1968, Democrats undertook a series of reforms designed to make the party's nomination process more open and more representative of party constituents. Beginning with the McGovern-Fraser commission, Democrats changed the party's rules for selecting delegates and established procedures ensuring that state parties would comply with national party rules. Efforts to reform the nomination procedures were not settled easily, however. The Democrats set up additional reform commissions after the 1972, 1976, 1980, and 1984 elections that were designed to remedy defects perceived in the previous election nomination.

Although Democrats focused on the nomination process, leaders in the Republican party chose to improve the performance of their central party organization. The linchpin of this strategy has been to raise more money for the national party and to use the cash to provide services for candidates and state parties. Under the leadership of party chair Ray Bliss (1965–1969), the Republicans essentially invented the service party organization.

Although the two parties pursued different paths in the 1970s and 1980s, developments in one party led to changes in the other as well. Because changes in the Democratic party led states to modify their nomination procedures, the Republican nomination process often had to change to meet new state requirements. More dramatically, Democratic party leaders realized by the mid–1980s that they were seriously behind the Republicans in the ability to raise money and provide services to candidates. The Democratic party then made a concerted effort to catch up with Republican innovations in party organization. Thus, the national parties retain their traditional structures, adapted to the realities of contemporary politics.

Party Conventions

Formal authority for both major political parties is vested in a national convention that meets every four years. The delegates selected to attend the Republican and Democratic conventions are responsible for choosing the party's nominee for president, approving the party's platform, and approving any changes to party rules or organization. Though formally the supreme authority in party matters, the national conventions are clearly less important today than they were prior to World War II.

One reason for the diminishing importance of conventions is the growing number of state primaries (a point discussed in more detail in the next chapter). Since the 1970s, the process of selecting each party's nominee for the presidency has been determined by the selection of pledged delegates in state primaries rather than at the convention itself. Another change concerns control over the party's platform. Although delegates can still influence the party platform, the process of writing the platform is usually carefully monitored by supporters of the presidential nominee. Since the nominee is usually known prior to the convention, supporters of the nominee try to prevent the party from adopting potentially damaging platform planks on the eve of the general election campaign. Finally, even though the national conventions decide the organizational structure and rules of the party, the responsibilities of running the party's increasingly complex affairs are handled by the national committee and the chairperson of the national committee.

Although the national conventions have become less important as decision-making bodies, they are still important as symbols of the parties. They bring together representatives from across the United States to perform the party's most significant functions—selecting the presidential ticket and writing the platform.

In practice, the contemporary conventions have stopped being a mechanism for selecting the party's nominee and have become a showcase for the party's presidential candidate. Because television coverage of the conventions allows candidates to present themselves and their major campaign themes to viewers virtually unchallenged, the nominee's supporters script the party convention to control the candidate's and the party's image with the attentive electorate. Debates regarded by party insiders as divisive or overly technical are relegated to nontelevised times; speakers who appear in prime time are carefully selected and coached to emphasize particular themes. At the 2004 Democratic National Convention, for example, the Kerry campaign sought to neutralize the expected Republican advantage on national security issues by repeatedly emphasizing Senator Kerry's military service in Vietnam. The convention included speeches from Kerry's Vietnam crewmates, it had former Georgia senator and Vietnam veteran Max Cleland introduce Kerry's acceptance speech, and Kerry began his acceptance speech with a military salute and the line: "I'm John Kerry, and I'm reporting for duty." This example helps to illustrate the general point that party leaders see their conventions as a way to present a carefully crafted view of the party and its candidates to the voters.

Do such efforts to control the convention help the party's nominee? There is little evidence to suggest that voters are attracted to a party simply based on its convention, but there is some anecdotal evidence to suggest that a poor convention may hurt. For instance, in contrast to the carefully scripted 1984 and 1988 conventions, the 1992 Republican convention that nominated President George H. W. Bush for reelection was marked by considerable controversy over the speech given by Patrick Buchanan. Although controversy over the Buchanan speech probably did not contribute to Bush's defeat in 1992, it certainly did not help the Bush-Quayle ticket focus attention on the themes the campaign wanted to communicate to voters.

Another way to assess the effect of a party convention is to examine the **convention bounce**—the difference in a candidate's intended vote before and after the party's nominating convention. Prior to the 2004 Republican convention in New York City, for example, about 46 percent of registered voters in a Gallup poll indicated they intended to vote for George W. Bush. In weekend polling after the convention that nominated Bush and running mate Dick Cheney, 48 percent of registered voters said they intended to vote for the Bush-Cheney ticket. Thus, Bush got a two-point convention bounce (see table 3.4). Because the candidates and party receive several days of nearly exclusive attention from

the national media, including hours of prime-time television coverage, the candidate's intended vote usually jumps immediately after the party's nominating convention.

As table 3.4 shows, since 1964, when Gallup first asked the intended vote questions just before and after the conventions, the average convention bounce has been 5.4 percent. Republican candidates have fared slightly better on average, at 5.5 percent, than Democratic candidates, at 5.3 percent. Between 1964 and 2004, the "out party" (the party not holding the presidency) generally received a higher bounce because it traditionally holds its convention first. On average, the out party has a convention bounce of 6 percent, whereas the party in power has an average bounce of 4.8 percent (with the eight incumbent presidents averaging a 4.6 percent bounce).

Of course, the size of the bounce depends on how the candidate was perceived before the convention as well as what happened at the convention. In 1964, for example, Republican Barry Goldwater got a respectable 5 percent bounce after the Republican convention, whereas President Johnson got no discernible bounce. But President Johnson's lack of bounce was due, no doubt, to the fact that he had a 69 percent approval rating prior to the convention. In recent years, candidates representing the party out of power have done particularly well. Prior to 1992, the Gallup poll recorded only one double-digit increase— Jimmy Carter's 10 percent bounce in 1980. In 1992, Bill Clinton recorded the largest convention bounce measured by Gallup at 16 percent, attributable in part to the dramatic exit of Ross Perot from the presidential race just prior to the Democratic convention (Saad 1996). Republican Bob Dole got an 11 point convention bounce in 1996.

The summer nominating conventions have been an important ritual for American parties since the nineteenth century and have been broadcast on television since 1952. Yet, in recent years, there has been growing dissatisfaction with the conventions and a decline in the number of hours shown on

TABLE 3.4 Convention Bounce for Major Party Presidential Candidates, 1964–2004

Year	Candidate	Party	Bounce
2004	Kerry	Democrat	0
	Bush, G.W. (I)	Republican	2
2000	Bush, G.W.	Republican	4
	Gore	Democrat	8
1996	Dole	Republican	11
	Clinton (I)	Democrat	5
1992	Clinton	Democrat	16
	Bush (I)	Republican	5
1988	Dukakis	Democrat	7
	Bush	Republican	6
1984	Mondale	Democrat	1
	Reagan (I)	Republican	4
1980	Reagan	Republican	8
	Carter (I)	Democrat	10
1976	Carter	Democrat	9
	Ford (I)	Republican	4
1972	McGovern	Democrat	0
	Nixon (I)	Republican	7
1968	Nixon	Republican	5
	Humphrey	Democrat	2
1964	Goldwater	Republican	5
	Johnson (I)	Democrat	0

Average Bounce, 1964–2004

All Candidates	= 5.4	Out-Party Candidates	= 6.0
Republican Candidates	= 5.5	In-Party Candidates	= 4.8
Democratic Candidates	= 5.3	Incumbent Presidents	= 4.6

Note: (I) denotes an incumbent president. For each election year the out party traditionally holds the first convention and so is listed first.

Source: Created by authors using data on convention bounce for 1964 to 1992 from Saad (1996, 8–9) with post-1992 convention bounce calculated from Gallup Poll data by the authors.

television. With the growth of state primaries and pledged delegates, the party's nominee is generally known well in advance of the convention. As a result, instead of being the climax of the nomination process, conventions have become the opening of the general election campaign. Party leaders may regard a strong show of party unity as a valuable opportunity, but the increasingly choreographed convention proceedings shown on television have resulted in fewer viewers and dissatisfaction among journalists with the lack of "real" news stories. As veteran ABC news anchor Ted Koppel put it during the 1996 Republican convention in San Diego, "This convention is more of an 'infomercial' than a news event. Nothing surprising has happened. Nothing surprising is anticipated.

Frankly we expect the Democratic convention in Chicago to be much the same" (quoted in Laurence 1996, 4). The heyday of extended hours of television coverage for national conventions is undoubtedly over, but it is unlikely that there will be major changes in the convention system any time soon due to its importance to the parties.

The National Party Committees

Both major parties rely on a **national committee** to conduct party business between conventions. The two national committees are similar in function, but they differ markedly in membership. The Republican National Committee (RNC) uses a traditional method of representation based on states. According to the rules of the Republican party, three members are selected from each of the fifty states and six additional areas: the District of Columbia, Virgin Islands, Guam, Northern Mariana Islands, American Samoa, and Puerto Rico. The three representatives are the party chair and one national committeewoman and one national committeeman selected from each state. The RNC thus has a total membership of 168, representing all the states and additional areas equally, regardless of state population or party performance. In contrast, the Democratic National Committee (DNC) is far larger than the RNC and its membership criteria are more complex. Prior to 1972, the structure of the DNC was similar to the current RNC structure. In 1972, however, as part of the reforms recommended by the McGovern-Fraser commission, the party convention approved a change in representation on the DNC to increase participation in the party and enhance the representation of groups that had previously been underrepresented. Members of the DNC are selected from four constituencies: (1) the states and territories, (2) elected officials, (3) special constituency organizations, and (4) at-large members. The most numerous group of representatives is the one selected from states.

Membership in the DNC is not apportioned equally to all states but is based on population and past support for Democratic candidates. According to the Democratic party charter, each state has at least two members on the DNC, but larger states and states that have elected Democrats to office are apportioned additional seats (using the formula for apportioning national convention delegates discussed in the next chapter). In addition, the DNC consists of the state party chair and the next highest Democratic party official of the opposite sex from each state and six other areas: the District of Columbia, Virgin Islands, Guam, American Samoa, Puerto Rico, and "Democrats Abroad." The DNC also includes members who are elected officials from the national, state, or local level. The DNC reserves places for Democratic leaders in the House and Senate, as well as members of the Democratic Governors Association, the Democratic Mayors Conference, and other state and local elected officials. The DNC also includes members who are Democratic party officials and representatives of affiliated groups such as the Young Democrats, College Democrats, and the National Federation of Democratic Women. Finally, the DNC includes places for additional members to increase the representation of women, young people, and minority group members. Its total size varies, but the DNC usually has in excess of four hundred members.

Both Democrats and Republicans leave the selection of national committee members from the states to the state parties and state laws. In some states, national members are selected by the state party central committee or at a state party convention, whereas other states use primary elections to select members for the national committees.

The full national committee for each party is too large and meets too infrequently to govern the party effectively. Management tasks for the national committees, such as approving budgets, are handled by an executive committee. In keeping with differences between the parties, the RNC has a relatively small executive committee whereas the DNC has a larger executive committee. The RNC executive committee consists of the RNC chair and cochair and other RNC officials, members appointed by the chair of the RNC, and eight members elected from four regional caucuses of states. The Democrats' executive committee includes members of the DNC from the state regional caucuses as well as DNC officials and the chairs of various affiliated organizations.

In practice, the chairperson of the national party committee is primarily responsible for running the party between elections. The chair of each major party's national committee is formally elected by the full national committee, although in practice the selection of the party chair is heavily influenced by the incumbent president or presidential nominee. Typically, only when the party not holding the presidency replaces its chairperson after the presidential election is there a competitive election for party chair. After Democrats lost the 2004 presidential election, for instance, members of the DNC elected Howard Dean—the former governor of Vermont and a candidate for the 2004 Democratic presidential nomination—as the new chairman in 2005. In contrast, when the party wins the White House, the president usually chooses the chairperson.

The position of national party chair can be a demanding one. The goals for the chair of the DNC or RNC depend to a large extent on whether the party currently holds the White House. For the party in power, the party chairperson is selected by the president and is expected to be a strong public advocate for the administration. The chair of the party out of power has more freedom to target the administration for political criticism while preparing for future elections. Generally, it is the job of the party chair to raise money to pay off debts or build up funds for future campaigns, get a team in place for upcoming congressional or presidential elections, assist state parties to recruit candidates, and develop issue positions and campaign themes for the

party as a whole. For example, DNC chair Howard Dean launched an initiative termed the "50 State Strategy." This initiative was an effort to help build the strength of state and local Democratic parties across the United States by using the resources of the national party to provide paid organizers to assist local party activists. As part of Dean's strategy, veteran party workers were sent to each state to assess the party's organization and to try to ensure a basic level party personnel. Dean's initiative was generally popular with state Democratic parties but was criticized by some elected officials and political consultants who felt the party should concentrate its resources in those areas where it was most likely to make gains rather than spread resources across all states (Bai 2006; Kamarck 2006).

The Congressional Campaign Committees

The **congressional campaign committees** (CCCs) are an important element of both major political parties. These groups are not a formal part of the national party organization for either party but exist in order to promote the election goals of the Democratic and Republican members of the U.S. House and Senate. Each party in both houses of Congress maintains a campaign fund. The House committees are the National Republican Congressional Committee (NRCC) and the Democratic Congressional Campaign Committee (DCCC). The Senate committees are the National Republican Senatorial Committee (NRSC) and the Democratic Senatorial Campaign Committee (DSCC).

The CCCs have been in existence for some time. The first congressional campaign committee was formed by House Republicans shortly after the Civil War, whereas the Senate committees were created after the ratification of the Seventeenth Amendment in 1913, which provided for direct election of senators (Kolodny 1998). Although they have existed for a number of years, these committees have

FIGURE 3.1 Fund-Raising by Party Committees in 2003–2004 and 2005–2006 Election Cycles

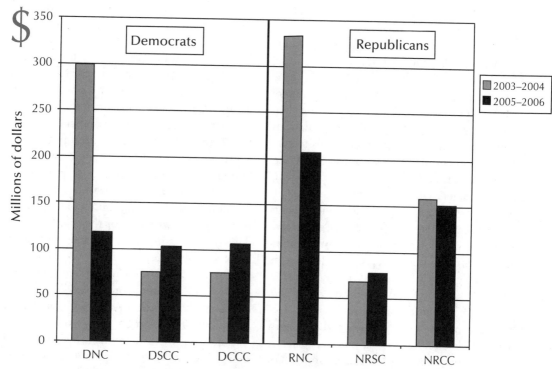

Source: Created by authors using data from Federal Election Commission (2006).

become more prominent in recent years because of the increasing importance of money in congressional campaigns. The CCCs are led by members of the House and the Senate. Leaders are usually chosen based on their ability to raise funds and implement a campaign strategy to help incumbent members get reelected and get new members of their party elected. Since the 1980s, the CCCs have employed a fairly large number of professional staff especially in election years.

The primary function of the CCCs is to use the advantage of incumbency to raise money to assist the party's candidates in House or Senate elections. Especially in recent years the parties have been highly effective at raising money, and the congressional committees have been an important part of the fund-raising effort for both parties. Figure 3.1 shows the amounts

raised in recent election cycles by the national party committees as well as the congressional campaign committees for both the Republicans and Democrats. Figure 3.1 illustrates two features of party fund-raising that generally hold true. First, the Republican party usually raises more money than the Democratic party. Second, the national party committees—the DNC and the RNC—typically raise larger amounts than the congressional committees. Still, the congressional committees are able to raise impressive sums of money—the DSCC and the DCCC both raised more than $100 million in the 2005–2006 election cycle, and the NRCC raised more than $150 million in both of these election cycles.

The congressional campaign committees raise money from individuals and from political action committees. Increasingly, a major source of money for the CCCs has been their own incumbent members of Congress (Larson 2004). Once the funds are raised, the committees provide direct contributions to congressional candidates, both incumbents and challengers, and may spend money independently in key states or districts to help their candidates. The leadership and staff of the congressional committees try to use their money as strategically as possible. All four committees attempt to use their funds to protect incumbent members who may be vulnerable to defeat and to promote the campaigns of challengers who have a good chance to win. As a general rule, established incumbents in safe seats should be less likely to receive help from their campaign committee than incumbents who face tough reelection fights or challengers in competitive contests. Studies of congressional elections indicate the CCCs allocate money primarily on the basis of electoral competitiveness (Damore and Hansford 1999; Nokken 2003). For a number of years, Republicans were more successful than Democrats in targeting money to competitive races (Damore and Hansford 1999; Dwyre 1994a), but Democrats have improved their performance in recent elections (Herrnson 2000, 95–97).

In addition to providing contributions directly to candidates' campaigns, congressional campaign committees may use "coordinated expenditures" by which the party spends money on behalf of its candidates. Coordinated expenditures often involve spending for campaign consultants, media time, production of campaign commercials, opinion polling, or candidate training. These services can often be used to help several candidates simultaneously, for instance, by conducting a statewide opinion poll or by holding a campaign seminar for congressional candidates. In addition to providing resources, the senators or representatives who are chosen to head their respective campaign committees are often active in recruiting congressional candidates well before the campaign season starts. A call from a well-known member of Congress with a promise of assistance from the congressional campaign committee can be a positive incentive for individuals contemplating a run for the House or Senate.

The recent prominence of the congressional campaign committees reflects an important lesson about the contemporary national parties: formal structure is often less important than control of resources. The idea of incumbent politicians collecting funds to assist all candidates from their party may appear to be the very essence of party commitment. Although organized by party, congressional campaign committees are not part of the formal structure of the major parties. That is, the campaign strategies and fundraising undertaken by the CCCs are controlled by members of Congress, not the party chair or the national committee. There is, of course, a very practical reason for members of Congress to assist their party's other candidates: Congress is organized by party, and being the majority party is tremendously advantageous (Kolodny 1998). Ambitious members of the same party may cooperate to promote their own good, which is not to imply that they are part of a strong hierarchical organization. Members of Congress and party officials seek the same goal and may coordinate their efforts, but neither group controls the actions of the other.

Conclusion: Contemporary Parties and the Service Party Role

The formal structure of American political parties is much the same today as it was at the turn of the century. Both major parties are composed of a loosely organized collection of state and local parties united through the mechanisms of a national party committee and a nominating convention meeting in the summer of presidential election years. But comparing only the outward similarity of the party structures misses the enormous changes that the parties have experienced.

The major political parties have changed because they had to adapt to new social and political circumstances. Quite apart from partisan concerns, American society has changed dramatically in ways that have affected the parties. In the nineteenth century, when there were high levels of immigration as well as internal migration from farms to cities, it was possible for strong local parties to organize masses of voters in an effort to control city governments. With immigration in decline and population movement going from the cities to the suburbs, urban political machines no longer dominated the political landscape. The development and spread of electronic broadcast media, first radio and later television, meant that citizens were no longer reliant on local newspapers or word-of-mouth communication for political information. Prior to the development of the mass electronic media, it made sense to campaign through organized rallies and candidate speeches. By using radio, television, and the Internet, candidates can communicate directly to voters and do not have to rely on a party organization as an intermediary. In sum, political parties, like other organizations, had to adapt to broader social changes.

There were also important changes in the political environment in which parties operate. Legislation passed during the Progressive era substantially changed party organization and operation. State adoption of the Australian ballot and subsequent passage of direct primary laws limited the control that party organizations had exercised over who appeared on the ballot under the party's label. Voter registration, limits on the ability of elected officials to hire and fire government employees, nonpartisan elections, and other laws took their toll on traditional party organizations. By the 1950s, state and local parties were no longer the dominant political organizations they had been in some areas, even though a few party machines managed to keep going in the 1960s (Mayhew 1986).

The combination of social and political change meant that party organization had reached its nadir just as new technology, especially television, was allowing candidates to speak directly to voters, bypassing the party organization altogether. The presidential election of 1952 was the first to feature televised advertisements for a presidential candidate; from that point on the medium became more accessible to candidates for a range of offices. An important consequence of the development of televised campaigning was that candidate's personal campaign organization became more central and the party organization became less important to candidates. The 1950s and 1960s thus marked a transition period. Party organizations were in the process of long-term atrophy, and candidates were beginning to take advantage of new technology to market themselves to voters.

The parties responded to these circumstances by adopting a "service party role." As service parties, the political parties have the primary function of providing services to candidates. Parties do not attempt to control or compete with the candidate's separate campaign organization; rather, the parties seek to recruit and assist candidates who can run under the party's label and win. In a sense, this has always been central to the role of political parties in the United States. What has changed, however, is the prominence of election contests. No longer do parties simply seek to mobilize "their" voters; now both parties and individual candidates must use sophisticated strategies to try to motivate party supporters and appeal to independent or swing voters at the same time. And increasingly political parties and candidates have been joined in these efforts to mobilize voters by a variety of interest groups. In the next chapter, we look at the rules that govern electoral contests.

CHAPTER 4

The American Electoral System

American political parties are something of a paradox. American political parties are among the oldest continuously established party organizations in the world and play a vital part in the conduct of American politics. Yet, by comparison with nearly any other democratic nation, American political parties are weak organizations that cannot control even such essential functions as determining which candidates run under the party's label.

Though seemingly contradictory, these two characterizations of American political parties are, in fact, quite compatible. American party organizations continue to exist and play an important part in American government because they have been able to adapt to the unique political environment of the United States. The American electoral environment itself is largely responsible for the type of political party system that exists in the United States today. In this chapter, we examine three important features of American election rules: the **plurality system**, the nomination process, and the **electoral college**.

Electoral Systems

One of the most fundamental features of any democratic system of government is the set of rules used to decide elections. The electoral rules help to determine the number of politi-

cal parties, the competitiveness of elections, the stability of government, and even how well citizens' policy preferences are translated into public policy. Before explaining the effects of the American electoral system, we need to discuss electoral systems in general.

The political consequences of various electoral arrangements have been carefully studied by political scientists (see, e.g., Lijphart 1990; 1994; Norris 2004; Rae 1967; Taagepera and Shugart 1989). Most scholars agree that the two most important features of any country's electoral system are the electoral formula and the district magnitude (Lijphart 1994, 10). Electoral formulas are the rules for deciding who gets elected. Most democracies in the world today use one of the following types of electoral formulas: (1) proportional representation systems, (2) plurality systems, and (3) semiproportional or mixed systems (Lijphart 1994, 10). Of these three types, the semiproportional system is the least common and will not be the focus of our attention. More important for our purposes is the distinction between proportional representation systems and plurality systems.

Most democratic nations use **proportional representation (PR)**. Proportional representation systems award seats in the legislature based on a party's proportion of the total vote. For example, a party that gets 40 percent of the popular vote should get about 40 percent of the seats in the legislature. There are a number of methods that may be used for determining how candidates are selected, but various PR systems share the idea that representation in legislative assemblies ought to be roughly proportional to overall support within the electorate. Some methods of PR are more favorable to parties that win relatively larger percentages of the vote; others treat parties relatively equitably.

The magnitude of electoral districts is the most significant determinant of how proportional a PR system is. Countries that use proportional representation have "multimember districts," meaning that two or more representatives are elected from the same geographic area. District magnitude, then, refers to how many representatives are elected from a particular district. Some PR countries, such as Ireland, have relatively small district magnitudes; the number of representatives per district is typically between three and five. Other nations have relatively large district magnitudes. In Israel, for example, the entire nation serves as one electoral district for the 120 members of the legislature. The relationship between district magnitude and the degree of proportionality in the electoral system is easy to identify: the larger the district magnitude, the more proportional the system can be (Lijphart 1990; Rae 1967; Taagepera and Shugart 1989, 112–125).

In contrast to PR, plurality systems are nearly always used in conjunction with single-member districts. A single-member district means that only one representative is elected from a geographic district. There is no logical necessity for using single-member districts with a plurality system. Two or three candidates with the most votes could just as easily be chosen from a given district; but, in practice, nations with plurality methods tend to use single-member districts. With a plurality formula, the decision rule is quite simple: the candidate with the most votes wins. The plurality formula, also known as "first past the post," is used in the United States, the United Kingdom, Canada, and India.

A related but slightly different electoral formula is the "majority-plurality" method that has been used at various times in France. The majority-plurality system requires the use of two ballots. On the first ballot, a candidate who receives a true majority of votes wins. If no candidate wins a majority in the first ballot, a second ballot is held and the winner is determined by a plurality of the votes. Although more than two candidates may participate in the second ballot, in practice the second ballot is a contest between the two strongest candidates, as weaker candidates withdraw and attempt to form an alliance with one of the remaining parties. In the United States, a similar type of electoral arrangement has been used in Louisiana (see the discussion on primary elections later in this chapter).

Since state governments in the United States are largely free to determine their own election laws, in theory a whole variety of electoral systems could be used. In practice, however, nearly all elections in the United States use a plurality system, although some states and localities have, at times, experimented with different systems.

Plurality elections are commonly used in the United States for several reasons. First, the plurality system is an efficient way to determine election outcomes. Because the candidate must simply win more votes than any other candidate, not a majority of the votes cast, the winner of the election is easily determined, whether two candidates or twenty candidates are competing for office. Of course, in a two-candidate election the results from a plurality system and a majority system would be the same. With three or more candidates, however, the plurality system still produces a clear winner, whereas a majority system may or may not produce a candidate with a majority of the votes. Another reason for the widespread use of the plurality system is tradition. The plurality system was used in England and has been commonly adopted by nations with a British colonial heritage.

Although plurality systems have advantages, they have limitations as well. One potential difficulty, particularly with multi-candidate elections, is that a plurality electoral formula tends to exaggerate the power of a plurality of voters. Consider the following hypothetical circumstance. Suppose that candidates from three parties (Party A, Party B, and Party C) were competing in ten single-member districts under a plurality electoral system. Further, suppose that the results in each district were the same: Party A's candidate got 35 percent of the vote, Party B's candidate got 33 percent of the vote, and Party C's candidate got 32 percent of the vote. Under a plurality system, Party A's candidate, who won the most votes in each district, would win *all* the seats in the legislature. That is, even though only 35 percent of voters supported it, Party A would get 100 percent of the seats. Thus, a plurality electoral system may transform a small plurality of support, 35 percent in our example, into a legislative majority.

Contrast the results just described with a PR system. If the ten seats had been part of one multimember district and the three parties had each earned the same percentages of the vote, Party A would likely get four seats and Parties B and C would each win three seats. Party A would still be advantaged by an electoral formula that translated 35 percent electoral support into 40 percent (four of ten) of the legislative seats; but the bias under the PR system would be much less than under a plurality method. Although PR would produce legislative representation more nearly matching the level of support within the electorate, it would not provide one party a clear majority in the legislature. In order to control a majority of the ten votes within the legislature, two of the parties would have to form a coalition.

The effects of a plurality electoral formula are readily apparent in real election results as well. Table 4.1 shows the outcomes from two recent British parliamentary elections to illustrate these effects. Notice that in both the 2001 and 2005 general elections in Britain, the Labour party got much less than a majority of the national vote but won a majority of the seats in parliament. Indeed, in the 2005 election, Labour received only 35 percent of the vote nationally, which was only 3 percent more than the Conservative party. But because Labour candidates won at least a plurality of the vote in 356 of the parliamentary districts compared to the Conservative candidates winning a plurality in 198 districts, the Labour party was able to control the House of Commons with 55 percent of the seats. These results illustrate how the plurality electoral system tends to result in a majority party in the legislature even if there is no majority in terms of the national vote.

The party that has fared least well under the plurality electoral laws in Britain has been the Liberal Democratic party. In 2005, for example, the Liberal Democrats got more than 22 percent of the vote, but won fewer than 10 percent of the seats in parliament. Because the party's base of voters is spread across large parts of the country and is not concentrated in a few constituencies, the Liberal Democrats have the curse of finishing second in many constituencies. In contrast, the parties that make up the "other" category tend to be small parties whose support is concentrated in a few constituencies. These parties include Scottish and Welsh national parties as well as the parties of Northern Ireland. Because their appeal is limited to certain constituencies, none of these parties gets a large share of the national vote, but they stand a better chance of getting a plurality of votes in those areas where their support is concentrated. For a third party in a plurality system, it is better to have support that is concentrated than it is to have support that is thinly spread over a wide area. Election outcomes in which seemingly more popular parties get less representation in parliament have led some political observers in Britain to call for changes in the electoral laws.

These examples show an important feature of electoral systems: the way that votes are

TABLE 4.1 Effect of a Plurality Electoral System: Election Results from the United Kingdom, 2001 and 2005

	Percent of Vote	Number of Seats	Percent of Seats
British Election 2001			
Labour	40.7	413	62.7
Conservative	31.7	166	25.2
Liberal Democrats	18.3	52	7.9
Other	9.3	28	4.2
Total	**100.0**	**659**	**100.0**
British Election 2005			
Labour	35.3	356	55.1
Conservative	32.3	198	30.7
Liberal Democrats	22.1	62	9.6
Other	10.3	30	4.6
Total	**100.0**	**646**	**100.0**

Note: The "other" category includes the Scottish National Party, Plaid Cymru (Welsh nationalist party), and the parties of Northern Ireland.

Source: Compiled by authors.

translated into seats has substantial political consequences. One of the best known statements of this relationship is "Duverger's Law," so named because it was proposed by French political scientist Maurice Duverger. Duverger stated, in effect, that plurality electoral methods were associated with two-party political systems and PR electoral methods with multiparty systems (1963, 217). Duverger also noted that plurality systems tend to result in more durable governments than PR systems because of the political difficulties associated with maintaining government coalitions (1963, 403–412). Of course, Duverger's Law does not hold in all cases. Canada serves as a contemporary example of a nation with a plurality electoral system but more than two major political parties.

Nonetheless, the logic of Duverger's analysis is still helpful in explaining an important feature of American politics. Despite the existence of a number of third parties at times in American history, the United States is correctly described as having a two-party system.

One of the chief reasons for the dominance of two large parties is that the plurality electoral system punishes minor parties. In a PR system, small parties that can attract 10 to 15 percent of the total vote stand a good chance of gaining representation in the legislature. With a plurality system, a party that cannot get the most votes in at least some districts will not be represented. Many third parties have discovered that in a plurality system it may be better to ally themselves with one of the major parties in order to have some influence, rather than go it alone and get nothing. In part as a result of our plurality system, American parties tend to be broad-based electoral coalitions designed to enhance their candidates' chances of winning.

Nominations

The plurality electoral system that predominates in American elections is not the most widely used, but it is employed in other democratic nations. When it comes to nominating candidates for office, however, the process used in the United States is unique: a state-run **direct primary**. It was not always that way, however. As discussed in Chapter 2, when parties began to organize in this country, candidates for office were chosen by means of a caucus of party supporters within the legislative branch. As parties began to develop "extra-parliamentary" organizations, however, the legislative caucus was replaced by a party convention in which supporters from across the state or the nation gathered to elect the party's nominee. Although the legislative caucus system and the convention system have flaws, they both have the advantage that the party's candidates are selected by people closely affiliated with the party itself. That is, the party controls its own nominations.

In most democratic nations, candidates are selected by the parties (Ware 1996, 257–288). Most political parties have developed their own internal rules for selecting candidates. In Britain, for instance, the selection of candidates to run for parliament is determined by the parties. The Conservative party provides a list of candidates who have met certain party criteria, but otherwise the selection of the party's candidate is made by members of the local constituency party. The Labour party has a more complex set of rules set by the central party, but candidates are nevertheless selected by the local parties. Other nations, such as Germany, have certain rules established by the government regarding the process that parties must use to select candidates. Yet, even in Germany, the selection of candidates for office is primarily a decision left to the parties.

In the United States, however, candidate selection is determined more by state government than by the parties themselves. The method for selecting party nominees used most widely in the United States is the direct primary. In a direct primary, it is the voters who decide the party's candidate for the general election rather than party officials or

party activists. It is not the primary itself that is unique; political parties in other nations have used **primary elections** to select candidates. What is unusual about the American system is that it is mandated by the states. As one scholar put it, "The distinctiveness of the American experience lies not so much in the use of primaries *per se*, nor in state regulation of the nomination process, but in the sheer extent of state involvement in this aspect of party activity" (Ware 1996, 260).

Extensive state government involvement in the nomination process in the United States stems from the Progressive era. The direct primary was championed by Progressive reformers as a way to make the selection of candidates more democratic and to limit the power of "party bosses." Wisconsin was the first state to adopt a statewide direct primary system in 1903. Wisconsin was a stronghold of the Progressive movement, but other states adopted the innovation and by 1920 a majority of states were using the direct primary. Today, some form of the direct primary is in place in every state, although there is considerable variation among states.

State Primaries

States have a variety of rules governing the nomination process. Further, the system used by a particular state at any point in time is subject to change as state officials and state parties attempt to improve the system or, in some cases, simply seek partisan advantage by altering the electoral rules. Despite the complexity of keeping up with current state law and party rules concerning the nomination process, several broad patterns are clear.

As with general elections, primary elections allow any legally registered citizen to participate. The criteria for determining who is eligible to vote in a primary represent a fundamental distinction in the primary election process. In general, there are two types of state primary elections: closed primaries and open primaries. States with closed primaries require voters to be registered as a Republican or Democrat to vote in that party's primary. For example, if you were a resident of New York and wanted to vote in the Republican primary, you would not only have to be a registered voter but also registered as a Republican to vote in the Republican primary. In states with open primaries, in contrast, voters are not required to register their party affiliation prior to the primary election.

Most states hold closed primaries, but there are differences among states as to when voters must register. The bulk of states that hold closed primaries, including the large states of Pennsylvania, New York, and Florida, require voters to register their party affiliation well in advance of the primary election. Other states with closed primaries allow registered voters to change their party registration at the polls on the day of the primary election. In addition, some state parties allow unaffiliated or independent voters to vote in the party's primary election. For example, Connecticut had a closed primary law that prohibited voters who were not registered partisans from voting in a party primary. But, in the case of *Tashjian v. Republican Party of Connecticut* (1986), the Supreme Court ruled that state law could not prevent the Connecticut Republican party from allowing unaffiliated voters to participate in its primary. Closed primaries are usually preferred by party officials because they are regarded as giving party supporters more control over nominations and limiting the opportunities for people who are not party supporters to play any part in selecting the party's candidates.

A smaller number of states use open primaries than use closed primaries. In some open primary states, voters are required to ask for the ballot of one party or the other when they appear at the polls. Although registered voters may participate in either the Democratic or Republican primary regardless of their own partisan affiliation, they must at least publicly request a party's primary ballot (some states allow these public declarations to be challenged by a party's poll watchers). In

an even less restrictive form of the open primary, registered voters are given the primary ballots of both parties and are allowed to choose, in the privacy of the polling booth, the primary in which they want to vote.

Although the primary elections used in most states can be classified as either closed or open, there are some variations on these practices that merit discussion as well. For many years, the states of Alaska and Washington used what was called a "blanket primary." A blanket primary is a variant of the open primary in which the primary contests of both parties are included on a single ballot. Unlike an open primary in which the voter must choose one party's ballot or the other, in a blanket primary the voter could shift between party primaries for different offices. The ballot for a blanket primary looked much like a general election ballot with voters free to vote for, say, a Republican candidate among all the candidates for governor and then vote for a Democratic candidate among the candidates for a House seat. A blanket primary thus allowed voters the maximum freedom to participate in interesting or hotly contested primary elections regardless of party, but it did so potentially at the cost of preventing the party's regular supporters from controlling the selection of the party's candidates.

Political parties generally opposed the blanket primary because it increased the chances that voters who were not affiliated with the party—and indeed may have been strongly opposed to the party's views—could select the party's general election nominee. Even though the major parties did not like the blanket primary, the states of Washington and Alaska were able to continue using them because of tradition and because the blanket primary was popular with the voters in those states. The beginning of the end of the state-imposed blanket primary, however, occurred in 1996 when voters in California passed a citizens' initiative, Proposition 198, that instituted a blanket primary for California in 1998. This initiative led to a court challenge to the new primary law by several state parties in

California including the Republican, Democratic, and Libertarian parties. This dispute over the primary election system went all the way to the U.S. Supreme Court. In the case of *California Democratic Party v. Jones* (2000), the Supreme Court ruled that the voters could not impose a blanket primary on the political parties because this action infringed on the parties' freedom of association.

The Court's decision not only meant that California could not hold a blanket primary, it also meant that Washington and Alaska could not require their political parties to continue to use blanket primaries to select their candidates for office. Alaska now allows the state Republican party to use a closed primary while the other parties in the state have voluntarily agreed to use a blanket primary, a decision that the Alaska Supreme Court has ruled is permissible (Aisenbrey 2006). The state of Washington has since adopted an open primary that requires voters to select the party's primary in which they will vote. The new primary system has not been popular with voters, however, and in 2004 voters approved a citizen initiative, Initiative 872, to create a new version of the blanket primary. The primary system created by this initiative, called the "top two" primary, would identify candidates by their party labels but it would send the two candidates with the most votes into the general election regardless of which party they represented (thus potentially allowing two Republicans or two Democrats to run against each other in the general election). This primary system has yet to be used, however, because its constitutionality has been challenged in court.

The primary system passed by initiative in Washington is based on another variant of the open primary that has been used in the state of Louisiana. Since 1978, Louisiana has used a "nonpartisan" or "all-party" primary in which all the candidates for a particular office are listed on the same ballot regardless of party. If one candidate wins a majority of the votes cast in the primary, usually held in October, there is no general election for that office. The winner of the primary is declared the winner based on obtaining a majority of votes in the primary. If no candidate wins a majority, then the general election features the two candidates who got the most votes in the primary regardless of party. Thus, a Louisiana general election may feature one Republican and one Democrat or even two Republicans or two Democratic candidates to determine the winner.

Louisiana's nonpartisan primary, however, has come into conflict with federal election law. In 1995, a group of Louisiana voters challenged the legality of the state's primary system for elections to U.S. House and Senate seats. These voters argued that Louisiana's system violated federal law requiring a uniform national election because by winning a majority of votes in the primary, federal officials were being elected before the federal election day in November. The U.S. Supreme Court ruled, in the case of *Foster v. Love* (1997), that Louisiana's primary system violated federal law mandating a uniform election day. In order to comply with federal law while still keeping its open primary system, Louisiana followed a court-imposed process for a number of years. With this system, the open primary for federal offices was conducted on election day in November and, if no candidate received a majority, the top-two vote-getting candidates competed in a runoff election in December. Some members of the Louisiana state legislature, however, argued that the potential for having Louisiana's members of Congress elected later than other states was a disadvantage. So, in 2006, the Louisiana legislature created a closed party primary for congressional elections while maintaining the state's nonpartisan primary for state and local elective offices (Anderson 2007). Thus, for federal elections, Louisiana has joined the majority of states using a closed primary while still maintaining its distinctive nonpartisan primary for state elections.

From the perspective of the party organizations, closed primaries are preferable to other types of primary election arrangements. Closed primaries are preferred because they effectively minimize the threat of "crossover" voting or, even worse, "raiding." Crossover voting occurs when voters who are not regular supporters of a party participate in the party's primary election. For example, if the Republican party in an open primary state were having a closely contested primary and the Democratic candidate faced no opposition, some Democratic party identifiers may be inclined to vote in the Republican primary. "Raiding" would occur if those Democrats chose to participate in the Republican primary with the intent of voting for the Republican candidate they believe to be the weaker general election opponent in order to improve the likelihood of the Democratic candidate winning the general election.

Proponents of strong parties argue that closed primaries are preferable because they prevent the threat of nonsupporters influencing a nomination. Despite this concern, studies of crossover voting in open primary states have found little evidence to suggest that the practice is widespread or that voters act strategically to try to weaken their opponents (Abramowitz, McGlennon, and Rapoport 1981; Hedlun and Watts 1986; Sides, Cohen, and Citrin 2002; Wekkin 1991). On the other side, advocates for open primaries maintain that they allow for higher levels of citizen participation and may even produce more moderate party nominees. Research on the impact of open primaries in presidential nomination contests suggests that "through the adoption of open primaries, Republicans' primary electorates often wind up less conservative than their party following and Democratic primaries less liberal than theirs" (Kaufmann, Gimpel, and Hoffman 2003, 471).

All states have provisions for primary elections to select candidates for the general election, and most states use only a direct primary election. A number of states, however, provide for a system of party conventions in place of, or in addition to, primaries (Council of State Governments 2004, 271–272). The most commonly used format is the "convention-first" method, which allows parties in Colorado, Connecticut, New Mexico, North Dakota, and Utah to hold state party conventions prior to the primary. The chief advantage of a convention, from the perspective of the party organization, is that party activists are able to exercise greater control in selecting nominees than if only a pure primary is held.

Other states use their party caucus-convention systems in different ways. One state, Iowa, requires a party to hold a convention after the primaries to select the party's nominee if no candidate in the primary receives more than 35 percent of the vote. Indiana, Michigan, and South Dakota use primaries for top state offices, such as governor, but let the parties select nominees for other offices at party conventions. Some states, such as Alabama, allow state parties to choose whether to hold a party convention or use the state primary to select nominees. These mixed convention-primary systems used in some states allow state party organizations and party activists a greater role in the selection of their party's nominees than does a pure primary election method.

Presidential Primaries

In addition to selecting nominees for state office, primary elections have also come to play a prominent role in the selection of presidential candidates. In primary elections for state offices such as governor, people vote directly for the candidate they prefer to be the party's nominee. The presidential nomination, however, is formally determined at the party's **national nominating convention**. Thus, what is actually being determined during a **presidential primary** is who the delegates to a party's national convention will be. The process for selecting delegates is complex because it involves the national parties, the state parties, and state laws.

The rules of the national parties determine the allocation of delegates to the states. Both the number of delegates and the allocation rules differ between the major parties. Republicans have fewer delegates at their national convention than Democrats. In 2004, for example, Republicans had 2,509 delegates and the Democrats had 4,322 delegates. Republicans allocate the number of delegates for a state or territory based on population and award additional or "bonus" delegates to states for support of the Republican presidential candidate in previous elections and for electing Republicans to national and state offices.

The Democrats allocate the number of base delegates to the states (and the District of Columbia) using a complex formula based on the proportion of the state's popular vote for the Democratic presidential candidate and the state's Democratic electoral college votes from the three preceding presidential elections. The Democrats also allocate additional delegates who are "party leaders and elected officials" (PLEOs), sometimes called "superdelegates." These PLEO delegates may be either pledged or unpledged delegates. The pledged PLEOs are similar to base delegates in the sense that they are publicly committed to a candidate for the party's presidential nominee. Unpledged PLEOs, in contrast, are free to support any candidate for the nomination. The original intention of the Democrats in devising the system of awarding PLEO delegates was to amplify the voice of delegates who would be most likely to select a nominee based on electability. But in practice, no nomination contest since the Democrats created this system has been close enough to have the votes of unpledged delegates be decisive.

The national parties can, if they choose, influence the selection rules that states use to award delegates to winning candidates. For the most part, Republicans have left the question of delegate selection to the states, whereas Democrats have tried hard to influence the selection process. Because the process is about selecting delegates to each party's national convention, the national parties have the leverage to influence the states by refusing to recognize delegates who are selected in ways that do not conform to party rules.

The traditional method used by states was "winner take all," in which the candidate who gets the most votes gets all the state's delegates. The winner-take-all system is based on the same logic that guides the plurality electoral formula discussed earlier in this chapter. Since the mid–1970s, however, the Democratic party has had a rule against using winner take all and has required states to use some form of proportional representation in awarding delegates. In 1992, Democrats again changed their rules to improve the application of proportional representation to ensure that any candidate who wins at least 15 percent of the vote receives some share of the state's convention delegates.

Within constraints imposed by the national parties, the states choose the method of delegate selection. The exact procedure by which convention delegates are selected differs from state to state. Currently most states use a primary election to determine delegate selection, with a small number of states using caucus-convention systems. Presidential primaries involve voters casting their ballots directly for their preferred candidate, who is then awarded delegates based on the vote. In a caucus-convention system, in contrast, the state parties hold a series of local meetings at which citizens who attend the meetings indicate their preference for the party's candidates and select delegates to attend the next level of meetings up to the state convention. National convention delegates are then elected at a state or congressional district convention.

Participation is considerably higher in primary elections than in caucus-convention meetings. In presidential primaries, much like general elections, candidates must emphasize a broad appeal to many different voters. As a result, candidates with name recognition and the resources to mount a media campaign usually do better than candidates without these advantages in states with primary elections. In caucus-convention states, on the other hand, campaign organization is an important factor. Candidates who have strong campaign organizations that can get their supporters to attend local meetings are much better off than candidates who lack strong organizations. Thus, the states of New Hampshire, which holds the first primary, and Iowa, which holds the first caucus, provide a demanding test for presidential campaigns. Though neither Iowa nor New Hampshire is particularly representative of other states, together they do provide an early test of both a candidate's voter appeal and campaign organization.

States also choose when to hold their elections, again in conformity with national party rules. Traditionally, the presidential primary season ran from late February to early June. Over the course of the last several elections, however, a number of states have moved up their primary or caucus dates in order to ensure having their election before the selection process is over. The shift to earlier primary dates is called "front-loading." Even though both major national parties have tried to discourage states from doing so, the front-loading of the primary process has continued as states seek to attract more attention from candidates and from the media by moving their primary election to an earlier point in the nomination season. The 2008 presidential primary calendar, for example, became heavily front-loaded as a number of states including California, Illinois, Michigan, New Jersey, New York, Pennsylvania, and Texas moved their presidential primary dates to early February. Some political observers believe that the front-loading of primaries has reached the point where there is a "de facto national primary" that helps well-known and well-funded candidates at the expense of lesser known candidates who need to win early contests to try to develop momentum (Milligan 2007).

Since 1968, there has been a marked increase in the number of states holding primary elections. In 1968, seventeen states held Democratic primaries and sixteen states held Republican primaries. By 2000, thirty-eight states held Democratic primaries and forty-two states held Republican primaries. As a result, most delegates to the national conventions are now selected in primaries rather than by caucus-convention. The chief reason for the shift to primaries was the internal reforms undertaken in the Democratic party after the 1968 Democratic National Convention. Although these reforms initiated by the McGovern-Fraser commission were not intended to compel states to use primary elections, in practice the new rules that the Democrats adopted led states to drop caucus-conventions to select delegates and use primaries instead. Moreover, even though these changes were initiated by the Democratic party, they also affected the Republicans. When states changed their laws to comply with Democratic party rules, the new procedures usually applied to both parties. Thus, primary elections, rather than caucus-conventions, have come to dominate the presidential selection process since the 1970s.

The Impact of Primary Elections

Progressive reformers urged the use of primary elections to open up elections to greater citizen participation and simultaneously weaken the power of party leaders over their organizations. Has the widespread adoption of primary elections brought about these intended consequences? For the most part, the answer is yes. Certainly, primary elections increase the number of citizens participating in the selection of party nominees. It is abundantly clear that more citizens vote in primary elections than participate in caucus meetings. Yet, in most states the turnout for primary elections is considerably below that of general elections. Thus, although citizens can involve themselves in the selection of party nominees, many voters choose not to do so. In a sense, then, the intent of the Progressive reformers has been only partially achieved; more citizens participate in primaries than in caucuses, but those voters who participate in primary elections are still a minority of those eligible to participate.

The effect of primaries on party structures, however, is more clear-cut. The widespread adoption of primary elections for state offices weakened the control of party leaders and ultimately the power of state and local party organizations. By the 1950s, state and local political parties were clearly weaker organizations in most states than they had been at the turn of the century prior to the adoption of the direct primary. Factors such as changing demographics and laws limiting patronage appointments also played a role, but the impact of direct primaries on the weakening of party organizations should not be overlooked. Although some states allow the parties greater latitude to use a caucus-convention system, the candidate selection process is still very much guided by state regulation.

The move to primary elections in the presidential nomination process, on the other hand, can be seen as more of a consequence of the weakening of party organization than a cause. The growth of presidential primaries was largely an unintended consequence of efforts by the Democrats to modify their internal party operations. Indeed, the ability of the national parties, both Democrats and Republicans, to influence state laws with regard to delegate selection can be interpreted as a sign of vigorous party organizations.

Of course, even after the parties make their nominations, the states continue to play an important role in election politics. Next we examine the role that states play in the general election due to the electoral college.

The Electoral College

When citizens cast their ballots for governor, senator, or state legislator, the winner is the candidate who receives a plurality of the votes cast. The only exception is the office of the president. The president, of course, is chosen by the vote of the electoral college rather than the popular vote. Perhaps because it is a unique institutional arrangement, the electoral college has attracted a good deal of attention. Since the impact of the electoral college on presidential elections is often not well understood, it is worth discussing in some detail.

The origins of the electoral college are rooted in the Constitutional Convention of 1787. During the debate over the new Constitution, Charles Pinckney and others spoke in favor of the president being selected by members of Congress so that states would be represented in the process. James Madison and others argued in favor of electing the president directly by popular vote. The idea of having a group of prominent individuals from the states, later known as electors, be responsible for selecting the one nationally elected official was a compromise (Mead 1987, 73; Glennon 1992, 7–10). To meet Pinckney's concerns, the electoral college provided a way for states to be central to the election of the national executive, since the selection of electors would be left to the states. To meet Madison's concern with keeping the president distinct from Congress, the electors were to convene in the states, and members of the House and Senate were prohibited from serving as electors.

Equally important, the electoral college provided a way to avoid the obvious practical difficulties of holding a national election in a predominantly rural nation in which citizens had limited access to information about political events in their own state, let alone information about what was happening in distant states. Thus, the local notables who were expected to serve as electors would meet in their states to cast their votes for president, and those votes would be sent to Congress to be counted. Recalling the antiparty sentiment common to political elites of the day, the electoral college was regarded as a practical way for state elites to select a national leader.

Problems with the workings of the electoral college were exposed by the election of 1800. As specified in Article 2, section 1 of the Constitution, electors were to cast two ballots. The candidate with a majority of electoral votes would become president and the person with the next highest number would become vice president. By the election of 1800, however, political parties had appeared. The Jeffersonian Republican party had organized a ticket of Thomas Jefferson for president and Aaron Burr for vice president. Republicans had a clear majority in the electoral college, but when Republican electors in the states dutifully cast one vote for Jefferson and one vote for Burr, it left the two candidates tied. Because of the tie vote, the election had to be decided in the House of Representatives. Although Jefferson prevailed, it was not without a good deal of political maneuvering by both Federalist and Republican supporters.

The election of 1800 led to the ratification of the Twelfth Amendment in 1804. It specifies that electors "shall name in their ballots the person voted for as President, and in distinct ballots the person voted for as Vice-President." The Twelfth Amendment sought to avoid the problem that arose in 1800 by requiring distinct votes for president and vice president. The amendment also limited the number of candidates the House could consider to the top three in the event that no candidate had a majority (originally the top five were considered by the House).

The Twelfth Amendment solved the problems of 1800, but subsequent elections have raised questions about the functioning of the electoral college. In 1824, another hotly contested presidential election had to be decided by the House of Representatives. Four presidential contenders won electoral votes but none had the required majority: Andrew Jackson had 99, John Quincy Adams had 84, William Crawford had 41, and Henry Clay had 37. Because only the top-three candidates would be considered by the House, Clay knew that he could not win. As Clay disagreed with Jackson on several key issues of the day and was closer in political outlook to Adams, he asked his supporters to back Adams. When the decision was made in the House, John Quincy Adams was elected president despite the fact that Jackson had won more electoral votes initially. After the election, John Quincy Adams named Henry Clay to be his secretary of state. Jackson's supporters denounced Clay's appointment as evidence of a "corrupt bargain" between Adams and Clay.

Later elections have illustrated another concern with the workings of the electoral college—when a candidate gets fewer popular votes than his opponent but is still elected president because of the electoral college. This circumstance has occurred three times in U.S. elections. In 1876, Democrat Samuel J. Tilden appeared to have defeated Republican Rutherford B. Hayes by winning 260,000 more popular votes. Disputes over electoral votes cast in Louisiana, South Carolina, and Florida, however, prevented either candidate from obtaining a majority of electors. Because the votes from the three southern states were disputed, the election was not decided in the House. A special electoral commission was set up to resolve only the contested ballots. The actions of the electoral commission were shot through with partisan politics, and ultimately Rutherford Hayes was elected president in one of the most questionable presidential elections in American history. In 1888, Democrat Grover Cleveland was defeated by Republican Benjamin Harrison in the electoral college, even though Cleveland had won about 90,000 more popular votes. Cleveland's revenge came in 1892 when he was reelected to the White House with a Democratic majority in Congress. Most recently, in the 2000 election, Republican George W. Bush defeated Democrat Al Gore by winning 271 electoral college votes to Gore's 267 even though Gore had some 540,000 more popular votes nationally than Bush. Of course, the important point to recognize is that presidents are not elected based on the total number of popular votes but by winning a majority of electoral college votes (or, if there is no electoral college majority, by winning a majority of the states in the House of Representatives as we saw in the election of 1824).

In spite of the controversy surrounding a few elections, the workings of the contemporary electoral college are fairly straightforward. Each state has a number of votes to cast in the electoral college that is equal to its combined number of representatives in the House and Senate. For example, Colorado has nine electoral college votes because it has seven members in the House of Representatives and two Senators. Because the number of House members from a state can change after a census, the number of a state's electoral votes can also change. No state, however, has fewer than three electoral votes because that is the constitutional minimum of representatives in the House and Senate. Representation in the electoral college for residents of Washington, DC, was established by the Twenty-third Amendment, ratified in 1961. The District of Columbia currently has three electoral votes, so there are 538 electoral college votes (435 members of the House plus 100 Senators plus 3 for the District of Columbia). Thus, 270 electoral votes constitute the majority required to be elected president.

Article 2, section 1 of the Constitution specifies that each state legislature determines the selection of electors, except that members of the House or Senate may not be appointed electors. Prior to the development of political parties, members of the state legislatures themselves chose the electors. After 1832, however, all the states adopted a system for allowing electors to be chosen by popular vote (with the partial exception of South Carolina, which continued to select electors by the state legislature until 1860).

Today, states rely on state parties to provide lists of nominees to be electors should that party's candidate win a plurality of the popular vote in the state. Most states require that the party's elector nominees be chosen at the state party convention, whereas a few states require the nominees to come from the state party central committee. Twelve states, including Alabama, Kansas, Texas, and Washington, allow the parties to use whatever method they wish to provide nominees (Berns 1992, 11).

Who are the electors? Because potential electors are selected by the state parties and cannot be members of the House or Senate, they are most often prominent state or party officials. Governors, members of the state legislature, state party chair and vice chair, or retired officeholders are often nominated to serve as electors should the party's candidate carry the state. Because electors are chosen by the parties and are usually individuals with a history of service to the state and party, the problem of "faithless" electors is rarely encountered. A faithless elector is one who votes for a candidate other than the candidate who carried the state. Some states have laws that require electors to vote for the candidate who carries the state, though only a few states specify a penalty for not doing so. As one scholar has noted, "the faithless elector phenomenon is an occasional curiosity rather than a perennial problem" (Berns 1992, 13).

Electoral college votes are awarded using the winner-take-all method, meaning that the candidate for president who wins a plurality of the popular vote in a state gets all of that state's electoral votes. The only exceptions currently are Maine and Nebraska, in which some of electoral college votes are based on the popular vote in the congressional districts (thus it is possible to split the electoral votes of Maine and Nebraska). It is this process of awarding electoral votes on a winner-take-all basis that exaggerates the majority of the winning candidate. For example, in 1996 President Clinton was reelected with just 49 percent of the popular vote, but he won 379 electoral votes—a full 70 percent of the electoral college votes. Clinton's plurality of the popular vote was thus translated into a convincing majority by the electoral rules. It is also the winner-take-all system that allows the potential for an "undemocratic" result in which a candidate wins fewer total popular votes but carries enough states to win an electoral college majority as occurred in the 2000 presidential election.

Does it matter whether or not the United States uses an electoral college? One common complaint about the electoral college is that the winner-take-all system tends to encourage presidential candidates to concentrate their attention on the largest states. A candidate could secure an electoral majority by campaigning in, and winning, only eleven states. A candidate who carried just the eleven largest states could secure 271 electoral votes, one more than the majority needed to win.

Is the electoral college system to blame for the attention that presidential campaigns lavish on large states? Oddly enough, the electoral college tends to slightly overrepresent less populated states such as Wyoming, Delaware, Alaska, and North Dakota because each state gets two votes for its senators regardless of its population. Thus, states with small populations actually get more weight in the electoral college than they would get based purely on popular votes. In other words, if there were no electoral college and the presidential elections were decided by the national popular vote, campaigns would still concentrate on the largest states because that is where most of the voters are.

Still, the existence of the electoral college does influence the conduct of presidential campaigns (Bartels 1985; Hill and McKee 2005; Holbrook and McClurg 2005). Although it is theoretically possible for a candidate to secure an electoral college majority by concentrating on only eleven states, in practice no candidate would be sufficiently sure of winning the largest states to campaign in such a fashion. The structure of the electoral college affects how candidates allocate their campaign resources, since winning the presidency is ultimately a matter of getting a majority of electoral college votes.

To illustrate the effect of the electoral college on campaign strategy, consider the circumstances of the Kerry-Edwards campaign in September 2004. Following the nominating conventions, the Democratic ticket of John Kerry and John Edwards trailed the Republican ticket of George W. Bush and Dick Cheney in most national opinion polls. Although examining national polls can help some aspects of campaign strategy, by September the campaign is a battle for the states. Table 4.2 shows how, according to our calculations, Kerry's strategists might have evaluated the likelihood of their candidate's winning various states. The states are arranged in five categories from "sure loss" to "sure win," with the "toss-up" states in the middle. Note that if Kerry were to carry all the "sure win" and "likely win" states he would have 190 electoral votes (74 + 116 = 190) and would still need 80 additional electoral college votes to reach the 270 votes needed to get a majority. The Kerry campaign would know that it needed to get at least 80 votes out of the 126 electoral votes available in the "toss-up" category.

In deciding how to classify their chances of winning a state, campaigns typically take many factors into account: past voting patterns, current polls, the strength of the state party, the strength of state candidates such as a governor or senator, key issues, and, of course, the home states of the presidential and vice-presidential candidates. But, arranging the states in this fashion might help the campaign to make difficult decisions about allocating campaign resources. For example, in 2004 should the Democratic campaign buy time in the North Carolina media market in order to try to win John Edwards's home state? Table 4.2 shows that North Carolina is not part of Kerry's winning coalition of states and suggests that campaign resources would be better used to pursue the electoral votes of states such as Ohio, Michigan, Pennsylvania, and New Mexico that would be needed to get to 270 electoral college votes. This type of calculation also suggests why states such as Massachusetts or New York, even though they have large numbers of electoral votes, would receive few resources from the Kerry campaign because his strategists would expect their candidate to carry those states. If the candidate were to be in danger of losing such staunch Democratic states, no amount of

TABLE 4.2 How the Electoral College Affects Campaign Strategy: Hypothetical Kerry-Edwards Campaign State List for 2004

Sure Loss		Likely Loss		Tossup		Likely Win		Sure Win	
Alabama	9	Arkansas	6	Florida	27	California	55	Connecticut	7
Alaska	3	Colorado	9	Iowa	7	Delaware	3	DC	3
Arizona	10	Missouri	11	Michigan	17	Illinois	21	Hawaii	4
Georgia	15	N. Carolina	15	Minnesota	10	Maine	4	Maryland	10
Idaho	4	Tennessee	11	Nevada	5	New Jersey	15	Massachusetts	12
Indiana	11	Virginia	13	New Hampshire	4	Oregon	7	New York	31
Kansas	6	W. Virginia	5	New Mexico	5	Washington	11	Rhode Island	4
Kentucky	8			Ohio	20			Vermont	3
Louisiana	9			Pennsylvania	21				
Mississippi	6			Wisconsin	10				
Montana	3								
Nebraska	5								
North Dakota	3								
Oklahoma	7								
S. Carolina	8								
S. Dakota	3								
Texas	34								
Utah	5								
Wyoming	3								
Totals:	**152**		**70**		**126**		**116**		**74**

Source: Constructed by the authors.

campaign resources could prevent an electoral college defeat. Knowing what states are crucial to getting the necessary majority within the electoral college can help campaign strategists use their resources effectively.

All presidential campaigns are aware of the workings of the electoral college and have a strategy to win enough states to gain an electoral college majority. Of course, in some elections, such as Reagan's landslide victory in 1984, the calculations are a mere formality. Yet in competitive presidential elections, careful use of limited resources may help win a crucial state and secure a winning majority. In the excitement and uncertainty of a presidential campaign, it is not always possible to conduct all activities according to the best overall strategy. Nevertheless, the electoral college does influence how candidates conduct their campaigns and may affect the outcome of elections as well.

Conclusion: The Impact of Electoral Rules

The theme of this chapter is that the rules of the electoral game matter. Elections in the United States are dominated by two big political parties in large part because of the plurality electoral system. If states were to adopt proportional representation, the number of political parties that could compete effectively would undoubtedly increase. With the widespread use of the plurality rule, however, it makes sense that the two dominant parties are broad-based electoral coalitions. By allowing state parties and state politicians the freedom to pursue election based on local issues, the national parties do not present a clear and coherent ideological message. They do, however, maximize their chances of winning control of both state and national governments by letting Arizona Republicans and

Massachusetts Republicans, or Wisconsin Democrats and Mississippi Democrats, seek election according to what will win in their state.

American political parties are organizationally weak in comparison to parties in other democratic nations, in part due to state control of nominations. Direct primary laws make it impossible for state parties to control even the seemingly essential function of selecting party candidates. The adoption of the Australian ballot and the direct primary by the states was largely responsible for transforming political parties from essentially private organizations into "public utilities" closely regulated by state law (Epstein 1986). In sum, state election laws passed in the late nineteenth and early twentieth centuries have profoundly altered the political environment in which the parties operate.

Of course, it is not just state laws that matter. Two features of the Constitution, federalism and the electoral college, have had a decided impact on the nature of political parties and electoral competition in this nation. The American federal system leaves control over the matter of elections largely to the states. In recent years federal legislation, such as the Voting Rights Act of 1965 or the Help America Vote Act of 2002, has introduced some federal control over the conduct of elections. Still, the bulk of election rules are left to the states to determine. As our discussion of the electoral college has shown, even in presidential elections the states are still central to the American electoral process.

CHAPTER 5

The American Electorate

Political parties, campaigns, and interest groups all share the need to get members of the American public to participate in the political process. For parties and campaigns, the focus is on getting people to contribute money to candidates and to encourage supporters to vote. Interest groups also work to mobilize people for election activities, but they more commonly seek to motivate their supporters to participate in the policy-making process more broadly. In this chapter, we focus on citizens and the nature of political participation in America. We address two questions that are fundamental to the study of political participation: who votes? and how do voters decide?

Political Participation in the United States

Most Americans believe that it is important to participate in the political process. Indeed, a poll conducted just before the 2006 congressional elections found that 90 percent of those surveyed agreed with the statement "I feel it's my duty as a citizen to always vote" (Pew Research Center 2006a). Yet, despite this widespread sense of civic duty, the level of voting in the United States is generally less than turnout in other economically advanced democratic nations. Figure 5.1 shows the average level of turnout in national elections

between 1945 and 1999 in fifteen democratic nations. This figure shows that turnout in U.S. elections, which averaged 55.8 percent, was much lower than most other nations. Among these nations, only Switzerland, with an average turnout of 56.6 percent, is similar to the United States in its level of turnout. Scholars have identified a number of reasons why turnout in the United States is lower than in other established democracies. Among these are the frequency of elections in America, the nature of the U.S. party system, and legal requirements such as voting registration (Norris 2004, 151–176; Powell 1986).

Another possible reason is that Americans have a variety of ways in which to participate in politics, and not all involve voting. In a classic study called *Participation in America*, political scientists Sidney Verba and Norman Nie identified four "modes" of political participation that Americans use to influence government legally: (1) voting, (2) campaign activity, (3) citizen-initiated contacts, and (4) cooperative activity (1972, 44–55). Voting in local, state, or national elections is, of course, one of the most common ways of attempting to influence government. Campaign activity is closely associated with voting but includes actions such as attempting to persuade other people to vote for a certain candidate, attending a political meeting or campaign rally, displaying a yard sign or bumper sticker for a candidate or party, or

FIGURE 5.1 Average Voter Turnout in Selected Nations, 1945–1999 (in percent)

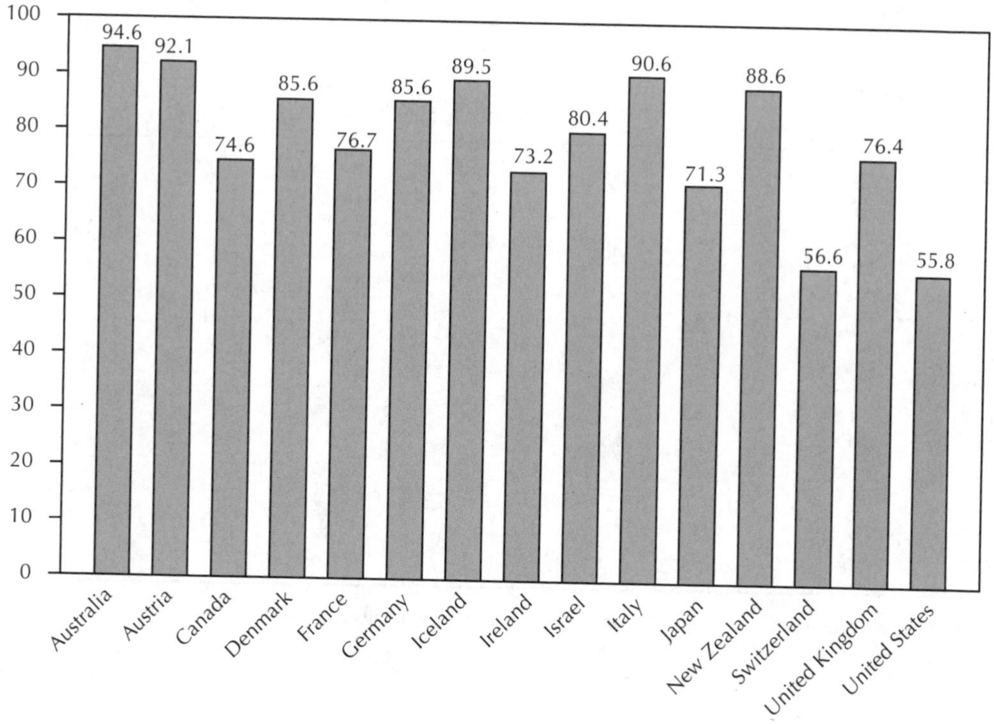

Source: Created by authors using data from Franklin (2004, 11).

giving money to a candidate. Verba and Nie also noted that some people participate in politics in a much more direct and personal way by contacting government officials to deal with a particular problem such as getting a pothole in a street filled or expressing support for (or opposition to) actions or proposed actions by government. Finally, Verba and Nie recognized that many Americans participate in politics in ways that are very different from the competition and conflict of elections. For example, a person may join the Parent Teacher Association (PTA) to try to improve their neighborhood public school or may contribute time or money to an organization seeking to create a public park. Verba and Nie called such actions cooperative activities because they often involved efforts to influence government policy by getting people to cooperate to achieve a com-

mon goal. Although our focus in this chapter will be on voting and campaign-related participation, it is important to recognize that a great deal of political activity in the United States takes the form of cooperative efforts. Indeed, Verba and Nie found that about 20 percent of the people in their survey could be classified as "communalists"—people who are "quite active in affairs of one's community, while staying out of the relatively conflictual realm of campaigning" (1972, 80).

The work of Verba and Nie helps to broaden our understanding of the nature of political participation in America. Still, voting and campaign activities are vitally important to many citizens as a way to express their views to political organizations such as parties and interest groups that need citizen involvement to function effectively, and for the overall health of our democratic system

TABLE 5.1 Types of Electoral Participation in Presidential Election Years, 1952–2004 (in percentages)

Year	Reported Voting	Persuade Others How to Vote	Campaign Button or Sticker	Contributed Money	Attended Meetings	Worked for Party or Candidate
1952	73	27	na	4	7	3
1956	73	28	16	10	7	3
1960	79	33	21	12	8	6
1964	78	31	16	11	9	5
1968	76	33	15	9	9	6
1972	73	32	13	10	9	5
1976	72	37	8	16	6	4
1980	71	36	7	8	8	4
1984	74	32	9	8	8	4
1988	70	29	9	9	7	3
1992	75	37	11	7	8	3
1996	73	28	10	8	5	2
2000	73	34	10	9	5	3
2004	77	48	21	13	7	3

Source: Created by authors using data from the American National Election Studies. Available at: www.electionstudies.org.

of government. How many Americans vote and participate in campaign activities? Table 5.1 shows the percentages of Americans who say they voted or participated in any of five other election activities for the presidential election years from 1952 to 2004 from the **American National Election Studies**.

Several results are evident from these data. First, it is clear that voting is the most commonly reported electoral activity with more than 70 percent of respondents reporting that they voted in the presidential election in every election shown. A second pattern that is clear from the table is that no other campaign activity is as common as voting and that the more difficult or costly the activity is in terms of time or money the fewer people report doing it. Trying to persuade another person how to vote or displaying a campaign button or yard sign is less costly than contributing money to a candidate or spending time working for a candidate. Consequently, more people report that they tried to persuade someone else how to vote or that they dis-

played a campaign sign than report the more costly activities of giving money, going to political meetings, or working for a candidate or party. In the hotly contested 2004 presidential election, for example, 48 percent of those surveyed reported that they tried to persuade someone else how to vote, but only 13 percent reported that they contributed money to a candidate or party. Finally, we should note that while the percentage of people who report engaging in these campaign activities varies over time, there is no evidence of a general decline in the willingness of Americans to participate in campaign activities. Though it is true that only a small percentage of Americans report working for a candidate or attending a political meeting, those percentages have not declined markedly over this time period.

One problem with using surveys to investigate turnout is that the percentage of people who report having voted is typically higher than the percentage of votes actually cast. For example, taking the total number of

FIGURE 5.2 Turnout in U.S. Presidential and Congressional Elections, 1920–2006

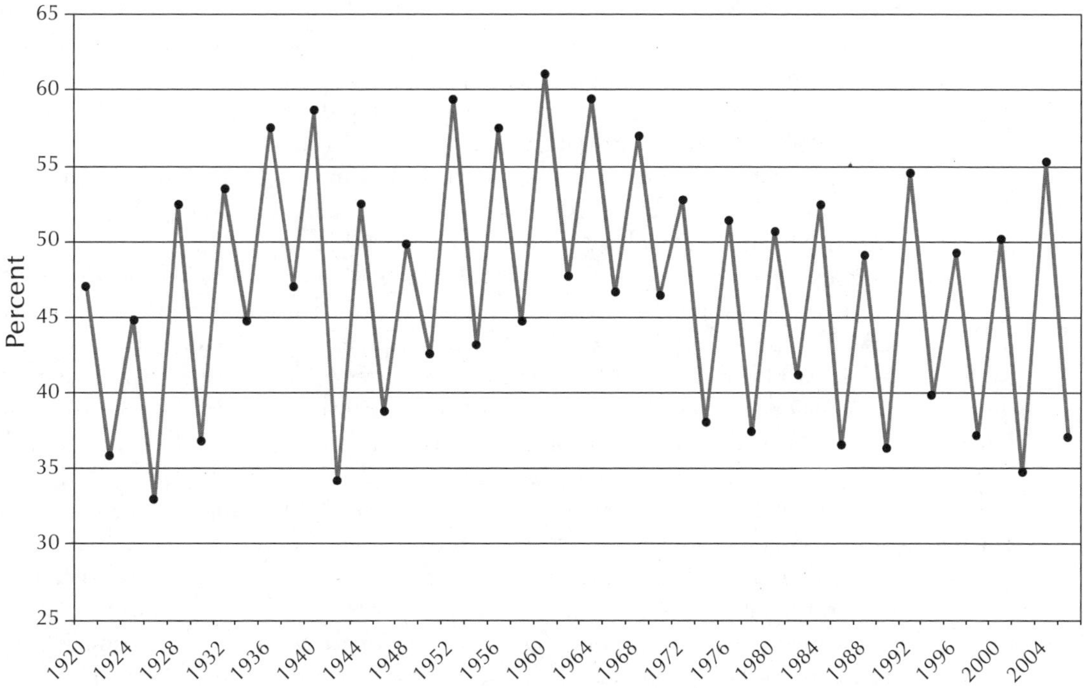

Source: Created by authors. Data for 1920–1998 are from Rusk (2001, 54), 2000–2004 data are from the U.S. Census Bureau (2005, 265), and 2006 data are from McDonald (2007).

votes cast in the 2000 presidential election and dividing it by the total number of people old enough to vote, yields a turnout rate of 50.3 percent. But, as table 5.1 shows, 73 percent of the people surveyed in the 2000 National Election Study reported that they voted. This problem, known as "overreporting," has been studied by scholars for some time and is generally considered to be due to people providing the "socially desirable" answer to a survey question (Bernstein, Chanda, and Montjoy 2004; Silver, Anderson, and Abramson 1986). But we can also look at turnout in American elections by examining the number of votes cast as a percentage of the voting age population.

Figure 5.2 shows turnout in presidential and congressional elections from 1920 to 2006 using the number of votes cast divided by the total voting age population. Several

patterns are evident when we look at turnout in the United States over this span of time. First, the up and down pattern that is evident over this entire time span reflects the fact that turnout in presidential election years is higher than in congressional election years. Average turnout in presidential election years during this period is 53.6 percent while in the congressional elections years it is 39.9 percent. This difference between turnout in presidential election years and congressional or midterm elections is usually attributed to the fact that presidential elections, as the only truly national election contests in the United States, attract more attention from voters than congressional elections alone. In addition, the major political parties put more effort into getting voters to the polls in presidential elections because of the importance of winning the presidency.

Figure 5.2 shows that, while there is considerable fluctuation in **voter turnout** in the United States over time, there is not simply a downward trend. Political scientists and others have been greatly concerned about the declining level of turnout in presidential elections that began after 1960 and continued through the 1980s (for example, Abramson and Aldrich 1982; Miller 1992; Putnam 2000, 31–47; Teixeira 1992). Other scholars, however, have suggested that much of this apparent decline in voting after 1972 is a consequence of how the number of people eligible to vote is calculated rather than being a real decline in participation (McDonald and Popkin 2001). In any event, there has been some improvement in turnout in recent presidential elections, notably 1992 and 2004. Also, by looking at turnout over this longer period of time we can see that the 1950s and 1960s appear to have been a time of unusually high turnout (with the presidential election of 1960 marking a high point in U.S. turnout for this period at 61 percent). Of course, any decline in political participation is troubling to those who desire a more inclusive democracy. But the pattern of turnout over this time period does not suggest a fundamental change in the nature of U.S. electoral politics.

Turnout: Who Votes?

We now turn to a topic of importance to the political parties, candidates, and their campaigns, as well as political scientists: who votes? Stated more formally, are there identifiable characteristics that are associated with people voting or not voting? The answer to this question is that there are a number of characteristics that are clearly associated with voting. Still, political scientists do not have a complete understanding of why people vote or do not vote.

Of course, one factor that is crucially important in determining whether or not citizens vote is whether they are registered to vote. Voter registration laws exist in order to ensure that only citizens who are legally eligible to vote are allowed to do so. Because states administer their own elections, however, the extent of registration requirements depends upon state law. All states except one, North Dakota, require some form of registration. But a number of states allow for "same day" registration in which an eligible citizen can both register and vote on election day. Most states, however, require that citizens register to vote well before election day in order to ensure that the person has met the state's residency requirement at the time of the election.

The system of state-based voter registration requirements has generally been found to reduce voter turnout especially among people who moved (Nagler 1991; Squire, Wolfinger, and Glass 1987; Wolfinger and Rosenstone 1980, 61–88). To address the concern that some citizens were not voting because they were unaware of voter registration requirements, Congress passed the National Voter Registration Act (NVRA) of 1993. This legislation is often called the "motor voter" law because it requires states to offer voter registration at motor vehicle registration offices as well as at other government offices. Although the NVRA has made it easier to meet voter registration requirements, especially for people moving from state to state, it has not resulted in a marked increase in voter turnout (Brown and Wedeking 2006; Fitzgerald 2005).

Socioeconomic Status and Voting

The most important factor for explaining political participation in the United States is a person's socioeconomic status (Verba and Nie 1972; Verba, Schlozman, and Brady 1995). The nature of this effect is clear: people with higher socioeconomic status participate in politics more than people with lower socioeconomic standing. The same is true if we look only at voter turnout instead of at political participation more generally (Wolfinger and Rosenstone 1980). **Socioeconomic status (SES)** is a concept that expresses the complex differences in social standing and economic position that exist among individuals in a society, which are sometimes referred to as "social class." In social science research, we typically measure SES using a person's level of education and income. (Occupation is also commonly used as part of the measure of SES, but it is less relevant to differences in political participation than education and income.)

We can illustrate the effect that education and income have on turnout using survey data collected by the U.S. Census after the 2004 presidential election. Figure 5.3 shows the percentage of turnout by categories of education and income. As we expect, this figure shows that as education and income increase, so does turnout. Education has generally been found to have a stronger effect than income on whether a person turns out to vote (Wolfinger and Rosenstone 1980, 13–36). Figure 5.3 illustrates the stronger effect of education as the increase from the lowest to the highest category of education shows a nearly 45 percent difference in turnout, with 39.5 percent of those people with less than a high school education reporting that they voted compared to 84.2 percent of those with an advanced degree reporting that they voted in the 2004 presidential election. Although the effect of income is similar to the effect of education, the difference between the lowest and highest levels of income is only 33 percent.

Why do education and income affect turnout? The explanation is that higher levels of education help to develop the cognitive and bureaucratic skills necessary to participate in politics and to cultivate attitudes that are conducive to participation such as an interest in public affairs. Similarly with income, people with higher levels of income often have greater opportunities in terms of both time and financial resources to participate in politics. For example, people with higher incomes are more likely to be contacted by political groups or candidates about contributing money. This sort of involvement helps to reinforce the importance of voting and other forms of participation.

In sum, SES has a marked impact on who votes in the United States. The effect of SES on turnout is generally stronger in the United States than in other nations in large part because the United States has never had a tradition of a strong working-class political party with a vested interest in encouraging turnout among lower SES people (Powell 1986; Verba, Nie, and Kim 1978).

How much does it matter that turnout in the United States is influenced by SES? On the one hand, we should point out while income and education influence who votes, they do not determine it. That is, not everyone who is well educated or has a high income will vote and it is certainly not the case that people with less education or income cannot or do not vote. On the other hand, the impact of SES does matter in the sense that the electorate, the people who actually vote in an election, has a greater proportion of more highly educated and higher income people than the American population in general. A more difficult question to answer is whether the SES differences between the population and the electorate have a decided impact on who gets elected or what policy decisions are made. Some research into this question suggests that the impact of demographic differences between voters and nonvoters is likely to be quite small (e.g., Wolfinger and Rosenstone 1980, 109–114), while other research suggests that demographic differences may matter more (e.g., Verba, Schlozman, Brady, and Nie 1993).

Other Factors Affecting Turnout

Although education and income are generally the most important characteristics influencing turnout, other factors matter as well. One factor that has been shown to influence how likely someone is to vote is age. Generally, young people are less likely to vote than people who are older. Figure 5.4 illustrates how age affects turnout, using data from the 2004 presidential election. As the figure shows, reported turnout is lowest, at 46.7

FIGURE 5.3 Effect of Education and Income on Turnout, 2004 (in percent)

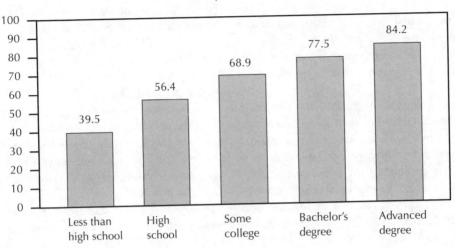

Turnout by Level of Education

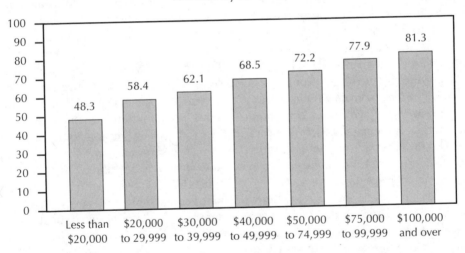

Turnout by Level of Income

Source: Created by authors. Data from U.S. Census Bureau (Holder 2006, 4).

percent, in the youngest age group (18 to 24 years old) and increases with each category of age until it tops out at nearly 72 percent among those 55 and older. This pattern is typical of the effect of age on turnout, although using data from the 2004 presidential election underestimates the usual effect somewhat since turnout was higher among 18- to 24-year-olds in 2004 than it was among the other age groups (Holder 2006, 2–3). Political scientists generally identify age as one of the factors that is important for turnout, even though in some ways the effects of age may be attributed to various other factors that are associated with voting such as residential stability (since younger people are most likely to be mobile) and marriage (since younger people are less likely to be married).

FIGURE 5.4 Effect of Age on Turnout, 2004 (in percent)

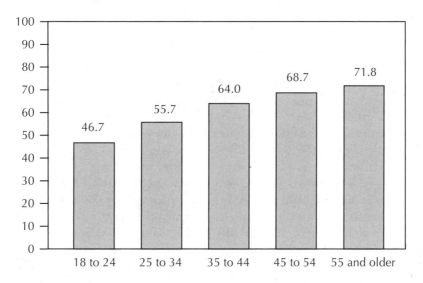

Source: Created by authors using data from U.S. Census Bureau (Holder 2006, 4).

Historically, two other demographic factors—gender and race—have been important influences on who voted in the United States. Thanks to legal and social changes over time, however, the differences in turnout between people based on their gender or race have been reduced considerably. Even after ratification of the Nineteenth Amendment in 1920, women were less likely to vote and participate in campaign activities than men. By the presidential election of 1984, however, a higher proportion of women than men voted. Since then, women have typically turned out to vote at levels equal to or slightly higher than men. In 2004, for example, 65.4 percent of women reported voting compared to 62.1 percent of men (Holder 2006, 4).

Differences in turnout between white and black Americans have also diminished over time, although the effects of race and ethnicity continue to be important in the story of who votes in the United States. In general, individuals who identify themselves as white report voting at higher levels than people who identify themselves as black, Asian, or Hispanic. In the 2004 election, for example, 65.4 percent of people who identified themselves as white reported voting, while 60 percent of blacks and 44.1 percent of Asians reported voting (Holder 2006, 4). According to the Census Bureau, 47.2 percent of people who identified themselves as Hispanic reported voting in the 2004 presidential election (Holder 2006, 4). Studies have found that African Americans tend to vote at the same or slightly higher levels than whites when differences in socioeconomic status are taken into account (Tate 1991; Wolfinger and Rosenstone 1980, 90–91). The same cannot be said of the differences among other groups, however. Thus, while the historical differences between blacks and whites have narrowed considerably in recent decades, racial and ethnic differences between Americans are still important when considering turnout in contemporary elections.

Among the other factors that may influence whether or not a person votes, two deserve special mention. One of these is "political efficacy" and the other is a person's connection to the community. Political efficacy is a term used to describe the belief that a person can effectively participate in politics. Generally, people who have a stronger sense of political efficacy are more likely to vote regularly and, indeed, to participate in politics in other ways. Political scientists also distinguish between "internal" and "external" political efficacy (Balch 1974; Craig and Maggiotto 1992). Internal political efficacy is an individual's sense of being able to understand politics and effectively express political views. External efficacy is a person's view about how responsive government is to people. External efficacy is of particular interest as an explanation for why turnout changes over time because it is seen as being a product of political events. If political events, such as a bribery scandal involving a prominent elected official, make people think that government is not responsive to them, we would expect political participation to decline. Indeed, studies of the decline in turnout between the 1960s and the 1980s found that a diminishing sense of external efficacy among Americans was part of the explanation (Abramson 1983; Abramson and Aldrich 1982; Rosenstone and Hansen 2003, 141–145).

People who are closely connected to a community also tend to vote more regularly than people who do not have well-established social ties. Among the indicators that reflect the extent of a person's social connectedness are years in the community, home ownership, marital status, talking politics with friends and neighbors, and church attendance. Citizens who are more closely tied to the social structures of family and community are more likely to vote than people with fewer community ties (Miller and Shanks 1996, 101).

Nonvoters: What Do We Know?

To this point we have focused on individual characteristics that are associated with voting. Another way to look at this topic is to ask: what do we know about citizens who do not vote? To the extent that we ask this question at all, we often think of nonvoters as all alike—people who are uninterested in politics or who feel alienated from government. An innovative series of surveys conducted by the Medill School of Journalism was designed to learn more about nonvoters. These surveys found that nonvoters are not all alike (Doppelt and Shearer 1999; 2001). Based on surveys of nonvoters conducted in 1996 and 2000, Doppelt and Shearer report that nonvoters can be classified as belonging to one of five groups. Box 5.1 presents some of the distinguishing features of each of these different groups of nonvoters.

One of the striking findings from the Medill surveys was that the largest proportion of nonvoters have attributes that are very much like those of people who vote. This group, labeled the "Doers," is similar to voters in its levels of education, income, and interest in political news. People in this group have generally positive views of government and politics and are more likely than other nonvoters to have contacted a government official. From this group, it is clear that a sizeable proportion of nonvoters are people who could readily become voters if they were motivated to do so by a candidate, political party, issue, or the people around them.

The next largest group of nonvoters demonstrates the importance of community involvement in getting people to vote. This group, the "Unplugged," tend to be disproportionately young and very likely to say they follow politics "hardly at all." Because they move often, they do not feel connected to their communities and, not surprisingly, the people in this group are very likely not to be registered to vote.

People in this group are less likely than other nonvoters to pay attention to political news and thus tend not to participate in politics in any form. A similar group to the "Unplugged" is the group called "Don't Knows." People in this group tend to be older and are distinguished primarily by their lack of interest in public affairs and a tendency to say they "don't know" when asked for their views of candidates, issues, or political institutions. Because of their inattentiveness to

BOX 5.1 A Profile of American Nonvoters

The Doers (29 percent of total in 2000)
- Young, nearly half of this group is under 30 years old
- Higher income
- College educated
- More likely than other nonvoters to contact politicians or volunteer
- Follow what is going on in government some or most of the time
- Generally positive in their outlook on government

The Unplugged (25 percent of total in 2000)
- Young, more than half of this groups is under 30 years old
- Lower income
- High school educated
- Rarely read a newspaper or watch television news
- Rarely discuss politics or pay little attention to the campaign

The Don't Knows (12 percent of total in 2000)
- Over 45 years old
- Lower income
- High school educated
- Have little interest in politics and few political opinions
- Most likely among nonvoters not to be registered to vote

The Irritables (14 percent of total in 2000)
- Middle-aged
- Higher income
- College educated
- Follow politics and public affairs closely in the media
- Have negative view of politics and see little difference between the parties

The Alienated (20 percent of total in 2000)
- Over 45 years old
- Lower income
- High school educated
- Have the most negative view of government among nonvoters
- Most believe the country is "off on the wrong track"
- Most say they "choose not to vote"

Sources: Constructed by the authors based on Doppelt and Shearer (1999; 2001).

political information, both of these groups would be relatively difficult for parties or candidates to encourage to become voters.

The final two groups of nonvoters identified in the Medill surveys are called the "Irritables" and the "Alienated." These groups are similar in that members of both groups tend to have negative views of politicians and political institutions. The key difference between these two groups, however, is their level of attention to political news. The "Irritables," unlike those in the "Alienated" group, tend to follow political news and election campaigns closely, even though they say they see little difference between the parties.

The Medill studies of nonvoters serve to reinforce several points about turnout: people who are younger, less educated, less prosperous, uninterested in politics, and have fewer ties to the community are less likely to be voters. People who fall into the "Unplugged," "Don't Knows," and "Alienated" groups would be difficult to reach with a political message and perhaps unlikely to be convinced, even if they were contacted. Still, the Medill surveys also help us to understand that not all nonvoters fit these images. Some nonvoters, in particular those in the "Doers" category, have many of the same attributes as voters and thus might be relatively easy to mobilize to become regular voters. Similarly, those nonvoters in the "Irritables" group might well be encouraged to vote if parties or candidates presented them with a sufficiently appealing message.

Mobilizing Voters

In their study of political participation, political scientists Steven Rosenstone and John Mark Hansen (2003, 161) summarized the essence of electoral politics as follows:

> People participate in electoral politics because someone encourages or inspires them to take part. The very nature of elections motivates political leaders to mobilize public involvement: More votes than the opposition means victory. Accordingly, in

any election campaign, candidates, political parties, campaign organizations, interest groups, and other activists do their best to muster participants. Candidates appear at factories, offices, and service clubs, parties canvas and staff phone banks, campaigns troll for contributors, and interest groups rally their troops. In any election campaign, moreover, the efforts of candidates, parties, campaigns, and interest groups are magnified by the subsequent social interactions of the people they reach. Families discuss campaigns, friends debate the options, and co-workers convey expectations. The essential feature of electoral politics, in short, is electoral mobilization.

As Rosenstone and Hansen make clear, elections are all about getting people involved and sufficiently motivated to vote. Indeed, such efforts are commonly referred to in campaigns as GOTV, an acronym for get-out-the-vote. In examining the topic of mobilizing voters, we should distinguish between two types of mobilization: nonpartisan and partisan. Nonpartisan efforts are designed to increase the overall number of people who are registered and who vote, even though many such efforts are aimed at particular groups of people—college students, Asian Americans, or people living in a particular neighborhood, for example. Partisan efforts to mobilize voters are also intended to increase turnout but are meant to do so only selectively: the key to successful partisan mobilization is to get people out to the polls who are likely to support a particular party, candidate, or position.

Nonpartisan efforts to encourage registration and turnout have been undertaken by a variety of organizations such as the League of Women Voters, the California Student Public Interest Research Group, Rock the Vote, and the NAACP National Voter Fund. These groups typically seek to educate citizens on the importance of voting and the need to be registered in advance of the election to be able to vote. In addition, some groups contact registered voters prior to the election to encourage them to vote. Do such actions increase turnout? In general, the answer is yes, but not all methods work equally well. A large-scale test of three ways of contacting registered voters—in person, by telephone, and by mail—found that personal contact with registered voters did increase turnout, while mailings had only a slight effect, and telephone calls from a professional call center had almost no effect (Gerber and Green 2000). Subsequent studies of the effects of telephone calls made by either volunteers or professional callers suggest that calls can increase voter turnout if they are done in a personalized manner and if they occur just before election day (Nickerson 2006; 2007). Indeed, personal contact appears to be the key element in many of the studies of voter mobilization. As Green and Gerber (2005, 7) put it,

> . . . the effectiveness of voter mobilization efforts depends on their personal touch. Impersonal approaches, such as direct mail and robotic calls, seem to have small effects; more personal approaches such as door-to-door canvassing and volunteer phone banks, do more to increase voter turnout—provided that voters have not already been saturated with personal contact.

Many of the lessons learned from the study of nonpartisan mobilization also apply to the partisan efforts. But, by far, the bulk of the efforts at voter mobilization are partisan in nature. Traditionally, getting voters to the polls was a job for political parties, and it still is today, although parties are now joined in these efforts by the campaigns of candidates as well as interest groups. In campaign parlance, get-out-the-vote efforts are part of a campaign's "ground war"—the tough house-by-house and call-by-call work to contact potential supporters and make sure they go to the polls—in contrast to the "air wars" fought out through advertising.

In some ways, the efforts of parties and campaigns to get their voters to the polls have come full circle. During the period when political parties were mass organizations, mobilizing voters at election time was their most important activity. The parties used as many party workers as they could muster to get their voters out to the polls, and virtually all of this effort was through face-to-face contact. As political party organizations became more regulated by the government and the nature of campaigning changed, with more emphasis on candidate advertising, the amount of personal contact declined over time. Although it never went away entirely, the highly labor-intensive, personalized contacting to get party supporters to the polls did decline in importance as parties became service organizations and candidates became more central to the conduct of election campaigns. In recent elections, however, the parties have once again recognized the importance of investing in the "ground war" (Mesrobian 2004). In large part, the renewed emphasis on mobilization is a result of the highly competitive nature of elections nationally and in many states. As a result of the use of new database and communication technologies, parties and campaigns are able to target their likely supporters and potentially "persuadable" voters ever more accurately.

We can see the impact of this renewed emphasis on party contacting in survey data from the National Election Studies from 1972–2004. Figure 5.5 shows the percentage of people who report having been contacted by one of the parties during the campaign (top line) as well as the percentage reporting which party contacted them (bottom two lines). As is clear from the figure, the number of people reporting that they had been contacted by one of the major parties has increased in the most recent elections. From 1972 to 1998, the average number of people who were contacted was 25.4 percent, or about one out of every four potential members of the electorate. In the closely contested 2000 presidential election the percentage increased to 35 percent and then climbed

FIGURE 5.5 Percentage of People Contacted in Total and by Major Party, 1972–2004

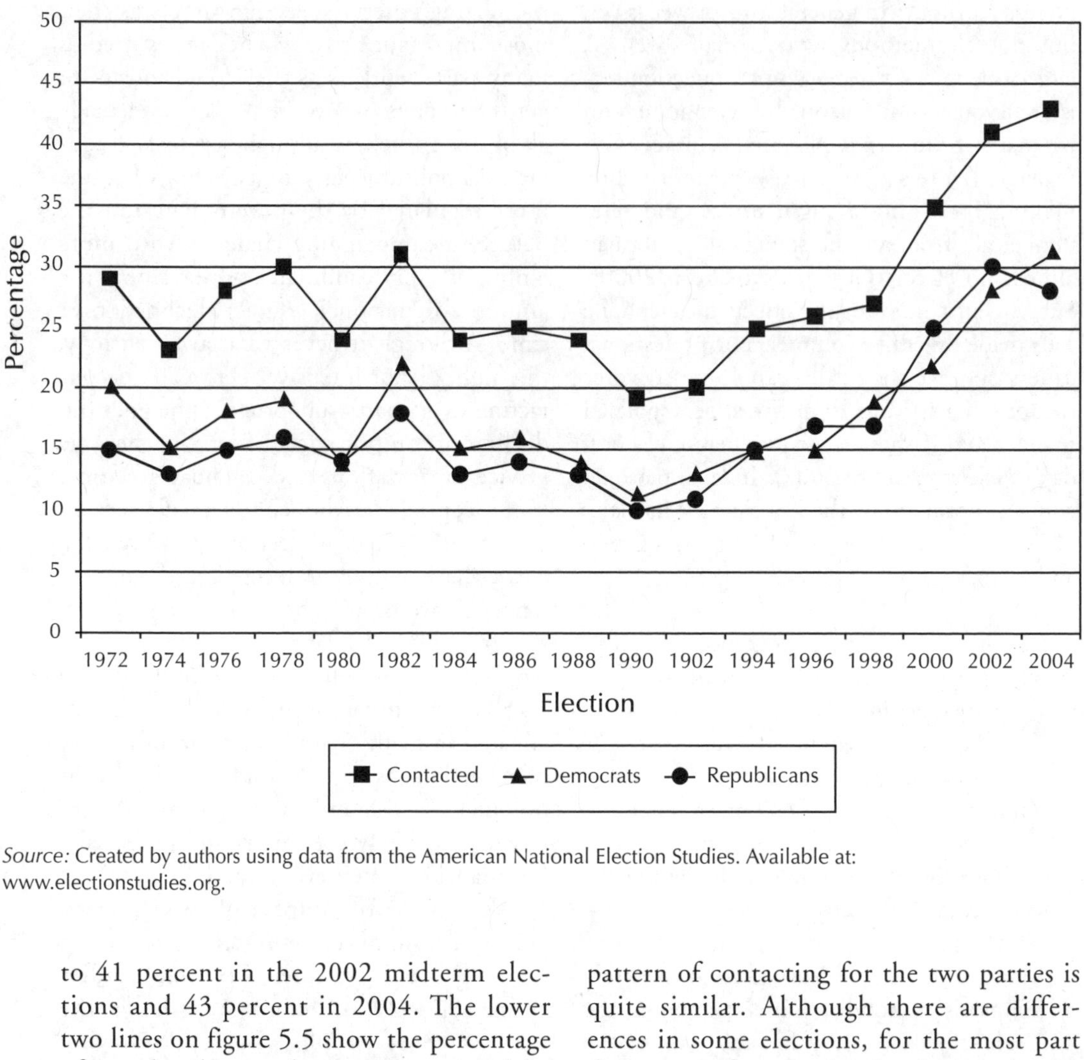

Source: Created by authors using data from the American National Election Studies. Available at: www.electionstudies.org.

to 41 percent in the 2002 midterm elections and 43 percent in 2004. The lower two lines on figure 5.5 show the percentage of people who say they were contacted by either the Democratic party or the Republican party. Two features of these lines are especially notable. First, prior to 1994, more people reported being contacted by the Democrats than the Republicans, suggesting that the Democrats had a consistent advantage in the "ground war" over this period. After the Republican takeover of Congress in 1994, however, the Democrats no longer enjoyed this advantage as partisan competition intensified and Republicans improved their GOTV activities. Second, we can see that, overall, the

pattern of contacting for the two parties is quite similar. Although there are differences in some elections, for the most part the extent of contacting by the two parties appears to rise and fall together. This pattern suggests that the two parties are reacting similarly to the political environments of specific elections as well as working to match the efforts of the competition.

Do these efforts at partisan mobilization increase turnout? Research on this question indicates strongly that partisan mobilization does increase turnout (Abramson and Claggett 2001; Goldstein and Ridout 2002; Rosenstone and Hansen 2003; Wielhouwer 2003; Wielhouwer and Lockerbie 1994). In general, these studies show that a higher proportion of people who are contacted by a political party during the campaign turnout to vote. To illustrate this point, based on the 2004 National Election Study sample, the level of reported voting in the presidential election was 21.7 percent higher among people who said they had been contacted by a party compared to people who had not been contacted. And this effect has been even stronger in recent congressional elections (Lefkowitz 2004). Turnout among people who were contacted by a party was 28.2 percent higher than people who were not contacted, according to data from the 2002 National Election Study of voting in congressional elections. Of course, not all of the difference in turnout between these groups is due to being contacted. Both parties tend to contact people who are very likely to vote anyway—strong partisans and people who have lived in a community for years (Gershtenson 2003). Still, even when other factors are taken into account, partisan mobilization does appear to increase turnout.

The political parties, along with the campaign organizations for various candidates in specific elections, have traditionally been responsible for partisan mobilization activities. In keeping with the theme of this book, however, the parties have been joined in these activities by a variety of interest groups. In the 2004 campaign, for example, not only did both major parties and presidential campaigns devote resources to their GOTV efforts, so did a number of interest groups. On the Democratic side, groups such as AFL-CIO, Service Employees International Union, Sierra Club, and America Coming Together reported that they used door-to-door canvassing, telephone calls, and direct mail to try to get people out to vote for John Kerry. On the Republican side, the Chamber of Commerce reported making 2.1 million telephone contacts, sending out 3 million pieces of mail, and 20 million emails in support of George W. Bush (Bergan, Gerber, Green, and Panagopoulos 2005, 765). Most of this activity was concentrated in the states that were the most competitive in 2004, states such as Ohio, Florida, Pennsylvania, Iowa, New Mexico, and Wisconsin. Still, all these GOTV activities are estimated to have produced about four million additional votes nationally in the 2004 election (Bergan, Gerber, Green, and Panagopoulos 2005, 771).

Although partisans work hard to try to ensure that their voters participate, not all efforts are equally effective. In a study of the 1992, 1996, and 2000 presidential elections, Holbrook and McClurg (2005) found that neither the number of visits by the presidential candidates to a state nor the amount of television advertising in a state increased turnout. What did increase turnout among partisans in a state was the amount of money that the national parties transferred to their state parties to conduct GOTV activities. Although the amount of money is only an indirect indicator, this result seems to support what was also true about nonpartisan mobilization efforts: the activities that work best are those that involve old-fashioned direct personal contact. As we see in figure 5.5, the parties have increased their efforts in recent elections. If the parties reduce these activities, we would expect turnout to decline, as it has in past elections (Rosenstone and Hansen 2003). Even though parties and campaigns have the intent of mobilizing only their voters, the overall impact of active party competition is a positive one for democracy—more citizens voting.

Vote Choice: How Do Voters Decide?

Getting people to the polls is one important aspect of a campaign. Another important part of campaigning is persuasion. Because an election ultimately comes down to a contest of one candidate against another (or perhaps several others), success is often a matter of persuading people how to vote. In some elections, the winner may do nothing more than appeal to voters' long-standing party loyalties, while in other elections the decisive factor may be a candidate's image as a strong leader or the candidate's position on a critical issue—bringing an end to war, returning the nation to economic prosperity, or restoring moral values. While the outcome of some elections may be foregone conclusions, in many elections voters have to sort out the advantages and disadvantages of each candidate. How do voters choose which candidate to vote for? This question has been one of the most studied topics in political science. Even with all the attention that has been devoted to this topic, there is no single best answer nor are there any answers that hold for all voters or in all elections. In this section, however, we provide a general outline of some of the consistently important features of how voters decide.

Because the topic of how voters choose has been widely studied, there are several contending theories that seek to explain **vote choice**. The approach that we present here is based on a well-established and widely accepted theory of vote choice. This approach is the social-psychological theory, often called the "Michigan model" of vote choice after the university affiliation of the scholars who developed it. The Michigan model was developed primarily to explain voting in American presidential elections beginning in the 1950s (Campbell, Converse, Miller, and Stokes 1960), but it has been applied to later U.S. elections as well (Markus and Converse 1979; Miller and Shanks 1996).

Figure 5.6 presents a basic conceptual model of vote choice. In the figure, the right-hand element is vote choice, the variable we are trying to explain. For our purposes, vote choice is simply whether someone chooses to vote for a Republican candidate, a Democratic candidate, or a third party candidate. As the figure shows, there are three important elements (or variables) that help to explain how voters make their decisions: partisan identification, candidate image, and issues. We will discuss each of these variables in more detail.

Partisan Identification

A central premise of the social-psychological approach is that people think of themselves in terms of social groups or, put another way, they identify with certain social groups. A person might, for example, think of herself as being young, or Catholic, or liberal. In other words, this hypothetical person thinks of herself as being similar to other people who are young, or other people who are Catholic, or other people who are liberal. If this person were to encounter political information on an issue such as, say, a proposal to increase Social Security payments, she would likely use her identification as a young person and a liberal to help her decide what her position on this issue would be. On another issue, such as abortion, her identifications as a woman and Catholic may be more important to her attitude on this issue. Of course, nearly everyone has multiple social groups that they may identify with, although some groups are likely to be more relevant to political decisions than others. According to the social-psychological approach, these social identifications are central to how people interpret politics and how they make decisions about political matters such as how to vote or whether they think the president is doing a good job.

In electoral politics, one of the most important of these identifications is **partisan identification (PID)**. PID is also called party identification or just partisanship. Within the Michigan model, PID is defined as being an individual's sense of identification with a political party. That is, a person's sense that he or she is "like other Republicans" or "like other Democrats." PID is not the same as being a dues-paying member of a political party nor is it the same as how a person votes in a particular election. Rather, PID is an affective or emotional attachment to a political party that is learned during the process of pre-adult political socialization. Young people generally learn to identify themselves with a political party from their parents or other close family members. In addition to parents,

FIGURE 5.6 Conceptual Model of Individual Vote Choice

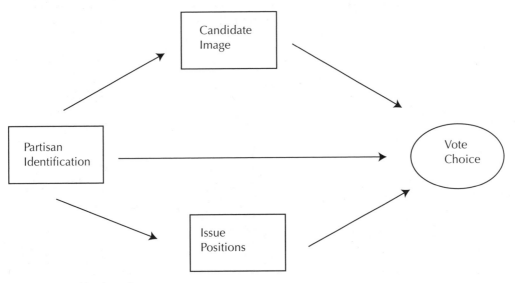

Source: Created by the authors.

a person's developing sense of partisanship may also be influenced by their friends, their schools, and other organizations such as religious or community groups (Beck 1977). Although PID is usually learned from parents, it is not true that party identification is perfectly shared between parents and children. A major study of political socialization showed that 57 percent of parents and children shared the same PID, meaning of course that 43 percent of parents and children did not share the same views as Republicans, Democrats, or independents (Jennings and Niemi 1981, 90). Further, even though people can and do change their attachments to a political party over time, most people do not change their PID easily. "The typical ebb and flow of political fortunes associated with scandal, war, and economic performance tend to have little enduring influence on the partisan identities of voters. And when these events do move partisans away from their long-term attachments, they tend to reequilibrate rapidly once the short-term tide has subsided" (Green, Palmquist, and Schickler 2002, 83–84).

In the National Election Study, a person's partisan identification is measured by two questions. The first question asked is, "Generally speaking, do you usually think of yourself as a Republican, a Democrat, an independent, or what?" For those people who say Republican or Democrat, the second questions is, "Would you call yourself a strong [Republican/Democratic], or a not very strong [Republican/Democratic]?" For people who say that they think of themselves as an independent, the follow-up question is, "Do you think of yourself as closer to the Republican party or to the Democratic party?" The answers to these two questions can then be combined to place a person on a continuum that ranges from "strong Democrat" to "strong Republican" (with a small number of people classified as "apolitical"). People classified as true independents on this continuum are those who answered that they are independents on the first question and say that they are not closer to either the Democrats or Republicans on the second. People who say they are independents in response to the first question and then say they are closer to one party or the other on the second question are called "independent Democrats" or "independent Republicans" (also called "leaning

TABLE 5.2 Partisan Identification in Presidential Election Years, 1952–2004 (in percentages)

Year	Strong Democrat	Weak Democrat	Independent Democrat	Independent	Independent Republican	Weak Republican	Strong Republican	Apolitical
1952	22	25	10	6	7	14	14	3
1956	21	23	6	9	8	14	15	4
1960	20	25	6	10	7	14	16	2
1964	27	25	9	8	6	14	11	1
1968	20	25	10	11	9	15	10	1
1972	15	26	11	13	10	13	10	1
1976	15	25	12	15	10	14	9	1
1980	18	23	11	13	10	14	9	2
1984	17	20	11	11	12	15	12	2
1988	17	18	12	11	13	14	14	2
1992	18	18	14	12	12	14	11	1
1996	18	19	14	9	12	15	12	1
2000	19	15	15	12	13	12	12	1
2004	17	16	17	10	12	12	16	0

Source: Created by authors using data from the American National Election Studies. Available at: www.electionstudies.org.

Democrats" or "leaning Republicans"). Thus, as table 5.2 shows, this measure captures both the direction of a person's party preference (Republican or Democrat) as well as the strength of that partisan attachment (strong or weak).

The data in table 5.2 provide a snapshot of the partisan composition of the American public in each presidential election year since 1952, when the first of the National Election Studies was conducted. Two of the changes over this time period are especially noteworthy. The first is the gradual erosion of the Democratic advantage in partisan identification. If we combine the three categories of Democrats together, we see that 57 percent of Americans identified with the Democrats in 1952 compared to 35 percent who identified as Republican and 6 percent independent. By 1988, however, this advantage had declined to 47 percent for Democrats and 41 percent for Republicans with 11 percent independent. Currently, the balance of the two parties is considerably closer than it was in the 1950s with the Democrats having lost ground and Republicans having gained

some. Still, in 2004 the Democrats maintained an advantage with 50 percent of Americans identifying themselves as Democrat, 40 percent as Republican, and 10 percent as independent. What accounts for this change in partisanship over time? In broad terms, this change is due to the erosion of the Democratic New Deal coalition that dominated electoral politics in the 1930s and 1940s. The decline of the Democratic coalition was most notably in the South, which shifted from being a bastion of the Democratic party to a predominantly Republican area today (Black and Black 2002).

The other notable change over time has been the overall weakening of party attachment and a slight increase in the percentage of true independents. On the Republican side, while the overall percentage of Americans who identify themselves as Republican has increased, this growth has occurred mostly among those classified as "independent Republicans." Even more dramatically on the Democratic side, the percentage of people who are strong or weak Democrats has declined and, like the Republicans, the increase has come among "independent Democrats." That is, in the aggregate, the American public has fewer people who identify themselves first with either the Democratic or Republican parties and more people who identify themselves as either true independents or leaning toward one of the parties.

Why have party attachments weakened over this period? Political scientists Warren Miller and Merrill Shanks point to generational change as the primary reason (1996, 151–185). Miller and Shanks note that the generation of people who became eligible to vote for the first time during the 1970s and 1980s were less inclined to adopt a strong partisan identification than earlier generations. In part, these generational differences again reflected the demise of the New Deal Democratic majority, particularly in the South. Young people who grew up in the 1950s and 1960s did not see political parties or the conflicts of the New Deal period as germane to them and thus they tended not to adopt partisan identities in the ways their parents had. The impact of the lower levels of partisan attachment among younger adults was magnified by the increased number of young people eligible to vote after ratification of the Twenty-sixth Amendment in 1971, which guaranteed the right of people eighteen years old or older to vote.

As the model of vote choice shown in figure 5.6 indicates, a person's partisan identification has a direct effect on how a person votes as well as influencing how a person views the candidates and issues in a campaign. Table 5.3 displays the relationship between PID and vote choice in three recent presidential elections. What is evident from these results is that partisanship has a substantial impact on the voter's choice in each election. For example, nearly 97 percent of the voters who identified themselves as strong Democrats voted for John Kerry and more than 98 percent of those who identified themselves as strong Republicans voted for George W. Bush in 2004. In that same year, true independents split nearly equally between candidates with 53.3 percent of independents voting for Kerry and 46.7 percent voting for Bush. Yet, for independents who lean toward the Democrats, 87 percent voted for Kerry, and 89 percent of independents who said they were closer to the Republicans voted for Bush. The general pattern is that the stronger a person's attachment to one of the major parties, the more likely that person is to vote for the candidate of that party. The other pattern worth noting in table 5.3 is that weak partisans and independent partisans tend to behave similarly when making their vote choice. In sum, a person's PID is a good, though not perfect, predictor of how that person will vote. Even among strong partisans, there is a small percentage in each party who votes for another candidate. Although the data shown in table 5.3 does not take into account other variables that might affect a person's votes, the general impact of partisan identification remains a strong influence on vote choice, even when other factors are controlled (Green, Palmquist, and Schickler 2002; Miller and Shanks 1996).

Candidate Image

While partisanship represents a relatively enduring orientation toward electoral politics for most individuals, other factors that can influence how a person votes are products of particular election campaigns. One such factor is the image that citizens form of the presidential candidates. By **candidate image** we mean the personal qualities that citizens believe to be true of the candidates. Of course, the comparison of rival candidates and the efforts to create a more favorable public image for candidates is a central feature of presidential election campaigns. Since the vast majority of citizens have no opportunity to meet a presidential candidate, the process of learning about the personal qualities that each candidate possesses is largely a result of information provided by the media and especially television (Keeter 1987). Consequently, campaigns put substantial resources

TABLE 5.3 Effect of Partisan Identification on Presidential Vote (in percentages)

Candidate	Strong Democrat	Weak Democrat	Independent Democrat	Independent	Independent Republican	Weak Republican	Strong Republican
1996							
Clinton (D)	95.6	84.5	78.1	39.3	20.5	19.7	4.8
Perot (I)	2.4	6.5	15.6	19.6	11.1	9.8	1.0
Dole (R)	2.0	9.0	6.3	41.1	68.4	70.5	94.2
2000							
Gore (D)	97.6	89.0	72.0	46.8	13.5	14.0	2.1
Nader (I)	0.0	0.5	8.3	6.4	6.5	0.7	0.5
Bush (R)	2.4	10.5	19.7	46.8	80.0	85.3	97.4
2004							
Kerry (D)	96.7	82.9	87.1	53.3	11.0	10.7	1.8
Bush (R)	3.3	17.1	12.9	46.7	89.0	89.3	98.2

Source: Created by authors using data from the American National Election Studies. Votes for presidential candidates with less than 1 percent of the vote nationally excluded. Percentages based only on candidates listed.

into managing how candidates are portrayed in the media—for example by staging campaign events in time for the pictures to make the evening news with the candidate in front of a cheering crowd and a giant American flag. Events such as the party's nominating convention and debates between candidates are a focal point for campaign professionals because of the media attention and the opportunity to convey the candidate's image to the public.

Does all this concern with a candidate's image really matter? It does in the sense that most citizens will form their impression of a candidate's personal qualities—and to a certain extent, qualifications for the job of president—from information provided through media. Table 5.4 illustrates the nature of candidate image using data from the 2004 contest between George W. Bush and John Kerry. Table 5.4 shows two aspects of candidate image: the personal qualities that citizens see in the candidates, and the affective feelings that candidates evoke in citizens. By comparing the two candidates in 2004, we can see that Kerry had an advantage in being seen as knowledgeable, intelligent, and caring, while

Bush had the advantage in being seen as a strong leader and better able to make up his mind. The candidates were similar with regard to the qualities of morality and honesty. In most presidential elections between 1980 and 2004, the Republican candidate tended to hold an advantage in terms of strong leadership and morality, and Democrats tended to have the advantage on caring (Hayes 2005). Looking at the affective responses from citizens, we see evidence that the 2004 contest was more about the incumbent than the challenger. President Bush was more likely to have made people angry or afraid, and he also was more likely to have made people hopeful or proud. Senator Kerry simply evoked less emotion from the public, either positively or negatively.

While campaign professionals place a heavy emphasis on managing their candidate's public image, there are two reasons to be cautious about the importance of candidate image. The first reason is that, as our model of vote choice in figure 5.6 indicates, the image a citizen has of a candidate is heavily influenced by the person's partisan identification. Not surprisingly, partisans tend to see

TABLE 5.4 Candidate Images in the 2004 Presidential Campaign (in percentages)

Candidate Qualities	Bush	Kerry
Moral	68.7	68.3
Provides strong leadership	64.5	51.9
Cares about people like you	46.0	57.0
Knowledgeable	58.9	79.7
Intelligent	60.5	85.1
Dishonest	32.3	25.0
Can't make up his mind	27.3	47.0

QUESTION: "In your opinion, does the phrase ['he is moral'] describe [George W. Bush/John Kerry] extremely well, quite well, not too well, or not at all?" Responses are the combined percentage of respondents saying "extremely well" or "quite well."

Affect toward Candidate	Bush	Kerry
Angry	56.1	31.4
Hopeful	55.4	46.5
Afraid	43.9	22.8
Proud	61.1	34.6

QUESTION: "Has [George W. Bush/John Kerry]—because of the kind of person he is or because of something he has done—ever made you feel [angry]?" Responses are the percentage of respondents saying "yes."

Source: Created by authors using data from the 2004 American National Election Study.

their party's candidate more favorably and the opposing candidate more negatively on all aspects of candidate image. We can illustrate this using another measure of candidate image from the National Election Studies called a "feeling thermometer" (because the question asks people to rate how cold or warm they feel toward a candidate on a scale of zero to 100 degrees). In 2004, true independents gave both Bush and Kerry an average rating of 52 degrees, indicating a slightly more warm than cold view toward both candidates. Strong Democrats, however, gave Bush an average rating of only 23 degrees while they rated Kerry at 77 degrees. Similarly, strong Republicans gave Bush an average rating of 90 degrees and rated Kerry at only 25 degrees. Thus, much of how citizens regard the qualities of the candidates is heavily colored by their PID.

A second reason to be cautious about the importance of candidate image is that, when partisanship and other factors are taken into account, it tends to have a small impact on a person's vote choice (Bartels 2002; Hayes 2005). Other things being equal, voters do tend to prefer candidates who they regard as strong leaders and as caring about people like themselves. But, the impact of a candidate's image is, by itself, rarely substantial enough to sway the outcome of a presidential election (Bartels 2002). Of course, there have been elections in which a candidate's appealing image clearly helped. A classic example of positive candidate image was in 1952 when the Republican candidate, Dwight Eisenhower, won the presidency, even though Democrats had a substantial advantage in terms of partisan identification. Eisenhower, of course, had a highly positive image as a leader because he was a military hero during World War II who had served as the Supreme Commander of allied forces in Europe. Although a candidate's image can on occasion be extremely beneficial, the way people see candidates is closely connected to their partisanship, and candidate image has only a modest independent effect on the decision a voter makes at election time.

Issues

The **issue positions** that the candidates take on important topics are another factor that may influence a person's vote choice. As with candidate image, where a candidate stands on particular issues tends to be the focus of a great deal of attention during presidential campaigns as candidates attempt to use issues as a way to motivate their partisan supporters and win over undecided voters. In recent presidential campaigns, Republican candidates have generally attempted to use their positions on issues such as lower tax rates, less government regulation of business, and support for military spending to their advantage, while Democratic candidates have usually focused on their support for education and job training as well as the defenders of popular social programs such as Social Security and Medicare.

The regularity with which candidates and parties have stressed their positions on particular issues intended to help them with the electorate has been termed the theory of "issue ownership" (Petrocik 1996; Petrocik, Benoit, and Hansen 2003). As Petrocik, Benoit, and Hansen (2003, 599) summarize this theory,

> Democrats "own" some issues; Republicans "own" others. Democrats have an electoral advantage when problems and issues associated with social welfare and intergroup relationships are salient. Republicans have an advantage when issues related to taxes, spending, and the size of government are high on the public agenda. Performance

issues, such as the conduct of government officials, the state of the economy, or the country's status and security among other nations, are not automatically owned by a single party, but can provide an advantage to a candidate when events, official behavior, and policy successes and failures allow the candidate to claim credit for good times or blame the opposition for bad times. Thus, candidates campaign on issues that confer an advantage in order to prime their salience in the decisional calculus of the voters.

The theory of issue ownership suggests that candidates have a built-in advantage with voters on issues "owned" by their party and it is thus beneficial to the candidate who can frame the election debate in terms of those issues. Other issues, such as the economy, are not owned by one party or the other but are a function of how people see the current state of affairs. For example, when the economy is doing well, voters will often credit the party of the incumbent president; and, if the economy is not seen as doing well, voters will blame the incumbent's party.

This theory also implies that candidates should seek to avoid talking about issues that the opposition party "owns." An analysis of statements made in campaigns between 1960 and 2000, however, indicates that most of the time candidates talk about the same issues as their opponents rather than avoiding issues that the opponent's party has used to advantage (Sigelman and Buell 2004). Moreover, candidates may even find it useful to emphasize issues owned by the opposition. The tactic of a candidate "trespassing" on an issue that has traditionally been owned by the opponent's party may neutralize a potentially damaging issue or even turn the issue into an advantage for the trespassing candidate (Damore 2004; Holian 2004). When Republican candidate George W. Bush talked about education reform as one of his priorities in the 2000 campaign, this was an example of trespassing on an issue traditionally owned by

Democrats. Similarly, when Democrat Bill Clinton raised the issue of crime in the 1992 election, he was able to trespass successfully on an issue that Republicans owned and had used against Democrats in previous elections (Holian 2004).

Clearly, an important element of any presidential campaign is for a candidate to emphasize issues that will resonate with voters and provide reasons for voters to support the candidate. The question that remains, however, is how much do issues affect how voters decide? The view that emerged from early studies of American voters tended to be that issues were not terribly important. The authors of *The American Voter*, a classic study of U.S. elections, found that less than one-third of voters could be classified as "issue voters" (Campbell et al. 1960, 168–187). In part, the conclusion that issues had a limited impact on voters was the result of the way these researchers studied this topic. Most importantly, the authors asked questions about issues that they identified before the election as issues that should be important to voters. The authors also established strict criteria to identify which voters could be influenced by issues. As these researchers saw it, voters could have their vote choice influenced by an issue only if the person had an opinion on the issue, knew about government policy on the issue, and saw a difference between the parties on the issue. Other scholars, however, have approached this topic differently and have found evidence that issues influence voters (Aldrich, Sullivan, and Borgida 1989; Carmines and Stimson 1980; Gopoian 1993; RePass 1971). For example, RePass (1971) argued that the approach used by the authors of *The American Voter* did not take into consideration what issues citizens considered to be salient, or important, to them. Using an open-ended question that allowed survey respondents to identify which issues were most important to them personally, RePass found that salient issues did affect vote choice (1971, 399–400).

We can use data from **exit polls** conducted during the 2000 and 2004 elections to illus-

trate the role of issues. Table 5.5 shows the results from the following question on the exit poll: "Which *one* issue mattered most in deciding how you voted for president?" The percentages in the first column are the results from all voters while the following three columns show the results for people who identified themselves as Democrats, independents, and Republicans. In the 2000 election, the economy, education, Social Security, taxes, and world affairs were the issues identified as being the most important in voting, followed by health care and Medicare. As table 5.5 shows, Democrats were more likely than Republicans to see the economy and Social Security as the most important issue, while Republicans were more likely to regard taxes and world affairs as the most important issue in determining their vote for president. The 2000 results reflect a fairly typical pattern of differences by partisanship for recent U.S. presidential elections. One exception to the typical pattern is education. Education is usually a topic that Democrats see as more important than Republicans. In 2000, the differences between Democrats and Republicans on the importance of education were quite small, perhaps reflecting the success of George W. Bush in trespassing on this traditionally Democratic issue.

The pattern of issues in 2004 reflects the particular circumstances of that election contest. In 2004, moral values, the economy, terrorism, and Iraq were the four most important issues followed by health care, taxes, and education. In contrast to 2000, the issue agenda in the 2004 election reflected the importance of new issues that had been thrust to the forefront—terrorism and the U.S. invasion of Iraq. The effect of partisanship on issue identification is even more evident in 2004. Republicans clearly identified moral values or terrorism as the most important issue, while Democrats saw either the economy or Iraq as the most important issue to them.

Clearly, a person's partisanship can influence what campaign issues they see as most

TABLE 5.5 Most Important Issue in the 2000 and 2004 Elections (in percentages)

Most Important Issue	All	Democrat	Independent	Republican
2000				
Economy/Jobs	18.2	22.3	17.2	14.8
Education	14.5	15.5	14.6	13.7
Social Security	13.7	17.6	9.4	11.1
Taxes	13.6	6.3	14.6	22.8
World Affairs	12.1	9.7	14.8	13.0
Health Care	7.9	9.4	8.2	5.6
Medicare	7.1	9.4	5.8	6.0
None	12.9	9.8	15.3	13.0
2004				
Moral Values	21.8	9.5	21.0	34.8
Economy/Jobs	19.7	33.2	19.3	8.2
Terrorism	18.9	8.1	18.0	30.5
Iraq	14.7	19.4	18.6	8.9
Health Care	8.0	13.2	7.2	3.6
Taxes	5.2	3.7	4.5	6.5
Education	4.4	6.2	2.1	3.7
None	7.3	6.7	7.6	5.5

QUESTION: "Which *one* issue mattered most in deciding how you voted for president?"

Source: Created by authors using data from the 2000 Voter News Service National Election Day Exit Poll and the 2004 National Election Pool General Election Exit Poll.

important. The next step is to examine how issues may influence a voter's decision. Table 5.6 shows the effects of the most important issue identified by a voter and the voter's choice in the 2000 and 2004. Once again, the 2000 election looks like a typical U.S. election pattern. The Democratic candidate, Al Gore, did better with voters who identified either the economy or social issues (health care, Medicare, Social Security) as the most important issue. The Republican, George W. Bush, clearly did better among voters for whom taxes or, to a lesser extent, world affairs were the most important issue. In 2004, George W. Bush did best among voters who regarded either terrorism or moral values, and to a lesser extent taxes, as the most important issue. John Kerry did best among those people who saw the economy, health care, Iraq, or education as their most important

issue. One of the most striking results from the 2004 election is that people who saw the Iraq war as the most important issue voted strongly for the Democratic candidate, while those who saw the most important issue as the war on terrorism overwhelmingly voted for the Republican incumbent.

Summary of the Influences on Vote Choice

The simple model of vote choice shown in figure 5.6 suggests that the process of deciding how to vote begins with a person's partisan identification, that affective attachment to one of the major political parties. Citizens do not start afresh in their political views with each new election campaign. Rather, citizens view the candidates and issues that

TABLE 5.6 Effect of Issue Importance on Vote Choice in the 2000 and 2004 Elections (percentages)

2000

Vote Choice	World Affairs	Medicare	Health Care	Economy/ Jobs	Taxes	Education	Social Security
Gore (D)	41.1	60.1	64.2	60.0	17.0	52.4	59.1
Bush (R)	54.8	38.6	32.9	37.7	81.2	44.4	40.1
Nader (I)	4.1	1.3	2.9	2.3	1.8	3.2	0.8

2004

Vote Choice	Taxes	Education	Iraq	Terrorism	Economy/ Jobs	Moral Values	Health Care
Kerry (D)	43.1	73.4	73.6	13.9	81.2	18.5	76.8
Bush (R)	56.9	26.6	26.4	86.1	18.8	81.5	23.2

Source: Created by authors using data from the 2000 Voter News Service National Election Day Exit Poll and the 2004 National Election Pool General Election Exit Poll.

become the focus of presidential campaigns through the lens of their own partisan preferences. While each of these factors—partisan identification, candidate image, and issue positions—influences how an individual chooses to vote, the most important of these factors in a typical election is partisan identification. People with strong partisan preferences tend to see the candidates and the issues in accordance with that strong pre-existing orientation. Independents and weaker partisans, however, are more likely to be influenced by campaign events such as the nominating conventions and debates (Hillygus and Jackman 2003). Because partisanship for most people is relatively stable, it may seem that the outcomes of presidential campaigns are largely determined by the established partisan preferences of most voters. Yet, it is important to recognize that what happens in presidential campaigns still matters (Campbell 2000). Campaigns matter because the support of even the most dedicated party supporters cannot be taken for granted; it must be revived and encouraged during each campaign by the party and candidate. Moreover, campaigns matter because neither party has a sufficient advantage in

partisan loyalty to be able to win an election with its supporters alone. From the perspective of the parties, then, the central task of any campaign is to mobilize their core partisans and at the same time present an appeal to independents or weak partisans that will be persuasive.

Of course, there are other factors that may influence how an individual decides to vote. In addition to the factors we have discussed, there are several other individual characteristics that can influence how a person votes. For example, both a person's gender and race usually have an effect on vote choice. In recent decades, women have been somewhat more supportive of Democratic candidates and men have tended to be more supportive of Republicans. This difference, called the "gender gap," is usually not that large in any given election, but it has persisted since the 1980s (Chaney, Alvarez, and Nagler 1998; Kaufmann and Petrocik 1999). With regard to race, a consistent pattern has been that African American voters are much more supportive of Democratic candidates than other voters. While about 41 percent of Asians and whites voted for John Kerry in 2004, nearly 87 percent of African Americans voted for

Kerry according to the National Election Study. Since blacks are also more likely to identify with the Democratic party, part of this difference is accounted for by partisan identification. Still, a person's racial identification continues to be an important influence in shaping how Americans vote.

Another important identity that can influence voting is a person's ideological identification as a liberal, moderate, or conservative. This sense of identification is, like partisan identification, a learned attachment to an ideological group. Unlike partisan identification, however, a sizable proportion of people, often between 20 and 30 percent, say that they do not think of themselves in ideological terms at all. Among people who do identify with an ideology, this identification is a predictor of how people vote with conservatives generally supporting Republican candidates and liberals supporting Democrats. While PID is a better predictor of vote choice than ideology in most presidential elections, ideology was nearly as strong as partisanship in 2004.

Conclusion: The Nature of American Political Participation

Political participation in the United States is something of an anomaly. As we noted at the beginning of the chapter, most Americans regard participation in politics as important, and Americans are proud of their democratic traditions. Yet, in comparison with other democratic nations, fewer Americans vote. On average, fewer Americans vote in presidential elections than people in other countries vote in national elections. And, the turnout rate in congressional election years tends to be even lower than turnout in presidential elections.

In part, as we have seen in this chapter, the decision not to vote may be a consequence of the many other opportunities that Americans enjoy to try to influence public policy that do not require a person to engage in the conflictual nature of campaigns and elections. Another substantial part of the explanation resides in the nature of the American electoral system. In the United States, more so than in other democratic nations, the burden of becoming an active participant in politics is placed on the individual. This tends to fit with the generally individualistic orientation of American culture. But it also means that, to a greater extent in the United States than in other democratic nations, political participation is a function of a person's socioeconomic standing. People who have more educational and financial resources are much more likely to vote and to participate in politics generally. The actions of political parties, campaigns, and interest groups can help because their activities do tend to increase participation among those people who are contacted.

Among citizens who vote, the evidence shows that a person's long-term attachment to a political party plays a central role in deciding how to vote. Not only does PID influence how a person votes, it also influences how that person looks at the candidates and the issues in an election contest. While campaigns seek to establish that their candidate has the better personal qualities and issue positions, professional campaigners also recognize that their ability to persuade voters is limited. Thus, most campaigns devote resources to getting out the vote among those people most likely to support their candidate and focus their efforts at persuading those independents or weak partisans who might be won over. In the next chapter, we turn to a topic that is central to all of these campaign endeavors: money.

CHAPTER 6

Campaign Finance

During election periods, hardly a week goes by without allegations of a candidate's violating campaign finance laws, and heated denials by the accused. Election financing is an important topic, but it is often discussed in terms that are difficult for the average citizen to understand. Whether intended or not, the combination of large amounts of money and the barrage of technical terms such as "federal" and "nonfederal" accounts, as well as "independent expenditures," produces in many citizens a "MEGO effect"—my eyes glaze over. To minimize this effect, our focus will be on four issues. The first issue is the effect of campaign contributions on representative government. Are campaign costs rising so rapidly that election outcomes are skewed toward those who can afford generous campaign contributions? In short, does the role of money in campaigns make a mockery of representative government? The answer to that question depends on whether influence in the nation's capital is viewed as unilateral (from donor to decision maker only) or bilateral (a two-way flow of influence).

A second issue is the goals that reformers have in designing and implementing campaign finance laws. What are these goals, and are they internally consistent with one another? How have the goals been modified or negated by decisions of the courts and the Federal Election Commission (FEC)?

A third issue is the importance of campaign finance law for candidates, parties, and interest groups. For candidates, the finance laws are of critical importance in determining who runs for public office, the campaign strategy that is used, and who gets elected. More recent innovations such as soft money and issue advocacy ads provide new opportunities for parties and interest groups, but a firestorm of criticism can arise if the public perceives them as mechanisms allowing improper access to decision makers.

The final issue is campaign finance reform, an area where Congress and the courts have taken recent action. Several broad approaches to reform and their potential consequences are explored. Disagreement about the impact of recent campaign finance laws, as well as whether additional action is needed, is largely due to the clash of goals among reformers, the Congress, the courts, and the public.

Campaign Finance and Public Decision Making

Given the many charges of campaign finance abuse after each election, it is not surprising that most Americans view the role of money in politics as a unilateral or one-way application of influence. Funds flow from the individual or interest group to the decision maker for the purpose of improperly influencing public sector decisions. Philip Stern, whose book *The Best Congress Money Can Buy* reflects this view, suggests "the line between a campaign contribution and a bribe is only, as one senator put it, 'a hair's breadth'" (1988, 18).

The assumption about the unilateral flow of money and influence underlies the four major goals of reformers. The first goal is to raise citizen confidence in representative government. The key principle stated by Senator Russell Feingold (D-Wisconsin), cosponsor of the McCain-Feingold reform legislation, is that "principal input should come from the people back home. . . . Money cuts the link between the representative and the represented" (Shulte and Enda 1997). Accepting the unilateral view of the role of money in politics forms the basis for other goals as well.

Linked with raising citizen confidence in government is a second goal: preventing corruption or the appearance of corruption. The first definition of corruption is that of quid pro quo: the position or votes of legislators are improperly influenced by campaign contributions. The second type of corruption is giving contributors improper access to decision makers in exchange for campaign contributions. Reducing the role of money in politics, it is assumed, will do much to accomplish the first goal, restoring the severed link between the representative and the represented.

The third goal is to increase equality in the political system. Even if those making large contributions to campaigns do not have as their primary focus "buying the vote" or undue access to decision makers, large contributions are seen as a form of "multiple voting" in which individuals and groups seek influence beyond the political system's central premise of "one person, one vote."

A final goal of reformers is increasing citizen knowledge about, and participation in a government. Party labels and candidate speeches offer clues about a candidate's future behavior once in office; knowledge of who has contributed the most to a candidate is yet another means of evaluation for those who wish to use it.

The key assumption behind each of the goals then, is that by reducing the role of money in politics, reform legislators can do much to restore that severed link between the representative and the represented. An opposing view to that of the reformers, which is the perspective adopted in this chapter, is that contributing money is a bilateral or exchange relationship (Keleher 1996; Schlozman and Tierney 1986; Sorauf 1992, 60–64). Campaign donors seek information, access, and influence on both current and future public policies. Legislators, in addition to using campaign donations to maximize constituent vote totals at the next election, have other goals, including using interest group members to lobby other congressional members to support a member's bill, or using the legislator's upcoming vote to cause the interest group to modify its stance on an issue. Political scientist Frank Sorauf (1992, 63–64) describes the process:

> It is not only a transferring of goods or services for something of equal value. It is also a mutual relationship in which the actions, goals, and strategies of one participant interact with those of the other. The sum of all the exchanges creates a market that defines alternative options, a range of "prices," and the viable and negotiable terms of individual exchanges.

Although scholars know the general goals of both groups and candidates, the lack of knowledge about the specifics of alternative options, or the range of "prices," leads to a more cautious evaluation of campaign reform efforts. Groups will always seek an unequal bargaining relationship with decision makers and will use loopholes or unintended consequences of reforms to negotiate a new "price." Although campaign reform may be able to temporarily modify the most outrageous abuses of the system, expecting campaign finance legislation to restore faith in representative government single-handedly places too high a burden on the reform vehicle.

Skyrocketing Campaign Costs or Underfunded Campaigns?

One of the most common complaints by the public is that elections cost too much. When the amounts expended for federal offices are considered, table 6.1 illustrates the increasing costs from the 2000 to the 2004 elections. Spending by 527 groups led the way, with four times the amount spent in 2004 compared with 2000. Amounts spent for presidential candidates nearly doubled between the two election years. With the control of Congress up for grabs in 2006 spending again increased. The nonpartisan Center for Responsive Politics estimates a record $2.8 billion was spent, averaging $59 per vote in Senate races and $35 per vote in the House of Representatives (Center for Responsive Politics 2006).

An opposing point of view contends that election spending is not out of control. Part of the funding disparity between 2000 and 2004 is due to changes in campaign funding law. Specifically, the ban on soft money contributions and "issue advocacy" ads led to a shift in funds from political parties to 527 groups. The impact of inflation needs to be considered as well. When the non-presidential years of 2006 and 2002 are compared, congressional campaign costs increased by 18 percent, slightly greater than the rise of inflation of 13 percent.

Sorauf (1992) contends that the claim of overspending on campaigns is one of the major "myths" of campaign finance. Former House Speaker Newt Gingrich, who is often critical of government, has called modern politics "underfunded" (Carney 1996, 1521). Moreover, in an era when about half of voters cannot identify their representative in Congress, advocates contend that money is a proxy for information. Whether the message is in the form of direct ads, advocacy ads, or

TABLE 6.1 Total Spending in Federal Elections, 2000 and 2004 (in millions of dollars)

Spending by:	2000	2004
Presidential candidates	671	1,230
Congressional candidates	1,007	1,259
National parties (federal)	497	542
National parties (nonfederal)	498	na
State and local parties (federal)	161	176
State and local parties (nonfederal)	330	67
527s	101	424
PACs	299	475
Issue Advocacy	248	na
Total	**3,812**	**4,173**

Source: Patterson (2006, 71).

independent expenditures, any increase in the number of messages leads to a more informed electorate. Critics of the current system, however, respond that the quality of information is the issue rather than the quantity. If the content is simply hurling charges and countercharges, the result is a less enlightened electorate and lower participation rates.

Reform Goals and Campaign Finance Laws

The means by which money is raised and how it is spent in political campaigns have been issues since the beginning of the republic. Early on, campaign financing was handled by the candidates themselves and one major expense was providing whiskey to increase turnout on election day. With the arrival of Jacksonian democracy in 1828, costs increased as the electorate broadened, and elements of modern campaigning appeared, such as parades and speeches at mass meetings. To pay for campaigns the Democratic party began the practice of requiring payments from government workers, who in the period before the civil service laws owed their positions to the patronage provided by the party machine. In the economic expansion that occurred after the Civil War, wealthy individuals and businesses became a major source of campaign money. In 1896, the Republican party chair, Mark Hanna, systematically assessed banks and corporations based on their financial worth (Mutch 1988, xvi–xvii).

Early legislation, including the Federal Corrupt Practices Act enacted in 1925, required disclosure of contributions, spending limits, and quarterly reports. That law was widely ignored by candidates and enforcement was nil. Thus, there was little by way of effective regulation of campaign finance. The most recent campaign finance legislation has three overriding goals: to establish greater equality in political campaigns; to protect the integrity of the electoral system; and to increase participation in the political system by candidates, individual citizens, and political parties (Corrado 1992, 13–15).

Major efforts to change campaign finance law did not resurface until 1971 when Congress passed the Federal Election Campaign Act (FECA) and the Revenue Act. The Revenue Act created the tax check-off system to allow citizens to earmark use of their tax dollars for public financing of presidential campaigns. The FECA of 1971 limited the amount that could be spent on advertising, limited the amount that candidates could contribute to their own campaign, and required disclosure of the names and addresses of those donating more than $100. While the disclosure provisions in the FECA have largely remained intact, the limits on spending and self-contributions were later changed in response to court rulings. The FECA also provided the legal framework for political action committees (PACs), originally defined as campaign funds that could be established by corporations or unions (FEC 2005, 4–5).

The 1971 FECA, however, did not provide for a single agency to enforce the law and did little to stem the tide of corrupt practices.

Fifty-one millionaires contributed a total of $6 million to political campaigns in 1972, capped by W. Clement Stone's $2 million gift to Richard Nixon's campaign. Executives from twenty-one corporations were convicted of making illegal $100,000 contributions. When these developments were combined with the revelations of the Watergate scandal, the result was a series of important amendments to the FECA passed in 1974. One of the important changes resulting from the 1974 law was the creation of a bipartisan agency, the **Federal Election Commission (FEC)**, to enforce federal campaign finance laws. The 1974 amendments also expanded the system of public financing for presidential campaigns. The new public financing provisions built on the system authorized in the 1971 Revenue Act. Public funding was provided for candidates who could qualify in the primary elections on a matching basis. After an initial amount was raised by the candidate, private contributions of $250 or less would be matched on a dollar-per-dollar basis by public funds. The public financing system also provided for a lump sum to be paid to the nominees of each of the major parties for the general election, provided that the candidate agreed not to exceed the federal spending limits. The intent of the system of public financing was to try to equalize available resources by allowing candidates to maximize the value of small contributions through the public matching funds and also to restrain the growth of campaign spending by requiring candidates who accepted public funds to limit their spending.

Court interpretations of the FECA and development of major loopholes, such as the proliferation of "soft money," ultimately led reformers to push for the passage of the Bipartisan Campaign Finance Reform Act of 2002 (BCRA). BCRA is often referred to as McCain-Feingold after its two chief sponsors. Table 6.2 summarizes the major provisions of BCRA as interpreted by the Supreme Court in the case of *McConnell v. FEC* (2003).

TABLE 6.2 Major Provisions of the Bipartisan Campaign Reform Act of 2002 (BCRA)

	What BRCA Does	Supreme Court Decision	Impact of Decision
National Party Soft Money	Prohibits national parties from raising or spending soft money	Prohibition upheld	National parties may not raise or spend soft money
Soft Money Fund-Raising by Federal Candidates and Officeholders	Prohibits federal candidates and officeholders from raising or spending soft money (with certain exceptions)	Prohibition upheld	Federal candidates and officeholders may not raise soft money (with certain exceptions)
"Federal Election Activities" by State and Local Parties	Requires state and local parties to pay for federal election activities with hard money or a mix of hard money and "Levin funds"*	Requirement upheld	State and local parties must use hard money (or a mix of hard money and Levin funds) for federal election activities
Prohibition of "Sham" Issue Ads	Prohibits corporations and unions from using soft money to pay for "electioneering communications"**	Prohibition upheld	Corporations and unions may not use soft money to pay for "electioneering communications"
Disclosure of "Sham" Issue Ads	Requires disclosure of "electioneering communications" in excess of $10,000 per year	Disclosure requirement upheld	"Electioneering communications" must be disclosed to the FEC
Contribution Limits	Increases the dollar limits on contributions from individuals to federal candidates or parties	Increased limits upheld	Individuals may make larger contributions to candidates or parties
Independent and Coordinated Expenditures by Parties	Requires a party spending money in a general election to choose between making coordinated expenditures or independent expenditures	Choice of expenditure rule declared unconstitutional	A party may make both coordinated and independent expenditures on behalf of its candidates in a general election
Contributions by Minors	Prohibits minors from making contributions to federal candidates and parties	Prohibition on contributions by minors declared unconstitutional	Minors may make contributions to candidates and parties

Notes:
* Levin funds are contributions made to state and local parties that can be spent on voter registration and voter mobilization in federal elections and are not subject to usual limitations on campaign contributions.
** "Electioneering communications" are broadcast advertisements that mention a federal candidate or officeholder within thirty days of a primary or sixty days of a general election and are targeted to that person's constituents.

Source: Center for Responsive Politics (2003).

The FEC defines "federal expenditures" (or the more commonly used term **hard money**) as contributions used for "cash, equipment, or services that go directly to a candidate's campaign committee for use at its discretion." Under the FECA, once a candidate formally declares for a federal office, individuals could donate $1,000 each in hard money to a candidate's primary, runoff, and general election campaigns. BCRA raised that to $2,000 and required that amount to be indexed for inflation. The total cap on individual spending for all federal campaigns during an election cycle is now more than $100,000 and is adjusted for inflation every two years. The amount an individual may contribute to the national parties has been raised to $26,700, again adjusted for inflation. PACs are limited to $5,000 each in direct contributions or hard money per election, an amount that remained unchanged in McCain-Feingold. But PACs can contribute that amount to as many candidates as they have funds for. The FECA also put a limit on how much an individual could contribute to his or her own campaign, but this provision was later struck down by the Supreme Court. To get around the Court's opinion, McCain-Feingold employed a so-called "millionaire's provision." Under a complicated formula, if a congressional candidate contributed more than the allowed amount to his or her own campaign, the opponent's supporters could exceed the individual hard money dollar limit. Among the other changes in BRCA were the "stand by your ad" provision requiring congressional candidates to state that they approved of the message and a ban on contributions by minors under seventeen years of age.

"Nonfederal expenditures," better known as **soft money**, came about as a result of changes in FEC regulations. Thus, by the 1980 elections political parties could solicit donations of any size provided that the money was used for "party building" activities, such as voter registration drives, at the state and local level (hence the origin of the term "nonfederal"). These funds were not, however, to be used to influence the conduct of federal elections by, for example, paying for a candidate's advertising. During the 1980s, the use of soft money by the political parties was not a major feature of campaign finance activities. By the 1996 election, however, the collection and use of soft money by the political parties had increased dramatically, and it became clear that both Democrats and Republicans were using these funds in ways that were, in fact, intended to influence elections. For example, the parties used these funds to pay for what were called "issue advocacy" ads that were thinly disguised ads to promote Democratic or Republican candidates. As soft money funding grew, reformers demanded a ban on soft money contributions in federal elections. A ban on soft money was one of the major provisions of the BCRA.

The McCain-Feingold legislation also tackled the issue of groups engaging in "independent" spending close to election day. Within thirty days of a primary or sixty days before a general election, ads in any broadcast medium that mentions a federal candidate and is targeted toward the electorate, falls within a "federal funding period" and must be paid for in federal or hard money funds. Any ads outside this period could be financed by soft money.

The complex regulatory system set up by the FECA and BRCA did make substantial progress in accomplishing the three major goals of reformers. The goal of greater equality in the political system was furthered by legal limits on individual contributions, as well as partial public funding of presidential elections, but these provisions did not create the proverbial "level playing field" for all candidates. The law did, however, result in a playing field somewhat less tilted toward those who were independently wealthy.

The second goal of increasing the integrity of the political system and decreasing the perception of corruption, was implemented by mandating a full and public disclosure of the funds raised and spent. The two laws required registration of one central campaign committee, and that committee was responsible for filing timely reports of campaign spending. The laws operated under the premise that "sunlight is the best disinfectant." Because campaign committees know that the news media, and hence the public, would closely examine their campaign reports, the chances of spending irregularities would decrease. The laws also assume that information flowing to the public increases their knowledge of campaign finance practices and allows for a more informed choice among the candidates. However, a substantial gap exists between the premises of the laws and actual practice. Even among the "attentive public," who pay close attention to politics, information about campaign finance is often scattered, provided only after the election, and difficult to put into perspective. The FEC now provides a comprehensive Web site, however, and several independent organizations provide information to assist interested citizens as well. Box 6.1 provides an evaluation of several sources of campaign finance information.

Campaign Finance Laws and the Courts: A Tumultuous Relationship

Several of the provisions in the 1974 FECA amendments were quickly subjected to court challenges. Because campaign finance laws can become mind-numbingly complex in very short order, an overview of two key constitutional questions will be of assistance before examining specific cases. The first question is, what are the various types of speech, and how do political contributions relate to the types of speech? The second question is, given the First Amendment's protection of freedom of speech, are limits on campaign contributions constitutional?

In general the Supreme Court has recognized three types of speech: pure speech, speech plus conduct, and symbolic speech. Pure speech is often defined as expressing a

point of view, and the Court has historically given this type of speech the highest degree of protection. In *Eu v. San Francisco County Democratic Central Committee*, the Court declared: "Indeed, the First Amendment 'has its fullest and most urgent application' to speech uttered during a campaign for political office" (1989, 223). Several justices, most notably Antonin Scalia and Clarence Thomas, have consistently contended that campaign contributions come closest to pure speech, and thus deserve complete First Amendment protection. In contrast, the concept of speech plus conduct adds an activity, such as walking a picket line, with speech in the form of a message on a sign. The message on the sign may well be protected, but conduct such as hitting an opponent with that sign could be regulated. Justice Stevens argues that adding money to speech in the form of a contribution implies conduct, as it allows one's voice to be amplified as the speech is carried on the airwaves or repeated over and over as an advertisement, far beyond that of an individual voice.

The second question then becomes, if limits are put on contributions, what kind of test should the Court apply to determine the constitutionality of such limits? Often in First Amendment cases the Court has decided that there must be a "compelling state interest" before limits on speech will be accepted. Thus any limits on speech will be given very close examination, which is termed "strict scrutiny." Again Justices Scalia and Thomas, focusing on the speech elements of political contributions, argue there is no compelling state interest in limiting campaign contributions, and any limits fail the test of strict scrutiny. In contrast, Justices Souter, Stevens, and Ginsburg would defer to Congress's judgment about the need for campaign limitations and would subject any law to "closely drawn" but not strict scrutiny.

The first court challenge occurred in 1976 in the case of *Buckley v. Valeo*. Basically, this decision upheld restrictions on political contributions (such as the FECA's

BOX 6.1 Campaign Finance Information Sites

There are a number of sites providing information or commentary on campaign finance at the federal and state levels. Here are a list of some useful sites, with descriptions taken largely from the mission statements of each.

1. The Federal Election Commission [fec.gov]. As the agency in charge of enforcing federal campaign finance laws, the FEC is an authoritative source of information. Prior to the 1996 election, however, the FEC site was not well organized and slow to provide information. Since that time the site has provided timely press releases as well as detailed information on candidate expenditures, PAC spending, and national party committee spending.

2. The Center for Responsive Politics [opensecrets.org]. This nonpartisan, nonprofit research group is based in Washington, DC, and tracks money in politics. The Center conducts research on campaign finance issues for the news media, academics, activists, and the public at large. The Center's work aims to create a more educated voter, a more involved citizenry, and a more responsive government.

3. Political Money Line [moneyline.cq.com/pml/home.do]. This organization was founded by Kent Cooper and Tony Raymond and became a leading independent source of campaign finance information. In 2006, Congressional Quarterly purchased the Political Money Line. The site is easy to navigate, but some of the information requires a paid subscription to access.

4. The Center for Competitive Politics [campaignfreedom.org]. The Center is a nonprofit organization founded in 2005 by former FEC chairman Bradley A. Smith, a professor of law at Capital University Law School, and Stephen M. Hoersting, campaign finance attorney and former general counsel to the National Republican Senatorial Committee. The Center's mission is to educate the public on the effect of money in politics through legal briefs, studies, historical and constitutional analyses, and media communication. The Center advocates a more free and competitive electoral process.

5. Public Campaign [publicampaign.org]. This organization is a nonprofit, nonpartisan group dedicated to reforming the role of money in American politics.

6. Common Cause [commoncause.org]. Common Cause is an advocacy organization that provides information on recent reform actions at both state and federal levels, and supports reform efforts.

7. The National Institute on Money in State Politics [followthemoney.org]. This nonpartisan organization bills itself as the "nation's most complete resource for information on state money and politics" and the Web site supports this claim.

The Institute's site provides elections summaries, top industry contributors, average dollars spent per voter in various races, and comparisons of labor, business, and party contributions for various offices.

8. Campaign Finance Information Center (CFIC) [campaignfinance.org]. This site was created for journalists and provides a comprehensive collection of state level data from both official and unofficial sources as well as information on using federal campaign finance information.

9. Citizens Research Foundation (CRF) [igs.berkeley.edu/research_programs/CRF]. Under the leadership of Herbert Alexander, the Foundation pioneered the study of campaign finance and provided the first reliable data on contributions to candidates. With many organizations now providing campaign finance data, the CRF fell behind. Although current output is scarce, the focus of this site is on analysis and providing a neutral forum to review and debate the latest research on campaign finance. CRF is now part of the Institute of Governmental Studies at the University of California, Berkeley.

10. Other useful university related sites include:
    American University Campaign Finance [www1.soc.american.edu/campfin.ind]
    Brennan Center at New York University Law School [brennancenter.org]
    The Campaign Finance Institute at George Washington University [cfinst.org]

11. State government Web sites provide information on state campaign finance laws and reports. As examples:
    California [cal-access.ss.ca.gov/campaign]. The Web site of the California Secretary of State provides data for the state.
    New York [www.elections.state.ny.us]. The State Board of Elections is the source of data.

$1000 contribution limit for individuals) while striking down limits on political expenditures. The court explained that contribution limits entail only a "marginal restriction" on free speech, while expenditure limits "represent substantial rather than merely theoretical restraints on the quantity and diversity of political speech" (*Buckley v. Valeo* 1976, 19). Campaign spending limits directly affect "the quantity of expression" by influencing how many issues are discussed, how deeply they are explored, and the size of their audience. Contribution limits indicate only a "general expression of support for the candidate and his views," but do not indicate the reason for the support (*Buckley v. Valeo* 1976, 21).

The Court further discussed three possible justifications for the $1,000 contribution limit for individuals: to "mute the voices of affluent persons and groups" in elections and therefore to equalize ability of all citizens to affect election outcomes; to act as a brake on the skyrocketing costs of campaigns, thereby allowing citizens with modest financial resources the ability to run for public office; and finally the prevention of "corruption and the appearance of corruption" resulting from the "real or imagined coercive influence of large financial contributions on candidates' positions and on their actions if elected to Congress" (*Buckley v. Valeo* 1976, 25–26). The majority decision determined that only the last reason of preventing corruption was constitutionally acceptable, as it was narrowly targeted to an area in which corruption was most likely to occur: the exchange of money for a member's future vote. Unfortunately for advocates of reform, even if the first two reasons of greater equality in the political arena and increased participation in the political system led to electing decision makers who were more responsive to the public's will, such logic would not receive constitutional protection.

In addition, the Court took a negative view of several other limits imposed by the 1974 amendments. Restrictions on using a candidate's own money or family money in campaigns imposed "significantly more severe restrictions" on protected freedoms of political expression and association, and were therefore struck down. "The candidate," the Court asserted, "no less than any other person, has a First Amendment right to engage in the discussion of public issues and to vigorously and tirelessly advocate his own election" (Lockard and Murphy 1980, 209–210). Moreover, the Court pointed out that a candidate spending his or her own money would be *less* likely to be influenced by campaign donations, thus helping to accomplish the second reform goal of protecting the integrity of the political system.

The majority decision also bravely entered the thicket of "independent spending." Could individuals and groups engage in unlimited spending to promote a candidate as long as the money was not contributed directly to a candidate's campaign? The Court stated that capping the amount groups spend independently of candidates restricts the First Amendment right to engage in "vigorous advocacy" of ideas. The majority decision further assumed that "campaign advertising" (which

is subject to regulation) could be identified by whether the advertisements "in express terms advocate the election or defeat of a clearly identified candidate for federal office" (*Buckley v. Valeo* 1976, 44). In a footnote the justices defined the concept of "express advocacy" to mean using such terms as "vote for or against," "elect," "Smith for Congress," or "defeat." Groups could conduct "issue advocacy" campaigns and severely criticize a candidate's stance on issues, as long as they avoided the "magic words" specified by the Court.

On the issue of disclosing who contributed to a campaign, Chief Justice Burger did concede that disclosure impinges upon First Amendment rights. Burger noted, however, that because disclosure can reveal "political support that is sometimes coupled with expectations of special favors or rewards . . . I agree that the need for disclosure outweighs individual constitutional claims" (*Buckley v. Valeo* 1976, 236).

The Supreme Court eliminated one potential roadblock to party spending in the case of *Colorado Republican Federal Campaign Committee v. FEC* decided in June 1996. Nearly a decade earlier, Timothy Wirth sought the Democratic party's nomination for a Colorado Senate seat. Before choosing a candidate, the state Republican party ran radio ads and printed fliers attacking Wirth's record. When the FEC attempted to apply this spending to the overall limit in senatorial campaigns, the state Republican party argued it should be free to spend any amount, just like PACs, as long as it did not coordinate its efforts with the candidate. The Supreme Court agreed. Justices Stephen Breyer, Sandra Day O'Conner, and David Souter wrote, "We do not see how a Constitution that grants to individuals, candidates and ordinary political committees the right to make unlimited independent expenditures could deny the right to political parties" (*Colorado Republican Federal Campaign Committee v. FEC* 1996, 618). Three other justices in a concurring opinion were willing to go even further. Justices Antonin Scalia,

Anthony Kennedy, and William Rehnquist stated that any limits on political party spending, whether coordinated with the candidate or not, violated the First Amendment's guarantee of freedom of speech. Justice Clarence Thomas urged fellow members to reverse *Buckley v. Valeo,* stating that contribution limits "infringe as directly and as seriously upon freedom of political expression as do expenditure limits" (*Colorado Republican Federal Campaign Committee v. FEC* 1996, 640). The Court's decision in the *Colorado Republican* case left the parties free to spend unlimited amounts in the general election. New ground could be broken in the area of independent expenditures, and issue advocacy campaigns accelerated.

In 2002, Senator Mitch McConnell (R-Kentucky) led a filibuster against the McCain-Feingold bill. After the bill became law, he and such diverse interest groups as the Chamber of Commerce, the AFL-CIO, the National Rifle Association, and the American Civil Liberties Union brought the issue to the Supreme Court (Barnes and Mosk 2007). In *McConnell v. FEC* (2003), the most important issues facing the Court were the ban on soft money and the ban on "sham issue ads" before the primary and general elections.

The majority restated the belief that Congress has a compelling interest in preventing "the cynical assumption that large donors call the tune" (*McConnell v. FEC* 2003, 143). The ban on soft money was upheld because such funds "have a corrupting influence or give rise to the appearance of corruption" (*McConnell v. FEC* 2003, 145). The majority did not want to upset "Congress' eminently reasonable prediction" that "state and local candidates and officeholders will become the next conduits for the soft money funding of sham issue advertising" (*McConnell v. FEC* 2003, 185).

Justice Scalia's dissent emphasized that the motive for doing away with soft funds was incumbent protection: a fear that an opposing party could pour soft funds into a race and defeat the incumbent. Academic studies, particularly by "public choice" economists, have also argued that money does not "purchase" legislation, but provides access for lobbyists, or helps to ensure that legislators show up to vote (Boyce 2000; Evans 1988; Strattman 1998).

The majority of the Court found little practical distinction existed between "genuine" and "sham" issue ads. Both ads, the majority concluded

> were used to advocate the election or defeat of clearly identified federal candidates, even though the so-called issue ads eschew the use of magic words. Little difference existed, for example, between an ad that urged viewers to "vote against Jane Doe" and one that condemned Jane Doe's record on a particular issue before exhorting viewers to "call Jane Doe and tell her what you think." (*McConnell v. FEC* 2003, 184)

After the addition of Chief Justice John Roberts and Justice Samuel Alito, the Court had the opportunity to hear a case that would apply the precedents established by *McConnell v. FEC* to an actual election controversy. That opportunity appeared in 2007 with the Court's decision in *FEC v. Wisconsin Right to Life* (2007). The controversy began in 2004 when Senate Democrats filibustered several of President Bush's federal court nominees. Shortly before the election that year, an interest group called Wisconsin Right to Life ran ads stating that the filibuster was "politics at work, and it's causing gridlock. Contact senators Feingold and Kohl and tell them to oppose the filibuster" (Barnes 2007). Viewers were then given an Internet address to contact for further information. Senator Russ Feingold, co-author of the McCain-Feingold bill, was up for reelection, but Senator Herb Kohl was not.

The issues that arose were should the three spots be banned during the "blackout" period—thirty days before a primary election and sixty days before the general election—because they were "sham ads"? Was their purpose the defeat of Senator Feingold, a legislator who earned the wrath of interest groups by limiting their ability to advertise before primary and general elections? Or were the three spots "genuine" issue ads? The district court judge looked at the "four corners of the ads" and concluded that if the ads do not explicitly urge voters to "defeat Feingold," for example, the ads must be allowed, even if their broader purpose is exactly the defeat of the senator. A three-judge Court of Appeals panel agreed, ruling the ads were not "intended to influence the voters' decisions" and were "genuine issue ads" (L. Greenhouse 2007).

The case was appealed to the Supreme Court. In oral arguments before the Court, attention focused on the Court's newest members, Justices Roberts and Alito, as both justices stressed the importance of upholding past precedents in their Senate confirmation hearings. In oral arguments both justices appeared skeptical of banning issue ads before the primary and general elections. Justice Roberts stated, "I think it's an important part of their exercise of First Amendment rights to petition their senators and congressmen and to urge others" to do so as well (Barnes 2007). Justice Stephen Breyer, who was in the majority in *McConnell*, indicated the Wisconsin Right to Life ads were exactly the type of ads the law was designed to regulate. If the Court agreed with the Wisconsin Right to Life argument, Breyer stated, "goodbye McCain-Feingold. Maybe we should do it upfront. That's what you advocate. Very well. . . . [But] why should this court only a year or two after it upholds McCain-Feingold accept a position that either in fact or in theory overturns that case?" (Barnes 2007). In a 5–4 decision Justice Roberts stated that the Wisconsin Right-to-Life ads must be considered "genuine" issue ads. The only ads subject to the blackout are those that are "susceptible of no reasonable interpretation other than as an appeal to vote for or against a specific candidate" (*FEC v. Wisconsin Right to Life* 2007, 39).

Thus while the blackout period is not specifically overturned, the clear implication is that if unions, corporations, and ideological groups avoid the "magic words" they may advertise whenever they please. The dissenters argued that the decision did not follow the philosophy of judicial restraint, did not rely on the precedent established in *McConnell v. FEC*, and thus effectively overturned a central holding of that case. Three justices—Scalia, Thomas, and Kennedy—wanted to toss out the blackout concept completely. Justice Scalia, infamous for his pointed barbs, aimed one at Justice Roberts by stating "this faux judicial restraint is judicial obfuscation" (*FEC v. Wisconsin Right to Life* 2007, 88).

In sum, prior to the Robert's Court, the Justices found constitutional problems at the periphery of campaign finance law, such as limits on candidates giving to their own campaigns. Given the views of the two newest members, it appears that what began as a minority view with Justices Scalia and Thomas is fast becoming the majority view of the Supreme Court. The new majority is increasingly skeptical of the premises of campaign finance reform legislation, and on a case-by-case basis appears to be moving toward the position that central aspects of campaign finance legislation deny First Amendment protection to interest groups and political parties.

Political Parties and Campaign Finance Law: Assessing the Impact

In the years immediately following the FECA, reformers hoped that campaign contribution limits would encourage less well-known individuals to run for federal offices, provide voters with a wider range of choices, and thus encourage greater voter turnout. In the 1976 and 1978 campaigns, however, voter participation was lower. Turnout decreased in part because the limits on campaign contributions meant that candidates were less willing to spend on activities such as grassroots campaigning or party-building activities. Parties argued that they needed more financial resources to participate effectively in federal and state elections. Congress responded in 1979 with revisions to the FECA that increased the flow of soft money. Expenditures for such "party building" activities as voter registration and turnout drives were exempted. The funds could also be used to pay for a portion of a party's overhead and administrative expenses. The parties needed only to establish "reasonable accounting systems" to determine what part of an activity should be paid for by such funds. Although the 1979 amendment specifically prohibited the use of soft money in broadcast advertising, later FEC rulings allowed such spending if party themes or symbols were stressed, rather than a specific candidate.

Given the changes accepted by the FEC in the 1980s, the importance of soft money exploded in the 1990s. While soft money or "nonfederal expenditures" accounted for only 16 percent of party money expenditures in 1992, the percentage of soft funds used in federal campaigns jumped to 30 percent in 1996 and to 49 percent in 2002. Although a lawsuit filed by Common Cause resulted in a 1991 FEC requirement that parties disclose soft money contributions and expenditures, tracking the actual use of the funds was very difficult. Party officials contended the money was "spent on Mom and apple pie stuff" (Donovan 1993, 1198). Still, a liberal interpretation of the law meant the funds were used for a wide range of activities: administrative costs (such as sending campaign operatives and political consultants to assist in state races); coordinated campaigns (sharing costs for phone banks, door-to-door canvassing); generic media purchases ("Vote Democratic" campaign spots); transfers of money to state and local parties; and "building funds" used to purchase facilities and computers. For an innovative interpretation of the requirement, few could top the former chair of the Democratic Congressional Campaign Committee, who upon learning that building-fund expenses (including the cost of constructing the party's national headquarters) could be paid for by soft funds ordered the furniture in the headquarters to be bolted to the floor to qualify as part of the "building" (Dwyre 1996, 411).

A measured assessment of soft money reveals that the funds proved advantageous to the parties in several ways. The financial resources that soft money provided allowed national political parties to regain their role as intermediaries. Before the rise of soft money, if candidates did not agree with aspects of the party's platform, or the party was unpopular among voters for any reason, candidates could run basically independent of their party. After the FEC's interpretation of the 1974 amendments, national political parties were limited in the amounts they could spend in coordination with candidates. However, control over financial resources can lead to substantial influence. Parties could run ads that reinforced the themes of its candidates. In purchasing air time for campaign ads, they could follow the lead of presidential candidates' media buyers, or they could attempt to build the party's base among different groups.

Another major benefit was the impact of soft funds upon state parties. Early on, the use of soft money helped to rejuvenate many state parties that had atrophied. The money greatly assisted the state parties in revitalizing their organizations and moving into the era of modern campaigning (Adamy 1984; Herrnson 1988).

Two of the most important costs that soft money imposed on the political system were the difficulty of tracking the money, and the contention that the funds were "fat cat" money designed to restore the unique access and influence of wealthy individual, corporate, and union donors. As to the first cost, only with great difficulty could one implement the advice allegedly given during the Watergate scandal by secret source "Deep Throat" to two *Washington Post* reporters: "Follow the money!" Broad definitions of how the money can be used leads to ingenious interpretations. When vague definitions are combined with the federal, state, and local avenues through which soft money can flow, this category of funds is more likely to provide continued employment for campaign finance specialists than enlightenment for the average citizen.

As to the contention that soft money was "fat cat" money, the Center for Responsive Politics found that 50 percent of the soft money in the 1992 election came in the form of checks larger than $20,000 (Donovan 1993, 1196). The perception that soft money was just another means for the wealthy to gain access was provided by the Clinton Administration and the Democratic National Committee in 1996. Still smarting from the Republican takeover of the Congress in 1994 and fearing a Republican sweep in 1996, Clinton vowed to dramatically increase the party's soft money funds. On a memo from his chief fund-raiser, the president wrote that he was "ready to start overnights [sleepovers in the Lincoln Bedroom] right away" and ordered the fund-raiser to "get other names at $100,000 or more, $50,000 or more" (Mitchell 1997).

When reports of the White House "sleepovers" surfaced in the press after the election, the public perceived a connection between the contributions and later political favors. In his 1992 book *Putting People First*, Clinton termed it deplorable when "political action committees, industry lobbies and cliques of $100,000 donors buy access to Congress and the White House." Yet in 1996, he found it necessary to state that "the Lincoln bedroom was never 'sold'" ("President's Remarks" 1997). Moreover, both President Clinton and Vice President Gore acknowledged contacting soft money donors on White House phones, but Gore claimed his calls were legal because they were made on a Democratic National Committe telephone calling card.

The Political Parties after BCRA and *McConnell*

Political scientist Michael Malbin (2004, 177) raised several key questions about life for the political parties after the Bipartisan

Campaign Reform Act and the *McConnell v. FEC* decision:

1. Will the parties in fact replace at least a significant part of the forbidden soft money with hard money? . . . How difficult will it be and how long will it take?
2. If the parties do raise the money can they—and will they—continue to pay for the same kinds of party activities as they did during the soft money years . . . ? If they do not replace all the lost money, how important will be the loss of activities they can no longer afford?
3. Will pre-BCRA activities and funding sources simply be displaced from party to non-party organizations?

The available data allow at least preliminary answers to these questions. The answer to whether parties would be able to replace soft money with hard money is positive, and the time frame for doing so proved to be about four years. As seen in table 6.3, both parties raised more hard money in the 2004 election cycle than the combined hard and soft money in the 2000 cycle ($576 versus $470 million for the Democrats, and $657 to $620 million for the Republicans). The three organizations of the GOP developed a more successful small donor base and maintained a lead in party fund-raising. The Democrats, however, were able to narrow the "contribution gap" in 2004 to $81 million compared to $150 million in 2000. Where the parties missed soft money contributions the most was during the congressional cycle of 2006 compared with 2002. Democrats raised $16 million less in 2006, while Republicans faced a $92 million difference.

If BCRA required the parties to depend on hard money contributions only, and the parties must compete with 527 groups and issue advocacy campaigns, how could parties raise the funds needed? A study by the Campaign Finance Institute (2003) found that only

TABLE 6.3 National Party Fund-Raising, 2000–2006 (in millions of dollars)

Committee	2000 Federal (Hard)	2000 Nonfederal (Soft)	2000 Total	2002 Federal (Hard)	2002 Nonfederal (Soft)	2002 Total	2004 Federal (Hard)	2006 Federal (Hard)
Democrats								
DNC	124.0	136.6	260.6	67.5	94.6	162.1	394.4	130.8
DSCC	40.5	63.7	104.2	48.4	95.1	143.5	88.7	121.4
DCCC	48.4	36.7	105.1	46.4	56.4	102.8	93.2	139.9
Total	**212.9**	**237.0**	**469.9**	**162.3**	**246.1**	**408.4**	**576.3**	**392.1**
Republicans								
RNC	212.8	166.2	379.0	170.1	113.9	284.0	392.4	243.0
NRSC	51.5	44.7	96.1	59.2	66.4	125.6	79.0	88.8
NRCC	97.3	47.3	144.6	123.6	69.7	193.3	185.7	179.6
Total	**361.6**	**258.2**	**619.7**	**352.9**	**250.0**	**602.9**	**657.1**	**511.4**

Note: DNC = Democratic National Committee; DSCC = Democratic Senatorial Campaign Committee; DCCC = Democratic Congressional Campaign Committee; RNC = Republican National Committee; NRSC = National Republican Senatorial Committee; NRCC= National Republican Congressional Committee.

Source: Federal Election Commission (2007a).

775,000 donors gave to all the presidential candidates combined in 2000. Of that number about 110,000 gave $1,000 or more. By 2004 the dynamics of giving had changed in two important ways. As previously noted, BCRA had banned soft money, while increasing the limit of individual giving from $1,000 to $2,000 (and the $2,000 amount was to be indexed for inflation). Supporters of reform reasoned that both of these changes, while keeping the amount that PACs could contribute at $5,000, would force parties and candidates to look harder for smaller contributions. Critics believed the opposite would occur; doubling the amount that individuals could contribute would lead to more money arriving in the form of large contributions.

A subsequent Campaign Finance Institute study by Malbin and Cain (2007) found some validity in both predictions. As seen in figure 6.1, for political parties small contributions (less than $200) made up 24 percent of the parties' receipts before the passage of BRCA. After BCRA, small contributions made up 43 percent of the money con-

tributed to political parties. For congressional candidates, however, the opposite trend occurred. Small contributions provided 20 percent of the funds before BCRA, but only 13 percent after the legislation went into effect. The increase in the percentage of money raised from large contributions to congressional candidates is mostly a result of the fact that BCRA raised the amount that individuals could give to a candidate's campaign. Still, this change is important. As Malbin and Cain show, the percentage of money raised by candidates from individuals donating more than $1,000 after BCRA is up 80 percent for Senate candidates and 85 percent for House candidates (2007, 10).

Another way for parties to obtain hard money was to seek funds from members of Congress. While reelection is the primary goal of the members, the narrow margin by which the majority party controlled both houses of Congress in recent years has the members' full attention. "Nothing focuses a politician's mind more clearly than being on the edge of control whether he or she is out of

FIGURE 6.1 Percentage of Receipts from Small and Large Contributions, Before and After the Bipartisan Campaign Reform Act

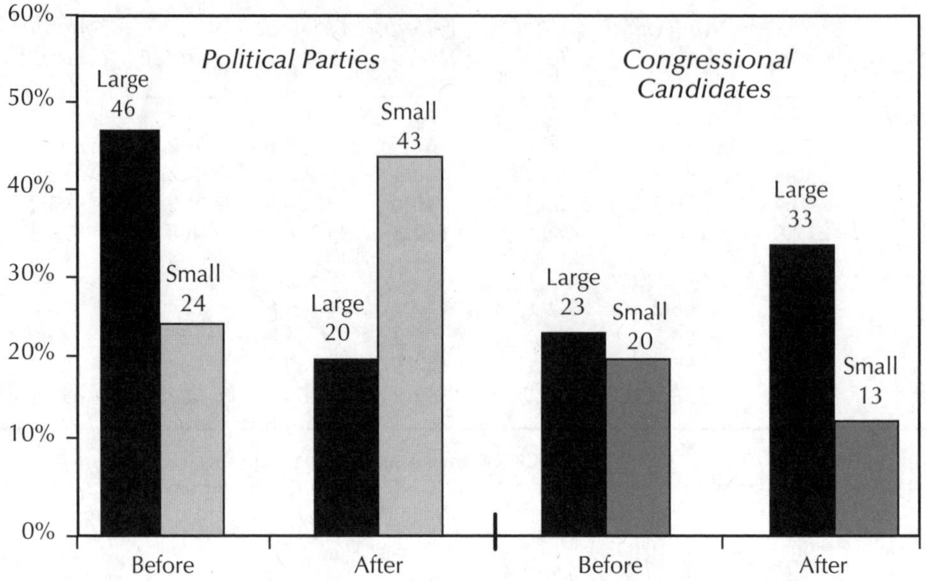

Note: For political parties "small" is less than $200 and "large" is more than $20,000. For congressional candidates "small" is less than $200 and "large" is more than $1,000.

Source: Malbin and Cain (2007, 4).

power and looking up, or in power and feeling threatened" (Malbin 2004, 178). The FECA allows a candidate's committee to make unlimited contributions to party committees. In addition, entrenched incumbents often do not lack for campaign funds. Thus beginning in the 1990s, House members became more willing to transfer money to the parties from their own campaign committees or from PACs they created. Senate majority leader Trent Lott's New Republican Majority Fund gave $1.3 million to forty-three GOP Senate and House candidates in 1996, while House representative Dick Armey's Majority Leader's Fund weighed in with $1.6 million in receipts (Wayne 1997a). Not to be outdone, former Speaker Newt Gingrich's fundraising innovation was the "Incumbent Protection Fund." Members made payments to the fund based on seniority, and the money was redistributed to members in tight races.

Gingrich distributed nearly $2 million to House members in 1996 from his own campaign money and his Monday Morning PAC (Wayne 1997b).

By 2002, House members' own campaigns or their leadership PACs contributed 13 percent of the National Republican Congressional Committee's hard money and 24 percent of hard funds for the Democratic Congressional Campaign Committee (Malbin 2004, 180). Table 6.4 concentrates on key lawmakers in the House and Senate whose PACs raised more than $500,000 for the 2005–2006 cycle. Leadership PAC names often lack originality (appearing to require some combination of terms such as "freedom," "progress," "hope," or "values") when compared to lesser known PACs such as the "Gumbo PAC" or the "Jazz PAC." Contributing to the party and its members does create a claim to move up the chain of

TABLE 6.4 Top Leadership PACs, 2005–2006

Member	Leadership PAC Name	Amount (dollars)	Leadership Position 2005–2006
Eric Cantor (R-VA)	Every Republican Is Crucial	1,240,842	Republican Deputy Whip
John Boehner (R-OH)	Freedom Project	1,033,831	Majority Leader House
Thomas Reynolds (R-NY)	Together for Our Majority	965,000	NRCC Chair
Dennis Hastert (R-IL)	Keep Our Majority	954,830	Speaker
Roy Blunt (R-MO)	Rely on Your Beliefs	925,981	Republican Whip
Steny Hoyer (D-MD)	AmeriPAC: The Fund for a Greater America	916,000	Minority Whip
Jim MCrery (R-LA)	Committee for the Preservation of Capitalism	817,500	Ways and Means
Deborah Pryce (R-OH)	Promoting Republicans You Can Elect	778,500	Repubican Conference Chair
Rahm Emanuel (D-IL)	Our Common Values	723,000	Co-chair DCCC
Spencer Bachus (R-AL)	Growth & Prosperity	698,961	Banking Committee
Pete Sessions (R-TX)	People for Enterprise/Trade/ Economic Growth	672,500	Budget
Buck McKeon (R-CA)	21st Century	656,584	Armed Services
Barack Obama (D-IL)	Hope Fund	595,169	Environment and Public Works
Mike Rogers (R-MI)	Majority Initiative-Keep Electing Republicans	593,000	Agriculture
Charles Rangel (D-NY)	National Leadership	566,000	Ways and Means
Michael Oxley (R-OH)	Leadership 2000	518,250	Financial Services Chair

Source: Created by authors using data from Center for Responsive Politics. Available at: www.opensecrets.org.

leadership, whether that occurs in congressional committees, in party leadership, or ultimately as a candidate for the presidency. Most of the Republican leadership in 2006 appears on the list, as do rising Democrats such as Rahm Emanuel and Barack Obama. While those who raise the largest amounts of leadership PAC money often become visible candidates for the top leadership spots, simply having the largest cash machine does not guarantee selection to a top leadership spot. When Democrats gained control of the House after the 2006 election, Representative Steny Hoyer (D-Maryland) challenged then Minority Leader Nancy Pelosi (D-California) for the Speaker's position. Hoyer was sixth in table 6.4, with more than $900,000 distributed to fellow Democrats (compared to only $300,000 for Pelosi). Pelosi, however, prevailed in the Democratic caucus to become the first female Speaker of the House.

The Rise and Impact of the 527 Groups

One answer to Malbin's question about what organizations might arise to fill the void left by the demise of soft money was answered very quickly in the form of the 527 groups. While the impact of these groups is addressed in greater detail in Chapter 9, this section focuses on several issues. First, to what extent was the creation of the 527 groups a direct result of campaign finance law? Are the election activities of 527 groups truly independent from the efforts of the political parties? If they are independent of parties, have the 527 groups substantially weakened the parties by taking over such key party functions as fund-raising and get-out-the-vote drives? Finally, based upon the 2004 and 2006 elections, do the 527 groups pose a realistic threat to the role of the two major parties in campaigns?

The 527 groups took their name from a provision of the federal tax laws. Indeed, the prominence of the 527s was a direct result of campaign finance reform. Public Citizen (2002), a public interest group associated with Ralph Nader, publicly predicted that campaign reform would cause soft money to flow from political parties to 527 groups. Private concerns were raised at an earlier stage. Harold Ickes, a former chief of staff to President Clinton, was worried about the large advantage the Republicans enjoyed in raising hard money for the 2000 election cycle. In a twelve-page letter written to key Democrats in March 2001, Ickes warned about the potential effect of campaign finance reform: "The ban on the use of soft money by national political parties will greatly advantage the Republicans. . . . Were the Republicans smart, they would vote to a person to enact [McCain-Feingold] word for word, and laugh all the way to the next election" (Grimaldi and Edsall 2004). The chairperson of the Democratic National Committee at the time, Terry McAuliffe, agreed and set up a task force to find a substitute for the anticipated loss of soft money. Several wealthy, but low profile individuals listed in table 6.5 were instrumental in the formation of the 527 groups. Ironically, as this effort was taking place, most Democrats in Congress repeated their support for campaign finance reform.

Immediately after the passage of McCain-Feingold, questions about the independence of the 527 groups were raised by the press and Republicans. Both noted the close relationship between key Democratic party members

and the 527 groups. In addition to Harold Ickes, top officials of EMILY's List (a group supporting mostly Democratic candidates), the Sierra Club, and the AFL-CIO resigned from the Democratic National Committee and became active in America Coming Together (ACT), the Media Fund, or the Joint Victory Campaign (Cigler 2007). The Republican party filed a legal challenge with the FEC claiming an absence of independence between these three 527 groups and the Democratic party. That challenge was rejected by the FEC, however.

The functions undertaken by the 527s, including advertising and get-out-the-vote, were historically the responsibility of political parties. Among the Democratic groups listed in table 6.5, a division of labor emerged. The specific task of the Media Fund was to spread a Democratic message across the mass media. A later meeting created ACT and assigned it the task of mobilizing the party's voters in the battleground states. Yet another group, the Joint Victory Campaign 2004, concentrated on fund-raising, with the money raised split between the Media Fund and ACT.

After losing the legal battle about the legality of 527s, the Republicans quickly turned to creating their own 527 committees, ignoring charges that the GOP was against the 527s before they were for them. As is evident from table 6.5, Republicans were not able to close the gap in 527 funds in 2004. The gap persisted for several reasons. In addition to the early start of Democratic-leaning 527s, the Republican party was awash in hard money for 2004 and only later became concerned with the 527 activities of the Democrats. Moreover, given the number of corporate scandals that occurred in 2001 and 2002, many business executives were leery of contributing to anything that might bring legal challenges or further scrutiny of their activities.

Do the efforts of 527 groups represent a significant challenge to the campaign activities of political parties? Although the 2004 and

TABLE 6.5 Top 527 Groups and Individual Donors to 527 Groups, 2004 and 2006

2005–2006 Group	Total Expenditures (millions)	Party Preference	Individuals	Total Contributions (millions)	Party Preference
Service Employees International Union	28.2	Democrat	Bob Perry	9.8	Republican
America Votes	14.1	Democrat	Jerrold Perenchio	5.0	Republican
Progress for America	12.5	Republican	George Soros	3.5	Democrat
EMILY's List	11.8	Democrat	Linda Pritzker	2.1	Democrat
College Republican National Committee	10.3	Republican	John R. Hunting	1.6	Democrat
Club for Growth	8.2	Republican	Peter Lewis	1.6	Democrat
America Coming Together	7.0	Democrat	John Templeton	1.3	Republican
Intl Brotherhood of Electrical Workers	5.5	Democrat	Timothy Gill	1.3	Democrat
September Fund	4.9	Democrat	Jon L. Stryker	1.3	Democrat
Economic Freedom Fund	4.8	Republican	Pat Stryker	1.3	Democrat
Total: All 527 Groups	**426.5**				
2003–2004					
America Coming Together	79.8	Democrat	George Soros	23.5	Democrat
Joint Victory Campaign 2004	71.8	Democrat	Peter Lewis	23.0	Democrat
Media Fund	57.7	Democrat	Steven Bing	13.9	Democrat
Service Employees International Union	47.7	Democrat	Herb Sandler	13.0	Democrat
Progress for America	35.6	Republican	Bob Perry	8.1	Republican
Swift Boat Veterans for Truth	22.6	Republican	Alex Spanos	5.0	Republican
MoveOn.org	21.6	Democrat	Ted Waitt	5.0	Democrat
College Republican National Committee	17.3	Republican	Dawn Arnall	5.0	Republican
New Democrat Network	12.5	Democrat	T. Boone Pickens	4.6	Republican
Citizens for a Strong Senate	19.2	Democrat	Andrew Rappaport	4.3	Democrat
Total: All 527 Groups	**612.1**				

Sources: Created by the authors using data from the Center for Responsive Politics (opensecrets.org), Glover (2004), Grimaldi and Edsall (2004), and Simon (2006).

2006 elections can provide a basis for only tentative conclusions, the 527 groups appear to be motivated more by ideology or a desire to defeat a specific candidate than a desire to supplant a political party's agenda. Wealthy individuals desire to maintain influence over candidates and issues, rather than promote an industry (Briffault 2005, 1719). If this is the case, we should expect to see a change in the specific mix of individuals and groups providing the greatest contributions. The close battle to control the House and Senate in 2006 sparked the interest of the 527 groups to the tune of $425 million. George Soros, the individual with the most generous checkbook in the 2004 election, became concerned about his decreased influence due to large donations by 527 groups such as labor (the Service Employees International Union and the International Brotherhood of Electrical Workers) and women's groups (EMILY's List). Soros remained among the top three individual contributors for 2006. The same could not be said about other prominent Democratic supporters two years earlier, such as Stephen Bing, Herb Sandler, and Ted Waitt who were not among the top ten contributors in 2006. Similarly, several Democratic-leaning groups fell from the top ten spenders in 2006. The Joint Victory Campaign 2004 was inactive and the Media Fund and MoveOn.org did not reclaim top spots in 2006. On the Republican side, the Swift Boat Veterans for Truth completed its mission of torpedoing the candidacy of John Kerry and disappeared just as swiftly. Committees such as Progress for America and the College Republican National Committee increased their efforts and were joined in the top ranks by the Club for Growth and the Economic Freedom Fund.

Reform groups continued to push for regulation of 527 groups, first by the FEC and then by Congress. The FEC agreed on a regulation in August 2004, too late to affect the 2004 election cycle (Hayward and Smith 2005). Under the FEC rule, 527 groups could not solicit donations if any of that money would be used to campaign for or against any candidate in a federal election (Hrebenar, Jowers, and Peery 2006, 108). That same month, Senators John McCain, Russell Feingold, Joseph Lieberman, and Charles Schumer introduced a bill called the 527 Reform Act, with identical legislation sponsored by Representatives Christopher Shays and Martin Meehan in the House. However a competing bill splintered support in the Congress, and the two sides spent more than a year accusing each other of "sneak attacks" and "sham" legislation. After being foiled in the Congress, House members Shays and Meehan filed suit against the FEC to force regulation of the 527s. In the case of *Shays v. FEC* (2004), the district court found the FEC must either provide a rationale for case-by-case decisions or provide a specific rule covering all 527s. The FEC levied $630,000 in fines against MoveOn.org Voter Fund, the League of Conservation Voters, and the Swiftboat Veterans for Truth. The FEC held that because the groups had used the forbidden "magic words" and their major purpose was to influence federal elections, they should have registered as political committees. This case-by-case approach to regulating the actions of the 527 groups did have its supporters (Feuer 2006). But many reform groups criticized the FEC for fining only those three groups and not providing a clear standard for its decision. On the other side, groups opposed to regulation cited First Amendment concerns and raised the specter of thousands of citizens groups facing regulation as "political committees." When *Shays v. FEC* (2005) was appealed, the Court of Appeals for the District of Columbia struck down the regulations on solicitation and direction of contributions as contrary to congressional intent. Legal wrangling continues over whether case-by-case regulation is possible, or whether a rule on all 527 groups must be written.

In sum, 527 groups have assumed some of the financial and get-out-the-vote responsibilities of political parties. Although rules implementing BCRA seem to forbid coordination between political parties and 527 groups, the role of party activists in several of the 527 groups suggest that they do more to supplement than to hinder party goals. Moreover, any potential threat to the durability of the parties is lessened by the substantial turnover already evident among the top spending 527 groups.

Finance Laws and Presidential Campaigns

The degree to which campaign finance law shapes election campaigns—who runs for the presidency, when they run, the amounts that are spent, and most importantly who gets the party's nomination—is difficult to overstate. A major innovation of the FECA amendments of 1974 was the creation of a system of partial public funding for presidential elections. This section focuses upon whether the trends of increasing campaign costs, the "frontloading" of primaries and caucuses, and mounting public indifference make the public financing system, at best, under siege or, at worst, irrelevant. Related issues include the mounting costs and the rigors of the "invisible primary" and the rise of entrepreneurial and issue-oriented candidates.

The public funding provisions provided a flat grant of $20 million to the major party candidates in the 1976 general election, with that sum to be adjusted for inflation for future elections. A proportional amount was available to minor party candidates who could qualify under the law for public funding. By 2004, the amount available for a major party presidential candidate was $75 million, but it also meant that the candidate's campaign had to agree to limit spending to that amount. For the primary election the formula provided public matching funds for contributions up to $250. That total amount was about $37 million, but additional amounts were allowed for fund-raising, legal, accounting, and compliance costs, bringing the total to $49 million (Malbin 2006). The

formula for allocating public funds has not been changed, but as noted previously, the BCRA increased the maximum individual contribution from $1,000 to $2,000.

Campaign finance law creates formidable obstacles for what has been called the "invisible primary" or the "money primary" in presidential elections (Jackson 1997, 230). This contest occurs in the year before the first scheduled primary in New Hampshire as candidates compete to raise money for the primary elections. Over the years, the expectations for how much serious candidates need to raise have risen dramatically. In 1995, campaign experts estimated that to be competitive, candidates had to raise at least $20 million during that year to build strong campaign organizations in fifty states and buy media to gain name recognition. Twelve years later, in 2007, candidates Hillary Clinton, Barack Obama, and Mitt Romney had all raised more than $20 million in the first quarter of the year. Viewed another way, the $20 million in 1995 required a candidate to raise $55,000 per day, while the frontrunners in 2007 needed to generate $222,000 per day in the first quarter to remain competitive. In this context editorial cartoonist Pat Gorrell's depiction of the leading candidates in figure 6.2 is not surprising.

Given the realities of fund-raising for the primaries, 2004 candidates George W. Bush, John Kerry, and Howard Dean all opted out of public funding of the primary elections. Candidates who opt out of the public financing system do not receive public money, but they are then free to raise and spend as much money as they can. After Dean dropped out, Bush and Kerry spent five times more than would have been allowed under public funding.

Various reforms have been proposed to deal with the candidate funding issues of the "money primary." A task force from the Campaign Finance Institute has recommended changing the current system to a 3-for–1 public match on the first $100 in private donations (indexed for inflation). The

FIGURE 6.2 Bob Gorrell Editorial Cartoon

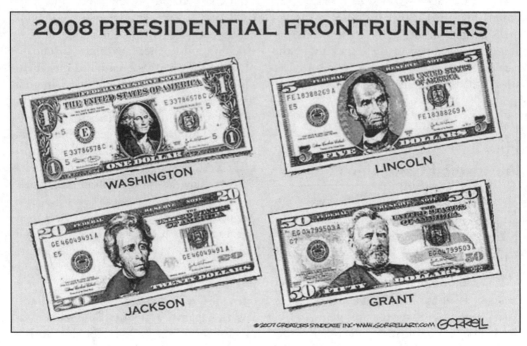

Source: By permission of Bob Gorrell and Creators Syndicate, Inc.

Institute believes that since most donations are under $100, this would raise the total amount available to candidates, and increase the significance of smaller donors compared to larger donors (Campaign Finance Institute 2005).

Yet another factor increasing campaign costs is the "frontloading" of primaries, as many states try to move to an earlier date hoping for greater influence over who is selected and for additional media attention for their states. Frontloading the calendar may increase spending as well. Malbin (2006) contends that public funding was designed to fit the elections of the 1970s. In 1976, the contests began with the Iowa caucus in January and continued until late June. Thus, an unknown candidate like Jimmy Carter could invest the small contributions received along with public matching funds into the Iowa caucus. A victory in Iowa would attract new backers and the campaign could "snowball"

into the New Hampshire contest five weeks later. In 2008, however, the Iowa caucus is followed by a Democratic caucus in Nevada less than a week later and the New Hampshire primary only days after that. By early February, a large number of delegate-rich states such as California, Michigan, New York, and New Jersey, hold their primary elections. This compressed schedule means that candidates cannot build momentum by using early primary victories to raise funds for later. It also means that candidates must have the money in advance to compete in numerous large states simultaneously and cannot rely on meeting the public funding criteria for resources.

Although the exact amounts of public funding for the 2008 election remain to be determined by the FEC, early estimates set a base of $40.9 million for the primary and $81.8 million for the general election (Federal Election Commission 2007b). Given these constraints, candidates Hillary Clinton, Barack Obama, John McCain, and Rudolph Giuliani indicated they would not take public funds for the primary elections and not be bound by federal spending limits. Candidates Obama and McCain did have a convoluted, and perhaps largely symbolic, promise that if either became their party's presidential nominee, and their opponent agreed to do the same, both would accept the public funding limit for the general election.

Another concern for proponents of public funding is the apparent declining support for public funding by taxpayers. Fewer citizens are opting to have a portion of the taxes they pay go to the election fund by checking off the box on their taxes. When the system began in 1976 as a reaction to Watergate, 27.5 percent of taxpayers marked the $1 check-off. By 1980, that number had increased to a high of 28.7 percent. Since then, participation by taxpayers has declined, prompting the FEC to increase the check-off amount to $3 in 1994. The decline has continued, dipping to 9.2 percent of taxpayers in 2004 and 7.3 percent in 2006 (Shouten 2007). Various reasons have been put forward for this drop. Many Americans choose to file their taxes with TurboTax or a similar program. The default choice for TurboTax is not to check off the $3 box, and taxpayers have to opt-in to do so. An equally plausible explanation is that voters are subjected to a barrage of campaign ads through the media and may not feel inclined to use tax money to pay for more of them.

The notion that taxpayers increasingly appear to reject the concept of public financing is alarming to advocates of campaign reform. A 2007 Gallup Poll asked respondents what effect the record amounts of money being raised by the 2008 presidential candidates would have on the quality of the next president. More than 68 percent felt the money spent would make no difference, with 20 percent saying the result would be a "worse" president. When offered two financing choices for the election—"taking public funding and accepting spending limits or not taking public financing and spending whatever they can raise on their own"—39 percent favored accepting public funding while 56 percent favored candidates raising their own funds (Saad 2007). Partisan differences on this issue were small, as 24 percent of Democrats favored public financing, compared to 17 percent of Republicans. Education levels resulted in the largest difference in opinion, as 55 percent of those who had a college degree agreed with relying upon public financing, compared with 35 percent for those people with "some college," and 29 percent for those without a college education. When the choices of financing were expanded to three, the public's preferences were: 46 percent favored private funding, 22 percent favored public funding, and 28 percent favored a combination of the two (Saad 2007).

Campaign finance laws may also influence who runs in elections. Political scientist Anthony Corrado defines an "entrepreneurial candidate" as one who is willing to forgo public financing and commit vast personal amounts to the presidential race (1997, 140). Entrepreneurial candidates have several initial advantages. They can focus on the message of the campaign and not be diverted by fundraising responsibilities. The campaigns can hire the best personnel and do not lack resources to buy advertising. Candidates can promote messages they believe in rather than modify them to gain contributors. Once they attain stature and name recognition, the option exists for future elections that rely upon the more traditional route of public financing.

The prototype for entrepreneurial candidates was independent candidate Ross Perot, who in 1992 provided $63.3 million of his own money (and 93 percent of the campaign's funding) to obtain 19 percent of the vote. Considerable modification of the self-financing strategy occurred in 1996, however. Perot used up to $9 million of personal funds to get his party, the Reform party, organized and qualified for the ballot in most states. Because of his previous vote total, Perot qualified for $29 million in public funds in 1996, but the FEC determined it was Perot the "independent" who qualified for the funds and not the Reform party, which did not exist in 1992. Still Perot got the Reform party nomination by defeating former Colorado governor Dick Lamm and stayed within the FEC guidelines to receive public funding. Although he received only 8 percent of the vote in 1996, this assured the Reform party of a place on the ballot in most states in 2000, as well as 50 percent of the public funds given to the major party candidates.

Assuming the role of entrepreneurial hopefuls for the GOP nomination in 1996 were Malcolm S. (Steve) Forbes and tire manufacturer Maurice (Morrey) Taylor, who loaned their campaigns $37.5 million (90 percent of the total receipts), and $6.5 million (99.9 percent of receipts) respectively. Both candidates spent huge sums for the number of votes received ($408 for each Forbes vote and $725 for Taylor in the Iowa caucuses), Forbes provided a striking example of how the use of personal money can raise public awareness and acceptance of their issues. Forbes finished first only in Delaware and Arizona, but his theme of "hope, opportunity, and growth" resonated with Republican primary election voters and his call for a 15 percent "flat tax" was later incorporated into candidate Bob Dole's call for tax cuts.

The financial resources of New York Mayor Michael Bloomberg, combined with his 2007 decision to change party affiliation from Republican to unaffiliated, provides yet another possibility for a well-financed entrepreneurial candidate. Although Bloomberg spent $70 million on his first mayoral race and $85 million on his second race, the total spent barely made a dent in his personal wealth estimated at more than $5 billion (Cardwell and Steinhauer 2007). Personal wealth thus remains a major factor in determining who can credibly run for office, who can saturate the airwaves with their message,

and which issues play a central role in the election.

If candidates survive the "invisible primary" and the actual presidential primaries, the focus of the campaign quickly turns to the effect of federal campaign laws on general election funding. Challengers who spend heavily in the early primary states to win the nomination may lack sufficient funds for the general election phase. Bob Dole in 1996 and John Kerry in 2004 are prominent examples. To avoid exceeding the federal spending limit, the Dole campaign resorted to staff reductions, as well as all kinds of creative accounting techniques including a "yard sale" at which items ranging from two-way radios to VCRs were sold to raise $1.2 million. John Kerry faced a similar situation. At the Democratic convention, Kerry had emphasized his record of service during the Vietnam war. The Kerry campaign then made a strategic decision to limit spending in August, so that he would not be at a disadvantage in key states in the crucial period several weeks before the election. Thus no money was spent on television ads through much of August. A 527 group, Swift Boat Veterans for Truth, ran ads in a small number of states attacking Kerry's service in Vietnam just after the Democratic convention. Media coverage expanded the influence of these ads. By the time counter ads were run at the end of August, the damage to Kerry's claim of leadership during a time of war was substantial (Corrado 2006).

Campaign Finance and the States

It is difficult to make generalizations about the effects of campaign spending in the states for a number of reasons. In addition to differences in size and population, comparisons are affected by such factors as state election laws, the number of candidates for gubernatorial or legislative positions, the extent of media markets, and whether spending data is gathered

TABLE 6.6 Campaign Amounts in Selected States by Office, 2006 Elections

State	Governor Average	High	N	State Senate Average	High	N	State House Average	High	N
California	4.7 mil	46.0 mil	29	468,000	3.3 mil	64	306,000	5.9 mil	293
New York	3.8 mil	31.0 mil	12	275,000	2.0 mil	126	76,000	719,000	287
Pennsylvania	4.6 mil	27.0 mil	9	202,000	2.9 mil	72	81,000	5.8 mil	604
Oregon	1.1 mil	5.0 mil	14	122,000	740,000	43	76,000	1.0 mil	156
Colorado	1.4 mil	4.4 mil	6	65,000	308,000	45	38,000	269,000	136
Maine	260,000	732,000	10	15,000	42,000	90	3,000	15,000	364
New Hampshire	177,000	270,000	2	21,000	57,000	52	147	8,000	783
Wyoming	373,000	1.0 mil	4	5,000	49,000	34	1,800	23,000	109
New Mexico	1.4 mil	8.2 mil	7	na	na	0	14,000	155,000	124

Note: "Average" is the average dollar amount collected, "High" is the highest total reported, and "N" indicates the number of candidates.

Source: Created by authors based on data from the National Institute on Money in State Politics. Available at: followthemoney.org.

and reported in a timely manner. Table 6.6 shows a sample of data on campaign funding amounts from the National Institute on Money in State Politics. While the data provide a consistent basis for comparison, the average amounts reported for obtaining an office are lower than past published reports for states like California. This result is due to the National Institute reporting fund-raising by all candidates who declared for office, rather than only the two major candidates who squared off in the general election. An additional issue is incomplete reporting by the states. For example, for the 2006 election, California assembled 95 percent of candidate data while in New York was able to obtain only 50 percent. Within these constraints several patterns are evident.

For gubernatorial races, as expected, states with larger populations led in campaign fund-raising. "The Governator" (also known as Arnold Schwarzenegger) led the pack by raising $46 million in California. The winning candidates in states with mid-range populations, such as Colorado and Oregon, collected between $4 and $5 million. But the table also illustrates the importance of unique political circumstances. Normally, the winning candidate in New Mexico would not need to raise $8.2 million to be elected governor. But Governor Bill Richardson used the election for governor to stockpile financial resources for an anticipated run for the presidency.

The National Conference of State Legislatures groups legislative bodies into three types based on length of the session, salaries, and size of staff. "Professional" legislatures work full-time, pay high salaries, and have a large staff. At the opposite end, "citizen" legislatures are part-time, have low pay, and only a small staff. "Hybrid" legislatures fall in between. In all three of the "professional" states in the table—California, New York, and Pennsylvania—average amounts raised for state senate races were substantially above that of house races. Yet house seats in key urban districts can be very expensive, with the top amount raised in California and Pennsylvania nearing $6 million. Greater variation in campaign costs is found in states with hybrid legislatures. The average amount raised for a state senate seat in Oregon was $122,000, while in Colorado the amount needed was about half that amount. A similar ratio exists for house seats in the two states, but the top amount of $1 million raised in Oregon again reinforces the costs in important urban districts. Conversely, for the four "citizen legislatures" listed in the table the amounts needed to run for office are much lower. Maine limits campaign spending, and the result was a reasonable $15,000 and $3,000 for senate and house seats, respectively. The $147 needed for the New Hampshire state house was the absolute bargain basement; the drawback occurs from being one of 783 candidates running for the legislative body containing the largest number of members in the country.

After passage of the FECA in 1971, campaign finance reform at the national level stalled for thirty years. Several states stepped into the vacuum, focusing on two components of reform: (1) contribution and expenditure limitations, and (2) public financing provisions. Wisconsin and Minnesota entered the arena first, by regulating campaign spending in the late 1970s. By the early 1990s, interest groups such as Common Cause, the U.S. Public Interest Research Group, and the League of Women Voters used state initiative and referendum processes to enact strict contribution limits in such diverse states as Florida, Arkansas, Nevada, California, Colorado, Missouri, Montana, and Oregon.

The question of how low can states go on limits for campaign contribution was certain to be challenged in the courts. A partial answer came in the Supreme Court's decision in the case of *Randall v. Sorrell* (2006). This case arose after Vermont imposed campaign contribution limits as low as $200 for state legislative races and $400 for such statewide elective offices as governor. Limits on campaign expenditures were also a part of the state law, including a $300,000 limit on the governor's race. The case was important for several reasons. First, it modified some aspects of past precedent and, second, it offered the

first glimpse of the views of Chief Justice John Roberts and Justice Samuel Alito, the two newest members of the Court.

Previously the majority in the *Buckley* case had argued that limits on expenditures posed a greater danger to First Amendment protections than limits on contributions. Some legal experts believed *Randall* offered the best chance of explicitly overturning the *Buckley* precedents (Huff 2003). Yet only Justices Scalia and Thomas persevered in their belief that *Buckley* was wrongly decided. Justices Roberts and Alito joined Justice Breyer in a plurality decision, declaring both the expenditure and contribution limitations unconstitutional. As to the former, Breyer noted that no governmental interest had been found that would justify expenditure limits, and that subsequent court decisions were based on this precedent. "Special justification" was needed to overturn precedent, and "We can find here no such special justification that would require us to overturn *Buckley*" (*Randall v. Sorrell* 2006, 2489). Concerning contribution limits, the plurality declared the Vermont limits to be so low as to inhibit advocacy of a candidate's views. Three dissenters, Justices Stevens, Ginsburg, and Souter used *Buckley* to uphold contribution limits but voted to send the case back to the appellate court to determine whether enough evidence existed to uphold the expenditure limits. In sum, this case may parallel the results of recent abortion cases, in which the Court resolutely declares that the precedent is upheld, but exceptions or "loopholes" in the precedent are generated when applied to specific issues (Shultz 2006, 175).

The second focus of state reform, public financing of campaigns, is found in what supporters call the "clean election" movement (and what opponents call "government funded elections"). The movement is based on several of the reform assumptions stated at the beginning of the chapter: (1) political spending is exorbitant; (2) politicians spend too much time fund-raising rather than leading; (3) special interest groups have too much influence over politics; (4) potential candidates with insufficient finances cannot compete (Schneider 1999). The states of Arizona and Maine and some local governments provide public financing to candidates agreeing to play under rules requiring that candidates not take anything beyond token individual contributions and not use their personal wealth in their campaigns. Using Arizona as an example, a 1998 citizen initiative passed by a slim 51 to 49 percent margin specified that funding for public financing would come from surcharges from parking tickets and voluntary check offs on individual tax returns. For statehouse races, candidates needed to collect just over two hundred individual $5 contributions, while a gubernatorial candidate had to get four thousand contributions of $5 each. Public money is then distributed in segments for the primary and general elections. For the gubernatorial race each candidate received $680,774. Other elective offices receive lesser amounts, ranging from $143,000 for Arizona's secretary of state and attorney general, to $18,000 for state legislative candidates The system is voluntary to meet the requirements of the *Buckley v. Valeo* decision. But if a clean candidate is being outspent by an opponent relying solely on private contributions, public funds will be provided to fill the gap up to a certain point (a limit of $53,000 for Arizona state house races in 2006).

Conclusion: The State of Campaign Finance

This chapter has concentrated on the values that guided campaign reform efforts, the laws that resulted, and the courts' interpretation of such laws. As campaign finance law evolved, it initially allowed the national parties to transfer funds to strengthen state and local party organizations. This chapter suggests that the relationship between money and politics is not merely a unilateral one in which PAC contributions corrupt politicians, but a bilateral relationship in which members of Congress utilize interest groups not only to fund campaigns but as resources to successfully enact their own programs. Successful reforms must take this relationship into account.

After the passage of the BCRA, parties and interest groups faced a new set of rules. The key questions of whether parties would be able to replace soft money with hard money, and whether new organizations would come along to take up the slack once soft money was banned have been answered in the affirmative. Reformers, who undertook the long, hard battle to enact McCain-Feingold now face the very real possibility that a Supreme Court increasingly inclined to view political contributions as a protected form of speech will overturn major portions of that law.

CHAPTER 7

Campaigns and Political Parties

An Altered Role

This chapter explores the nature of contemporary American election campaigns and the changing role of political parties in campaigns. As campaigns became more candidate centered, parties had to adapt to this new reality and develop ways to help their candidates win. In this chapter, we examine the recruitment and motivation of candidates as well as how campaigns are organized. We also consider how campaigns design and transmit their message to potential voters. Finally, we return to the topic of the role of political parties by examining how parties have developed into organizations capable of offering highly specialized campaign information.

The Purposes and Impacts of Campaigns

From a candidate's point of view, the purpose of campaigns is simple: get your message out to potential voters. But, more broadly, campaigns are as much a means of producing political stability as producing political change. Consensus is reached on what programs are legitimate, as well as providing an orderly succession to office. Campaigns fill a range of needs for individuals, including watching commercials to see what issues are important, signaling political activists to become involved, and making fun of people

at conventions wearing elephant noses or donkey ears (Gronbeck 1987, 141–147).

Research over the past fifty years reveals a substantial difference between what office seekers intend campaigns to do and their actual impact on the citizenry. In the late 1940s and early 1950s, researchers developed a "limited effects model" of political mass communication. Campaign messages were broad, aimed at many groups. People gained most of their political information from family, friends, and coworkers who shared the same social and economic status. The impact of all these messages was to reinforce existing party preferences. Thus the major impact of campaigns was to increase turnout. Occasionally, campaigns would produce minor changes in voters' preferences, but conversion to the opposing party or candidate occurred very rarely (Berelson, Lazarsfeld, and McPhee 1954; Lazarsfeld, Berelson, and Gaudet 1948).

By the late 1970s, the work of Dan Nimmo and Robert Savage was instrumental in emphasizing the significance of campaigns. Nimmo's (1970) book *The Political Persuaders* outlined a "field theory of campaign effects." The mass media, and particularly television, were instrumental in changing the field or context in which people view politics. According to this view, campaigns should target those with low involvement in politics because they are more susceptible to images of a strong leader onto whom people can project their own needs or wants. Indeed, Nimmo and Savage (1976) were concerned that television would be so powerful a tool in manufacturing candidate images that campaigns would be all style and no substance.

Yet another challenge to the impact of campaigns arises from recent research on the seemingly predictable nature of presidential election outcomes (Campbell 2000, 13–22). Political scientists have developed statistical models that are quite accurate in predicting the popular vote in November using information available prior to the start of the general election campaign (Campbell 2004, 2005). For example, one predictive model uses the incumbent president's Gallup Poll approval rating in June of the election year, a measure of national economic performance in the first half of the election year, and a measure of whether or not the incumbent president has been in office for one term or more to predict how the candidate of the incumbent party will do in the November election (Abramowitz 2004). Of course, if the results of the November election can be predicted with accuracy in the summer, it raises the question of whether the conduct of the campaign actually influences voters or whether the conditions for the election outcome are in place long before the general election campaign even begins. Despite the apparent predictability of presidential elections, few political scientists or political observers would argue that what happens in the campaign does not matter to voters.

Although the debate among political scientists about the impact of campaigns remains heated, most scholars would not agree with the idea that campaigns can sell candidates like soap. Whenever a campaign successfully uses a technique to influence voters in the short term, opponents eventually mimic or counteract the technique. It is more accurate to say that campaigns can have a major effect, provided that the candidates propose a set of themes with widespread appeal ("broadcasting") and then tailor those themes to specific audiences ("narrowcasting"). By personalizing their messages, office seekers distinguish themselves from one another and offer a skeptical electorate a reason to vote for them (Baer 1995, 61).

The Changing Roles of Parties in Campaigns

The role that political parties play in campaigns has undergone vast changes. As described in Chapter 2, the organizational nature of political parties has changed over American history and, as parties have changed, so has their role in campaigns. In their earliest form as elite caucuses, political parties played a very limited role in the campaign process. Parties generally consisted of groups of office holders who worked together to promote common political views. But campaigns were largely local affairs and the conduct of campaigns was left to the candidates and other local notables. There was little need for an elaborate party organization because the electorate was small, and there was little campaign communication.

As the electorate grew, however, political parties developed into stronger mass organizations, and they became central to the campaign process. Especially in those locations with large numbers of potential voters and an expanding local bureaucracy, political parties often developed into highly organized election machines. These party machines needed to win elections in order to control government contracts and patronage jobs to reward their supporters. The party thereby controlled municipal jobs and public works projects such as street repair and garbage collection. In some places, the party even functioned as a sort of social service agency by providing food and clothing to the poor as a way to maintain support for the party's candidates at election time. Local party organizations completely controlled the electoral process. At the recruitment stage, candidate selection was dominated by the infamous "smoke-filled room" where party leaders evaluated possible candidates and chose the ones who fit the party's needs. At election time, party workers made sure that their voters got to the polls and, if the election outcome might be in doubt, often took measures to ensure that the other side's supporters did not.

Economic, social, and political changes in the United States eventually led to the weakening of the party machines and loosened the control of parties over campaigns. In particular, a series of political reforms such as the introduction of the direct primary and the enactment of civil service laws gradually weakened party organizations. Over time, parties were no longer able to dominate elections and increasingly became organizations that were regulated by state laws. The decline of political parties did not occur quickly nor uniformly in all places, but by the 1960s the campaign organizations of individual candidates had become more central to the conduct of campaigns, and parties had become less central. Parties declined because many of the methods used to recruit candidates and win votes in the past no longer worked. Weak parties shared recruitment functions with issue-oriented interest groups, notably labor, business, and civic groups. In some campaigns, professional consultants had become bigger power brokers than party chairpersons.

During the 1970s and 1980s, however, both major parties began to adapt to the new realities of political life. This adaptation began first with the Republican party at the national level, and later the Democratic party adapted as well. These changes meant that parties began to provide the services that candidates needed in order to compete in elections. Unlike the old days when party bosses could dictate who the candidates would be and could ensure votes on election day, in this new era political parties help candidates to raise money, conduct polls, design Web sites, advertise, and get people out to vote. Since the 1980s, the parties have attempted to offer "one-stop" campaign services in five areas: recruiting candidates, managing campaigns,

fund-raising, providing information about voters, and developing voter turnout programs. In the contemporary era, political parties are an important element of most election campaigns. But parties no longer dominate the process; now they work with candidates, political consultants, and interest groups.

The Candidate: Recruitment and Motivation

The area of recruitment is still largely the responsibility of the individual. What motivates a person, then, to cross the threshold from being interested to becoming a candidate? Is it concern for a particular issue, or is it self-aggrandizement? Researchers studying the "why" of candidacy have offered differing explanations. Chief among these explanations are the sociological approach, the psychological approach, and the structural approach.

The sociological approach assumes that background, particularly occupational background, facilitates entry into public office. Within this approach, researchers have classified public officials according to occupation, educational experience, and their fathers' occupational status. It is assumed that certain occupations and social backgrounds carry with them a socialization process that influences individuals to run for political office. Political scientist Donald Matthews (1960) concluded that a particular type of social environment is what produces a candidate.' Matthews maintains that given a background of position, wealth, security, and a family tradition of activism, a candidate will emerge. This perspective applies quite well to the Kennedys, the Rockefellers, the Roosevelts, and the Bushes.

But this theory assumes women and minorities have less political ambition because they tend to have lower education and income levels, and their socialization process places less value on aspiring to or holding public office. A major question is whether gender roles continue to influence the election of women to local offices, thus reducing the pool of qualified candidates who will run for state or national offices. The research results are divided.

One set of results finds potential female office seekers can come from families in which the mother is politically active, is employed outside the home, or volunteers in a nonpartisan interest group (Sapiro 1983; Sapiro and Farah 1980; Fowlkes 1984). Although women do exhibit less political ambition than men, the "ambition gap" has narrowed over time (Clark, Hadley, and Darcy 1989, 203; Constantini 1990, 751; Fowlkes, Perkins, and Rinehart 1979). Research involving Arizona state and local officials finds that only 25 percent of women express political ambition in their first or second term, but by the third or fourth term the figure increases to 42 percent. Moreover, men with higher incomes and education may approach political ambition with an "up or out" attitude. If they do not immediately run for a higher office, they may return to the private sector. Women, with less challenging opportunities available outside public office, begin to enjoy their success and decide to seek higher office at a later stage (Burt-Way and Kelly 1992, 19).

A second set of results is far less optimistic about current and future recruitment of women candidates. A study of eight southern states revealed that while women were recruited to run for county offices, women held few local offices involved in fighting crime or of an executive nature (Lublin and Brewer 2003). On the other hand, women routinely won election to process-oriented offices with less discretion. Thus, women candidates may find it more difficult to move on to high profile state and national offices given the nature of the lower level offices they held.

A large-scale study, the Citizen Political Ambition Study, surveyed 3,800 individuals in four professions that often lead to a career in politics. Respondents were asked about the possibility of running (or not running) for public office. The key findings were that a politicized upbringing, combined with a sense of efficacy, motivates individuals to seek a public office. Conversely, belonging to a group historically excluded from politics greatly decreases the chances of becoming a candidate (Fox and Lawless 2005). Among men and women who share the same personal characteristics and professional credentials, women were significantly less inclined to become candidates. This "gender gap" persists for two reasons: women receive far less encouragement to seek office from spouses/partners, family members, and friends; secondly, women perceive themselves to be less qualified to run (Fox and Lawless 2004). Only the most qualified women decide to enter the political ring, but they are as successful obtaining office as their male counterparts when they do (Burrell 1994).

The work of Fox and Lawless (2004) suggests that because of currently existing patterns of socialization, under-representation of women at the recruitment stage is likely to persist into the future. Politically ambitious women often mention running for office only after child-care duties are not pressing. Because of the delayed entrance into the political field, they are less likely to advance very far on the political ladder (Lawless and Fox 2005).

A second approach to understanding why certain people decide to run for public office is psychological—the individual's personality traits and personal ambitions. Joseph Schlesinger (1966) argued that personal ambition both motivates people to seek office and determines what level of office they seek: "Ambition lies at the heart of politics." Schlesinger identified three degrees of ambition: (1) discrete ambition, whereby the officeholder aspires only to a local office and then retires; (2) static ambition, whereby an officeholder seeks a particular office and wants to make a career in it; and (3) progressive ambition, whereby an officeholder's current position is viewed simply as a stepping-stone to higher office. Because of the high turnover among state legislators who do not move on to other offices, this group exhibits more discrete, limited political ambitions. On the other end of the scale are those who progressively seek higher office. Few better examples of a rapid rise through the political ranks exist than Barack Obama. The son of a black father from Kenya and a white mother from Kansas, Obama's childhood was divided between Hawaii and Indonesia. He began as a community organizer with black churches in the south side of Chicago in 1985. He graduated from Harvard Law School in 1991, where he was president of the *Harvard Law Review*. He spent eight years in the Illinois state senate (1997–2004), where he often found a middle ground between the two political parties, and between liberals and conservatives. Obama gained national attention in 2004 when he gave a rousing keynote speech to the Democratic National Convention. That same year, he was elected to the U.S. Senate from Illinois. After only a short time in the Senate, Obama began planning for a presidential race, which opened with an announcement in Springfield, Illinois, on the very site where Abraham Lincoln had spoken.

A third approach to understanding why people become candidates emphasizes political opportunities. The structural approach contends that personal political ambitions are molded by the "opportunity structure" presented to the office seeker. Running for office is perceived as a risk, with the magnitude of the risk partially determined by the structural characteristics of the electoral system. What New York's Tammany Hall Boss Plunket said many years ago about graft also applies to ambition: "I seen my opportunities and I took 'em!" Sometimes opportunities for political candidacy and electoral success are beyond the control of the individual. Structural factors, such as the size of the election district, the degree of party competition within that district, and the presence of an incumbent, affect one's chances for moving up the political ladder. According to Gordon Black (1972, 145): "The theory rests on the idea that office-seekers attempt to behave in a rational manner in selecting among alterna-

tive offices. Rather than being driven by excessive ambition, they tend to develop ambition slowly as a result of their changing circumstances." For example, a political novice's decision to run against an incumbent is a very difficult one. The incumbent, due to position, staff, and public recognition, usually enjoys enormous financial and personnel advantages over all challengers. The great majority of incumbents who seek reelection are successful. For example, in most elections well over 90 percent of the incumbent House members up for reelection have been successful. The structural approach, therefore, emphasizes an individual's immediate circumstances at the time of the decision to seek office, rather than personal background or personality. Ambition is believed to develop in relation to political opportunities (Fowler and McClure 1989). For example, large districts require large campaign expenditures; there is usually more intra-party competition, and the possibilities are more limited. Another important factor affecting one's chances for election is the relative strength of the parties in the district. Obviously, there are more political opportunities for a candidate in a "safe" district (where one's party usually wins) than for a candidate in a more competitive district.

None of these three approaches claims to offer a total explanation. James David Barber (1965) suggests an approach that combines personal ambition, opportunity, and resources. Barber points out that all three elements should be considered in decisions to seek public office, and he suggests that potential candidates must give an affirmative answer to the following questions:

1. Do I want it? (ambition)
2. Can I do it? (resources)
3. Do they want me? (opportunity)

Noting that these factors are interrelated, Barber says that if any one of them is missing, the prospective candidate usually will not enter an election race.

While recruitment, in general, occurs through self-selection, the parties are not entirely absent in this process. For House and Senate seats the national party committees are involved on a selective basis, working with local party officials to encourage candidates in elections that are either very competitive or uncontested. Parties have undertaken both passive and active recruitment efforts. Passive recruiting simply seeks to make individuals aware of election opportunities. It is done through newsletters and "training colleges" for candidates and managers on such subjects as fund-raising and use of the media. Both the Republican National Committee (RNC) and the Democratic National Committee (DNC) give particular emphasis to making opportunities known to women and minorities, including such programs as the RNC Women's Outreach Program and the DNC Eleanor Roosevelt Program (Herrnson 1988, 49). The programs are low-key and the participants usually receive a small stipend for their participation. In active recruiting, the parties usually search for candidates to run for the House and Senate. If an announced candidate is viewed by the party as a disaster waiting to occur, negative recruitment may be subtly employed to discourage the person from running, perhaps showing him or her discouraging polling results.

Campaign Organization and Management

An example of the basic structure of a campaign, that of George W. Bush in 2004, is presented in figure 7.1. Although the central purpose of campaigns remains mass persuasion, campaigns are increasingly specialized in their organization and operation. As candidates try to maximize their chances to win, they put less stock in party loyalty, bumper stickers, or handshaking. In trying to get the greatest return for their time and money, candidates have sought the help of specialists and their professional techniques. Unlike the ama-

teurs of the past, candidates must now surround themselves with professional managers, statisticians, pollsters, advertising specialists, and lawyers.

While anyone can print a business card with the title of **political consultant**, Sabato (1981) defines the term as a campaign professional who is engaged primarily in providing advice and services (such as polling, media creation and production, direct mail fundraising, and issue and opponent research) to candidates and other political committees. The first modern political consulting firm was founded in 1934, and consultants were first used in 1936 by the Republican presidential nominee, Alfred Landon (Baumgartner 2000). The first professional organization, the American Association of Political Consultants, was founded in 1969 with twenty-five members and currently exceeds four thousand members out of the estimated thirty-five thousand political consultants in the United States today (Baumgartner 2000). A number of universities recognize the importance of this specialty by offering degrees with an emphasis in campaign management.

Academic studies of the impact of political consultants find that campaigns who hire consultants as fund-raisers are more successful than those which do not (Herrnson 2000). Having a political consultant on the campaign can increase a candidate's share of the vote by as much as 5 percent, even after controls are imposed for candidate quality and campaign spending (Medvic and Lenart 1997). The same study found that vote share rises by 2.5 percent for each additional political consultant hired. The number and type of political consultants hired depends upon several factors. Consultants were employed by candidates who were running for open seats (75 percent) and incumbent candidates (66 percent). Democrats were more likely to hire consultants than Republicans (Medvic and Lenart 1997). Pollsters ranked as the first hire, followed by media consultants and fundraisers (Herrnson 2000; Medvic and Lenart 1997).

FIGURE 7.1 Campaign Organization for Bush-Cheney Campaign, 2004

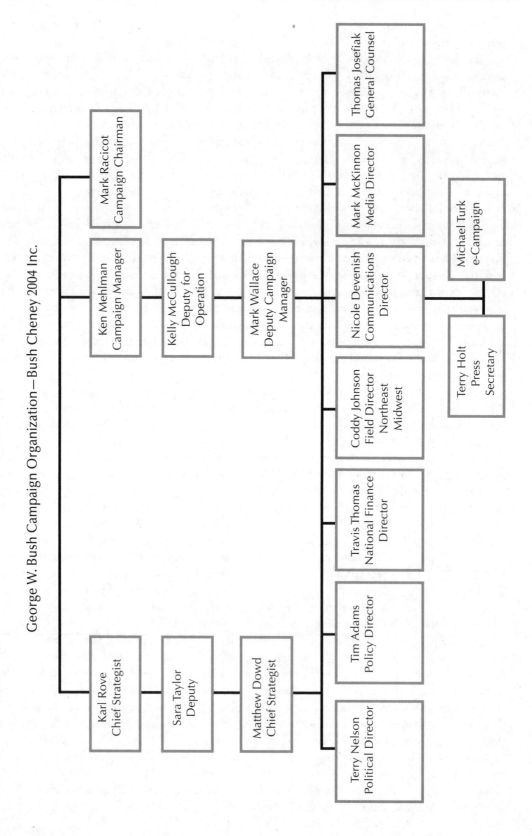

George W. Bush Campaign Organization—Bush Cheney 2004 Inc.

Information Needs: Research

Consultants are needed for research (issue and opponent research), advertising, fund-raising, and polling. Campaigns rely on two concepts: geodemographics and narrowcasting. Geodemographic refers to the gathering of information about specific segments of the electorate. Narrowcasting is the process of choosing specific issues that appeal most to each group and then disseminating that information primarily to that group.

Research consultants first gather information to provide the candidate with a candid profile of his or her district. This, in turn, suggests guidelines for making key strategic decisions. More specifically, information must be gathered about the social, economic, and political makeup of the district or the state, as well as the past record of both the opponent and the candidate. Although the lists vary, issue and opponent research must provide the candidate information on a minimum of five factors:

1. Voting behavior—the patterns of voter turnout, ticket splitting, and party loyalty of the district;
2. Demographics—the income, education, occupation, race, age, and residential characteristics of the district;
3. Party affiliation—strength of the voters' party identification and participation in party organizations and activities;
4. Issue and concerns—current and likely future political issues in the district and how these fit with the candidate's own priorities and positions;
5. Opposition—a profile of group support, issue positions, skills, strengths and weaknesses with the voters, and likely campaign tactics.

Statistics of past elections are important in predicting future voting behavior, identifying the relative strength of party registration in a particular district, and determining voter turnout levels. Election statistics such as levels of voter turnout, registration lists, and candidate vote totals are available from county, municipal, state, and federal governments.

Information Needs: Public Opinion

Polling, or survey research, is the most common means of gathering up-to-date information about the electorate. Candidates for public office rely on their polling firm to identify voter priorities and preferences, assess voter expectations of the officeholder, and measure voter familiarity with the candidates and issues. Indeed, the polling firm plays such an important role in the organization that candidates are often accused of being driven by polling numbers rather than principle.

In planning campaigns, candidates are advised to allocate 10 to 15 percent of the total budget to polling. Pollsters offer different types of polls, often presented to the candidate in the form of a package. The most basic question of "Should I run against this opponent" can be answered by the vulnerability poll. The poll is short, usually under five minutes, and focuses on name recognition, job approval ratings for the incumbent, potential issues for the campaign, and the positive and negative aspects most associated with the incumbent (Cohen 2004).

The benchmark poll is the basic planning document for the campaign, as it contains important issues to stress during the campaign: how to campaign among various groups; where to place the campaign's geographic focus; candidate personality information (including which personality factors to stress in advertising); how much emphasis needs to be given to familiarizing people with the candidate's name; what is known and unknown about the candidate's past record; potential areas of appeal that might increase the number of vote switchers; which voters are undecided—their characteristics and issue preferences; and the media that each voter group utilizes most often. This poll should include a minimum of six hundred respondents, and often it will be much larger, in the range of fifteen hundred to two thousand respondents. With the larger number of questions, such a poll typically requires a respondent thirty minutes or more to complete. Given the benchmark poll's central role in the campaign, up to 50 percent of the total polling budget should be allocated for this task (Cohen 2004; Varoga 2001). Presidential and senatorial candidates are often advised to complete benchmark polls up to two years before the election. The open seat in the 2008 presidential race attracted a large number of candidates, making a benchmark poll critical for determining how a potential candidate could differentiate himself or herself from the pack. Yet, few voters give serious thought to an election nearly two years in the future. A December 2006 poll found only 23 percent claimed to "give serious thought" to the 2008 candidates (Pew Research Center 2006d).

Benchmark polls help candidates develop their themes and sharpen their images, but campaigns use a trend poll to determine whether these messages are getting through to the electorate. These surveys act as a kind of "report card" for candidates by probing more deeply into a narrower range of subjects. Trend polls have a smaller sample size, often five hundred respondents, and may be carried out as often as once a month.

Early in the history of election surveys, in 1948, pollsters predicted that Thomas Dewey, rather than Harry Truman, would win the presidential election. This specific error was largely due to the pollsters' failure to detect a last-minute shift in the preference of the electorate because of the time delay between asking the question and publishing the results. To avoid such surprises, tracking polls are used the last two to four weeks of the campaign. To detect shifts in voter sentiment, one hundred to two hundred likely voters are called each night. They are asked very specific questions about changes in their perceptions of the issues and the candidates (Traugott and Lavrakas 2004, 17–18). The small sample size raises questions about how well the results can

be generalized. In an attempt to overcome the limitation of the small samples but also capture a sense of the movement in voter sentiments, data analysts may use a type of "moving average." The results for the first three nights are added together to increase the number of interviews available for analysis. From that point, as each new night's results come in, the oldest night's results are dropped (Sabato 1981, 76).

Focus groups are another basic tool used by polling organizations. Such groups are not a random sample but usually consist of ten to twenty people who are chosen to represent the target groups the campaign is trying to influence. Among the groups targeted in the past have been "soccer moms," "Wal-Mart shoppers," or "NASCAR dads." The questions are often open-ended to uncover more deeply embedded responses that might be missed by questions designed by pollsters. Potential commercials are often screened by focus groups in order to try to determine how people react. Such pretesting may help campaigns learn which ads will not work and thus avoid costly mistakes with expensive media advertising.

Some marketing firms now employ the Internet as a way to conduct a larger focus group. After sorting individuals for party affiliation or independent status, approximately five hundred participants are shown a speech or advertising on their computer and asked to rate the believability as they watch it. Participants rate the video at any given moment on a sliding scale that ranges from +100 to -100. A graph can then be generated with the average responses from everyone of that party affiliation (Bowers 2007).

The polls used by candidates have a strategic purpose as well; they try to find out how the public will respond to political trends that grab the headlines. Whether the top story is Democratic candidates contesting a presidential "surge" of troops in Iraq, or determining a stance on a controversial issue such as immigration reform, polling information is critical to determine whether the headlines are of real concern to constituents (and thus can affect election chances) or if their impact is confined "inside the Beltway" (that is, to people in Washington, DC).

Pollsters can also use public opinion results as a strategic weapon. Announcing the results of candidate preference polls almost automatically gets coverage in newspapers, radio, and television. Dramatizing one candidate's standing may also effectively knock an opponent from the race, since a poor showing tends to demoralize volunteers and discourage potential contributors. The wide open presidential race for 2008, for example, attracted a large number of early candidates. Very early polling showed John McCain as a Republican frontrunner. When McCain supported President Bush's "surge" of troops in Iraq, as well as immigration reform legislation, his poll numbers declined, and his campaign had a more difficult time raising money.

Polls have been criticized for both the methods they use and the undesirable effects they can have on election outcomes. Several reasons exist for healthy skepticism about poll results. Interest groups give polls a bad name by relying on thinly disguised SUGs, or "selling under the guise of polling." With such techniques, questions are heavily biased toward the group's point of view and the real purpose is to attempt to obtain a contribution.

Another problematic technique is the use of "push polling" (also called negative persuasion phoning or negative canvassing). Although several different definitions of a push poll exist, the key characteristic is the intent of the sponsor. If the purpose is to shape public opinion rather than to measure it, the effort is a push poll. One infamous example reportedly occurred in the 2000 South Carolina Republican presidential primary between John McCain and George W. Bush. Possible Republican voters were called by an unidentified organization and asked such questions as: "Would you be more likely or less likely to vote for John McCain for

president if you knew that he had fathered an illegitimate black child?" (Center for Media and Democracy 2007). McCain was campaigning with his adopted Bangladeshi daughter. Though asked in the guise of a poll question, the intent was clearly to attempt to shape the views of likely voters in the Republican primary. Senator McCain denounced the use of such a campaign tactic, and the Bush campaign denied being involved (Johnson 2000).

A more subtle method of introducing a push-poll question into the mind of the public occurred with Barack Obama. An article in *Insight,* a conservative magazine, began with the question, "Are the American people ready for an elected official who was educated in a Madrassa [a Muslim seminary] as a young man and has not been forthcoming about his Muslim heritage?" ("Hillary's Team Has Questions" 2007). The "question," attributed to Senator Hillary Clinton's camp, was discussed by Fox News. The question was soon repeated in the *New York Post,* CNN, and a number of political blogs. A CNN investigation found that while Obama did attend school in Malaysia, it was a regular school and not a Madrassa ("CNN Debunks False Report About Obama" 2007). Fox News later indicated that some of its network hosts were simply expressing their own opinions and had relied on *Insight* magazine for information. In this instance, however, the news report of a push-poll question was more effective in creating doubt about the candidate than was an actual poll.

Responsible pollsters face several additional problems. The first issue is that given the busy schedule of many Americans, it is difficult to find people who will take the fifteen or twenty minutes necessary for the average phone poll. The American Association for Public Opinion reports that as many as eight phone calls are necessary for a completed survey. A second problem arises because telephone capabilities are now standard in a range of technologies from cell phones to personal digital assistants (PDAs). An increasing number of citizens and their families have substituted the newer technologies for the traditional telephone lines. Polling firms must make a special effort to search for these phone numbers, and in the case of families to screen among several different members that have the same number.

A last concern is that the rise of instant and overnight polls forces respondents to make snap judgments on complex issues, whereas considerable information and time are necessary for a person to form a stable opinion. As a result, polls may show either contradictory results or a volatile public opinion that is heavily dependent on the next round of news bulletins and candidate statements. For this reason, political scientist James Fishkin (1995) had advocated the "deliberative opinion poll" in which a representative group of citizens are gathered together, provided with substantive information on public issues, and given time to hold discussions before their more informed views are polled. Deliberative polls have been conducted a number of times in the United States and in other countries, including during the 1996 presidential election (Merkle 1996). Although this technique can supply a missing component within public opinion, an artificial element is introduced into the process as campaigns take place amid heated political battles in which few citizens have the time or energy to undertake the kind of deliberation Fishkin desires.

Polls have been criticized for exerting several undesirable influences on elections. One is the so-called bandwagon effect that occurs when citizens decide to vote for a candidate who is leading in the polls rather than vote for the candidate they most prefer. On the opposite side of the coin is the underdog effect that leads a voter to support a candidate precisely because he or she is trailing in the polls. Although there are reasons to be cautious about both the accuracy and purpose of polls, they are still widely read, quoted, and believed by politicians and the public.

The Campaign Manager

Campaign organizations vary in size from a group of three or four who are trying to elect a friend to a minor office to a team of thousands who work in a presidential campaign. Whatever the size or complexity of the organization, the basic task remains the same: to coordinate the efforts of the three groups of campaign workers—the professionals, the party workers, and the nonparty volunteers. The person primarily responsible for this task is the campaign manager.

The professional campaign manager of today differs from past managers in two distinct ways: the relationship with the party organization, and the sophistication of the skills employed. The traditional campaign manager, who had many years of party experience, relied heavily on the organization and the skills of party workers for the traditional vote-getting procedures—door knocking, canvassing, and personal voter contact in the precincts. In general, the professional, however, operates largely from an established, private, profit-making firm that is relatively independent of the political party.

The professional campaign manager also differs from the traditional one in his or her personal background, which will determine the skills the professional uses. The professional is well versed in marketing, public relations, and communications rather than door knocking and backroom dealing. By the early 1970s, one study found that more than two-thirds of campaign managers had a background in public relations, advertising, journalism or media, and only 11 percent came from a traditional political party or campaign staff position (Rosenbloom 1973, 67).

Although a campaign manager is likely to work for candidates of a single party, a campaign manager often views campaigns from a business perspective rather than a party perspective. Bill Roberts, of the Spencer-Roberts team, emphasized this at a meeting sponsored by the Republican National Committee: "As a

Campaign manager, your sole purpose is to win. There is absolutely no other goal. You are not trying to prove a cause or sell a philosophy. You are trying to win a campaign in the most expeditious manner possible, using every legal and moral way to do so" (Rosenbloom 1973, 104).

There is no single path to becoming the campaign manager for a major presidential campaign as the following reports on three campaign managers illustrate. In 2004, the campaign manager for the Bush-Cheney reelection team was Ken Mehlman. Mehlman's story offers a contemporary example of one tried and true path to the top of a major campaign. While in law school at Harvard, Mehlman worked for William Weld's successful campaign for governor of Massachusetts. After graduating from Harvard in 1991, Mehlman went to work in Washington, DC. Mehlman worked first for Akin Gump Strauss Hauer and Feld, a prominent legal and lobbying firm in Washington, DC, and later served as a senior staff member for two Republican members of the House of Representatives. Mehlman gained additional campaign experience working for Michael DeWine's Senate campaign in Ohio in 1994 as well as in the 1992 and 1996 Republican presidential campaigns of George H. W. Bush and Bob Dole. In 1999, Mehlman joined the presidential campaign of George W. Bush and became the national field director for the Bush-Cheney campaign in the 2000 election. After the election, Mehlman was appointed as the director of political affairs in the Bush administration. Given his success in the 2000 campaign and his knowledge of the Bush administration's political agenda during the first term, Mehlman was an obvious choice to be campaign manager for the Bush-Cheney reelection in 2004. After the successful 2004 election, Mehlman was President Bush's choice to head the Republican National Committee. Mehlman served as chair of the RNC until shortly after the 2006 midterm elections.

On the Democratic side in 2004, John Kerry's first campaign manager, Jim Jordan, lasted only nine months and was replaced by Mary Beth Cahill. Cahill had been a long-time staff member for Senator Edward Kennedy and later the executive director of EMILY's List, a political action committee which supports the election of women and pro-choice candidates. Like Mehlman, Cahill had a long list of prior campaign experience working for Democratic candidates in Massachusetts, Vermont, and Oregon. As manager for the Kerry campaign, Cahill's priorities were to introduce John Kerry to the public, to make the case as to why a change in the presidency was necessary, and finally to show what a Kerry presidency would look like. When Kerry's poll numbers dropped later in the campaign, John Sasso became the senior campaign strategist, even though Cahill retained the post of campaign chair.

In contrast, Hillary Clinton's campaign manager for 2008, Patti Solis Doyle, does not fit the standard profile of a campaign manager (Romano 2007; Zuckman 2007). While coming from a politically active family—her brother is Chicago alderman Danny Solis—Solis Doyle joined Bill Clinton's presidential campaign in 1991 after having worked on the mayoral campaign of Richard M. Daley in Chicago (Romano 2007). Unlike other campaign managers who have worked for numerous candidates in a variety of campaigns, Solis Doyle joined Hillary Clinton's staff after the 1992 election and has remained a close aide. Solis Doyle did leave for a job with a Washington media relations firm, but returned after several months because she found the work for Clinton to be more fulfilling. Solis Doyle's strengths are organizational as opposed to strategic or political. She has extensive fund-raising experience, as she headed Senator Clinton's HillPAC and Friends of Hillary (Senator Clinton's reelection committee). Reports about the workings of Clinton's organization describe it as tightly run with few information leaks.

Designing the Campaign Message

The campaign manager, along with the creative director and a few key advisors have the responsibility of creating the message and designing the campaign's strategy. Republican strategist Mary Matalin stresses the need for a candidate to emphasize why he or she is running. Matalin defines "message" as "short hand for a coherent, cohesive philosophy of governance and a set of comprehensive principles underlying the formulation of policy or, in political parlance, *what you stand for*. It is your link/bond/compact with the citizenry" (Carville and Matalin 1994, 487). Her husband and political opposite, James Carville, stresses the consequences of a campaign that has no rationale or reason for existence. "You can plaster your candidate's face and name all over the state, but if he or she is not saying anything, you're not going to make a dent" (Carville and Matalin 1994, 74). The message must also be distinct from the strategy. "A *message* answers the question: why are you running? A *strategy* answers the question: how will you win?" (Faucheux 1993).

For the 2000 election George W. Bush's election message was that he was a "compassionate conservative." This message appealed not only to conservatives who wanted tax cuts, but also to a broader base who favored education reform. Incumbency and the events of 9/11 dictated a different message for 2004. The Bush team, led by creative director Mark McKinnon, determined the message would be the president's strong leadership, humanity, and steady predictability. As McKinnon put it,

> We began to focus on this idea of steady leadership. We recognized that one of the things people liked about President Bush, even if they disagreed with him, they felt he was a guy of strong conviction who was steady and predictable. People like that, particularly in times of change. . . . We were trying to communicate strength, trust, and values. (Devlin 2005b, 282)

To convey this message, one of the first ads McKinnon devised was "Safer/Stronger," which used an actual flag scene from 9/11. Although the footage was controversial, McKinnon believed it communicated the campaign message because "This was the defining moment—certainly of this president, of our decade, and our generation. . . . We discovered that 9/11 was not only powerful, but also positive; it was something that people felt that we had gone through together that tested us" (Devlin 2005b, 282).

The Bush campaign received help from a 527 group in communicating the message of the president's humanity. Late in the campaign the group Progress for America Voter Fund aired a spot called "Ashley's Story." The ad was based upon an article in the *Cincinnati Inquirer* in which the president gave a sixteen-year-old girl a hug because her mother had been killed in the World Trade Center collapse. In the ad, the president says, "I know that's hard. Are you all right?" Ashley repeats the president's words, and then says, "He's the most powerful man in the world, and all he wants to do is make sure I'm safe." Her father ends the ad by stating, "What I saw was what I want to see in the heart and soul of the man who sits in the highest elected office in our country." The creative director for the Kerry campaign, Bob Shrum, acknowledged the impact of the ad. "'Ashley' was real, was human, people could relate to it. 'Ashley' probably cost us Ohio and cost us the presidency!" (Devlin 2005b, 296).

Shrum had the difficult task of conveying who John Kerry was and what drove him to seek the presidency. The message was that Kerry was both a war hero and a war opponent. Shrum turned to chief ad creator Jim Margolis who designed a spot showing a young John Kerry, who after serving in Vietnam came home to testify against the war before the Senate Foreign Relations Committee. "How do you ask a man to be the last one to die in Vietnam? How do you ask a man to be the last one to die for a mistake?" Margolis explains:

That story really conveyed why this person was presidential timbre . . . after coming home a hero, having served, volunteered, having done his duty, having taken shrapnel and saying "this is wrong" was compelling. It shows the depth of this person at a couple of levels—one, in terms of conscience, two in terms of maturity. (Devlin 2005a, 453)

The decision to portray Kerry as thoughtful and nuanced would clearly set the two candidates apart, but it could also alienate voters seeking clarity as opposed to complexity.

On the campaign trail, John Kerry did not show the kind of focus or the ability to stay on message as did George W. Bush. Kerry's desire to address many topics served as a metaphor for his entire campaign. Bob Garfield (2004, 53), a columnist for *Advertising Age* magazine, spared few words in describing John Kerry's inability to stay on message:

Not since George H. W. Bush's failed 1992 re-election campaign have we witnessed such fecklessness, such indecision, such flailing attempts to define a candidate's positions, his qualities and his overall brand image. It's actually worse than that; the Kerry campaign has taken the candidate's profound political advantages and squandered them.

Transmitting the Campaign Message

Media consultants, who often have previous experience in either commercial or political advertising, are a vital part of a candidate's team. Media advising is an inexact science; techniques and themes that work well in promoting one candidate do not always transfer to another candidate. In 1984, for example, Ronald Reagan's campaign assembled an all-star "Tuesday team" of commercial advertisers to design the reelection spots. The team used lush spots of family reunions, parades, and weddings to push the Reagan campaign's message of optimism, featuring the slogan "It's morning again in America." In 1992, George H. W. Bush adopted a similar strategy in hiring a team of advertisers, called the "November Company," with limited experience in the political arena but an impressive list of commercial clients that included BMW, Pontiac, Budweiser, Burger King, Kraft Foods, Stanley Tools, and—perhaps appropriately for a political campaign—Milk of Magnesia (Wines 1992). In contrast, Mark McKinnon, the creative director of George W. Bush's 2004 campaign, assembled a team of all-star political advertisers, including Alex Castellanos, who had created ads for the RNC in 2000, and Scott Howell, known for his controversial ads supporting Republican candidates.

The fact that many media consultants are trained in advertising and bring the tricks of the advertising trade to their political work raises questions of whether they are creating false images of candidates or distorting issues. In short, the complaint is that these advisors are marketing the candidate like a box of cereal. Some critics of the consultants complain that voters are being entertained and duped rather than informed. These critics claim that the purpose of the short TV spot is to sell the voter an illusion, to move the voter to act without analyzing the material presented, to "con" the voter psychologically. Most consultants responsible for the commercials reply that they do not fabricate a message. Legendary Democratic consultant Tony Schwartz contends that the most successful political commercials are "similar to Rorschach patterns. They do not tell the viewer anything. They surface his feelings and provide a context for him to express those feelings" (1973, 93). Schwartz prefers the term "partipulation" to "manipulation"— maintaining that voters must be willing to participate in their own manipulation by bringing certain emotional feelings and reactions to a particular commercial. As to informing the voter about what a candidate

TABLE 7.1 Primary Sources of Campaign Information, 1992–2006 (in percentages)

Sources	1992	1996	2000	2002	2004	2006
Television	82	72	70	66	78	69
Broadcast					29	24
NBC					13	11
ABC					11	9
CBS					9	9
Cable					40	30
Fox					21	16
CNN					15	13
MSNBC					6	5
Newspapers	57	60	39	33	38	34
Radio	12	19	15	13	17	17
Internet	na	3	11	7	18	15
Magazines	11	11	4	15	3	2

QUESTION: "How have you been getting most of your news about the November elections?" (up to two answers were accepted from each respondent).

Note: Survey data from 2000 include registered voters only.

Sources: Created by the authors using data from Pew Research Center (2006b, 2007a).

will do about an issue, Schwartz (1985) contends that listing a candidate's stands on the issues will confuse voters, but voters can evaluate a candidate's feelings about an issue.

The media advisor must be aware of where people get their information and be able to select the right medium that will transmit the campaign's message effectively and affordably. Overall, the number of Americans seeking news and information has declined slightly over the last decade. In 1994, 90 percent of Americans reported obtaining news from either television, radio, newspaper, or online compared with 81 percent in 2006. For those who do seek information, however, the amount of time spent gathering news has changed little. The public spends a little more than an hour a day (sixty-seven minutes) obtaining news from various sources, almost exactly the amount spent in the 1990s (Pew Research Center 2007b). This section will explore five of the most essential means of communications: (1) television, (2) radio, (3) newspapers, (4) the Internet, and (5) direct mail.

Television

Television remains the most important source of information about news in general. On any given day in November 2006, 61 percent said they watched a television news program, compared to 38 percent who read a daily paper, and 21 percent who received news online (Pew Research Center 2007a, 7). Television is the medium people turn to when there are breaking national or international events, such as the 9/11 attacks, the Iraq war, and Hurricane Katrina. For such events, television as a source spikes; newspapers show the most significant decline, followed by the Internet and radio (Althaus 2007).

As shown in table 7.1, in 2006 citizens report that television is their preferred source for campaign information by a two-to-one ratio over newspapers. But over the last fifteen years, the percentage who report television to be the most important source of election information has declined by 13 percent. This decline occurred not just for network news, but for local news as well.

Increasingly the choices viewers make about where to get information on television are politicized. Partisan differences occur among cable viewers and to a lesser extent among broadcast viewers as well. Since 2000, the Fox News Network, with its slogan of "Fair and Balanced," has been the top choice of Republican viewers, and more than half of the network's viewers describe themselves as conservative (Pew Research Center 2004). Republicans and conservatives rate Fox as the most credible news source, while Democrats and liberals find it the least credible. Similarly, as table 7.2 shows, 24 percent of Republicans chose Fox Cable for 2006 election news, compared to just 10 percent for Democrats. The opposite trend is found for CNN Cable, which 17 percent of Democrats preferred for election news but only 8 percent of Republicans. Smaller differences occur for broadcast networks, with Democrats more likely than Republicans to tune into the NBC and CBS networks.

Media consultants find television is particularly useful in conveying a compressed ten-, thirty-, or sixty-second message to large audiences because it gives the viewer the illusion of immediacy as well as a sense involvement in the audio-visual presentation. As pioneering media advisor Joe Napolitan (1971, 48–49) stated,

> Television has an inherent mobility. It moves. It captures time and makes a record of it. A still photograph or a printed word is static, it does not move forward or backward. Furthermore, it takes a much more willful effort to ignore that which stimulates two of our senses than that which strikes only one. In other words, that which I see and hear involves me more than what I just see. Once I am involved, I become a participant and add something of myself to what I see and hear. I add my own impressions and attitudes. I have become part of a circle of communication.

Napolitan found that 80 to 90 percent of what people retained from television were the

TABLE 7.2 Media Choices for 2006 Election News by Republican and Democratic Voters (in percentages)

	Voted Republican	Voted Democratic
Television	69	74
Fox Cable	24	10
Local news	22	25
ABC Network	11	13
NBC Network	10	14
CNN Cable	8	17
CBS Network	7	11
MSNBC Cable	3	6
Newspapers	38	44
Radio	21	14
Internet	17	17
Magazines	2	2

QUESTION: "How have you been getting most of your news about the November elections?" (up to two answers were accepted from each respondent).

Source: Created by authors using data from Pew Research Center (2007a).

visual images. Thus how a person looks on television, or even the backgrounds used, are often more important than the stated audio message. Ronald Reagan's White House communications director, Michael Deaver, operated under the same principle. Deaver's rule was that "the visual beats the verbal." Thus even a story with a reporter's negative comments was welcomed, as long as the piece contained the gorgeous visual images designed by Deaver (Graber 1989, 202–203).

The firm PQ Media keeps watch on campaign spending on media for races at all levels. Table 7.3 reveals an almost insatiable appetite for spending on media. Even though the rates charged for media purchases increase each year, the amount spent on media of all types almost doubled to $3.14 billion in 2006 compared to the previous nonpresidential election in 2002 when $1.63 billion was spent. Despite the decline in the number of

TABLE 7.3 Total Campaign Spending on Media, 2002–2006 (in millions of dollars)

Media	2002	2004	2006
Broadcast Television	912	1,450	1,578
Cable Television	35	103	144
Direct Mail	335	648	707
Radio	155	175	256
PR Promotional	128	43	254
Newspaper	34	58	104
Outdoor	25	34	55
Online	5	29	40
Other	1	2	1
Total	**1,630**	**2,542**	**3,139**

Source: Created by authors using data from PQ Media reported in Lieberman (2006).

people who seek election information from television, a similar pattern of increase is evident for this medium. When broadcast and cable television are combined in table 7.3, in 2006 an estimated $1.72 billion was spent on races at all levels compared with $947 million in 2002.

Television is particularly important in introducing the candidates to potential voters. One poll found that 62 percent of people first learned about candidates through television advertisements (Times Mirror Center 1992, 48–49). Interestingly, many people identified several types of TV political programs—editorials, talk shows, educational programs, documentaries, and specials—as more influential sources of information than talks with friends, contacts with candidates, or discussions with party workers or one's own family.

Cable television, or its competitor satellite television, offers several benefits to candidates engaged in narrowcasting. Literally hundreds of channels are targeted to specific audiences ranging from financial news to cooking or gardening. Candidates find it easier to buy a spot targeted to a specific audience in a specific time period and for less money. Moreover, research on cable subscribers finds those

who tune into CNN, MSNBC, or the History and Discovery channels are more likely to vote, to be involved in political fund-raising, and to work actively for a political candidate. Those shows focused on political satire such as *The Daily Show* or the *Colbert Report* tend to attract audiences with greater political knowledge (Pew Research Center 2007b).

Given the demographics of cable then, George W. Bush's 2004 campaign devoted roughly 30 percent of television advertising to cable and 70 percent to broadcast television (Devlin 2005b, 289). Cable is format driven, and using resources there allowed the campaign to target a specific audience—men—and to do so in a cost efficient manner. Media advisor Mark McKinnon stated, "We could buy cable in the 18 states or buy national cable for less than it would cost for [broadcast] spot buys in the 18 states" (Devlin 2005b, 289). Conversely, the Kerry campaign spent 95 percent of the television budget on broadcast television. The campaign's primary target—women—were most likely to watch broadcast television.

Congressional campaigns also spend heavily on television, as that medium has accounted for almost half of Senate expenditures and a third of House candidates' budgets in recent elections. In large, populous states such as California it is not unusual for candidates to spend up to two-thirds of their funds on television (Luntz 1988, 82).

Despite the advantages of television in terms of visual images, market penetration, and narrowcasting opportunities, several constraints should be noted. For information about political campaigns, the qualities Napolitan cited that made this medium unique, such as mobility, seeing and hearing, a greater sense of involvement, and adding one's own attitude are no longer the sole domain of television. Talk radio and the Internet can both provide the same sense of immediacy and involvement.

Some critics also question the effectiveness of the political advertising run on television. Research on the effectiveness finds it has the greatest impact on low-level, nonpartisan, and state races (Swinyard and Coney 1978). When voters know little about the candidates, television ads convey the message more effectively than other types of media. For other races, massive television spending does not directly translate into votes. Particularly in high interest, high visibility races, voters receive substantial cues from other sources. Moreover, incumbency has proved to be a more important (if not the single most important) factor in determining election success.

Radio

Radio is found in 99 percent of American homes, 95 percent of cars, and in 61 percent of workplaces. About four in ten Americans say they listen to radio on a daily basis for news, a proportion that has changed little since 2000. Talk radio, which can be defined as any station that encourages listeners to call in to discuss public issues and politics, can count on substantial numbers of Americans tuning in on a daily basis. Also, radio news continues to attract a sizable audience. For example, 28 percent of Americans said they regularly listened to the news programs on National Public Radio (Pew Research Center 2007b).

Radio advertising offers several benefits for candidates when compared with television. First, the audience for radio, rather than television, is more interested in local politics and has more knowledge of it (Becker and Dunwoody 1982, 214–215, 218). Second, radio stations offer the same opportunities for narrowcasting that cable television does. Stations target segments of the population, ranging from classical music to continuous news broadcasts to alternative rock. Talk radio listeners are highly segmented, as polling shows that the audience is mostly male, middle-aged, well-educated, and conservative. This format both stimulates attention and engages its listeners (Hofstetter 1998, 283–285). Those who are more attentive are more likely

to become aware of and engaged with political issues (Bennett 2002). Research in the 1990s showed talk radio listeners more likely to have a particular world view (usually conservative) and to fit bits of information gained from this format into their existing world view (Hofstetter et al. 1999, 356). Since that time period, much less of a partisan tilt is evident in the talk radio audience, as nearly identical percentages of Republicans (21 percent), Democrats (20 percent), and independents say they regularly listen to such programs. The National Public Radio audience is young and also well-educated, but listeners have definite partisan preferences, with 41 percent identifying themselves as Democrats, compared to 24 percent Republican (Pew Research Center 2004).

For candidates, radio thus offers candidates the opportunity to tailor their messages to specific audiences. This medium also functions as an effective vehicle for negative advertising. Spots aired during drive-time commutes that bash an opponent resonate with the public, who are already angry at being stuck in traffic. Further, what was once thought to be a disadvantage of radio—that it does not provide a strong visual image to accompany the message—allows candidates to make negative attacks without becoming too closely associated with the attack. Such ads are difficult for the opposition to keep up with because of the large number of radio stations in any market (Kolbert 1992). Radio has several advantages in terms of costs. Because less technical and expensive production equipment is required, candidates can quickly and inexpensively respond to a recent event, the latest polling results, or an opponent's last-minute campaign attacks.

More recently, political consultants have questioned several of radio's benefits. While radio is seen as a prime example of narrowcasting to different groups, newer technology allows listeners to actively choose formats that reduce or eliminate commercial interruptions, such as satellite radio or FM stations promising "more music and less talk." Moreover, in commuter markets where people spend so much time in their cars, radio ads were seen as an effective means of reaching captive audiences. Now the audience is no longer captive, as campaigns must consider what proportion of that audience is instead using cell phones or PDAs.

Ironically, the increase in the number of formats may still not answer the question of how to reach specific voters. For example, younger listeners may prefer stations with a "rap" format, but should scarce resources be spent on a format where many listeners may not be of voting age, and where few politicians have mastered sounding authentic? Campaigns must also determine what resources to allocate to the growing number of Spanish language stations. Finally, the splintering of music formats into "micro-differentiated stations" has led to the radio version of "grazing"—a practice originated by television viewers where viewers exhibit such dexterity in changing channels with the remote control that it rivals a fast-paced video game (Wolff 1989, 34). In sum, campaigns buying radio advertisements must still be wary of whether their messages are reaching the desired segment of the public.

Newspapers

People who use newspapers as their source of information tend to have higher levels of education, which in turn is linked to a greater knowledge of politics and a greater likelihood of voting in elections (Becker and Dunwoody 1982, 214). Newspapers are therefore better than television for disseminating in-depth information on the candidates' background and issue positions. Newspaper readers are more likely to make up their minds earlier about the candidates or issues, and are less likely to change their decisions. The newspaper that a person chooses to read can influence voting behavior. A recent study of two Washington, DC, newspapers found that those who were randomly given a free sub-

scription to the *Washington Post* were eight percentage points more likely to vote for the Democratic candidate than a control group. This effect, however, was not evident among readers given a subscription to the *Washington Times* (Gerber, Karlan, and Bergan 2007).

The two greatest concerns about using newspapers for campaign purposes are the precipitous drops in both number of readers and time spent reading the newspaper. More than 78 percent of the adult public reported reading a newspaper just about every day in the 1970s, compared to 49 percent in 1994 and 40 percent in 2006 (Pew Research Center 2006b). The average amount of time spent with the newspaper is fifteen minutes. While newspaper readership is now holding steady, this occurs only when online readers are factored in. People who read the paper on the Internet are more likely to choose the national editions of the *New York Times*, *Washington Post*, or *USA Today*.

The decline in readership for newspapers is greatest among those under thirty, as only 24 percent read a newspaper daily. On average they spend about eight minutes reading the newspaper. The most loyal readers are those over sixty-five, who spend twenty-five minutes reading newspapers. But even this age group has seen some erosion in daily readership, dropping to 58 percent (Pew Research Center 2006b).

Voters rate newspaper editorials as more influential in their decision making than television editorials. Yet it is important to differentiate between national and local races. Little evidence exists of the ability of editorials to influence voter behavior at the presidential level, but their influence is likely to be greater at the state and local level.

Republican campaign consultant Frank Luntz contends that newspaper ads do not have much of an impact, even among those who claim to read the newspaper daily (1988, 109). One difficulty is that to get the most mileage out of a newspaper ad, candidates are cautioned that it must be "different." A typical daily newspaper includes at least three hundred ads, all competing for the reader's attention. The candidate's ad must catch the reader's eye as he or she proceeds to the comics or the sports section. Good artwork, "catchy" text, and large ads are necessary to attract attention. The cost of such advertisements varies with the newspaper's circulation, the size of the ad, and its location in the newspaper.

The Internet

The value of the Internet to campaigns as an efficient way to gather campaign contributions, especially from people giving relatively small amounts, is well established. The question remains, however, as to how successful the Internet is as a source for campaign information and whether it helps to increase individual political participation in campaigns. Because of its potential for interactive exchange, most scholars identify the Internet as part of the "new media" (Bimber 2003; Bimber and Davis 2003). While some studies have found that use of new media may have an independent positive effect upon political participation (Hardy and Scheufele 2005), others find that online media complement traditional media to increase civic participation (Shah, Cho, Eveland, and Kwak 2005).

In 2006, the Pew Research Center and its "Internet and American Life Project" estimated that 136 million adult Americans were Internet users. Generalizations about the effect of Internet usage are difficult given the wide variety of sources available, the different purposes for accessing sites, the tendency of Internet users to rely on more than one source, and the preferences of different demographic groups for different sites. Any evaluation must also consider the Internet as both a source for gathering information and as a means of disseminating information and opinions among others.

For most Americans, the Internet serves as a supplemental source of information. Only 23 percent reported getting any news online in a typical day, and the average amount of time spent retrieving the news is a mere six minutes a day (Pew Research Center 2006b). Table 7.1 indicates that about 15 percent of American adults said they used the Internet for information about political campaigns. As Table 7.4 shows, however, there are a variety of sources for gaining political information once users are on the Internet. Most Internet users who sought campaign information reported using news portals, national television network sites, local news organizations, or major national paper sites. Given the nature of these sources, the information encountered by a user is likely to be similar to campaign information from other sources such as television news or newspapers. Yet, sizable percentages of Internet users sought campaign information from sources likely to cater to highly particular interests such as issue-oriented sites and blogs. Still, only 4 percent of Americans said that they relied upon the Internet as the sole source for political information (Pew Research Center 2007a).

For those using the Internet the most, the Pew Research Center distinguishes between campaign Internet users and online political activists. The former category includes those Americans who received any type of political information online or who exchanged emails about the candidates. Online political activists were those who created political content online and shared it with others. In a study of Internet campaign use in the 2006 midterm elections, the Pew Research Center (2007a) found that 8 percent of campaign Internet users posted their own political commentary, 13 percent forwarded or posted someone else's political commentary, 1 percent created political audio or video recordings, and 8 percent forwarded or posted someone else's political audio or video recordings. According to the report, this "translates into about 14 million people using the Web to contribute to political discussion and activity" (Pew Research Center 2007a). Not sur-

TABLE 7.4 Major Sources of Campaign News among Internet Users

Internet Source	Percent
News Portals (such as Google News or Yahoo! News)	60
TV Network Sites (such as CNN.com or ABC.com)	60
Local News Organizations	48
Major National Newspapers (such as the *New York Times*)	31
State or Local Governments Sites	28
Issue Oriented Sites	24
Blogs (such as the Daily Kos)	20
International News Organization Sites (such as the BBC)	20
Sites Created by Candidates	20
News Satire Sites (such as *The Daily Show*)	19
Radio News Organization Web sites (such as NPR)	19

Note: Numbers are the percentage of Internet users who reported that they obtained campaign news during the 2006 election from Internet sources.

Source: Created by authors using data from Pew Research Center (2007a).

prisingly, a profile of this group finds them to be largely white and male, as well as younger and more politically knowledgeable than the general population.

While the number of online activists is small, the Internet allows them to have an impact far beyond their numbers. Those who create video recordings for or against a candidate can post them on YouTube or a similar site, and the most creative videos can draw a large number of hits. One example of such a spot, "Hillary 1984," is profiled in box 7.1. For candidates, these political videos serve as another example of their diminished control over defining their message and how that message is perceived by the public.

Direct Mail

As shown in table 7.3, direct mail is typically the second largest expense for campaign media spending. The spending for direct mail follows the pattern for other media, as expenditures more than doubled from 2002 to 2006. While the public may not welcome a mailbox full of literature from various candidates, this medium is viewed as a necessary, but not necessarily cost-effective, means of reaching certain segments of the electorate (Simpson 1996). In state legislative races, direct mail is often the only way to target just the district's eligible voters. In many cases, the reach of television or radio is too broad and often too expensive.

Because direct mail often lacks the impact of television or the Internet, it often requires numerous mailings. One campaign manager in California notes that at least five pieces of mail are necessary to inform voters of a candidate's existence and several more to persuade citizens to vote for the candidate (Gerber, Green, and Green 2003). The available evidence also suggests that direct mail does little to increase voter turnout and indeed may even decrease turnout if the mailings are negative in tone (Gerber and Green 2000; Gerber, Green, and Green 2003). Moreover, if direct mail usually generates only one additional voter per eight hundred mailings, the cost of that extra voter is very high (Gerber, Green, and Green 2003).

BOX 7.1 "Hillary 1984" or the Potential and Pitfalls of Technology

One of the best examples of the debate over the impact of new technology in campaigns occurred with the "Hillary 1984" or "Vote Different" video that appeared on YouTube, attributed only to "ParkRidge 47." The clip is a video remix or "mashup" of a controversial Apple computer commercial that appeared only once in the 1984 Super Bowl. The "Hillary 1984" spot follows the Apple commercial quite closely: robot-like men can be seen marching into a large arena and watching a giant screen. Rather than a speech by "Big Brother," this video shows Hillary Clinton. As in the Apple commercial, a young blonde athlete chased by police races into the auditorium. She wears a track outfit (with what appears to be a Barack Obama logo) and an iPod. Following the Apple script, she hurls a sledgehammer at the screen. The screen explodes, and the masses react in shock. The final line of the spot reads, "On January 14th, the Democratic primary will begin. And you will see why 2008 will not be like '1984.'" The closing shot of "Obama.com" features an "O" in the form of Apple's original multicolored logo, and the title of the spot, "Vote Different," parallels an earlier Apple slogan of "Think Different."

The video received more than 2 million "hits" and moved quickly from the Internet to being shown on cable news and network broadcasts. Speculation about the identity of "ParkRidge 47" was rampant, ranging from a member of the Obama campaign to a Clinton supporter attempting to generate sympathy for her by creating an "attack" from the Obama camp. Blogger Ariana Huffington (2007) soon revealed that "ParkRidge 47" was Phil de Vellis, who worked for an Internet company that supplied technology to several Democratic presidential candidates, including Obama. According to de Vellis, he created the video "on a Sunday afternoon in my apartment using my personal equipment (a Mac and some software)" (Huffington 2007). The purpose was "to show that an individual citizen can affect the process. . . . This shows that the future of American politics rests in the hands of ordinary citizens. . . . This ad was not the first citizen ad, and it will not be the last. The game has changed" (Huffington 2007). Simon Rosenberg of the New Democratic Network, an influential party advocacy group based in Washington, DC, contends the ad is proof that "anyone can do powerful emotional ads. . . . And the campaigns are no longer in control. . . . It will no longer be a top-down candidate message; that's a 20th century broadcast model" (Marinucci 2007).

Other commentators have a less positive view about YouTube, noting that this kind of outlet may further decrease the ability of candidates' political parties to control their own messages. Rather than increasing the role of individuals in politics, "Hillary 1984" should serve as a cautionary tale for traditional media that may spread material which is later found to be untrue or damaging to a candidate. Tom Rosenstiel of the Project for Excellence in Journalism states that on the Internet "You essentially have a public wall where anybody can put up a billboard and say anything. And if the wall attracts a crowd, mainstream media write about it" (Johnson 2007). The ability to attack another candidate anonymously (at least for a while) is another vehicle for negative politics, and thus raises questions about what the impact of these newer technologies will be.

(continues)

"Hillary 1984" or "Vote Different"

On January 14th,
the Democratic primary
will begin.
And you'll see why 2008
won't be like "1984."

The Impact of Negative Campaigning

One of the purposes of campaign communication is to project a positive image of a candidate to potential voters. Another purpose of campaign communication can be to raise concerns or doubts about an opposing candidate in the minds of potential voters. Campaign communication, especially television ads, that are intended primarily to portray an opposing candidate in a less-than-flattering light are often called "negative" ads or "attack" ads. Negative advertising, however, is not synonymous with false or deceptive advertisements. While ads that are negative may also contain deceptive or untruthful information, negative ads may also be completely truthful; similarly, positive ads may be either truthful or untruthful.

Public opinion polls show that most Americans do not like negative campaigning and many Americans believe that contemporary election campaigns are more negative than campaigns used to be. Studies by academics suggest a more complex picture of the frequency and impact of negative advertising (Ansolabehere and Iyengar 1995; Geer 2006; Lau, Sigelman, Heldman, and Babbitt 1999; Wattenberg and Brians 1999). For example, a study of 379 prominent campaign spots from 1952 to 1996 found 54 percent to be negative, with nominating campaigns slightly more negative than general elections (57 percent to 53 percent), and Republican spots more negative than Democratic spots (60 percent to 48 percent) (West 1997, 58).

Although citizens may believe that there are more negative ads today than in past campaigns, defining what constitutes a "negative" ad is not a simple matter. What may appear to be a negative attack to one person may be seen as simply "getting out the facts" to another. Karen Johnson-Cartee and Gary Copeland provide a more useful definition by breaking the concept of negative ads into three parts: direct attack ads, comparison ads, and implied comparison ads (1991, 38–51).

The sole purpose of direct attack ads, as the name implies, is to attack the opposition. The ad is structured to imply that the opponent is inferior, not to be trusted, or even a liar. Consultants advocating this type of ad believe that part of the electorate votes *against* one candidate rather than *for* the opponent.

Two powerful examples of the impact of direct attack ads upon a campaign occurred in the 2004 presidential campaign. The "Surfer" spot used actual footage of John Kerry on a windsurfer weaving back and forth in Nantucket harbor. The image of Kerry zooming from the left to right, while the narrator listed Kerry's "flip-flops on the issues" was imbedded in the public's mind, along with the fact that the candidate was engaged in an elitist sport that few could identify with.

The 527 group Swift Boat Veterans for Truth produced some of the most effective attack ads of the 2004 campaign. About thirty veterans who had some connection with John Kerry in Vietnam appeared in the ad "Any Questions." Four veterans called Kerry a liar, and three used some version of the term "dishonest." A second spot, entitled "Sellout," used Kerry's own voice where he testified about reports of alleged war crimes committed by U.S. military personnel in Vietnam. The Kerry campaign did not believe the ads would have much traction and did not prepare a response. Neither did any of the 527 groups supporting Kerry. Many campaign watchers viewed the decision not to respond quickly to these attacks as a serious mistake by the Kerry campaign.

Because direct attack messages do not provide any kind of comparison, they run the greatest risk of backfiring on the sponsor if the public feels the message is not credible or is in bad taste. By using other veterans or by using Kerry's own words, the Swift Boat ads appeared sufficiently credible so that they were not immediately dismissed by voters or by reporters covering the campaign, and thus the ads were effective in raising doubts about the image of Senator Kerry that his campaign wanted to promote.

In contrast, the direct comparison spot contrasts the candidates' records, experience, or positions on the issues, for the purpose of claiming superiority over the opponent (Johnson-Cartee and Copeland 1991, 42). The ad uses inductive logic in offering a few specific bits of information and asking the viewer to draw a broad conclusion about a candidate's superiority. As one example, a 1996 spot produced by the Democratic National Committee began with Bob Dole proclaiming, "We sent him the first balanced budget in a generation. He vetoed it. We're going to veto Bill Clinton." The announcer then continues, "The facts? The President proposes a balanced budget protecting Medicare, education, the environment. But Dole is voting no. The President cuts taxes for 40 million Americans. Dole votes no. The President bans assault weapons; demands work for welfare while protecting kids. Dole says no to the Clinton plans. It's time to say yes to the Clinton plans—yes to America's families" (West 1997, 32).

Implied comparison ads, the third type, are not negative in the sense of the words used, but in the conclusion that the viewer draws from the comparison. Two classic examples are the 1964 "Daisy Ad" and the 2004 "Wolves Ad." For the 1964 campaign of the incumbent president, Lyndon Johnson, Democratic advertising consultant Tony Schwartz designed a spot that had a powerful impact on viewers. A small girl in a field of flowers is plucking petals from a daisy. She counts the petals and reaches "nine." Then she is startled, and the camera zooms in for an extreme close-up of her pupil. A man's voice off screen begins a countdown, and when he reaches "zero," an atomic explosion fills the screen. Over the distinctive mushroom cloud, President Johnson's voice proclaims, "These are the stakes—to make a world in which all of God's children can live, or to go into the dark. We must either love each other, or we must die." The announcer then urges viewers to vote for President Johnson because "the stakes are too high for you to stay home"

(Schwartz 1973, 93–96). The Democrats ran the ad only once, but network news programs subsequently aired it. Schwartz (1973, 93) explained that the commercial had such an impact because it "*evoked* a deep feeling in many people that Goldwater might actually use nuclear weapons. This mistrust was not in the *Daisy* spot. It was in the people who viewed the commercial. The stimuli of the film and sound evoked these feelings and allowed people to express what they inherently believed."

Provoking a similar reaction was the goal of 2004 "Wolves" ad, which in turn was a remix of the 1984 Ronald Reagan "Bear" ad. As sunlight filters through the deep woods, an announcer states, "In an increasingly dangerous world, even after the first terrorist attack on America, John Kerry and the liberals in Congress voted to slash America's intelligence operations by $6 billion." The viewer sees fleeting images of wolves in the trees and hears their throaty growls. "Cuts so deep they would have weakened America's defenses. And weakness attracts those who would do America harm." In the last shot, a group of wolves has gathered against the forest background.

For the student of campaigns, negative spots raise several important questions: How effective are negative ads? How can candidates respond to this tactic? Most importantly, does the emphasis on negative spots increase voter alienation and lead to decreasing participation in elections?

As to the effectiveness of such campaigns, as Tony Schwartz indicated, the greatest limitation is that a spot must evoke an emotional feeling the voter can identify with. If the intended comparison is accepted, negative ads are effective. In the case of the Republican "Wolves" ad, many Americans could relate to the notion that shadowy figures were waiting to do America harm. Even if voters say they dislike negative advertising, the emotional impact of a negative message may result in the ad being better remembered than a positive ad. One survey of six southern states found that 65 percent of respondents did not favor the use of such ads, but two-thirds were able to remember specific negative ads (Johnson-Cartee and Copeland 1991, 11). Still, an analysis of numerous studies of the effects of negative political ads concluded that "*There is simply no evidence in the research literature that negative political advertisements are any more effective than positive political ads*" (Lau, Sigelman, Heldman, and Babbitt 1999, 857; emphasis in original).

Whether or not they have the intended effect on viewers, negative ads do exist and can influence the course of a campaign. So how can candidates respond? The best defense may be an inoculation campaign, combined with refutational preemption. Although these terms may sound like a combined press release from the public health service and the military, the inoculation concept attempts to raise a threat in order to motivate the viewer to defend against the attack. Simultaneously, the refutation provides material in a supportive environment to ward off the attack (Pfau and Kenski 1990, 75). In a 2006 ad, Republican congressional candidate Michael Steele, leaning atop a television set, stated, "You knew they were coming. Nasty ads from the Washington crowd. We don't think much of that." The camera zooms in on a small dog who growls. "I think you deserve straight talk . . . If you're ready for change, I'm your man." Steel's opponent, however, resumed the attack with an implied comparison ad that stated, "It's nice that Michael Steele likes puppies . . . but he *loves* George Bush." The spot then named the times Steele agreed with the policy stands of President Bush. Research has shown that inoculation must be started early to be effective and that the effect is likely to help the candidate much later in the race. Television is a particularly appropriate medium for inoculation spots because the viewers tend to be passive and thus more receptive to the message (Cundy 1986; Kern 1989).

One short-term check on negative ads is that they do run in cycles. Given a constant diet of negative ads, voters may express increased dissatisfaction with the tone of the election. When negative campaign ads become *the* focus of the election, candidates will abruptly switch tactics. Polls taken for Representative Ron Wyden (D-Oregon), for example, who ran for a Senate seat in a 1996 special election, indicated that voters' primary concern was the negative tone of the election. Wyden had relied on negative campaigning in the past but began having himself introduced at campaign events with a song recorded by Bing Crosby and the Andrews Sisters: "*Ac-cent-tchu-ate the positive / E-lim-in-ate the negative*" (Elving 1996, 440). Wyden continued this theme throughout the campaign.

As to whether an abundance of negativity in campaigns drives voters from the polls, the studies to date are inconclusive. Stephen Ansolabehere and Shanto Iyengar (1995) contend that negative campaigns do have a measurable effect on both turnout and political efficacy. Advertising can mobilize or demobilize voters, depending on the type of messages that are transmitted (Ansolabehere and Iyengar 1995). A major difficulty is isolating the impact of campaign ads on the voter from the effect of other influences. To accomplish this, a control group that saw no political advertisements was compared to groups that saw actual campaign spots that candidates aired, as well as the authors' professionally produced fictional ads that used actual candidates' names. They found that exposure to positive ads increased intention to vote by 2.3 percent, whereas viewing negative ads reduced it by 4.6 percent (Ansolabehere and Iyengar 1995, 104–105; Ansolabehere, Iyengar, Simon, and Valentino 1994, 835). The greatest impact occurred with nonpartisans, who are likely to have a more pessimistic view of politics in the first place. For partisans, the greatest effect was on deciding which candidate to vote for rather than whether to vote (Ansolabehere and Iyengar 1995, 110–112). A similar effect was observed on political efficacy. Among those who saw the negative ads there were 5.2 percent fewer people who felt that their vote counted, compared with the control group.

The effect of negative ads on voter turnout and political efficacy is still under debate, however (Kahn and Kenny 1999; Lau, Sigelman, Heldman, and Babbitt 1999; Wattenberg and Brians 1999). One study determined that campaigns based on negative advertising do not have a major effect on decreasing political trust (Martinez and Delegal 1990). Others critique the research of Ansolabehere and Iyengar, contending that negative ads have very little effect on turnout (Finkel and Geer 1998; Wattenberg and Brians 1999). For example, when negative spots are broken down into issue attacks and character attacks, Finkel and Geer find that ads that target issues decrease participation slightly, character attacks mobilize voters slightly, and the net effect is very small (1998, 577). Although the finding that attacking character actually entices more voters seems counterintuitive, one explanation is that these spots give more information to voters, and the new data is given greater weight. Furthermore, Geer (2006) contends that negative ads provide viewers more evidence than positive ads typically do, and that negative ads often serve an important purpose by raising national issues. In sum, it may be both convenient and satisfying to blame lower turnout in part on the use of negative ads, but conclusive statements about their impact must await further study.

Political Parties as Campaign Specialists

While the role of political parties in campaigns has changed over the years, the highly competitive nature of contemporary American elections means that both parties do what they can to help get their candidates elected. Both major political parties aid their candidates in identifying voters through a process called microtargeting, and both parties spend resources on get-out-the-vote (GOTV) drives in key states.

As noted previously, in the 1980s and 1990s private consulting firms would provide information about geodemographics, gathering information about the social, economic, and political makeup of the district or the state. The major assumption was that demographic characteristics strongly influence issues of concern to voters. A district with a large proportion of aged citizens would undoubtedly be interested in federal health care policies for the aged. Similarly, districts with low per capita income would be more concerned with job opportunities and social welfare benefits. The notion that group demographics have the main impact on voter interests and decisions was modified after the 2000 election.

Gertner (2004) describes the new situation facing political parties. As he puts it, imagine being called into the boss's office to determine how to sell the public on a presidential candidate and being told:

> Forget about TV commercials, forget about radio, forget about debates. . . . Think voters—just voters. And don't think only in terms of big demographic groups like senior citizens, middle-class white men or young single women; don't think of them only in terms of geographical areas like districts or precincts or even neighborhoods. Think about what they like, what they do, what they consume. Think about them one by one. Name by name, address by address, phone by phone. (Gertner 2004, 43)

It is this process of identifying individual potential voters and getting them to the polls that solidifies the role of the parties in campaigns. Thus after the very close and extremely controversial presidential election results of 2000, both the DNC and the RNC vowed to place more emphasis on information gathering and GOTV programs. This required identifying potential voters, determining the "pitch" or message, and ensuring that the targeted people get to the polls. To identify voters, the RNC relies on a program called "Voter Vault," while the DNC primarily uses a software program called "Data-Mart." While the RNC worked on Voter Vault in the mid–1990s, the program was not ready for field use until the 2002 election. Voter Vault is believed to contain about 168 million registered voters, with up to one hundred different data points per individual. DataMart, the DNC program, has also been in use since 2002 and contains the records of 166 million registered voters. The Democrats also use a smaller database, called DemZilla, for fund-raising and organizing volunteers (Tynan 2004).

These programs use "data mining," which is a process of gathering a great deal of information on people and searching for patterns that may be useful. The first step in examining voters "one by one" is to compile state voter files, which campaigns have always used to determine residence, elections voted in, absentee voting, party registration, and party donations. Then, data on political views may be added by party canvassers who knock on voters' doors and use PDAs to access the Internet and update the party's database immediately after each voter interview (Gertner 2004; Wallsten and Hamburger 2006). Relevant data may also be collected from other sources. For example, in the 2004 election, Ralph Reed, the southeastern chairman for the Bush-Cheney campaign, asked supporters to supply the Republican party with membership rolls from churches, clubs, fraternities, and PTA organizations. Next comes data purchased from commercial marketing companies such as magazine and newspaper subscriptions, automobile type, type of computer used, catalogs received, and home financing information. Even such consumer preferences as favorite toothpaste, beer, or soda are catalogued. Finally, other publicly available information may be added such as census data that includes the race and income mix of your neighborhood, how many people own their homes, the size of homes, and length of commute to work.

To demonstrate the power of the software, the chair of the DNC can turn to his "director of targeting" and ask for a list of voters: "We can go right down to the county and precinct level and pull up any person who now lives in any of those precincts . . . with high-quality lists for targeting, testing, fund-raising and organizing for a master mobilization effort. . . ." (Benson 2003). In addition to identification of the party's base voters, people who are not active in politics but might lean toward one party can be discovered. One result is that voters can be identified who would be missed by previous software programs, either because their demographic profile may have contradictory characteristics or because they see themselves as nonpartisan.

Both parties see the strategy of gathering information through data mining as paralleling in some respects, the "retail politics" of the era before television ads blanketed the airwaves. In that era, the precinct workers were the foot soldiers who went door to door and knew the district best. Ken Mehlman, chair of the RNC in 2004, called the current strategy "neighbor-to-neighbor" campaigning (Republican National Committee 2007). While granting that the current system does have some parallels with the past, microtargeting has several advantages. Party supporters can be identified more accurately, potential supporters can be uncovered, and individualized messages can be produced. Microtargeting can save campaigns precious dollars to be used for other purposes.

While party leaders may see only the positive aspects of data mining and microtargeting, the normative questions posed by Voter Vault and DataMart deserve attention as well. In gathering such detailed information on individuals, do these programs invade privacy, or perhaps even limit the public dialogue between voters and the candidates and thereby curtail the ability of democratic government to deliver on its promises?

Civil liberties organizations have expressed alarm about the loss of privacy and the potential abuses of government agencies involved in data mining operations, but only a few organizations focusing on privacy issues such as the Electronic Privacy Information Center and the Privacy Rights Clearinghouse have expressed concerns about data gathering by political parties. Privacy rights advocates generally acknowledge that while law enforcement agencies have legal limits on the kind of data that can be collected, political parties are not subject to the same limitations. Still, the parties do risk the potential of a negative response from individuals who may feel that a highly targeted political appeal may invade their sense of privacy.

The power of microtargeting also raises a broader concern about its effects on the democratic process. This concern stems from the sense that this technology could diminish rather than enhance the dialogue between candidates and the voters. Such highly individualized communications might result in a series of appeals to each potential voter based on that person's individual concerns rather than developing an appealing collective vision. "The nightmare vision means that the public debates lack content, and the real election happens in the privacy of these mailings. The candidate knows everything about the voter, but the media and the public know nothing about what the candidate really believes. It is, in effect, a nearly perfect perversion of the political process" (Gertner 2004, 47). A similar view is expressed by Beth Givens, director of the Privacy Rights Clearinghouse: "Think about the possibilities for abuse, for manipulation—democracy suffers when you tailor your message 12 different ways depending on who you want to reach out to" (Benson 2003). If voters are segmented into so many categories that a party can, in effect, take multiple different stands on an issue, how can the party have an effective legislative strategy, much less deliver on its election promises? Would frustrated voters decrease voter participation in the future?

Despite such concerns, campaign experts in both political parties have not lost sleep over issues of voter privacy or effective governing and instead have focused on the task of making sure that the citizens identified by the software do make it to the polls.

Both parties have sought to use their databases to assist with their voter mobilization efforts. Under the leadership of Karl Rove and Ken Mehlman, the Republican party developed a sophisticated GOTV plan. This "72-hour plan" combined the use of high-tech microtargeting with volunteers to contact voters by phone or go door to door. This strategy relied upon volunteers from states that were not competitive to go to battleground states where a presidential election or control of Congress might be decided. Party officials and political consultants believe that intensive voter mobilization efforts can change election outcomes. The difficulty however, is separating the impact of the volunteers from all the other factors influencing the election. Supporters of the concept point to a 2006 special election in California. The resignation from his House seat and imprisonment of Republican Randy "Duke" Cunningham required voters in his San Diego–area district to choose a replacement. Democrats relished the opportunity to focus on a Republican "culture of corruption." Four days before the election, more Democratic absentee ballots were turned in than by Republicans. Voter Vault was searched for sympathetic GOP voters who requested absentee ballots but had not yet submitted them. Then, the seventy-two hour strategy began as activists poured into the district. By election day, the GOP secured ten thousand more Republicans than Democrats voting absentee. Not only did a Republican lobbyist win the election, but the Democratic nominee's vote count was only slightly better than that of presidential candidate John Kerry two years earlier (Wallsten and Hamburger 2006).

With the success of Republican GOTV efforts in the 2002 and 2004 elections,

Democrats sought to match GOP efforts (Chaddock 2006a). Within the Democratic party, however, there was considerable debate over whether GOTV efforts ought to be modeled after the GOP strategy of focusing resources on key states or as part of a broader strategy of building party capacity as advocated by DNC chair Howard Dean (Bai 2006; Chaddock 2006a). After the Democrat's election triumph of 2006, Dean contended that his approach, known as the "50 State Strategy," had forced Republicans to spend resources in districts that the GOP usually considered to be safe, leaving fewer funds to pour into the heavily contested districts (Shepard 2007). Critics within the Democratic party downplayed Dean's role, contending that in an environment where voters were concerned about an ongoing war, a slowing economy, and wage increases that barely kept up with inflation, an increase in Democratic seats was to be expected. In truth, one election cycle is not sufficient to offer a definitive evaluation and the outcome of this debate will be decided by future election results.

Conclusion: A New Balance for Parties and Campaign

In this chapter we have examined the changing nature of campaigns and the role that political parties play. For many years in American politics, political parties dominated candidates' campaigns. By the 1950s, however, campaigns had become increasingly candidate-centered, and many candidates were able to mount independent operations, raising both the money and the personnel necessary for the campaign. Today, in keeping with their adaptation to the service party role, both major political parties tend to serve their candidates as campaign specialists. Both parties have attempted to develop stronger party organizations at the national, state, and local levels in order to be able to assist candidates with such activities as get-out-the-vote drives. As such, parties are better able to compete for

influence, with both the political consultants hired by the campaigns and with interest groups.

Most candidates today generally combine traditional methods of campaigning with newer methods. A party organization, when it is available, can be an important source of personal contact with the voters—through door knocking, canvassing, and telephoning. Consultants, too, rely on party organization when it is advantageous for their candidate. Most political consultants align themselves with one party by working exclusively for its candidates and are often available to work for the party organization itself or for traditionally supportive interest groups.

Television remains the candidates' preferred medium of communication. Despite a decrease in the number of citizens who use television as their primary source of information, candidates have increased the amount of spending on television in recent elections. While newspaper readers are better educated and tend to retain information better, campaigns are rightly concerned about using newspapers to communicate their message given the declining number of regular readers and less time spent reading newspapers. For most Americans, the Internet is a supplemental source of news and political information, rather than a revolutionary means of increasing the public's level of information and political participation. For a smaller group of online activists, however, the Internet serves as a vehicle for creative political participation that can have a greater impact on public opinion than their numbers suggest.

Negative campaigns continue to constitute a sizable portion of political advertising. Negative campaigning may be viewed as the advertising that citizens "love to hate" because at the same time that people denounce negative advertising, they also rely on it to evaluate the worst that can be said about a candidate. Whether tactics such as negative campaigning have harmful influences on American democracy, for example by reducing citizen participation in politics, remains the source of a lively debate among election observers.

In the tumultuous relationship between the media and contestants for public office, candidates often seek to bypass journalists and present their messages more directly to the public, whether by well-established techniques such as a relentless focus on the campaign's "message of the day" or by using new technology such as Internet blogs. Despite the efforts of candidates to exert ever more control over their campaign environment, American campaigns are becoming more difficult to control. Interest groups have come to provide substantial competition for parties because groups have also mastered these new technologies in order to raise substantial amounts of money, contact voters, and directly influence Washington politics. Clearly, the present is an uncomfortable period of transition for candidates, political parties, and professionals in campaign politics.

CHAPTER 8

Interest Group Politics

Building Campaign Power on Organizational Strength

In this chapter, we turn our attention to the nature of interest groups in American politics. Along with parties and candidates, some interest groups have become significant actors in American political campaigns. While some interest groups are actively involved in campaigns, other groups do not—indeed, legally cannot—become involved in campaigns. In order to understand why some groups can and do take part in election or advocacy campaigns, we first need to understand what interest groups are and what they do. In this chapter, we examine the identity, resources, leadership, and other attributes of interest groups that help us understand how these organizational characteristics fuel the political activities that affect public policy decision making.

Let us begin with some definitions. Over the years, interest groups have been called trusts, vested interests, special interests, single interest groups, and pressure groups. These names carry certain unsavory connotations; even the more neutral term "lobby" has some negative baggage. We define political interest groups as groups based on one or more shared attitudes and making political claims on other groups or organizations in the society (Truman 1971). From this definition come two characteristics that are important to our understanding of interest group politics. First, groups are composed of individuals (or organizations) who share some common characteristics and interests. Second, some groups choose to become involved in the political process and seek to have an impact on public policy.

Social and political movements that seek social change but have not formed into lasting organizations may be called pre-interest groups. Social movements arise from the unfulfilled demands of a group of people and are persistent, organized expressions of collective behavior differing from fads, riots, or panics. Herbert Blumer defines social movements as developing by "acquiring organization and form, a body of customs and traditions, established leadership, an enduring division of labor, social rules and social values" (1951, 199). Some social movements may evolve into political interest groups with a well-defined membership, regular funding, permanent staff, and knowledge of how to operate within the political system. Freeman (1983) views social action in terms of a continuum from contagious spontaneity and lack of structure (a crowd or a riot), to social movements having some structure, to well-organized interest groups. Movements may have elaborate ideologies that argue their political agendas, and they often rely on unorthodox politics to advance their cause. Normal politics does not offer an effective set of tactics for movements. The postwar era has seen several movements, including the civil rights movement, the women's rights movement, the antiwar movement, the antinuclear weapons and antinuclear power movement, the abortion rights movement (both for and against), animal and children's rights, and environmentalist concerns. Failed movements gradually disappear; successful movements often evolve into powerful interest groups.

Interest groups interact with political parties but are very different types of political organizations. Both parties and interest groups operate as communication conduits between citizens and government; parties seek to capture government, whereas interest groups want government to give them certain governmental policies. Parties live for elections, are highly regulated by state laws, and are broad-based coalitions of individuals who want to win elections. Interest groups want policy outcomes and are the least regulated organizations in the nation.

Not all potential interest groups exist at any given moment. So-called potential groups are groups of people who are not organized, and many are not effectively represented, for example, children. There are several organizations that claim to represent children in the political process and hundreds, if not thousands, of groups that may at one time or another purport to represent the interests of children. The reality is that when the interests of children come into conflict with other established interests in our society, the lobbying power of children is far weaker. All is not lost, however, for many potential groups. Sometimes circumstances come into being that allow their interests to become well represented in the political process. Prior to the 1960s, senior citizens were largely underrepresented but now can select among a number of organizations, including the National Council of Senior Citizens (NCSC) and the American Association of Retired Persons (AARP), the nation's largest interest group in terms of membership numbers. AARP went from 1 million members in 1967 to more than 35 million members today. Another group that

was largely underrepresented in the 1960s consisted of fundamentalist, "born again" Christians. The Moral Majority was founded by Jerry Falwell and claimed hundreds of thousands of members and millions of dollars in revenue before it disappeared in the late 1980s. Another fundamentalist "entrepreneur," Pat Robertson, created the Christian Coalition, which became a major player in Republican and conservative politics during the Reagan administration. Today the Christian Coalition and other similar organizations represent the political agenda for many people. The fundamentalist Christian Right could become organized in such numbers (a possible 30 to 60 million people) that it might surpass even the senior citizen's lobby.

Lately, many journalists have divided political interest groups into two broad types: self-oriented groups and public interest groups. Self-oriented groups seek to achieve some policy goal that will directly benefit their own membership. These are the "selfish" groups and are viewed by journalists as not being particularly interested in the impact of their political agenda on the broader public. Public interest groups (PIGs) pursue goals that may not benefit their membership directly but will be enjoyed by the general public. Many such groups seek policies that will never specifically benefit their membership. A classic example is liberal group of highly educated professionals who seek to abolish the death penalty in criminal cases. Other public interest groups such as Common Cause, Ralph Nader's consumer organization, and many environmentalist groups pursue objectives that they believe will benefit the public in a general sense. Many interest groups now claim to be public interest groups, but, in reality, many of these groups are really self-oriented in their political goals and their funding sources.

James Madison was one of the first to write about interest groups and their effect on American politics. Madison's essay in *The Federalist Papers,* no. 10, noted his concern about the negative influence of groups (or as he called them "factions"). Madison's factions were pre-interest groups characterized by their temporary nature, but his concerns apply easily to contemporary interest group politics. He defined factions in a negative way by arguing that they were "adverse to the rights of citizens or . . . the interests of the community." No matter how Madison felt about these factions, he recognized that they were inherent to the nature of a democracy and impossible to eliminate. What Madison tried to do was to create in the new federal government's Constitution a set of mechanisms that could control the negative effects of factions. One such mechanism was a republican form of government in which no single faction could control political decision making.

Another early political analyst was Alexis de Tocqueville, a French citizen who wrote of Americans' tendency to join together in interest groups when participating in domestic politics, which differed from the style of politics found in Europe at that time. "Whenever at the head of some new undertaking you see government in France, or a man of rank in England, in the United States you will be sure to find an association." He also concluded that "in no country in the world has the principle of association been more successfully used, or applied to a greater multitude of objects, than in America" (de Tocqueville [1835–1836] 1956). Studies by political scientists in the post–World War II era concluded that this tendency persisted. Compared to citizens in other selected democracies such as Britain, Germany, Italy, and Mexico, Americans were more likely to have interest group memberships and use them for political activities (Almond and Verba 1963).

The exact number of interest groups operating in the United States is unknown. On the national level, the *Encyclopedia of Associations* lists more than twenty-two thousand national nonprofit organizations. The largest category of groups is, as expected, business groups (17 percent). Political groups had the greatest growth in terms of numbers of new groups formed since 1980. Business, agricultural, environmentalist, social welfare, health, educational, cultural groups, and hobby groups have all added five hundred or more new groups since 1980. Labor unions and Greek letter societies are the only two categories that lost numbers. It should be noted that the summary of national groups includes many organizations that never become actively involved in normal patterns of politics. How many of the twenty-two thousand-plus groups are frequently active is simply unknown at this time.

A major change in the American interest group pattern has been the continuing trend among groups to move their headquarters to Washington, DC. Jack Walker's (1983) sample of national-level interest groups discovered that half of the groups had been founded since 1945 and that the nation's capital was the home of most of them. In 1960, Washington was home for 67 percent of the nation's voluntary associations; by 1980 it was over 88 percent (Walker 1983). By 1995, the National Trade and Professional Associations of the United States counted seventy-four hundred national associations with headquarters in Washington, DC ("A Nation" 1995). A walk around the northwest quadrant of that city would reveal building after building of offices for one to dozens of groups or associations.

A clearer picture is emerging of the number of groups on the state level as a result of lobby registration laws that various states have enacted, especially California. One interesting finding is the numerical domination of business, banks, and economic groups among the state-level registrants. The number of local-level groups is impossible to determine because of the ephemeral nature of many of them. Many deal with specific local problems and may be founded and dissolved within the same calendar year. Finally, there are almost no reporting requirements for local-level groups in the United States. Despite these problems, it has been estimated that more than two hundred thousand different organizations exist on the state and local levels of American politics.

What Causes Interest Groups to Form?

Political interest groups appear in American history in waves, specifically four major "waves" (Truman 1971, 30). The first of these waves began in the period between 1830 and 1860, when the first great national organizations were created, such as the Grange farm group. The second wave began in the 1880s when many new national groups emerged from the industrialization process, such as the American Federation of Labor. The third wave occurred during the 1900–1920 period when a large number of powerful organizations were founded, including the U.S. Chamber of Commerce, the American Medical Association, the NAACP, the American Farm Bureau, and the American Cancer Society. Finally, the fourth wave began in the 1960s with the explosion of many specialized groups reflecting the growing micro-nature of interest groups in recent decades. Among the groups founded in the 1960s were environmental groups such as the World Wildlife Fund and Friends of the Earth, civil rights groups such as the National Council of La Raza, and policy advocates such as the National Taxpayers Union.

What forces are necessary for such large numbers of interest groups to be created in certain decades and not others? Wilson (1995) suggests that communications revolutions have been a major factor. In most of these eras, new communication technologies facilitated the ability of groups to seek new members and connect them to politics. Telegraphs, telephones, railroads, radio, national magazines, television, computers, faxes, and the Internet make such communications easier. Another important factor has been the changing role of government, particularly its attempt to regulate business activity, which forced businesses to organize to protect themselves. Other factors include the increasing division of labor, particularly in economic sectors, and the growing heterogeneity of the American population. Wilson also argues that

periods of great social unrest and social movements are also associated with periods of interest group growth.

Truman (1971) and Salisbury (1969) have offered a "disturbance theory," suggesting that interest groups arise from the increased complexity of society and a systemic drive to achieve equilibrium. As society inevitably becomes more complex and specialized, more specialized groups and interests form associations to articulate their needs (Salisbury 1969). Until recent decades, a broad umbrella organization such as the National Association of Broadcasters could effectively represent the general interests of the communications industry, but dozens of spin-off organizations have emerged to represent the many new technologies, such as cable and satellite television and Internet interests. A second version of this theoretical perspective suggests that disturbances undermine the political power relationships among various sectors of society, which are "disturbed" or altered by various forces, including technical innovation, international events, societal changes, new legislation, governmental decisions, the formation of new interest groups, and business cycles. The disturbance creates new advantaged and disadvantaged groups; the latter may seek to restore equilibrium by organizing in an effort to convert their immobilized resources into political influence. For example, groups representing men emerged in the 1990s to counter various women's groups such as the National Organization of Women, which had become a powerful lobbying force affecting many political, social, and economic issues as well as laws impacting employment, marriage, and many other issues.

Neither perspective of the disturbance theory offers a complete explanation of how groups are created. The equilibrium theory suggests a cyclical pattern of membership in groups; although this was true of agricultural groups and labor unions, it was not the case for professional or technical associations. Specialization does not explain why agricultural groups were almost all general farm organizations, such as the Grange or Farm Union, and does not explain why specialist crop associations are relatively modern. So we have to look to another theory. Salisbury offers another theory to explain group formation, entrepreneurial theory (or exchange theory), which suggests that the organizer is the key element in terms of why new groups are formed at a given moment of history (Salisbury 1969). Consumer and environmentalist groups are often the products of such entrepreneurs.

Political Science and Group Theory

The focus on interest groups as a part of political science began in the first decade of the twentieth century. Arthur F. Bentley's (1949) book *The Process of Government*, originally published in 1908, was the first major work to use groups as a central theme for understanding American politics. Previous organizing structures had been based on the Constitution or how public laws were made in governmental institutions. Bentley argued that groups were the key unit for studying American society and politics. In fact, Bentley concluded that groups explained American politics in its entirety. With David Truman's (1971) *The Governmental Process,* published after World War II, political science rediscovered Bentley's focus on groups. At that time social science, in general, was searching for a theory to explain many of the events of World War II in a different, modern way. Truman's group focus was positive, portraying groups as essential elements of a modern democracy. Earl Latham's (1952) *The Group Basis of Politics* argued that groups struggled in legislatures and that the balance of power among the various participating groups was reflected in the laws enacted or killed. Latham introduced the concept of governmental units as interest groups themselves, and subsequent researchers have broadened the concept of interest group politics to include the tens of thousands of American governments not only

as sites for interest group battles but as demanding interest themselves.

From these early works on group theory emerged two broad theories that tried to explain political power in American society in a group framework. Elitist theorists such as E. E. Schattschneider and C. Wright Mills argued that a relatively small elite controlled politics in the United States and manipulated the important decisions. Schattschneider (1975) pointed to an "upper-class bias" of business domination in our American political system. In *The Power Elite,* C. Wright Mills (1956) also perceived a small group of elites controlling real power in America. The second theory, pluralist theory, began with Robert Dahl's (1961) *Who Governs?* Pluralist theory emphasizes the importance of groups in policy decision making. Dahl saw power not concentrated in the hands of the elite but in a complex assortment of groups and governmental officials and structures. Dahl's image of political power crossed social and economic class lines and was moderated by a pattern of multiple memberships, which made for broader participation in the decision-making processes. This pluralist theory came to be (and still is) the dominant model in political science for explaining the nature of American political power. Rational choice theory from economics has also become an important model used in researching interest group politics. The most important work from this perspective was Mancur Olson's (1965) *The Logic of Collective Action,* which has driven much of the research in recent decades on internal group politics, leadership, and membership.

Leadership and Interest Group Power

High-quality leadership is an essential ingredient in the long-term success of a lobbying organization. Many organizational failures can be attributed to the crucial problem of inept leadership. Most interest group leaders are manager-lobbyists lacking charismatic or entrepreneurial skills. These leaders have to manage a budget and a staff and organize for an occasional lobbying victory or two.

The reality of many complex organizations is that paid staff members dominate the elected leadership. Some associations have huge staffs numbering hundreds of people and filling floors of offices in major Washington, DC, buildings. The National Rifle Association (NRA) and AARP have their own impressive buildings. The NRA's Washington staff includes nearly five hundred people, and the national Chamber of Commerce has more than twelve hundred employees in its Washington, DC, office, including eleven lobbyists and about forty persons who support them with research.

Staff members can have an important impact on an organization's policies and lobbying strategies. Robert Michel's (1962) "iron law of oligarchy" argues that the larger the organization, generally the larger and more specialized the staff. As an organization becomes better established, it becomes more conservative in its policies and tactics as it seeks organizational security. The staff is not selected from the general membership, since expertise not found among the membership is required for many staff jobs. Michel suggests that group-elected leadership, the general membership, and the staff often are driven by different motivations and goals and that this may cause serious problems in many organizations. One charge often heard in these situations is that the leadership has lost touch with the membership. Recent cases of this have occurred in the labor movement and the NRA. In the AFL-CIO, George Meany, a former plumber, was the longtime leader. Meany's successor, however, was Lane Kirkland, a graduate of Georgetown University's School of Foreign Affairs and the U.S. Merchant Marine Academy. Under Kirkland, the AFL-CIO's secretary-treasurer, chief organizer, and head lobbyist were all lawyers. Kirkland was replaced as AFL-CIO president in 1995 by John Sweeney, president of the Service Employees union, and Linda Chavez-Thompson became secretary-treasurer. Sweeney purged the AFL-CIO board and appointed new members so that twenty of its fifty-seven members were female, black, or Hispanic. Sweeney was only the fifth person to be president of the AFL-CIO dating back to 1881 (Victor 1995).

Is the staff of a large organization always more conservative and concerned about security than the general membership? Or, conversely, does a large organization have a staff that is more committed to the political goals of the organization than is the membership? The evidence is mixed, and good examples of each can be presented. The staff of the National Council of Churches (NCC) has been far more radical in its support for guerilla wars and social revolution in Africa and welfare and social policy reforms than its generally conservative membership. One explanation for this is the very low pay many NCC staff members receive: part of their compensation is paid in the form of policy actions. The huge and relatively low-paid AFL-CIO staff, headquartered in Washington, DC, is more liberal than the increasingly conservative rank-and-file union member, and the American Civil Liberties Union's (ACLU) leadership and staff much more liberal than its average member. Another explanation for this pattern is that maintenance of the rank-and-file membership and organization is done at the grassroots level, leaving the national level relatively free to pursue its own politics. The NRA, on the other hand, has been waging a civil war for decades, its ideologically hardcore member-zealots constantly attacking the staff for being too cautious and conservative in its defense of the Second Amendment and gun rights. Some lobbies (e.g., the ones mentioned above) are well organized and well off, a majority of lobbies have small budgets and very small staffs (Wilson 1995, 224). Margaret Fisk, editor of the massive *Encyclopedia of Associations,* warns individuals interested in corresponding with the listed voluntary associations that many are essentially one-person operations (*Encyclopedia of Associations* 1996, 1140). Many public interest groups are very small operations. Berry (1977) discovered that only half the public interest groups he studied had one or more full-time staff members.

The degree of democracy in the leadership selection and policymaking of interest groups can impact their ability to achieve their political goals. Since a democratic process is almost always regarded as preferable in American politics, nearly every interest group must at least try to portray itself as democratic. This does not mean that all groups are democratic. The Teamsters Union is a classic example of non-democratic leadership-selection processes. Other interest groups, such as Common Cause, tend to be democratic in their leadership-selection processes and policy decision making largely because it seems to be important to the membership. Both the League of Women Voters and the American Civil Liberties Union provide for membership input into the organization's policy agenda.

Regimes often experience crises as they make a transition from one political leader to another, and so do interest groups. Just as Yugoslavia collapsed following the death of longtime leader Josip Tito, the United Mine Workers never recovered from the death of its great leader, John L. Lewis. Successor after successor was unable to provide honest, effective leadership, and the union continued to deteriorate. Of course, there are many groups that have not only survived leadership successions but have prospered. Common Cause survived the leadership crisis that occurred when its founder, John Gardner, retired in 1977. Successors Nan Waterman, Archibald Cox, Fred Wertheimer, and Ann McBride provided more than adequate leadership, and the organization regained its former levels of influence.

Interest groups of all types may be vulnerable to leadership problems. But in terms of external threats, the purposive groups are the most vulnerable of all. Purposive groups are particularly vulnerable to changes in the political environment because often they cannot survive either success or failures. If a group is seeking to raise highway speed limits, what happens to the group after the government allows states to raise their speed limits to any level they choose? If a group supports welfare reform and it happens, what happens to the group? If a group is an environmental group that opposes a particular threat to the environment and the group is unable to stop it, can the group convince the membership to support it if it chooses a new cause?

Sometimes, a group can turn a failure into an internal, group-maintenance success. Many of the liberal groups that attempted to keep Clarence Thomas off the Supreme Court were able to use the defeat in their direct mail solicitation campaigns and gain new members and money for future campaigns. An earlier successful campaign that defeated the Robert Bork nomination to the Supreme Court brought millions of dollars and hundreds of thousands of new members to liberal groups.

A group's leadership must decide how the group is to be structured. Key to this decision is matching the group's resources, including membership, to its political objectives and lobbying goals. The group may choose between a federated structure and a unitary structure. A federated association is an organization made up of other organizations. The National Association of Manufacturers includes thirteen thousand member companies. The National Association of Broadcasters comprises many corporations and the major television networks. Many trade associations have corporations as their major members. Finally, almost all the coalitions that are created for a specific issue battle are largely composed of constituent companies, interest groups, and trade associations. Federations by their very design usually have members on the local level and are often organized by "federating" local organizations into a national group with headquarters in Washington, DC. As a result of this organization on the state and local level, federated groups have the ability to do grassroots lobbying on their own.

A unitary group locates its organization in Washington, DC, and has little, if any, organization on state and local levels. Some groups have state and local organizations, but they have no power and simply exist for the convenience of the national group. Common Cause started out as a purely unitary group and then added state chapters. It gave those chapters some independence to make their own policy decisions with national-level guidance after the local activists demanded more self-determination.

Federated associations are generally more effective in grassroots lobbying efforts, but they are also much more difficult to coordinate and lead in cohesive national campaigns. Unitary organizations, as a result of their national-level organization, are more effective in Washington lobbying because they can speak with a single voice, but they have limited grassroots capability unless they pay for it (Hall 1969, 136–140).

An important resource for many interest groups is the proportion of potential members who are enrolled as members in the group. A high proportion gives the group legitimacy as the "spokesperson" for the interest. A low proportion, or many groups having a fraction of the membership pool, calls into question the credibility of a group's claim to represent the interest. American interest groups represent a smaller proportion of the potential membership compared to interest groups in Europe, where large umbrella groups are common. Labor unions now represent less than 15 percent of the nonfarm working force. The American Medical Association represents only 36 percent of the five hundred thousand American physicians; the American Bar Association, only 45 percent of the nation's lawyers; and the American Association of University Professors, less than 20 percent of professors. The three major veterans' organizations (the American Legion, Disabled American Veterans, and Veterans of Foreign Wars) only represent one-sixth of the nation's 28 million veterans. Consequently, it is difficult for many of these "peak associa-

tions" to speak as true representatives of given interest sectors.

Although having high proportions of potential memberships is an asset for an interest group, in today's world it is also important for a group's survival to establish its niche and unique benefit in competition with other groups. Groups seek to develop autonomy. In the electric power industry, the various groups concentrate on statistics, lobbying, technical information on the industry, public relations, and media campaigns (Wilson 1995, 263).

A famous California politician, Jesse Unruh, once said that "money is the mother's milk of politics," and that certainly is true for interest group politics. Money is the most convertible of all resources in that it can buy leadership, technology, and even "volunteers." Yet the group with the most money does not always win. Some of the richest and most powerful interest groups (e.g., the AFL-CIO and the NRA) have lost important lobbying battles in recent years against opposition with much less money.

Another group characteristic that can greatly assist it in acquiring financial resources is tax-exempt status. The so-called 501(c)(4) of the Internal Revenue code qualifying it for income tax exemption is given to a group if it operates exclusively to promote the social welfare of the country and is engaged in substantial lobbying. However, individual contributions to 501(c)(4) groups are not deductible. Groups such as the National Right to Life and the National Taxpayers Union fall under this provision. Another important part of the IRS code to interest groups is Section 501(c)(3), which provides for tax-exempt status and the deductibility of individual donations if substantial lobbying is not performed. The 501(c)(3) groups (charitable) cannot legally lobby Congress but may advocate positions before administrative agencies and may give Congress information on pending legislation. The Heritage Foundation and the Religious Roundtable are 501(c)(3) groups. An interest group's 501 status can change if the group gets too involved in politics and the government decides to force it to follow the restrictions of its tax status. The Sierra Club got much more involved in lobbying and established the Sierra Club Foundation to allow it to generate additional income (Berry 1984, 46). The 527 groups, discussed in the next chapter, are essentially issue advocates and can buy unlimited amounts of TV commercials attacking various candidates or supporting them because of their positions on a given issue such as abortion. The 527s need only to report to the IRS various pieces of financial information, and the Federal Election Commission has very little control over them.

The United Farm Workers (UFW) has received millions of dollars in federal grants in recent decades, which it used to fund UFW programs in the areas of English-language instruction, education and retraining programs, and work surveys. Major veterans' groups are given free government office space in fifty-eight regional Veteran's Administration centers around the nation. Many interest groups receive large portions of their budgets in subsidies or grants from more established groups. Labor unions have been the financial "godfathers" of many of the new left groups as have various conservative foundations and research think tanks such as the Heritage Foundation for the right.

The National Association for the Advancement of Colored People (NAACP) has suffered through one leadership crisis after another since the 1960s. In 1994, the very survival of the oldest civil rights group in the nation came into question. Headquarters staff was cut by a third and several regional offices were closed. The budget was cut nearly in half, and the Ford Foundation refused to release a $250,000 grant to the NAACP while the leadership was in flux. In 1996, the NAACP named Kweisi Mfume, a former Maryland congressman and chair of the Congressional Black Caucus, to be the new president. Gradually, the organization began to recover and became more attractive to foundations while improving its financial situation and its tattered reputation. Mfume was suc-

ceeded by a successful businessman, Bruce Gordon, who resigned in 2007 after conflicts with the NAACP's board of directors (Sullivan and Glaude 2007).

Internal Organizational Strength and Lobbying Power

Lobbying power is largely based an interest group's characteristics and resources such as membership, formal organization, leadership, and the staff. Membership is the foundation of any organization. Every organization is both empowered and restricted by its membership. Middle-class organizations such as Common Cause gain lobbying power from the willingness of its membership to give it money for lobbying and to volunteer as lobbyists themselves on occasion. Such a middle-class membership base has high levels of personal efficacy and the ego strength, plus a good knowledge of the political process and a sense of obligation that encourages them to participate in politics. Groups with large numbers of lower-class members, such as welfare rights groups, tend to have many members who lack the aforementioned psychological characteristics and thus do not tend to participate to the same extent as their middle-class counterparts.

People join interest groups for a variety of reasons. Mancur Olson (1965) suggested in his *The Logic of Collective Action* that it was irrational (in an economic sense) for people to join an interest group unless one of several specific conditions existed: (1) coercion, or being forced to join; (2) the small size of the group means that the addition of even one more member may significantly affect its chances of success; (3) possessing extraordinary resources that strongly enhance the group's likelihood of achieving its goal; and (4) the benefits offered by the group exceed the cost of joining it. Salisbury (1969) and Wilson (1995) have used exchange theory to study people's reasons for joining interest groups. Exchange theory substitutes the idea of a businessperson and a customer for the leader-follower relationship. The leadership provides the "capital" or benefits that are offered to potential members. These benefits can be either selective or collective in nature. Selective benefits may be obtained only by those who are members of the organization. The members of an exclusive country club are the only ones who can use the amenities of the club and golf course in exchange for large amounts of money they have paid for the right. Collective benefits are available to all persons regardless of group membership. Usually so-called public interest groups seeking goals such as clean politics or clean air cannot restrict the benefits it achieves to its own members.

The three types of benefits are material, purposive, and solidary. Material benefits are items or services that have monetary value. These may include product discounts and political advantages that eventually convert into economic advantages. Some of the most common material benefits offered by many organizations are access to low-priced group insurance or charter air travel. Members of the AARP have access to low-cost home delivery of prescription drugs.

Purposive benefits usually tend to be collective in nature. They are the result of cause-related activities and include such things as clean air or politics or a prohibition of the death penalty. A general requirement for purposive benefits is that they not benefit the individual members of a group directly. Consequently, these benefits are almost always collective, since it is nearly impossible to restrict them to the formal membership.

Solidary benefits are defined as psychological rewards that come from associating with certain individuals. Collective solidary incentives are derived from the congeniality and the social attractiveness of the group. Many social groups, such as country clubs, ethnic groups, or fraternal groups, have restrictive memberships that focus primarily on social activities. Selective solidary benefits are given to specific individuals in the form of special honors or offices. Organizations that rely primarily on solidary incentives to attract and maintain membership frequently use selective benefits to encourage additional contributions from members. Some groups have established a fantastic hierarchy of exalted titles to artificially enhance the status of their members (for example, leaders of the Ku Klux Klan are known as "Grand Wizards").

The ideal interest group would combine all three benefit types to reinforce the recruitment and retention of members. Many groups are forced to rely more on one type of benefit than another, which may limit the group's political activities. Organizations that rely on material incentives have the greatest freedom of political action as long as the membership is happy with the benefits received. The great freedom of labor unions to support the Democratic party in elections despite the fact that many union members vote Republican is largely a function of the benefits (e.g., job security and personal prosperity) that many of their members enjoy. Data from the American National Election Studies reveal that 39 percent of people in labor households in 2000 and 36 percent in 2004 voted for the Republican presidential candidates. Material benefits are seldom effective in encouraging sacrifice by members. Solidary incentives must be selective to be effective. Prestige country clubs can accomplish this by stringent screening processes and high dues. Solidary benefits may also be distributed selectively within an organization to motivate extraordinary membership contributions. But groups relying on solidary benefits must avoid politics, which can be very disruptive to the social environment of the group.

Purposive organizations by their nature and benefit package can be very unstable because they rely on the attractiveness of "the cause" or "the goal" to attract or maintain their membership. When the group fails to achieve the goal or cause, the group is in danger unless it can alter members' perspectives and have them focus on a new cause. Even successful purposive groups are in danger, since once the cause is won, why would the members continue to belong to the group? Groups that survive such successes are able to switch to a new cause and build on their past success. Although the ideal situation for an organization is to have a mixture of the three types of benefits, interest groups that last long enough to become part of the establishment generally discover that material benefits are the most important.

Political scientist John Mark Hansen (1985) argues that a group must be subsidized to be organized. Economic groups or trade associations are relatively easy to organize and tend to be subsidized by their industries or by the government. Some groups, such as consumer and environmentalist groups, have proven to be difficult to subsidize and must rely on support from charities, foundations, and governments (Hansen 1985). In recent years, conservative foundations or sources of money have supported many of the new conservative groups that have emerged to change the style of American politics. Richard Mellon Scaife has been a major financial contributor to as many as twenty-five of these new conservative political groups, including the Heritage Foundation and Americans for Effective Law Enforcement (Rothmeyer 1981). On the liberal side, labor unions have been major sources of support for liberal public interest groups. Investigations into campaign finance practices after the 1996 election brought to light this pattern of funding when it was discovered that for years a reform group, Citizen Action, had been taking money from labor unions for its normal annual budgets.

Let us look at a major interest group and see how all these pieces fit together. The AARP, with more than 35 million members, is the largest interest group in America. Yearly dues are low and in return members receive the AARP magazine, a monthly newsletter, low-cost pharmacy services, dis-

counts at hotels and car rental agencies, special insurance programs, and access to a mutual fund. But its lobbying operation on issues important to senior citizens has been effective for a much longer time. It has computerized age files on nearly everyone in the nation and mails an invitation to join the organization to everyone shortly before his or her fiftieth birthday. AARP calls the membership application "a certificate of admission" and lists fifteen membership benefits including representation in Washington, DC. However, new benefits have been added in terms of solidary appeals such as AARP Online—where members can chat with other members—volunteer opportunities through the AARP Volunteer Talent Bank, and four thousand local chapters where "members can meet new people."

The Nature of Interest Group Membership in the United States

Not all Americans play the interest group game in the same proportions. According to Schattschneider (1975), our interest group system has an "upper-class bias," but in reality, it is heavily dominated by the middle class. The middle class has sufficient income and education to facilitate their interest group activities. A majority of the lowest economic class do not belong to any organization (except maybe religious groups). According to data from the 2004 General Social Survey, only 24 percent of people in the lowest income category belonged to two or more groups, whereas 45 percent of people in the highest income category belonged to multiple groups.

The reasons behind this pattern are quite simple. The richest people can afford to belong to more organizations because they have more resources such as money, time, distant time horizons, personal political efficacy, social status, and desire. The lowest socioeconomic classes do not seem to have these characteristics in the same proportions as the highest. Even the aspect of money would seem to confirm this pattern. Many lower-income people belong to a church that accepts voluntary contributions as opposed to an interest group that mandates dues. The problem for potential entrepreneurs of groups aimed at the lower social economic classes is constructing an attractive set of benefits. Immediate monetary benefits might get such a person into the organization, but how does the leadership keep the member in the group over time? Consequently, many such groups start and then fail (Wilson 1995). Many groups that represent the interests of the lower classes tend to be started by middle- and upper-class leaders and are often dominated by these groups in terms of membership as well (Piven and Cloward 1977, 295–313).

Perhaps the classic example of a lower-class group that has been relatively successful is the United Farm Workers (UFW), organized by the late Cesar Chavez and composed of California's Mexican-American farm workers. The charismatic Chavez was very effective in leading the movement but proved to be much less effective as an interest group administrator. It is still not clear that the UFW will survive as an interest group. The UFW illustrates well the problems associated with lower socioeconomic class interest groups.

Churches and religious organizations are the most frequently joined voluntary associations in the United States. American religious organizations have been involved in politics in one manner or another throughout our history. Usually, such involvement took the form of periodic crusades against some vice such as alcohol, slavery, gambling, war, drugs, or sexuality issues. Since the mid–1960s, however, some churches have become more active in the lobbying process and consequently more significant to political scientists as political organizations.

Many religious organizations had become involved in the civil rights revolution of the 1960s and 1970s, but a significant change in the pattern occurred in the 1980s as evangelical Christians joined the political process first under Jerry Falwell's Moral Majority and then the Christian Coalition sponsored by another fundamentalist minister, Pat Robertson. The Christian Coalition and other organizations such as Focus on the Family, Tradition Values Coalition, and the American Family Association have become powerful political groups. Yet, the Christian Coalition has fallen on hard times due to leadership changes and mismanagement (Cooperman and Edsall 2006).

The second and third most frequently joined association types are sports groups and school service groups such as the PTA, groups that get involved in the political process only on rare occasions. Parent-teacher associations have in recent years broadened their interests beyond the quality of education produced by local school systems to include a nationwide campaign against sex and violence on commercial television. Other types of groups, such as hobby, literary, fraternal, youth, and service groups, seldom become involved in political activities. The major organizations involved in politics that people join are labor unions, professional, veterans, political, farm, and ethnic groups.

Robert Putnam (2000) began an interesting discussion on the question of the nature of American participation in interest group politics. Putnam's book, *Bowling Alone*, begins with the observation that while more Americans are bowling than in the past, the number of bowlers who participate in leagues is down. Putnam extends this to American politics by arguing that while more Americans are able to participate in politics, fewer people are actively participating in established organizations. This phenomenon is part of a broader pattern of what Putnam sees as "civic disengagement." Putnam argues that a number of causes have contributed to this, including a greater preoccupation of Americans with their personal lives, families, careers, and hobbies. All of these time pressures have resulted in less civic engagement. People have become so busy with their personal lives that they no longer even socialize the way they used to socialize before the 1960s. Particularly hard hit have been many of the locally based social organizations such as the Elks, the Masons, and civic associations such as the League of Women Voters. Among the national organizations Putnam examined, most seemed to peak in terms of membership before 1960, and since then membership levels have declined. Without involvement in such organizations, Putnam argues democracy may be diminished when citizens fail to acquire the participatory skills needed to play the political game. Putnam suggests that about half of the decline is due to generational change and the failure of the younger generations to value such participation (2000, 284).

Critics of Putnam's argument point out that citizens are engaging in politics in new and different ways. The old way of local group activities has been replaced by new forms of participation characterized by greater involvement in advocacy groups on the national level, more volunteering in community and nonprofit activities, participation in institutions of direct democracy (such as initiatives and referenda), and a greater use of the Internet to participate in political activities (Hudson 2006, 163–165). It remains to be seen whether these new forms of political participation promote greater levels of participation among American citizens or are simply different ways to participate using more informal structures.

Lobbying Resources Derived from Membership Characteristics

Is big powerful? The groups with the largest membership may not be the most powerful actors in issue campaigns. The two largest political organizations in the United States, the 35-million-member American Associa-tion of Retired Persons (AARP) and the 13-million-member AFL-CIO, have mixed records in recent years as lobbying organizations. It has been a long time since the AFL-CIO has won a major labor lobbying battle in Congress. Such a dismal record was understandable during the anti-labor Reagan and Bush administrations during the 1980s and early 1990s, but it was almost as bad with a Democratic Congress and president in 1993–1994. A nearly complete collapse occurred after the Republicans took control of Congress in 1995. Big labor has been declining in political power because its total membership has been declining, as well as its percentage of the workforce. In pure numbers, organized labor peaked in 1975 with 22.2 million members. By 1993, 16.3 million people were union members. In 1983, 20 percent of the labor force was unionized. The slide continued after the turn of the century when, in 2006, union membership dropped by 326,000 to 15.4 million representing 12.8 percent of the nation's workers. Even worse for organized labor is the fact that only 7.4 percent of the private sector work force was unionized in 2006. In recent years, the only growth of organized labor has been in the public sector (S. Greenhouse 2007).

The AARP is so huge that it has real problems gaining a sense of direction from its membership. It cannot lobby on many issues because its membership may not be interested in a given issue or may be split between Democrats and Republicans. Thus, it is a giant without real power.

Middle-sized organizations such as the American Bar Association, American Medical Association, and Common Cause, with memberships of several hundred thousand, have been able to convert membership characteristics into successful lobbying efforts. Legal skills, medical knowledge, and middle-class commitment to reforms have driven these often quite different lobbying efforts, but it is important to remember that large numbers alone do not guarantee lobbying success. Box 8.1 describes how even a large and well-funded lobbying effort may not be successful in getting Congress to change federal law.

Sometimes it is important for a group's success to have its members in the proper geographical distribution. One reason for labor's weakness in recent decades is that its membership strength is concentrated in the Northeast and Midwest and is weak in the South and West. The South has long been the most anti-union part of the nation, and this outlook has helped the revival of the Republican party in the South. Another group with a maldistribution of membership is the ACLU, the liberal defender of the Bill of Rights. Unfortunately, in exactly those states that pose many of the most serious threats to the defense of the First Amendment (the South and Mountain West), the ACLU has its smallest memberships and fewest resources. Other groups with a more even distribution of membership, such as real estate agents, school teachers, and small businesses, are able to function well anywhere in the nation.

Even small groups may have memberships with characteristics that can be converted into successful lobbying campaigns when necessary. High respect, prestige, and status of either individual members or the general membership can be utilized in lobbying. The National Rifle Association has millions of members. But how many of them were more useful than actor Charlton Heston and his willingness to become the organization's front man in its defense of its interpretation of the Second Amendment? On the left, Jane Fonda and Robert Redford greatly aided the anti-Vietnam War and environmentalist movements, respectively. The Business Roundtable, consisting of the CEOs of America's largest corporations, is literally the nine-hundred-pound gorilla of lobbying groups. American Medical Association doctors carry significant weight in any discussions of the medical industry. The fact that they represent a well-paid profession that is willing to donate millions of dollars for lobbying campaigns gives the AMA many political options. Some organizations have developed strong positive reputations (American Cancer Society, League of Women Voters, and Planned Parenthood) among the general public. Others, such as the Tobacco Institute, have real problems with their reputation.

Many people join a collection of organizations that can be described as overlapping. They usually tend to reinforce each other and produce a more effective member. Take, for example, a Utah man who happens to be a devout Mormon as well as a conservative Republican who works for an anti-union, high-tech firm in his home state. When a political issue emerges with a conservative-liberal dimension, the overlapping memberships all move such a person to action in support of the conservative cause. A relatively small number of people join groups with differing political agendas, such as the ACLU and the Christian Coalition. People who receive conflicting messages from their different groups are "cross pressured." Such members have to decide which groups are more important and which groups can be ignored. If this determination cannot be made, the person often tries to ignore the issue that is causing the different messages.

Another important membership characteristic that may impact lobbying effectiveness is the degree of commitment held by the membership or activists concerning the organization's policy objectives. Groups with intensely committed members may have a great advantage in asking these members to participate in various types of grassroots actions and meeting a very enthusiastic response. The National Rifle Association, for example, has perhaps thirty thousand to one hundred thousand of its 3.5 million members who are very committed to defending their "gun rights." The AFL-CIO, on the other hand, has millions of members who have joined for economic benefits and do not care at all about the group's political agenda. Many union members, in fact, may strongly oppose some parts of its political agenda.

BOX 8.1 Never Bet Against the Gambling Lobby?

Just before the November 2006 elections, the Republican-controlled Congress passed a law that threatened to eliminate Internet poker and other Internet gambling, a major industry that generates about $12 billion a year and is growing rapidly. "The Unlawful Internet Gambling Enforcement Act owed its momentum at least partly to a desire by Republican leaders to eradicate the specter of corruption lingering over their party from the gambling-tinged Jack Abramoff lobbying scandal" (Vogel 2007a). In response, the poker industry organized a celebrity lobbying campaign led by poker champions such as Chris "Jesus" Ferguson and sought to build a grassroots advocacy organization called the Poker Players Alliance with a reported membership of 135,000. The casino industry's powerhouse lobby, the American Gaming Association, took a neutral position on the Internet gambling issue. But, a variety of other powerful interests supported the proposed legislation including all the professional sports leagues, the NCAA, the credit card companies, the American Bankers Association, a wide variety of conservative family oriented groups, and forty-nine of the fifty state attorneys general. Because supporters of the bill were careful to exempt thoroughbred racing and greyhound racing and the various state lotteries, even the National Association of Convenience Stores— whose members sell most of the state lottery tickets—supported the bill.

After losing the first round, the poker interests returned to Congress to seek a removal of the ban in early 2007 hoping for better luck with the new Congress with Democrats in control. This time, the emerging poker lobby took a different approach to the lobbying. Poker took a lesson from the protections that horse racing had built up over the decades and argued that online poker was not just gambling but a form of entertainment that could also contribute lots of tax money to the federal budget. The Poker Players Alliance claimed to represent more than 70 million American poker players and 23 million online poker players. The Alliance hired a public relations firm and added former U.S. Senator Alfonse D'Amato (R-New York) as the chairman. The results of the fall 2006 congressional elections were thought to be great news for the poker industry. Some of the strongest opponents to online poker had been defeated in November 2006 and the new Democratic congressional leadership came from Nevada and California, two states with strong gambling industries. Still, the Poker Alliance faced long odds in an effort to get the ban repealed outright because it was strongly supported by conservative Christian and anti-gambling groups. When it was clear that little support could be found for a complete repeal of the ban, the poker lobby shifted its short-term strategy to seeking an exemption from the ban only for poker.

Sources: Caruso (2006), McCarthy (2007), and Vogel (2007a; 2007b).

Very committed or intense members may be too much of a good thing for some organizations. They are so committed to a goal or cause that they make it very difficult for the leadership of a group to engage in discussions, compromises, or "politics." Other intensively committed members may get frustrated easily with normal politics and lobbying and may engage in violence or other forms of extreme acts to further their cause. The eco-terrorists who burned buildings at the Vail, Colorado, ski resort in 1998 represented that type of challenge to more conservative environmentalist movements. The killing of a New York medical doctor who performed abortions and the hundreds of other acts of violence against abortion clinics or their workers also pose serious problems for those who are pro-life but also nonviolent.

Conclusion: Interest Groups in American Politics

Even though no one can say for sure exactly how many interest groups exist in the United States, we do know that interest groups have played and will continue to play a vital role in American politics at the local, state, and national level. In this chapter we have discussed some basic features of interest groups in the American context—why interest groups form, the nature of group membership and leadership, and how groups use their organizational attributes for political advantage. In the next two chapters, we continue our focus on interest groups by examining first the role that interest groups play in a range of political campaigns and then the role of interest groups in lobbying.

CHAPTER 9

Interest Groups and Campaigns

From Electoral Campaigns to Advocacy Campaigns

The distance between political campaigns run largely by and for political parties and political campaigns run largely by and for interest groups was bridged in the early 1990s. The political campaign that symbolized the merging of the two types of campaigns was President Clinton's unsuccessful health care reform efforts in 1993–1994. Obviously, many important elements of modern campaigns had been used in both types of campaigns in previous years, but the nearly complete merging of the types of campaigns was indicative of a new style of interest group politics. This new style of interest group campaign can be called the "total war" model. It has raised the stakes of interest group conflict significantly, as well as the costs.

Interest groups have been and continue to be frequent participants in the election game as well, playing two distinct roles. First, groups have come to dominate direct policymaking processes in many states as they have discovered the advantages of **initiative and referendum (I&R)** in the advancement of their policy objectives. These I&R elections have become more frequent in many states, especially in the West. Each election year hundreds of campaigns are contested among thousands of interest groups to influence an ever-growing range of public policies. Second, as the 2004 and 2006 elections demonstrated, interest groups have become increas-

ingly powerful political actors in election campaigns in support of political parties and their candidates. Groups such as the AFL-CIO have reasserted their once-powerful contribution to the Democratic party in the 2006 elections, and in the 2000 and 2004 elections, the Christian Coalition served as the Republican party's organizational equivalent to big labor. Additionally, dozens of other groups joined the electoral battles and made significant contributions. One of the more influential groups in the 2004 presidential elections was a group called Swift Boat Veterans for Truth. This group not only had a substantial impact on the tone of the presidential campaign, but it also represented a new development in interest group involvement in campaigns (see box 9.1). In this chapter, we will discuss the range of interest group strategies and tactics as they have been applied in electoral campaigns.

The "Total War" Campaign of Health Care Reform

The political "war" over health care reform was one of the defining moments in recent American political history. It was defining because it clearly established the previously suspected fact that interest groups could successfully withstand the power of a determined president and all the political resources he

BOX 9.1 The Rise of the 527s: A New Tool for Interest Groups in Party Campaigns

The tax code of the Internal Revenue Service has a section numbered 527 that refers to organizations operated for the purpose of influencing the selection, nomination, election, or appointment of an individual to federal, state, or local office. These 527 organizations have become powerful tools for interest groups to participate in federal elections without the restrictions that political action committees (PACs) have to follow. While section 527 was added to the IRS Code in 1974, the 527s have become significant actors in federal elections since the mid-1990s. In 1996, so-called issue organizations (especially the AFL-CIO) began to run "issue ads" in support of political candidates in congressional elections. The key limitation on these ads is that they do not expressly urge the viewer to vote for or against a specific candidate. Frequently, the ad urged the viewer to contact a candidate to ask for a desired action on a particular issue. In 2000, 527s were required to notify the IRS of their existence within twenty-four hours of organizing and to file periodic reports to the IRS of their activities.

After the Bipartisan Campaign Reform Act of 2002 was implemented for the 2004 elections, soft money donations could no longer be made to the political parties, and the 527s became more prominent as a way for interest groups or rich individuals to spend unlimited amounts of money during the campaign. In the 2004 elections, 527 groups spent more than $400 million in federal campaigns. About two-dozen wealthy individuals financed these groups with more than $145 million in contributions. Some interest groups such as the AFL-CIO, League of Conservation Voters, and the Planned Parenthood Action Fund have both PACs and 527s. In the 2004 presidential elections, the major pro-Democratic party 527s included America Coming Together, America Votes, and MoveOn.org. On the pro-Republican side, the major 527s in 2004 were the Club for Growth, Progress for America, and the Swift Boat Veterans for Truth. By the 2006 congressional elections, 527s spent about $220 million on the federal level. The Service Employees International Union funded 527s with more than $32 million in contributions. Bob Perry, a Texas homebuilder, and George Soros, a wealthy investor, were the top individual contributors to conservative and liberal 527s, respectively, in 2006.

Sources: Brookings Institution (2001), Common Cause (2006), Center for Responsive Politics (2007b).

could muster in a direct showdown on a policy issue. It was also defining in the sense that the outcomes of the issue war echoed throughout the nation and changed the course of American political party history by ending the New Deal era and giving Republicans control of Congress for the first time in almost fifty years.

The issue of health care reform had been raised to the status of a potential major issue in the 1991 U.S. Senate race in Pennsylvania. The underdog Democratic candidate turned to health care as his issue and won a dramatic victory. A year later, as Bill Clinton planned for his campaign to win the Democratic party presidential nomination, the potential of health care was acknowledged as powerful. After the general election campaign against the incumbent president, George H. W. Bush, health care grew to be the top new domestic program in the new Clinton administration. The battle over health care reform in 1993–1994 marked the formal beginning of the era of massive interest group participation in the "new style" of political campaigns. Interest groups had participated in various issue campaigns previously, but never with the intensity, commitment of resources, and wide range of strategies and tactics found in the health care reform effort.

Certainly, interest groups and movements have been periodic participants in some of the great political campaigns of American history. The abolitionist movement was active in the formation of the new Republican party in the 1850s and vitally important in Abraham Lincoln's successful presidential campaign in 1860. In 1896, the campaign of William McKinley was managed by Mark Hanna, a Cleveland industrialist, who raised between $35 million and $100 million (in current dollars) by "shaking down" America's largest corporations for campaign funds. Decades later, the suffrage movement tried to affect a series of elections in its efforts to secure the vote for women. Prohibitionists triumphed in the early twentieth century with their drive to ban alcoholic beverages. More recently, many

movements, including feminists, environmentalists, political reformers, "pro-choice," and "pro-life" groups, have been active in a wide range of political campaigns. Some of these campaigns have been interest group campaigns focusing on a specific legislative goal and containing a grassroots component. Others focused on political election campaigns as groups sought to elect friends of their cause to various public offices. Finally, interest groups have sometimes gone directly to the public in election campaigns to enact "direct legislation" using the tools of initiative, referendum, and even recall.

Clearly, interest groups have used campaigns to achieve their political objectives. But something different occurred in 1993–1994. For the first time, interest groups mobilized enormous resources to fight complete political campaigns on a national level. The campaigns were nearly identical in almost every aspect to the campaigns waged by successful presidential candidates such as Ronald Reagan and Bill Clinton. They had nearly unlimited resources to utilize, they recruited personnel from party campaigns to lend their expertise, they used highly centralized organizational structures and "war rooms" to coordinate the various participants, and they unleashed the multiple channels of modern communications media from television advertising to the Internet to battle for the favor of American public opinion. In the 1998 elections, dozens of interest groups spent a reported total of at least $260 million in television and radio advertisements, according to the Annenberg Public Policy Center, to advance their political agendas or to support or oppose particular candidates. Sixty-seven groups were identified as sponsoring such ads in the 1998 elections (Marcus 1998).

The line between interest groups and political parties has become blurred by recent events. Major interests use the techniques of modern election campaigns, and they share the same personnel, who offer their expertise to parties, candidates, and interest groups. As box 9.2 recounts, advertisements produced and aired by interest groups were among the most significant ads in the 2004 presidential election campaign. Of course, there are still differences between political parties and interest groups. Parties seek to win elections and govern. They use issues to put together strategies to win and occupy political offices. Periodic elections and campaigns make up the parties' main arena. Interest groups, on the other hand, seek primarily to impact public policy, and thus elections are just one of several types of campaigns that groups may use in order to achieve their policy objectives.

The Greatest Interest Group Campaign in American History?

After the Democrats won control of the Congress in the 2006 elections, many asked if it was time to address the universal health care issue again. As the 2008 presidential election unfolded in the following year, several of the Democratic candidates (Clinton, Obama, and Edwards) were making health care one of their top issues. The health insurance issue has risen to the top of the Democrats' agenda for several reasons. The cost of medical care had been skyrocketing in recent years—far ahead of the nation's rate of inflation. By 2007, 45 million Americans had no health insurance, and the United States remained the only industrialized nation on the planet with no system of universal health care insurance. But many remembered the last time the Democratic party had made health care the most important issue and their political disaster in the congressional elections of 1994.

In terms of the range of resources expended and the number of strategies and tactics employed, many political observers have anointed the 1993–1994 health care reform effort as the "greatest interest group battle in American political history. More importantly, given the fact that interest group

politics have emerged in its most complete and most expensive forms in the United States, one could then logically argue that it was the greatest such battle in world history" (Johnson and Broder 1996).

The issue, health care reform, emerged from the 1991 special Senate election in Pennsylvania. Democratic candidate Harris Wofford used the issue to win a stunning victory. Since Wofford's campaign advisers, James Carville and Paul Begala, went on to become strategists for the 1992 Clinton presidential campaign, it was not surprising that Bill Clinton grasped health care reform as one of his central themes. Relatively soon after the Clinton administration settled into the White House, the new president appointed his wife, Hillary Rodham Clinton, coordinator of the administration's health care reforms. Later, both supporters and detractors agreed that appointing the First Lady as the administration's leader on this crucial issue was a fundamental mistake that opposing interest groups utilized in their successful campaign to kill the reforms.

The *New York Times* declared that "Clinton's health care plan was the very centerpiece of his Presidency—'our most urgent priority' as [Clinton] told Congress in a grand unveiling of the plan in September 1993" (Wines and Pear 1996). As is well known, the reform initiative died in the late summer of 1994 after being assaulted by a powerful coalition of interest groups. When health care reform was declared the Clinton administration's top priority, it attracted a particularly large number of opponents operating with an impressive range of political objectives—not the least being the destruction of the Clinton presidency. The success of the anti-reform interest group coalition also had a significant impact on American political party history, since it set the stage for the 1994 House and Senate elections and the destruction of the Democratic party majorities in Congress.

The demise of the reforms proposed by Clinton did not mark the end of the health

BOX 9.2 Were Interest Group Ads Decisive in the 2004 Election?

Democrat John Kerry and Republican President George W. Bush both had millions of dollars for grassroots get-out-the-vote (GOTV) campaigns and had thousands of television ads in 2004. But there are grounds for believing that the decisive element for the reelection of President Bush were two series of TV spot ads produced by two 527 interest groups—the Swift Boat Veterans for Truth and Progress for America Voter Fund.

John Kerry's managers had scripted the Democratic nominating convention around the theme of John Kerry as a Vietnam war hero capable of leading the nation in dangerous times of the post–9/11 world and the Iraq war. A 527 group, Swift Boat Veterans for Truth, was formed for the purpose of attacking that foundation. The group, which seemed to represent several hundred naval veterans from the Vietnam war, spent more than $22.5 million dollars in the 2003–2004 election cycle. Three TV ads were produced and run in only a few selective markets, but many voters later noted the ads were probably the most influential of the campaign and probably decisive for the Bush victory. The first ad appeared just after the Democratic nominating convention and just prior to the Republican convention. It aired in only three states: Wisconsin, West Virginia, and Ohio. The ad stated that Senator Kerry had lied about his Vietnam record and betrayed his shipmates. The second ad ran several weeks later in West Virginia, Ohio, and Iowa. It carried video of Kerry testifying before Congress about the war crimes committed by Americans in Vietnam and implied that Kerry was dishonoring his country. The third and final ad noted that Kerry had renounced his medals in protest of U.S. policy in Vietnam and asked whether such a man could be trusted.

The Progress for America Voter Fund spent more than $26.4 million on advertising in battleground states in support of Bush's leadership. One of this group's ads was particularly powerful—an ad called "Ashley's Story." This ad ran during the final weeks of the campaign and pictured President Bush hugging a 16-year-old girl who had lost her mother on 9/11. The group spent more than $16 million broadcasting this ad in eleven states and on national cable television.

While the Swift Boat ads effectively attacked Kerry's military advantage over Bush, the Progress for America ads attempted to make Bush appear to be "one of us," in contrast to the cold and distant Kerry. While the political parties and candidates produced and ran thousands of advertisements, these important—and perhaps decisive—ads were produced by interest groups in support of the Bush campaign.

Sources: Cigler (2007) and Phillips (2007).

care war. It raged throughout 1995 and 1996 in various forms and returned in 1997 in the budget deficit debates and efforts to cut billions of dollars from the Medicare program. One group, the National Coalition on Health Care, took out *New York Times* ads in October 1997, warning that health care costs could rise nearly 90 percent in the coming decade and could prevent families from retiring comfortably or sending a child to college. The ad urged readers to join the coalition in calling for health care reform or to get additional information by visiting its Web site. The battle continued into 1998 as the issue changed to controlling some of the problems that have emerged as more and more Americans come under the health insurance system administered by health maintenance organizations (HMOs). Insurance companies and their allies spent $60 million in the first half of 1998 while their opponents (medical organizations, trial lawyers, unions, and consumer groups) spent $14 million. Another $11 million was spent on media advertising against managed care legislation; additional millions were made in campaign contributions to opponents of the reform legislation. During the same period, tobacco companies spent about $40 million to kill legislation to raise cigarette taxes to curb teenage smoking ("Opponents of Health Care Reform" 1998).

After 9/11, the nation's focus was on security, not health care. The issue returned again in 2005–2006 in terms of a huge new benefit to senior citizens in the form of a new, very expensive Medicare prescription drug program for seniors passed by the Republican Congress to assist its candidates in the 2006 elections. The program was written by the Republican Congress to pass hundreds of billions of dollars on to their pharmaceutical industry supporters, and they were very careful to include a provision in the law that prohibited the federal government from negotiating lower drug prices from the industry by using the massive purchasing power of the government. But, while it was a nice benefit

for the nation's older citizens, it did not address the growing problem of lack of insurance for so many millions of Americans.

Interest Groups Seek to Mold Public Opinion in Media Campaigns

"Appeals to the masses" are used frequently by interest groups as supporting tactics for broader lobbying campaigns. It is generally the tactic of large, wealthy groups and is based on a paid mass media campaign using extensive television commercials and major newspaper advertising. However, even the weakest groups can seek to mold public opinion by appeals to gain the attention of "free media."

Groups can use mass media campaigns to pursue four major objectives: group maintenance, public goodwill, defensive strategy, and offensive strategy. Many media appeals contain coupons to send to the lobbying targets such as senators, representatives, or bureaucrats, and other coupons that ask the reader to send money to the group to support future efforts. Some groups have significantly increased their membership bases during such media campaigns. Various liberal groups greatly increased their membership during the Nixon impeachment process in the 1970s, the Robert Bork Supreme Court nomination process in the late 1980s, and the Bush "war on terrorism" in the post–9/11 era. Another internal goal related to maintenance is providing evidence to existing members that the group is effectively representing them in the public policy process. Just having a high visibility media presence can help insulate interest group leadership from membership complaints.

The other three objectives relate directly to the policymaking process. A particular media campaign can have an offensive or a defensive strategic orientation or may be building a foundation for future media campaigns. "Goodwill" campaigns lay such a foundation for future lobbying. Mobil Oil, now ExxonMobil, has run numerous goodwill campaigns over the years. Many of these ads have nothing to do with Mobil's lobbying agenda. They urge such actions as parents getting inoculations for their children or citizens acting more responsibly within their communities.

Many goodwill ads are presented by interest groups seeking to refurbish somewhat tarnished images. Philip Morris, a giant corporation that produces a wide range of products, including Miller Beer, Kraft Foods, and tobacco products, bought a double-page ad in the *New York Times Magazine* entitled "Helping the Helpers: Victim Services." The ad addresses domestic violence and contains information on services to victims of domestic abuse. It should be noted that goodwill media ads are relatively rare, since most groups prefer to spend their scarce resources in defending gains already made or seeking new legislative goals.

A majority of issue advocacy ads in recent years seem to be defensive. This may be a function of the style of politics operating in the United States for the past three decades— a politics with little chance of new taxes or budgets for new programs and lots of attacks on existing programs to help cut the persistent federal budget deficits. The giant pharmaceutical company, GlaxoSmithKline, paid for full-page ads in the *National Journal* with the message line of "Experts say 10% of the world's drug supply is counterfeit. Can we be sure we import the 90% that isn't?" It was a very straightforward defensive tactic to defeat attempts in Congress to allow importation of prescription drugs from other nations where the price of such drugs is often much lower than in the United States.

Offensive ads are attack ads seeking to change some aspect of American society or politics or to pass a new law to that effect. In another recent media campaign, the AFL-CIO argued that Congress could reduce health care costs by passing new laws that

make generic drugs easier to get for America's patients.

Figures 9.1 to 9.4 exemplify advocacy ads. The first ad is for the American Civil Liberties Union's campaign, protesting the Bush administration's use of government surveillance without judicial authorization. The second ad is an appeal from the National Association of Realtors asking the government to help small businessmen with the rising costs of health care. The third ad is from the Pharmaceutical Research and Manufacturers of America (P*h*RMA) and is seeking to defend the clause in the Medicare prescription drugs law that prohibits the government from negotiating with the drug companies for lower prices based on bulk purchases. The fourth ad is a "good will" ad from ExxonMobil noting the progress that has been made in the war on malaria.

Media campaigns can be very expensive strategies for interest groups. A full-page ad in a national newspaper or a newsmagazine costs tens of thousands of dollars. The high cost of media advertising makes it a tool of business lobbies or rich, well-established lobbies like the National Rifle Association or the American Medical Association.

Often an interest group or, better still, a coalition pursues a coordinated media campaign in a variety of media in order to target a range of audiences. These audiences could include national opinion leaders, issue activists, corporate employees, stockholders, regional audiences, Congress, labor unions, and academics. To reach these targets, a coalition may place its ads in college newspapers, regional trade publications, specific magazines, and different types of newspapers. For example, national newspapers such as the *New York Times, Wall Street Journal,* and *Washington Post* may be included because their subscribers include people and businesses across the nation as well as many libraries in addition to their city and regional audiences. Even a one-day campaign could cost hundreds of thousands of dollars! Other interests target elite public opinion in Washington, DC, by placing ads

FIGURE 9.1 ACLU Advertisement

40 YEARS AGO, WIRETAPPING INNOCENT AMERICANS WAS AN ABUSE OF GOVERNMENT POWER.

IT STILL IS.

At the time Martin Luther King Jr. was championing the rights of all Americans, the government was violating his rights by secretly wiretapping him in the name of national security. The sorry history of the surveillance and wiretapping of dissenters—of those seen as "enemies" of the President—led to a law that specifically requires the President to seek court approval for wiretaps of Americans, even for national security investigations. George Bush believes that he is not bound by this law. An American can be under illegal surveillance by the Bush administration without any judicial check on that power. That's not the America in Martin Luther King Jr.'s dream.

Call the White House (202-456-1414) and tell the administration to stop the illegal spying on Americans.

ACLU
AMERICAN CIVIL LIBERTIES UNION

Paid for by the ACLU Foundation

JOIN US AND LEARN MORE. GO TO WWW.ACLU.ORG

FIGURE 9.2 National Association of Realtors Advertisement

It's Time the Senate Gives Small Businesses the Affordable Healthcare They Deserve

Right Here. Right Now.

They're shopkeepers, mechanics, farmers—America's small businesses and the self-employed. They've been saying it loud and clear: they need affordable health plans. Last year, the House was listening and passed needed legislation. Now, it's time for the Senate to do the same.

The over 1.2 million members of the National Association of REALTORS® urge the Senate to pass Small Business Health Plans legislation. *Not later. Not down the road. Right now.* Millions of hard working American families would finally be eligible for the affordable healthcare they deserve.

NATIONAL ASSOCIATION
OF REALTORS®
The Voice for Real Estate®

For more information, visit our website www.realtor.org

FIGURE 9.3 P*h*RMA Advertisement

Leading newspapers say...

"The Wrong Prescription"
"Government should not negotiate prices in Medicare."

The Washington Post 1/13/07

"...put brakes on drug plan 'fix'"

USA Today 11/13/06

"...the last thing patients need."

The Wall Street Journal 12/6/06

...don't rush to change
the Medicare prescription drug benefit.

Today, for the first time ever, 90% of seniors have comprehensive prescription drug coverage.

Millions of older and disabled Americans have peace of mind thanks to Medicare's new prescription benefit.

The program is only a year old, but it's already making a difference. Real savings for seniors. A wide choice of plans—not a one-size-fits-all. The medicines seniors need for the care they deserve.

The Medicare debate going on in Congress is really about patient choice. Restricting access to medicines for tens of millions of seniors and disabled Americans would be a huge mistake.

And it won't save any money either. The Congressional Budget Office (CBO) estimates "H.R. 4 would have a negligible impact on federal spending."

USA Today tells Congress to put on the brakes.

Change is the last thing patients need warns The Wall Street Journal.

We agree. Medicare's prescription drug benefit is working for seniors. Give it a chance to keep working.

P*h*RMA
www.PhRMA.org

FIGURE 9.4 ExxonMobil Advertisement

in small-circulation political journals such as *Roll Call, The Hill, National Journal,* and *Congressional Quarterly.*

Grassroots Interest Group Issue Campaigns

The objective of many interest group ads is to support grassroots campaigns. In most of these ads, the political targets are clearly identified so that the group's message can be communicated directly to the target. One way to accomplish this is to have "fill in the blank with your name" letters sent to the interest group offices and be "bundled" there for delivery to the targeted officials. Of course, in recent years, most groups use Web sites and email for communicating to supporters and getting messages back for delivery to political targets. Almost all print media ads have Web sites prominently noted for the reader to complete the communications feedback to the group.

Many lobbying campaigns with broad-based strategies and tactics in recent years have required resources from "outside the beltway." The beltway refers to the highway that encircles Washington, DC. It is the symbolic barrier separating "insider Washington politics" from those found in the rest of the nation. Such "outreach lobbying" is often called "grassroots lobbying." The standard definition of grassroots lobbying is mobilizing supporters on the sub-national levels of American politics to put pressure on targets at the national level.

Liberal interest groups such as labor unions, public interest groups such as environmentalists, and political reform groups such as Common Cause pioneered the modern development of grassroots lobbying in the 1960s and 1970s. Ironically, conservative interest groups refined the practices and made grassroots lobbying a major part of modern political campaigning. What corporate America added to the technique was money—lots and lots of money. With the infusion of money came the professional campaign consultants, the Washington, Los Angeles, and New York City public relations and media firms, and the various technologies such as direct mail and computers that have become the standard in the profession of grassroots campaign management.

Some have argued that grassroots lobbying campaigns are much more effective than traditional lobbying efforts, which are described in the following chapter. No less an authority than former Senate majority leader and 1996 Republican presidential candidate Robert Dole has suggested that the combination of money and mail from constituents will probably equal a lobbying victory. Senator John Danforth noted that when letter writing and newspaper ad campaigns are organized, "members of the Congress of the United States crumble like cookies" (Johnson 1984).

Grassroots victories are not quite as automatic as these quotes imply. Grassroots campaigning may be effective or ineffective, and many grassroots campaigns fail. Effective grassroots campaigns are usually able to appear to be natural and spontaneous. A lobby wants such a campaign to be perceived as thousands of concerned citizens (preferably voting constituents) communicating their political desires to their elected representatives. Ineffective grassroots lobbying is called "AstroTurf lobbying" because it is clearly artificial. Enhanced communications capabilities have brought grassroots lobbying to the forefront in contemporary lobbying campaigns. Activating grassroots members or sympathizers can be accomplished quite easily with computers, but even resource-poor groups can run an effective grassroots effort by using telephone trees consisting of one member calling ten members, and so forth.

Lobbies can activate either "rifle" or "shotgun" styles of grassroots campaigns. As the names imply, the two types of campaigns differ in terms of the number of communications activated by the group. The rifle tactic is to pinpoint a target and then bring specific resources to the target. This approach involves relatively few people to activate it. Sometimes, it is called "grass-tops lobbying." An example of this elite type of lobbying would be bringing local TV station owners to Washington, DC, to lobby to new FCC rules regarding the number of TV stations that can be owned by one company in a given market. The shotgun approach relies on activating large numbers of communications. A typical shotgun campaign is centered around either mass mailings or media ads urging a group's membership or the public to blanket Congress with letters or phone calls. An effective campaign can generate millions of communications to the Congress over a very short period of time. Several such campaigns can operate at the same time and may well generate several millions of messages to Congress in a day. In a classic campaign run by the banking lobby in the early 1980s, Congress was inundated by a massive grassroots letter- and postcard-writing campaign that totaled more than 22 million letters and postcards ("Statistic of the Week" 1983, 720).

The following are some classic examples of grassroots lobbying as it has been perfected by corporate America:

- Coca-Cola urged its stockholders to join its Civic Action Network (CAN) and recruited more than fifty thousand stockholder-grassroots activists.
- The American Bankers Association, one of the heavyweight lobbying groups, orchestrated an estimated 22 million postcards, letters, and mailgrams to force Congress to cancel a requirement that banks and other financial institutions withhold income taxes on interest and dividends.
- Delta Airlines distributed messages to its passengers on food trays and frequent fliers in the monthly mailings, urging them to "call or fax your U.S. congressional representatives today" to oppose congressional efforts to raise taxes on air travel and frequent flier miles.

- The National Restaurant Association flew in 150 restaurateurs from forty states to meet with congressmen to try to kill a drunk driving bill that the association believed could have a financial impact on their businesses. Mom and pop beer and liquor stores were also sending faxes and making phone calls to their congressmen.

There are a variety of ways interest groups can "help" connect a grassroots constituent with a government official. After being contacted by the group by telephone, the constituent can fax his or her letterhead with signature to the group and the group's message can be inserted on the letterhead and then sent to the governmental official. If the group determines that the constituent has a clear and desirable message to communicate, the group can immediately connect him or her to the Washington, DC, office of the official using "patch through" technologies. Some are asked if they would like the group to write a letter for them. Groups use different styles of stationary, envelopes, and stamps to make the letters appear as individual as possible. Sometimes, key constituents (or "grasstops") are singled out by interest groups because of their prominence in the home districts of important congressional members. They are brought to Washington (usually at the expense of the group) for personal visits with their representatives. Especially effective at the congressional level are powerful elites such as bankers or media executives who can be very important in helping produce future reelection victories for the congressmen.

The most effective grassroots campaigns are as personal and individualistic as possible. Congressional staff screen all incoming mail, and personal letters receive more attention than mimeographed postcards. Letters from "important people" and letters with unusually interesting arguments may be brought to the attention of members of Congress. Letters from groups that come into contact with the representative may be brought to his or her desk as well.

"Patch through" technology has also greatly facilitated the lobbyist's task of linking the public to the politician. One such computer program selects names and phone numbers from a database, makes a phone call to the name, delivers a prerecorded message about pending legislation, and then connects listeners to the office of their members of Congress. The program had a 25 percent success rate. If that seems low, it is much higher than the success rate of direct mail efforts, which usually have a success rate in the single digits.

Fax communication is another tool of successful grassroots campaigns and has also become the preferred method of internal rapid communications in many interest groups. Faxes can be generated one at a time by individuals, or "astro faxes" can be generated by computer (Browning 1994, 2450).

Among new technologies that have contributed to the enhancement of grassroots lobbying are desktop publishing, short-wave radio, citizen access television, computer-supported fax networks, independent video production, computer billboards, and the Internet. The Internet and email have become increasingly popular for lobbying communications. Groups set up a Web page, and members and other activists can "pull up the page" and receive instant communications. The group's Internet address can be communicated to the potential viewers in print or television ads or by in-house publications. More and more video clips are being featured as well as portal document files. By 2000, Web pages had replaced billboards on the side of the road as a "sign of seriousness" in that almost all the serious lobbies had them. The more sophisticated the Web sites were, the more seriously the lobby was taken as a major player in the interest group game. Hill and Hughes (1998) studied the use of the Internet by interest groups and noted that many groups were using the Internet for a wide variety of objectives, for example, posting group testimonies, conducting public meetings, posting in-house information, announcing legal actions, communicating to politicians, indicating support for sympathetic politicians, recruiting new members, fundraising, communications to and from members, and links to allied groups. The mean size of the Web sites studied was 82 pages, but the largest had 652 pages!

Manipulation of the news media to bring about a grassroots effect is yet another successful grassroots tactic. The goal is to generate newspaper editorials supporting the group's political position and put pressure on politicians dependent on the future support of the media in upcoming campaigns. The tactics appear to be particularly effective in "low salience issue" campaigns and in legislative (rather than executive) campaigns. A variety of tactics are effective in this area. A group can go for high-prestige newspapers such as the *New York Times, Wall Street Journal,* or a handful of other such newspapers. Sometimes the support of papers such as the *New York Times* or *Washington Post* may be sufficient to tilt the political balance in favor of an issue. The alternative tactic is to try to "tidal wave" key members of Congress with a series of editorial page statements on the issue from newspapers in their home districts or states. One lobby that has used the editorial page tactic was the liberal, free-speech lobby, People for the American Way.

The humble telephone remains a mainstay of many grassroots lobbying operations. Common Cause, for example, uses direct mail, the Internet, and a telephone network to activate its troops for grassroots campaigns. Common Cause's Washington, DC, headquarters calls coordinators in selected congressional districts across the country, who in turn contact several other Common Cause members, who each contact other members and so on down the action alert "communications tree."

The technology that made interest groups very aware of the tremendous potential of grassroots lobbying was direct mail. Richard Viguerie founded the technology in the late

1970s and provided conservative groups with a tremendous fund-raising tool and helped create a wide range of such groups. Today, almost every group in the nation uses some form of direct mail. The typical established citizen receives dozens of fund-raising letters and appeals, ranging from environmentalists to senior citizens. Most Americans probably receive in any given year dozens of "appeals packets" from interest groups.

Fine-tuning these direct mail appeals is not a casual operation. Everything that goes into the communications package is tested and retested: the size of the envelopes, the color of the paper, the type size and style, the number of pages, and the personal touches that are added to the letter, such as the recipient's name and address or the signature of the person who is supposed to have signed the letter. The content is also tested and refined to make it as powerful a selling mechanism as possible. A well-designed appeal can raise millions of dollars, whereas a poorly designed one can threaten the group's survival.

The central motivation of direct mail is fear. Frightening events or prospective events and political actors are used to frighten the recipient into joining the group or at least providing money to avoid the prospective bad outcome. Following the Republican takeover of Congress in 1995, liberal groups featured Newt Gingrich as the object of fear; conservatives presented a future negatively impacted by Ted Kennedy or Bill and Hillary Clinton. The sudden resignation of Newt Gingrich after the 1998 elections left the Democrats without an opponent to attack in their direct mail campaigns. After the election of 2000, however, direct mail campaigns for Democrats began to feature President George W. Bush, Vice President Dick Cheney, and Secretary of Defense Donald Rumsfeld. Direct mail frequently uses emotions, including "outrage, fear, guilt, pity or self-interest" (Eckholm 1995).

Groups combine direct mail, media ads, and some of the new communications technologies of the last several decades to maximize the possibility of getting the message to the grassroots target. Some groups began using toll-free telephone numbers for the public to call and request information on issues the groups were supporting. During the Clinton administration's health care reform crusade, for example, the American Medical Association (AMA) ran advertisements featuring its telephone number for people to get information on the AMA's health care plan. In an earlier battle, tobacco company Philip Morris pushed this tactic even farther when it hired a Washington polling firm to generate mail in opposition to a proposed law banning smoking on airline flights. The firm called smokers and read them a script that included a prewritten message. The caller asked smokers if they would consent to having the message sent to their state's senator on the smoker's behalf. If they received an affirmative reply, the message was sent at Philip Morris's expense.

Letter-writing campaigns are the most common grassroots campaign. The most effective ones use individually written letters or produce a huge flood of orchestrated mail. The targets of letter-writing campaigns—politicians and bureaucrats—frequently are so swamped by mail that they note only the quantity and quality of the letters. Huge deliveries of such mail may influence politicians who have not made up their minds on an issue or those who face a particularly difficult reelection campaign.

Another frequently used grassroots political tactic to influence public policy is the boycott. Boycotting involves asking supporters of some group or cause to avoid purchasing products from a company or industry being boycotted or to refuse to visit a boycotted place and thus reduce income from tourism, conventions, or normal commerce. A boycott can be used by both powerful and weak groups, but it is particularly useful for groups without the traditional routes of access. A number of prominent boycotts over the years have been successful, including the United Farm Workers boycotts against grape growers in California during the 1960s and 1970s, a boycott of Colorado by civil rights groups protesting a state law undermining "gay civil rights," and the boycott of the state of Arizona by civil rights groups after that state decided not to observe Martin Luther King's birthday as a state holiday. In recent years, some interest groups have boycotted corporations. People for the Ethical Treatment of Animals (PETA) called for a boycott against Kentucky Fried Chicken restaurants in protest over the methods used by the chain to kill chickens. PETA placed a billboard showing actress Pamela Anderson next to the tagline, "Boycott KFC—live scalding, painful de-beaking, crippled chickens" and a PETA Web site address(KentuckyFriedCruelty.com).

In recent years, dozens of boycotts have been organized by various groups, and some of them have been continuing for years. A political boycott can be successful if it accomplishes its main task of gaining media attention for the group and its cause and ultimately changes public opinion. Some boycotts are able to do this, but the vast majority of boycotts fail. A famous 1970s failure was a boycott of states that had failed to ratify the Equal Rights Amendment led by various feminist groups including the National Organization of Women. Despite tremendous efforts to enforce that boycott and the loss of many millions of dollars in business in three key states, the legislatures targeted never ratified the amendment.

Interest Group Campaigns Against Parties and Candidates

In most election years, some major political interest groups seek to defeat specific candidates in an effort to secure more favorable treatment for legislation they support. Organized labor did just that during the 1996 elections by targeting for defeat almost three dozen freshmen Republican members of the House of Representatives. Groups that declare war on a political party must carry out their threats of defeating their enemy or be able to withstand a hostile legislative environment dominated by their enemies. After the Republicans held on to Congress in 1996, labor found itself frozen out of power until it was able to help the Democrats win control of the Congress in 2006. Sometimes the existing political environment is so hostile that even if groups fail to defeat their enemies, the outcomes could not be any worse than what already exists. Such was the attitude of organized labor and many environmentalists during the period the Republicans held control of the House (1995–2007). As box 9.3 describes, such battles can also take place in local elections as well.

Groups may use an electoral retaliation strategy, which to be effective must be based on some evidence that a group can reward or punish a candidate in elections. Several lobbies have been perceived by politicians as being able to defeat their opponents. The anti-abortion movement, religious groups, environmentalists, and organized labor have all been given credit for defeating senators and house members in elections during the past several decades. Part of the myth of retribution lies in the groups not being shy about claiming credit for whatever victories may occur in an election. In the crucial 1994 congressional elections, liberal Democrat after Democrat was defeated, and the Christian Coalition claimed credit. Interest groups need to "deliver the vote" for or against a specific candidate. In 1998, however, the Christian Coalition was unable to deliver the votes to defeat Democratic candidates for Congress, and the group's status dropped as a result of this perceived failure. The National Rifle Association (NRA) claimed a great election victory in 1994 with the "defeat of 32 anti-gun politicians." *Campaigns and Elections* magazine declared that the NRA had "a lot more to do with the November [1994] elections than most pundits realized." According to its own count, the NRA spent money on twenty races. Nine of the ten NRA-backed candidates won in 1994; six of the eleven

BOX 9.3 Labor Unions versus Big Business . . . in City Council Elections?

Big business and big labor have frequently clashed in presidential and congressional elections across the nation since the 1930s. But such conflicts can extend down to local government elections as well. The city of Chicago has long been a stronghold of organized labor. The 2007 Chicago City Council elections became a battleground between the Service Employees International Union (SEIU) and the nation's largest employer, Wal-Mart. The battle had been raging prior to the 2007 elections because Chicago City Council passed a union-supported idea to allow the non-union Wal-Mart stores in Chicago, only if they increased the pay and benefits for their employees. A new ordinance was passed that mandated "big-box stores" (read Wal-Mart) to pay at least $10 an hour in wages plus an additional $3 an hour in benefits. Mayor Richard Daley vetoed the measure, and the city council failed to override the veto.

That set the stage for a classic business-labor confrontation in the 2007 Chicago City Council elections, especially in those districts with large numbers of minorities and desperate need for new employment opportunities. Labor unions, led by the SEIU, poured $2.6 million into a handful of key races in minority neighborhoods in an effort to get additional pro-labor candidates elected to the city council. In one district where an incumbent council member voted for and then against the ordinance, labor put more than $500,000 into defeating her. On the other side, Wal-Mart contributed at least $100,000 to Mayor Daley's political action committee, which supported many of the pro-business candidates.

Sources: Ciokajlo and Becker (2007), Mihalopoulos (2007), and Mihalopoulos and Pearson (2007).

targeted candidates were defeated (O'Leary 1994, 32). When George W. Bush defeated Al Gore and John Kerry in the 2000 and 2004 presidential elections, the Christian Coalition and the NRA claimed credit for turning out the crucial votes in critical states (Florida, Tennessee, West Virginia, and Ohio) that had helped Bush win the White House.

Organized labor has had difficulty delivering its vote as more of its membership gain middle-class income and identify with the values of the Republican party. For example, it has been estimated that about one-third of the National Education Association's nearly 2 million members are Republicans. More importantly, the number of union households has been steadily declining from 25 percent of the nation's households in 1952 to only 15 percent in 2004. One can see the impact of these declines in the proportion of the Democratic vote from labor voters in presidential elections. Between 1964 to 1984, labor was one-fourth of the Democratic vote, one-fifth from 1988 to 1996, one-sixth in 2000, although it rose to one-fifth again in 2004 (Abramson, Aldrich, and Rohde 2007).

In general elections, interest groups have an impact in terms of the range of services they can offer a favored candidate. Giants such as the AFL-CIO, AARP, women's organizations, the Christian Coalition, and single-issue groups such as the NRA can conduct voter registration campaigns and "get-out-the-vote" telephone efforts that can be invaluable to a candidate. The American Medical Association, beginning in the early 1980s, has made available to endorsed candidates the services of any of six national pollsters—a service that has been very popular with many national candidates. A variant of traditional election day strategies is the development of endorsement lists or candidate ratings. Many groups publish their ratings, and some of the most effective groups get a great deal of media attention when they announce their "dirty dozen," "heroes and zeroes," and "warriors for small business." Nearly a hundred groups rate the Congress yearly on a selected range of issues.

The largest lobby in the United States for small businesses—the National Federation of Independent Business (NFIB)—puts together its ratings each year by polling the group's six hundred thousand members about the stands the membership wants the group to take on issues before Congress (Broder 1995; Foster 1985). The polling information is then sent to congressional offices. Just prior to a crucial vote on one of the group's priority issues, a special green-edged postcard is sent to members of Congress warning them that the vote will be part of the NFIB's next report card. Approximately thirty votes constitute the NFIB ratings. To each member of Congress receiving 70 percent or higher rating on the report card, the NFIB awards a small pewter trophy inscribed with the words "Guardian of Small Business." The NFIB will also launch a media campaign in the politician's home district or state announcing the award.

In recent years, about a third of the House and half of the Senate have received such awards. Finally, the NFIB has a PAC that contributes hundreds of thousands of dollars each year to deserving congressional candidates. A 70 percent rating entitles an incumbent to the group's endorsement, as well as a monetary contribution if the race warrants it. Conversely, any incumbent with a score of less than 40 percent may see his or her challenger receiving such a PAC contribution from the NFIB.

Many interest group ratings are of little importance to the typical member of Congress. Most Republicans from rural or agricultural states are not concerned over a low rating from the AFL-CIO; in fact, a bad labor rating is usually a plus in conservative districts. However, strong ratings from labor and ethnic lobbies are very important to big city–based Democratic candidates. In the 2004 elections, for example, conservative Senator Orrin Hatch (R-Utah) received zero ratings from the League of Conservation Voters and the ACLU. On the other hand, Hatch got 100s from the Chamber of Commerce and the Christian Coalition (Barone and Cohen 2005). Will any of these ratings have an impact on Hatch's next election? Certainly, people trying to find out if Senator Hatch shares their preferences in a particular policy area can find some of that information in these ratings, but no discernible relationship exists between any of Hatch's low ratings and any future electoral problems.

Interest Group Efforts in Party Campaigns

Interest groups have participated in political party election campaigns throughout much of this nation's political history. The history of the Republican party in the pre–Civil War period of the 1850s was largely a history of various antislavery groups helping to elect Republicans to office in an effort to destroy slavery. The once powerful political machines that controlled many of America's major cities in the late nineteenth century operated effectively by working with a wide variety of interest groups—some business and others ethnic or religious in nature. However, our focus is on what political scientists and historians call the New Deal system, which began with the election of Franklin Roosevelt in 1932 and continued at least to the 1960s. During this period emerged the present pattern of interest group involvement in traditional party election campaigns.

The image problems that both Democratic and Republican parties have faced in recent campaigns highlight the extent of interest group participation in modern party campaigns. The Democratic party had a severe political image problem since the 1970s. Many viewed the party as captive to a number of powerful interest groups; various public opinion polls indicated that this subservient relationship—real or imagined—was costing the party votes in presidential campaigns. Any list of groups and movements that appeared to have a stranglehold over the Democratic party would include first, organized labor and specifically the AFL-CIO. The giant labor confederation emerged from its battles with American business in the first three decades of this century as a powerful force in American politics based on the number of members it organized and the money it could raise and spend in political campaigns. Gradually, it came to align itself with the Democratic party of Roosevelt and Truman (1933–1953), and by the 1960s, it had become the foundation of the party. Organized labor had become the core of the party because the party never spent resources developing its own viable structure for campaign support, fund-raising, or even volunteer administration. Whenever the Democratic party needed money, it turned to labor; when it needed volunteers in a specific campaign, it turned to labor; and when it needed administrative support such as computers, the unions would offer their computers to the party. In fact, it was not in the interest of the unions for the Democratic

party to develop its own independent resource base in these areas, since any enhancement of the party's resources would result only in a lessening of the political power of the unions in the party. Union power in the Democratic party had become so great by the 1970s that a number of seats were reserved for union representatives in the key Democratic party committees.

Other groups or movements have also been perceived by many as having extraordinary influence and access in the Democratic party. One such group is the "education lobby." Represented by the powerful National Education Association (NEA), an educational professional group, teachers and school administrators have become frequent participants in Democratic councils and conventions. Significant parts of the women's movement have also signed on with the Democratic party in recent decades, as have groups representing gays and lesbians and their political interests. All of these groups or movements became visible in Democratic party activities and came to symbolize to some the party's power core. Republicans successfully portrayed the party as the captive of these powerful interests, which represent policy agendas outside the mainstream of American politics. No mention of the powerful interests that support the Democratic party would be adequate without noting the financial contributions of the nation's trial lawyers that have become a very important money source for the party. The trial lawyers have sided with the Democrats because Republicans have strongly supported the goal of business to pursue tort reform that would severely cut back on the money generated from lawsuits brought against corporations.

The Republican party has had similar image problems. Since the beginning of the New Deal system in 1932, the interest that many felt dominated the Republicans was "big business." With the Democrats "in the pocket" of organized labor, the Republicans continued their pre-Depression, pro-business orientation. But their pro-business orientation was not the interest group relationship that has caused the party some political damage in recent years. The GOP has become the party of choice of "fundamentalist (or evangelic) Christians," and thus organizations such as Jerry Falwell's Moral Majority and Ralph Reed's Christian Coalition became powerful actors inside Republican political circles. The 1995 Christian Coalition campaign in support of Republican House Speaker Newt Gingrich's Contract with America spent more than $1 million on a lobbying campaign through phone banks, fax networks, satellite television, computerized bulletin boards, talk radio, and direct mail (Berke 1995).

Many within the party worried that this religious identification could be as dangerous for the GOP as identifications that the Democrats developed. Like the relationship between the Democratic party and organized labor (and militant women's groups as well as gay and lesbian groups), the symbiotic relationship between the GOP and fundamentalist Christians has been a mixed blessing. Since the 1970s, fundamentalist Christians have been escalating their activities in support of Republican candidates for public offices. By the time of the Bush presidential victories in 2000 and 2004, evangelic Christian voters accounted for about 40 percent of the Republican presidential total vote.

The resources that interest groups bring to a political party and its political election campaigns are, first and foremost, voters and dollars. Both labor and fundamentalist Christians have claimed the ability to bring large numbers of voters to party campaigns. The Christian Coalition and its nearly 2 million members and the NRA's 3 million members claimed to be the decisive element when the Republicans unexpectedly captured the Congress in the 1994 elections. More than 46 million pieces of pro-Republican literature were distributed by the Christian Coalition and its thousands of individual churches during the 1996 campaign. The conservative religious movement had one of the strongest pro-GOP votes during both the 1994 and 1996

elections. On the other hand, labor's voting loyalty had been declining since the 1940s. During the 1990s, although most labor families voted Democratic, the general economic prosperity evident since the 1940s had moved many of these families into the middle class and toward the Republican party and its more conservative candidates.

For decades, the Democrats have relied on "big labor" to get out the vote—especially in states in which unions are very strong, such as in those in the Northeast or the industrial Midwest. It was not unusual for AFL-CIO campaign specialists to lend their expertise to Democratic party campaigns in trouble as well as bring with them highly organized telephone "get out the vote" and volunteer operations. It was not until the 2006 elections and the ability of the Democratic party to raise hundreds of millions of dollars that the Democrats realized they could buy the campaign resources that would allow them to exert a bit of freedom from their labor allies.

Interest Groups, Political Parties, and Financial Support

Money is the second resource that interest groups bring to party campaigns. Modern political campaigns expend enormous amounts of money on the media, consultants, and technologies that have become part of almost every campaign level except the most rural or lowest levels. The national level of politics—presidential, congressional, and national party organizations—spent more than $2 billion in 2004 and $2.8 billion in 2006 (Toner and Laurenza 2007). Additional tens of millions of dollars were spent on state and local level races in 2006. The money had to come from somewhere, and the parties and various interest groups went to new levels of inventiveness to raise these huge amounts of political campaign funds.

Since 1932, big business has filled the coffers of both major parties. The reason for giving money to both Republicans and Democrats is found in the long-term Democratic

TABLE 9.1 Who Gives? The Twenty Largest Total Contributors in Federal Elections, 1989–2006

Organization	Total Amount (in millions of dollars)	Type	Preferred Party
1. American Fed. of State, County, and Municipal Employees	38.1	Labor	Democrats
2. AT&T	37.0	Business	Both
3. National Association of Realtors	30.3	Business	Both
4. National Education Association	27.1	Labor	Democrats
5. American Association for Justice	27.1	Professional	Democrats
6. International Brotherhood of Electrical Workers	25.8	Labor	Democrats
7. Laborers Union	25.0	Labor	Democrats
8. Goldman Sachs	24.9	Business	Democrats
9. Service Employees International Union	24.7	Labor	Democrats
10. Carpenters and Joiners Union	24.4	Labor	Democrats
11. American Medical Association	24.2	Professional	Republicans
12. Teamsters Union	24.2	Labor	Democrats
13. Communications Workers of America	24.1	Labor	Democrats
14. United Auto Workers	23.3	Labor	Democrats
15. American Federation of Teachers	23.2	Labor	Democrats
16. FedEx	22.7	Business	Both
17. Altria Group (formerly Philip Morris)	22.4	Business	Republicans
18. Machinists and Aerospace Workers Union	21.5	Labor	Democrats
19. United Food and Commercial Workers Union	21.2	Labor	Democrats
20. Citigroup	21.0	Business	Both

Note: Total contributions include money from the organization given to political parties, money from an organization's PAC, and individual contributions from employees or officers of the organization. Preferred party means that more than 60 percent of the organization's contributions went to that party.

Source: Created by authors using data from Center for Responsive Politics. Available at: www.opensecrets.org.

domination of the Congress. Between 1933 and 1994, the Democrats controlled the House of Representatives for all but four years (1947–1948 and 1953–1954) and the Senate for almost as many years. With the Democrats in control of the lawmaking branch of government, America's business community had to deal with them and finance their campaigns in order to get the access it desired. Big business strongly prefers to have Republicans in control of Congress but can usually work very nicely with Democrats, who may favor labor but understand that business campaign contributions come when Congress provides the legislation that business wants. Many large business contributions come from corporations and interest groups with on-going interests in the policies of the federal government such as tobacco companies, telecommunications firms, lawyers, and energy companies.

Table 9.1 shows data on the financial relationship between interest groups and the two political parties over a number of years. Table 9.1 lists the twenty organizations that have contributed the largest total amounts of money in federal elections between 1989 and 2006. The total amount includes money given by the interest group directly to a party, contributions from a PAC affiliated with the organization, as well as individual contributions from employees or officers of the organization. Labor unions are especially well represented

TABLE 9.2 How the Ten Biggest PAC Donors Distributed Their Contributions in the 2006 Election

Organization	Amount (in millions of dollars)	Percent to Democrats	Percent to Republicans
1. National Association of Realtors	3.76	49	51
2. National Beer Wholesalers Association	2.95	31	69
3. National Association of Home Builders	2.90	27	73
4. National Auto Dealers Association	2.82	30	70
5. Operating Engineers Union	2.78	78	22
6. International Brotherhood of Electrical Workers	2.78	97	3
7. American Bankers Association	2.75	36	64
8. Laborers Union	2.68	85	15
9. American Association for Justice	2.56	96	4
10. Credit Union National Association	2.41	45	54

Note: Contributions made by PACs connected with the organization in the 2005–2006 election cycle.

Source: Created by authors using data from Center for Responsive Politics. Available at: www.opensecrets.org.

among these consistent contributors with twelve of the twenty largest contributors being unions and most of their contributions going to Democrats. Business groups are more likely to give to both parties to help ensure access to whoever is in power. Professional groups such as the American Association for Justice, representing trial lawyers, and the American Medical Association, representing doctors, are also persistent contributors to parties and candidates. Table 9.2 shows the ten largest PAC donors in the 2006 congressional elections and the distribution of their contributions between the parties. Some groups such as the Brotherhood of Electrical Workers and the American Association of Justice direct nearly all their contributions to candidates from one party (Democrats for both these groups) because they believe their political goals will be best met with that party in power. Other organizations such as the National Association of Realtors and the Credit Union National Association gave money to candidates (and especially incumbent candidates) from both parties with the intent of maximizing their access to members of Congress. Figure 9.5 shows a summary of PAC and individual contributions to congressional candidates in the

2006 election according to whether the contributor represented business, labor, an ideological group, or some other group. It is evident from the figure that, as in most elections, the bulk of campaign contributions come from groups or individuals representing business. Business contributed more than $500 million to Democrats and more than $600 million to Republicans. Contributions from labor groups were much less than from business, although most labor contributions went to Democratic candidates. Contributions from ideological groups were roughly the same amount as labor but almost evenly split between Republicans and Democrats.

Following the congressional elections of 1994 when Republicans gained control of both houses of Congress, Republican leaders in Congress threatened business with reduced access if they continued to give campaign money to the Democrats. This "K Street Strategy," named after the Washington street that is home to many lobbying firms, was devised by Representative Tom DeLay (R-Texas). DeLay's strategy was intended not only to benefit Republicans, which it did by bringing hundreds of millions of dollars into Republican party coffers during the

FIGURE 9.5 Source of Contributions to Candidates and Parties in the 2006 Election

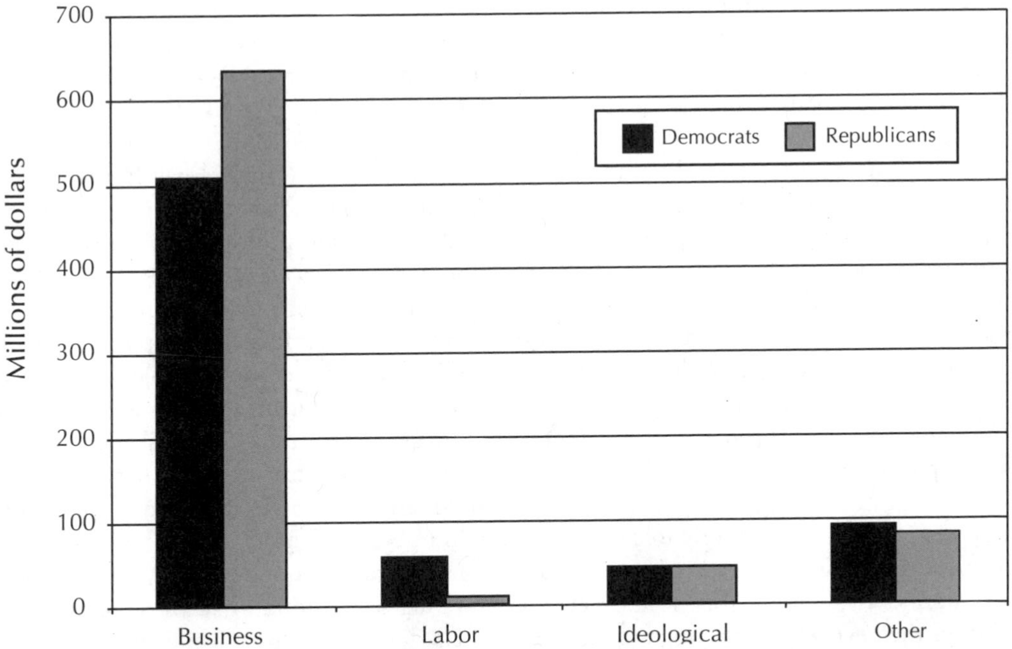

Note: Contributions from PACs and individual donors to a political party or candidate in the 2005–2006 election cycle.

Source: Created by authors using data from Center for Responsive Politics. Available at: www.opensecrets.org.

1996–2006 period, but was also to hamper Democratic efforts to regain power. Although some business interests adapted to this new reality of power in Washington, other business groups continued to give to Democrats. The strategy of these business groups was in part a recognition that even in the minority these longtime incumbents could be helpful and in part on the recognition that the majority party can change, as it did in the House and Senate following the 2006 congressional elections.

Corporations were also active in financially supporting both the Republican and Democratic national party conventions. For example, the 1996 GOP convention in San Diego was funded by contributions from Microsoft, Philip Morris, Time Warner, Lockheed Martin, and AT&T—which gave nearly $2.7 million. The Amway Corporation came up with

$1.3 million after it had given the party $2.5 million in 1994. The Amway money was used by the Republicans to buy television time on two cable networks (The Family Channel and USA Network), and for thirteen hours during their own convention, Republicans leaders favorably reported on themselves. Later that summer, the Democrats raised even more money than their rivals, with the largest contributions coming from Ameritech ($2.4 million), Motorola ($1 million), AT&T ($558,000), United Airlines ($432,000), and Kemper Securities ($339,000). Among the top ten convention-supporting interests that gave money to both parties were AT&T, Microsoft, United Airlines, and Philip Morris (Jackson 1997, 241). When the final totals were reported, the Republican convention was supported by more than $11 million in private contributions and the Democratic convention received $21 million. Larger business funding to the Republican conventions in 2000 and 2004 demonstrated the effectiveness of the "K Street Strategy" until the Abramoff lobbying scandal contributed to Republican losses in Congress in the 2006 midterm elections.

Major interest groups have already made substantial financial investment into the 2008 elections and promise to support the two party conventions in the summer of 2008. In the early going, lawyers and employees of the nation's major investment firms were the big contributors. Other top industries in the 2008 presidential races were real estate, entertainment, and health professionals (Center for Responsive Politics 2007).

After the Republicans won control of the Congress in 1994, they bluntly told corporate America that if they expect access and favorable business legislation, they would have to "change their evil ways" of giving the majority of their PAC money to the Democrats and switch their contributions to the GOP. Prior to 1994, business PACs gave most of their money to Democrats in the Congress. After 1994, business PACs continued to support those Democrats who survived that election but greatly increased business PAC giving to Republican members of Congress.

Business and business lobbyists have continued to give huge amounts of money to both parties, since divided government requires access to both parties. Washington, DC, is awash with daily party fund-raisers that raise millions of dollars from business and their lobbyists. Donations got lobbyists and their interests invitations to the White House or lunches with powerful congressional committee chairmen. Millions of dollars from interest groups got access and coincidentally, desired legislation or perhaps, desired legislative inaction.

Labor union PACs continued their overwhelming support for Democratic candidates in the 2006 elections. In 2006, 96 percent of the nearly $41 million given by labor PACs went to the Democrats. The AFL-CIO's $35

million campaign effort during the 1995–1996 election cycle was a mixture of media and services in support of the Democratic party. Reportedly, about two-thirds of that amount went for radio and television ads, with the rest being spent for organizing, get out the vote campaigns, and training political workers. Business made a half-hearted effort to directly counter labor advertising (about $5 million), but most of its 1996 financial support for Republican candidates went directly to the party in the form of soft money.

Interest group financing of political candidates and political parties exploded into the nation's consciousness during and after the 1996 general elections. The avalanche of revelations began with reports of large sums of Indonesian corporate money donated to the Clinton presidential reelection campaign. Some foreign and domestic contributions totaling $1.5 million had to be returned to their donors. Later exposures indicated that the Clinton White House regularly invited major contributors to spend the night in various historic bedrooms.

Republicans in Congress showed that they knew how to raise money in huge amounts, too. GOP contributors got access to the party's private skybox, pictures with the presidential and vice-presidential nominees, plus special assistance with political problems in Washington, DC. These special donors, called "season ticket holders in 1996," had become the new peak standard of party fund providers. The old standard in the 1992 elections was a mere $100,000. In 1996, the GOP recorded seventy-five contributions of $250,000 or more, and the Democrats had a total of forty-five. The Republican list included Philip Morris ($2.5 million) and four other tobacco companies (an additional $2.8 million).

Another example of ties between interest groups, political parties, and public policy is found in the case of the giant agricultural corporation Archer Daniels Midland (ADM). ADM, its executives, and its PAC gave more than $1 million to both Republican and

Democratic federal candidates in 1996. Those contributions bought access to key congressional decision makers on issues of major concern to ADM like the billions of dollars in ethanol subsidies it receives from the federal government. The companies that form the so-called China Lobby (the three hundred companies forming the United States-China Business Council) contributed more than $55 million to party campaigns in 1995–1996 ("Rights vs. Revenues" 1997) during the debates to grant most favored nation status to China. By the 2005–2006 period, new groups such as the pharmaceutical industry were deeply concerned over the decisions Congress was making on drug benefits for the nation's elderly. In the four election cycles prior to the 2006 elections, the pharmaceutical industry contributed $150 million to federal and state candidates and parties with 65 percent of it going to the Republican party. The Republicans passed new legislation for the industry and then protected it after the Democrats regained control of Congress in 2007 (Center for Public Integrity 2005).

The two major parties were prolific fundraisers in the 2005–2006 election cycle. During this period, the Democrats raised $483 million and the Republicans more than $602 million. Compared to the 2002 election cycle, the Democrats more than doubled their totals while the Republicans raised their figure by 42 percent (Federal Election Commission 2007a).

Usually, party donation solicitations strongly imply that the money would help buy special access to top congressional leaders. After the 1994 GOP takeover of Congress, the party concentrated its appeals to those corporations and individuals having pending business before the Congress. One corporation gave the Republicans a check for $500,000 and noted that a lot of money buys a lot of access. A Republican National Committee invitation to a fund-raising dinner in January 1996 promised those who gave $250,000 or more private meetings with Republican House chairmen and lunch with

Speaker Newt Gingrich and Senate majority leader Bob Dole. A record $17 million was raised at that dinner. When the Democrats took over as the majority party in Congress in 2007, Democratic House committee chairs put out almost the identical message that exceptional financial contributions will be associated with unusual access.

Interest Groups Campaigns in Initiatives and Referenda

The Progressive movement, which dominated the political agenda at the turn of the century, had a profound impact on the ability of interest groups to advance their agendas. Political parties were stripped of long-held powers to nominate candidates for elections, and other reforms allowed citizens the power to initiate legislation, void existing laws, and even throw publicly elected officials out of office prior to the next election. All of these new procedures were enacted to promote democracy, but in the case of the direct democracy reforms (initiatives, referenda, and recalls) the power often was transferred from political parties to powerful interest groups.

These reforms originated largely in California under Progressive reformist Hiram Johnson and then gradually spread eastward across the nation before losing political steam at about the Mississippi River. The first state to pass an initiative law was South Dakota in 1898, but the first state to have an initiative election was Oregon in 1904. As of 1995, most of the states having "direct democracy" laws are found west of the Mississippi; the most active states in terms of ballot propositions are west of the Rocky Mountains, especially Washington, Oregon, and California. Twenty-four states have initiative provisions, but only six (Florida, Illinois, Maine, Massachusetts, Michigan, and Ohio) are east of the Mississippi River. Thirty-four states have referenda laws, fourteen of which are east of the Mississippi. One explanation for this difference lies in the stronger position of political parties in the East, as opposed to the West, and their ability to resist lawmaking initiatives while agreeing to the less powerful law approving referenda demands.

The golden age of ballot propositions occurred in the 1910s, when 269 appeared and 98 passed in the various states. Only ten propositions passed in the entire decade of the 1960s. The 1990s had more than 350 measures placed on state election ballots. In the 1950s, California passed only two propositions. By the 1980s, Los Angeles County ballots averaged about thirty state and local propositions per election. As soon as the dust settles from a given year's proposition campaigns, the signature collectors are already on their way to the malls to collect names for the next campaign and the vote two years later.

In the 2006 elections, there were 163 initiatives and referenda in thirty-four states, and the most frequent ones dealt with prohibitions of gay marriages. The recent peak was 235 propositions on the ballots in forty-one states and the District of Columbia in the 1998 general elections. Sixty-one were citizen-initiated proposals and the remainder were referred to the voters by state legislatures as referenda. In the 1998 I&R contest, the voters passed thirty-eight of the sixty-one citizen-initiated propositions, a 62 percent success rate. Over the last hundred years of such propositions, around 40 percent have won in an average election year.

An industry grew up to service the needs of the interest groups seeking to use direct democracy to further their political agendas. Firms were formed to provide campaign management skills, petition signature collections, media strategies and production, and polling expertise. Later, additional expertise was required in the areas of litigation, direct mail fund-raising, and coalition building. There are three separate phases during which the industry must offer the right mix of services to interest groups: (1) qualifying, (2) campaigning, and (3) defending or challenging the results in the courts. Recent research on direct democracy campaigns in California,

Michigan, and South Carolina discovered massive interest group utilization of the techniques and very frequent interest group reliance on campaign consultants and service providers. In fact, in some states, interest groups are the major clients of campaign consultants rather than individual candidates or political parties.

Increasingly, proposition litigation has become one of the most significant areas of interest group campaigning. Almost every major initiative that wins at the polls is routinely challenged in court, which is often the only real check on interest groups' direct law writing. Court battles are fought at every stage of the initiative process: proposition titling, measure wording, official descriptions in voter guides, qualifying procedures, and defense and attack on the constitutionality of successful propositions. Between 1960 and 1980, only three initiatives approved in California were not entirely or partially declared unconstitutional by state or federal courts (Butler and Ranney 1994).

Direct democracy (initiatives and referenda) is significant in about fifteen states. Between 1950 and 1992, California led all the states in having 127 measures on the ballot, followed by Oregon's 97 and North Dakota's 95. On the other end of the continuum, among those states with direct democracy provisions, Kentucky held none, New Mexico held two, and Wyoming held three. California is the state that uses direct democracy with the greatest frequency on the state and local levels of politics. In any given election, there are a dozen or so statewide initiatives as well as dozens of county and city initiatives. California could be called "an interest group playpen" in the sense that almost all the statewide initiatives are sponsored by major groups or coalitions of groups.

Progressive reforms severely weakened California political parties in their role as campaign resource providers in regular election campaigns; the frequent initiative campaigns increasingly came to look just like office-oriented campaigns. Special initiative-supporting companies were born in California to organize initiative campaigns. These campaign management firms provided all the campaign-related services previously offered by the two major parties: workers, strategies and tactics, communications, advertising and media campaigns, polling, and other such parts of modern campaigns. Thus, two incentives for interest groups to use direct democracy were in place: enabling laws, dating from approximately 1905, and the private organizations that by the 1940s allowed groups to bypass parties and state government.

Why do interest groups find initiative campaigns to be an attractive strategy? The major advantage is that they can avoid the normal legislative process and literally write the exact law the group desires and then go out and make it law. They can avoid the uncertainty and compromise of the normal legislative process by going to the initiative campaign if they have the resources to pursue that path. Initiatives are also attractive to groups that have lost their issues in the legislative chambers, in the governor's office in terms of a veto, or even in the courts. Frequently an interest group can introduce a piece of legislation into the state legislature and have it emerge from the process as a new law that is very different from the law desired by the group. The initiative process allows interest groups to avoid this problem. Citizen groups are more likely to use these tools of direct democracy than business groups because business groups are more comfortable working through the legislative and executive branches.

What resources are necessary for success in initiative campaigns? No single essential resource can guarantee success. Various types of groups have used very different combinations of resources in victorious initiative campaigns. Perhaps the single most useful resource is money. In an initiative campaign environment, money can buy almost every other key resource, including leadership, management skills, media strategies and production advice, and lots and lots of media

access. It can buy "volunteers" to work the petition tables in shopping malls to qualify an initiative for the ballot. Money can even buy respect for a group if an expensive public relations campaign is carefully crafted. Groups with money have a very significant advantage in the initiative campaign process. One study indicated that groups with the most money won more often than they lost, but it did not explain why some very underfinanced interests were able to win as well (Magleby 1998).

Even the poorest interest groups can mount successful initiative campaigns if they have alternative resources such as numbers, public sympathy, or special membership characteristics such as respect or celebrity status. For small, poor groups, the existence of preexisting public support or sympathy may be an essential resource. For large, financially weak groups, membership numbers may be decisive in the petition phase or in the decision making election. Although it is easier for powerful groups to participate and achieve success in initiative campaigns, poorer and weaker groups have a chance to play the game.

The highest number of statewide propositions was recorded in 1996 when ninety-six were held in twenty states. This broke the 1914 record of ninety initiatives. The all-time low, twelve, was recorded in 1968. An estimated $200 million was spent on these ballot propositions in 1996. The best-known of the 1996 propositions were the California initiatives that sought to overturn state laws on affirmative action and another that sought to legalize the medical use of marijuana. These attracted enormous media attention throughout the nation and also the anticipation that if they were successful in California, other groups would attempt them in other states. This is the "agenda setting" role of initiatives. One interest group, U.S. Term Limits, spent more than $1 million supporting term limit measures in fourteen states. This group was supporting the requirement to identify whether or not candidates on future ballots support a constitutional amendment on congressional term limits.

Initiatives range from those with potentially profound impact on millions of Americans to those that impact only a handful of people. An example of the latter type was a measure on the Alaska state ballot in 1996 that banned hunting wolves, wolverines, foxes, or lynx on the same day that a hunter flies in an airplane. The purpose of this initiative was to prevent hunters from flying around the state, sighting an animal on the ground below, landing the plane, and then shooting the animal. The various immigration initiatives on ballots in several states after 2004 had the potential of impacting millions of people in those states.

Interest groups must qualify an initiative in order for it to reach the ballot for a popular vote. The proposed law must be titled and the various details written. In these early steps, the interest must have legal or at least legislative knowledge or expertise. The next major step is the petition drive to obtain sufficient signatures from a state's voters to qualify the proposed initiative. The number of valid voter signatures required varies from state to state, from 2.7 percent of those voting in the previous general election in North Dakota to a high of 15 percent in Wyoming. The higher the threshold, the fewer the initiatives on the ballot. The most common threshold is 6 percent, as found in California and Oregon. Some state legislatures have tried to block attempts at direct democracy. The Utah legislature passed a law that raised the number of signatures and to further require a certain number must be collected in about half the state's twenty-nine counties. This latter requirement for popular support in the state's most rural counties made qualification very difficult if not impossible for most issues.

Both conservative and liberal interest groups have used initiatives. During the 1970s and 1980s conservatives used the process to limit state and local governments' taxing power and to establish term limits. Environment groups have used initiatives to limit corporate use of certain lands and to limit hunters. After 2000, the emotional conservative issues such as the prohibition of gay marriage were found on a growing number of states' ballots. In general, voters tend to view propositions with general suspicion and tend to vote no if doubt exists. Thus the process tends to favor conservatives in their defense of the status quo.

The campaigns for some propositions have been quite inexpensive, whereas others rival the most expensive U.S. Senate and gubernatorial campaigns. A 1988 California initiative campaign financed by five insurance companies totaled $101 million. The same year saw a $21 million campaign by the tobacco companies and an $8 million campaign by the National Rifle Association in California. The 1998 California proposition dealing with Indian casinos recorded well over $100 million in total spending as Indian tribes poured about $85 million into their effort, and Las Vegas gambling interests spent more than $45 million in an unsuccessful effort to protect the billions of dollars at stake in their industry. Some less controversial propositions can get by on shoestring budgets with almost no expenditures for media. These campaigns largely rely on free media to communicate their arguments to the voting public. These campaigns can succeed only if they are unopposed, and even in that case there is no guarantee of victory, since voters will vote against propositions they have heard little about.

Conclusion: The Role of Campaigns in Linking Political Parties and Interest Groups

Contemporary interest groups are frequent campaigners. They campaign in initiative and referendum campaigns as they seek to pass laws that they desire while bypassing state legislatures and other governmental institutions that may obstruct their goals. Media campaigns are also important tactics for many interest groups. They seek to establish reservoirs of goodwill in the public for future issue campaigns, present their defense of existing policies, or argue their demands for policy changes. Grassroots campaigns are run to supplement insider campaigns by professional lobbyists working in Washington, DC, or the various state capitals. Grassroots efforts attempt to activate membership, selected publics, or the general public to exert pressure by forwarding supportive communications to the intended target—usually political but sometimes private organizations.

Many interest group campaigns proceed simultaneously. This is a major change in the general area of campaigns. At one time, the word "campaign" was understood to mean political party election campaigns. Now a campaign is more likely to mean an interest group campaign, since they seem to be part of every month of the year, unlike party campaigns, which are concentrated around our two-year cycle of fixed elections. The health care reform campaign, discussed at the beginning of this chapter, may be the greatest interest group issue campaign in American political history. But it is certainly not the last major issue campaign. It served as the model for other issue campaigns that followed it in the mid-1990s, and the unofficial announcement that party-oriented campaigns and interest group campaigns had finally come together.

The next chapter discusses the "inside" tactics of interest group campaigns along with their major participants, the lobbyists, and closes with an examination of internal interest group characteristics such as leadership, money, and membership and how they can be converted to valuable political lobbying resources useful in the issues and candidates' campaigns.

CHAPTER 10

Interest Group Lobbying

Campaigning Inside the Government

Lobbying in Washington, DC, and the various state capitals and other local governments is usually personified by the lobbyist. The lobbyist is the person sitting up in the gallery of the House of Representatives or in the back of the committee meeting rooms. The lobbyist is also the association representative who helps draft forthcoming legislation for a state legislator and then testifies at committee hearings on the value of the proposed law. Lobbyists often symbolize the interest groups for which they work. The late Jack Valenti, adviser to former president Lyndon Johnson, represented Hollywood in Washington for decades. Valenti was the president of the Motion Pictures Association and one of the most powerful and best paid ($11 million a year) of all the association lobbyists in the capital. All of the top fifty association heads were in the million dollar total compensation range in 2003–2004 (Vaida 2006, 24).

The Lobbying Profession

What types of people become lobbyists? Former U.S. Senate majority leader and unsuccessful Republican 1996 presidential candidate Robert Dole became a lobbyist in 1997. Dole joined the Washington law firm of Verner, Liipfert, Bernard, McPherson, and Hand. His fourteen-room office suite is located a couple of blocks from the White House. Dole earned his estimated $600,000 salary not by lobbying in the normal meaning of the word but by providing access and strategic advice to his clients. Dole was hired to help the firm erase its image as a "Democratic" law firm. Other former political heavyweights who joined Verner-Liipfert in recent years included Bob Dole's Democratic counterpart, former Senate majority leader George Mitchell, former Texas governor, Democrat Ann Richards, and former Texas senator and Treasury secretary Lloyd Bentsen.

The most visible lobbyists are retired politicians or heavyweight political activists. But they do not represent the typical lobbyist. Lobbyists come from a wide variety of backgrounds and occupations. Some are long-term interest group activists; others are associational employees who may do association office work during most of the year and emerge as lobbyists during the short legislative sessions common in many states. Others come from a governmental background, not as high-profile elected officials but as "faceless staffers" from obscure committees or governmental offices. Lobbyists used to be stereotyped as overweight males smoking long cigars, but the Gucci shoes and expensive suits are still part of the image for both male and female lobbyists. Research on the state level indicates the emergence of women as lobbyists across the nation, and that pattern holds in Washington as well. Boxes 10.1 and 10.2 tell the stories of two Washington lobbyists.

BOX 10.1 Meet Gerald Cassidy, Super Lobbyist!

In 2005, Gerald Cassidy hosted a party to mark the thirtieth anniversary of the establishment of Cassidy & Associates, a small lobbying firm that grew into the "most lucrative" lobbying firm in Washington, DC (Kaiser 2007b). Today, Gerald Cassidy, a true American success story, is reported to be worth more than $125 million. Cassidy's lobbying firm became so successful in part by devising a new kind of business—the "earmarking" strategy. Earmarking is a term used to describe the appropriation of money by Congress that is usually directed to specific institutions—public or private—even though no federal agency has proposed to spend the money to carry out its regular activities. After two years of lobbying, Cassidy's firm helped Tufts University secure earmarked federal funding for a nutritional research center in 1978 and later for a veterinary school (Kaiser 2007a). Once this process was established, earmarked appropriations became a standard tool for lobbyists, and a specialty of Cassidy's firm. In recent years, however, the use of earmarks has exploded and eventually became the subject of intense criticism as a way for special interests to get federal funding for projects that were not subject to the normal Congressional appropriation process (Chaddock 2006b; Kirkpatrick 2006).

Cassidy originally came to Washington, DC, in 1969 to join the committee staff of Senator George McGovern (D-South Dakota). Cassidy had been working as a legal aid lawyer for migrant workers in Florida when he met the senator whose staff had organized hearings on hunger among migrant workers. In 1975, Cassidy left the senator's staff and started a two-person lobbying firm with another congressional staffer. As the firm grew, additional lobbyists were hired on a 10 percent commission compensation plan that became the foundation for great growth in the firm's revenues. Later, Cassidy created Powell-Tate, a public relations firm, and acquired a polling firm and a grassroots lobbying firm as well as engaging in a number of business transactions to raise money.

The Republican takeover of Congress in 1995 hurt Cassidy's firm; however, because of its long-standing ties to Democratic legislators. Cassidy's firm also suffered because other lobbying firms began to specialize in earmarking. Still, Cassidy was able to compete and succeed in the new political environment by hiring key Republican operatives. For a person who was raised in a poor Irish American family in New York City and whose goal was to achieve personal financial security, the rise of Cassidy & Associates to become one of the most important and lucrative lobbying firms in the nation's capital is quite a story.

BOX 10.2 Who Is Jack Abramoff, and Why Is Everyone Saying Such Bad Things About Him?

By the end of President George W. Bush's first term, Jack Abramoff had reached super-lobbyist status in Washington, DC. Few had ever played the lobbying game so ruthlessly and so profitably as had Abramoff. From just his collection of American Indian tribe clients, Abramoff had raked in $80 million in lobbying fees. Yet, in March 2006, Jack Abramoff was sentenced to more than five years in prison and ordered to pay restitution of more than $21 million.

Just how did Abramoff manage to position himself to milk the Washington lobbying game so expertly? If one came up with one simple explanation, it would be the classic explanation of lobbying success: access, access, and more access. It was not "what" Abramoff knew; it was "who" he knew. Born in Atlantic City, New Jersey, Jack Abramoff grew up in Beverly Hills. As an undergraduate at Brandeis University, he organized colleges in Massachusetts for the 1980 Reagan presidential campaign. He later earned his JD degree from George Washington University Law School in 1986. His initial entry into conservative Republican party power circles was aided by his father, who was the president of Diners Club and had contacts with one of Ronald Reagan's close friends. Abramoff won the presidency of the College Young Republicans after a campaign managed by Grover Norquist. Later, Abramoff hired Ralph Reed as an intern with the organization. Norquist and Reed would go on to become two of the most powerful actors in the post–1994 Republican years in Washington. Abramoff rode these and other friendships to the peak of the Washington power game.

Prior to the November 1994 elections when Republicans won control of the House, Abramoff spent some time in Hollywood producing an "anti-communist" movie called *Red Scorpion*. After the Republican election victory, Abramoff was hired as a lobbyist at Preston Gates Ellis & Rouvelas Meeds, the lobbying branch of a major Seattle law firm. Abramoff was hired to add a conservative Republican with ties to the new Republican leadership. A year later, he used his relationship with Representative Tom DeLay (R-Texas) to help kill a bill to tax Indian casinos and began building an enormously lucrative lobbying specialty representing Indian tribes with gambling interests. He got additional millions of dollars representing businesses in the Northern Mariana Islands that wanted to keep Congress from imposing American labor laws on their textile and clothing factories. Other Abramoff clients included a Russian energy company, the Pakistani military, Tyco Corporation, the governments of Malaysia and Sudan, and an Israeli telecommunication firm.

Abramoff was appointed to the Bush administration's 2001 transition advisory team for the Department of Interior. Abramoff claimed close ties with the Bush White

House as well as with Tom Delay in the House. In addition, Abramoff remained close to his friends Ralph Reed, a prominent member of the fundamentalist Christian community, and Grover Norquist, an anti-tax activist closely connected with a number of the city's most powerful conservative groups. Since wining and dining help create access, Abramoff bought two Washington restaurants. He also rented four sky boxes at local sports arenas at a cost of more than $1 million per year. Finally, Abramoff arranged and paid for golf trips to the world-famous St. Andrews golf course in Scotland for powerful congressmen and their staff members. He paid various journalists to write glowing columns about how powerful and effective Abramoff was as a lobbyist. He bought a string of casino riverboats in the South and set up a "think tank" that existed only as a beach house and a site to wash money from various clients.

Political scientist Norman Ornstein (2007) noted that the crimes that Abramoff committed were not unique in American political history, but "the scope and brazenness . . . were on a wholly different scale . . . from anything in the last century." Ornstein concluded, "To anyone who cares about our political institutions and their integrity, this story is simply revolting" (2007). Another writer referred to Abramoff as a "living museum of corruption" (Taibbi 2006). Ornstein reminds us that unless the rules of the Washington system are reformed and carefully enforced, Democrats in Congress and Democratic lobbyists may be tempted to exploit the system in the same way as Jack Abramoff and his friends.

Sources: Continetti (2006), Ornstein (2007), Schmidt and Grimaldi (2005), Stone (2006), Taibbi (2006).

To be successful, a good lobbyist must have something to sell potential clients. Some sell subject matter expertise such as deep knowledge of a particular area, for example, the health care industry. Such knowledge can come from working in the industry or from governmental expertise gained as legislative staff on the health or tax-writing committees. Others offer a deep understanding of the legislative process, policymakers of all types, or the political process. This is the type of knowledge offered by the Bob Doles of the lobbying world. They can crack the political maze by offering strategic advice and personal access. Other lawyer-lobbyists can offer advice on the legal process—an area of lobbying that has become very important for many interest groups. A final type of knowledge is communications. This sector is dominated by public relations and political communications specialists and has spread far beyond New York City's Madison Avenue to major cities across the nation.

The pool from which lobbyists emerge is largely located in Washington, DC, or the various state capitals. Former government employees and elected officials make up a large part of the pool, as do the jack-of-all-trades lawyers and employees of trade associations, interest groups, and other such organizations.

However, in recent years, new professions such as public relations and accounting have become prominent in the lobbying field ("The Public Relations Industry" 2006).

The *Washington Post* and the *National Journal* are excellent sources to help understand the broad range of experts who make up the Washington, DC, lobbying corps. With billions of dollars at stake for America's major corporations, many lobbyists may be employed and millions of dollars spent in lobbying campaigns; almost all involved will consider it money well spent. One of the nation's largest pension funds, TIAA-CREF (which probably holds the money invested for your college professor's retirement), hired a corps of lobbyists to defend its tax-deductible status, including a former Republican member of the House, a former Bush chief legislative aide, and several heavyweights from the lobbying firm of Hill and Knowlton. Despite this firepower, it lost.

This lesson is an important one—lots of money and high-powered lobbyists do not always win because they are often opposed by other high-powered groups with lots of money. Indeed, competition between interest groups in the policymaking process is a consistent feature of American politics. Often, though certainly not always, the competing sides both have deep pockets. For example, a recent lobbying battle involved competition between internal medicine physicians and radiologists. The former were represented by the famous lobbying firm of Patton Boggs, and the losing radiologists retained another powerful law firm of Mannatt, Phelps, and Phillips. In another battle, a number of airline companies retained a significant part of the lobbying community as they fought over the distribution of the airline ticket tax that generated more than $33 billion in a five-year period. Delta (former Republican National Committee chair Haley Barbour), American (former Bush transportation secretary James Burnley IV and the wife of then Senate minority leader, Linda Daschle), and Southwest (several former congressmen and

aides plus Fred McClure, President Bush's top legislative adviser) used both lobbyists and CEOs as well as passengers as grassroots lobbyists. Perhaps the most important battles (in terms of the billions of dollars on the table) were over efforts to cut more than $100 billion in Medicare spending in the budget over a five-year period. The American Association of Retired Persons (AARP) defeated various proposals, including a proposal to raise Medicare premiums on wealthier seniors, increase the age for eligibility, and charge a set fee for each home health care visit. One interest group, the American Hospital Association, was concerned over so many budget issues that it hired an all-star team of lobbyists including Christopher O'Neill, son of the former House Speaker, former GOP head Haley Barbour, and a host of former staff aides of top congressmen and senators.

Voluntarily and involuntarily retired (i.e., defeated for reelection) politicians can become nearly perfect lobbyists. After all, they come to the job possessing the skills necessary for lobbying success: access to governmental decision-makers, knowledge of the legislative process, political skills, and even knowledge of the law, since many are lawyers as well. Many former members of Congress have become permanent residents of the capital, and after they leave Congress, they seek alternative employment in order to avoid returning to their home state. One incentive has lured more than two hundred former members of Congress to become lobbyists in Washington: money. One former congressman is reportedly earning almost $350,000 a year as a lobbyist for banking interests. Former senator Bob Dole's $600,000 a year salary is a bit on the high side for such former members, but his résumé is a bit better than others. A Dole-type lobbyist is called a "rainmaker" in that his role is to find clients and let them "rain money" down on the law-lobbying firm. For example, former vice president Walter Mondale was nominated to be the U.S. ambassador to Japan in August

1997. Prior to that appointment, he rained down more than 1 million dollars a year in billings on his law firm.

Not all of the former government officials who turn to lobbying come from the Congress or state legislatures. One of the most successful (and, incidentally, best compensated) is former Nixon administration secretary of state, Henry Kissinger, who so capitalized on his "special relationship" with the People's Republic of China that he has been called "China's single best lobbyist" (Sciolino 1996). Maybe Kissinger is China's best lobbyist, but he is only one of many. Among the big names who have lobbied for the People's Republic of China are four other ex-secretaries of state (Alexander Haig, Cyrus Vance, George Schultz, and Lawrence Eagleburger), former secretary of defense Richard Cheney, former national security adviser Brent Scrowcroft, ex-Senate Republican leader Howard Baker, and two former U.S. trade representatives, Carla Hills and William Brock (Grady 1997).

Former officials such as Kissinger are often eagerly sought out by foreign interests who assume that such people have extraordinary access and influence. A classic example of this type of lobbyist was Michael Deaver, a former White House staff member in the Reagan administration who landed three very lucrative clients—South Korea, Canada, and Philip Morris International—soon after he left his job with Ronald Reagan. Personal connections are the essence of Korean domestic politics, and thus hiring Deaver was a logical move for the South Koreans. Later Philip Morris, seeking to gain entry into the very restrictive and very rich South Korean tobacco market, hired Deaver to represent it in South Korea. Perhaps one of the major selling points such lobbyists have when they approach potential clients is the access they retain to their former places of employment. Deaver kept his White House access pass long after he moved to the private sector as a lobbyist. Former members of Congress have access to the floor of

Congress, its gyms and restaurants, and other gathering sites off-limits to ordinary lobbyists.

"Inside lobbyists," as the name implies, are informal lobbyists who are sitting members of a legislature or bureaucracy. An example of this type of hidden lobbyist would be all the lawyers or veterans who also sit in legislatures or governmental offices. In the 1980s, a majority of House and Senate members were veterans and always seemed to find money for veterans' causes. Although the number of veterans in Congress has declined in recent years, Congress finds it politically impossible to vote against veterans. Congress also has great difficulty passing laws that affect lawyers. Maybe the large numbers of former lawyers have something to do with those outcomes.

Inside lobbyists are frequently found in the executive branch. The George W. Bush administration was filled with hundreds of former lobbyists and association representatives who advanced their old interests in their new roles as federal government political appointees. It is the same in nearly every administration, but the groups that are represented change from Republican to Democratic administrations. Many lobbyists volunteer their time with the incoming presidential transition teams that select members of the new administration. Not surprisingly, many interest group advocates show up in the new administration when the appointments are announced. So common is this pattern that hundreds of such examples can be noted in all recent administrations.

Other interests with significant inside lobbies have included farmers, small businesses, and lawyers. Recently Alaskan seafood processors sought to increase their tax deductions for the costs of feeding employees located at remote sites in Alaska. The seafood companies wanted the same type of tax consideration given years earlier to the offshore oil drilling companies that had supporters on the Senate Finance Committee. Senator Frank Murkowski of Alaska was added to the tax writing committee and was able to introduce the equal tax break to a budget bill. For the first time, the seafood industry had an inside lobbyist.

Bureaucratic lobbyists are government lobbyists who lobby other parts of the government. In the White House, the presidential lobbying staff is called the Office of Congressional Liaison. These "liaison lobbyists" have become a powerful corps of hundreds of professional advocates with total lobbying budgets approaching $20 million. Approximately fifty liaisons lobby for the military before Congress, and another twenty-five represent the interests of the State Department. Many of these liaisons move on to the private sector after a few years of lobbying for the government.

Former bureaucrats and political appointees know the lobbying business because they are the targets of lobbying campaigns or help organize such campaigns to secure their objectives. Even more prized are former legislative staff members who possess many of the key lobbying skills: legislative and political skills, contacts, and, most importantly, subject matter expertise. The banking industry, for example, is always looking for experienced staff members from the Finance or Banking Committees and the pattern extends to almost every other congressional committee or governmental agency. When these staff experts switch sides to the lobbying community, their arrival is well announced in the various Washington, DC, media. Note the tone of the following three "announcements" in the *National Journal*:

- "Dutco Worldwide has just snagged the Education Department's Cristina Culver as vice president." (May 6, 2006, p. 75)
- "David Russell, who was chief counsel for the Republicans at the Senate Commerce, Science and Transportation Committee, is now a senior vice president with Bryan Cave Strategies, a bipartisan lobbying firm." (January 21, 2006, p. 60).

- "Tammy Cameron has joined Van Scoyoc Associates as a vice president. Cameron comes to the lobbying firm from Capitol Hill, where she worked on the Senate Appropriations Committee as majority staff director on both Energy and Water and the Military Construction and Veterans Affairs subcommittee." (May 20, 2006, p. 84)

Some of the highest paid lobbyists in Washington, DC, and the major state capitals are "lawyer-lobbyists" such as Bob Dole. Affiliated with the most prestigious Washington and regional law firms, these men seldom participate in the direct contacts that other lobbyists perform daily. Depending on the relevant laws, they resist registration as lobbyists by emphasizing the lawyer part of their hyphenated job title. Traditionally, many of Washington's most powerful law firms resisted putting significant resources in their lobbying sections. Since the 1980s, however, more of the mega-firms have hired personnel as their lobbying billings have multiplied. Washington is awash with lawyers. The number of lawyers admitted to practice before the federal courts of the District of Columbia increased from just under one thousand in 1950 to sixty-one thousand in 1990. Many of these are lawyer-lobbyists. A good example of this type of lawyer-lobbyist is Robert Strauss, former chairman of the Democratic National Committee, former trade representative and ambassador to Russia, and his law firm, Akin, Gump, Strauss, Hauer, and Feld.

The elite of these lawyer-lobbyists are often called "super lawyers." Their experience and knowledge are eagerly sought after by interests of all types. The very best of these have worked in the White House or as cabinet members. They personify the "revolving door" of private lobbying: government service followed by very lucrative career lobbying. Salaries for some of these super lawyers may run into the millions of dollars on an annual basis. The best way to describe the rationale behind these huge salaries is to note that a single provision inserted into a tax bill can be worth billions of dollars to a given industry. One bit of advice by super lawyer Clark Clifford was estimated to have saved the DuPont family more than $500 million in taxes. Clifford received a reported $1 million at the time—now worth more than $4 million when adjusted for inflation. Lobbyist Michael Deaver was earning about $400,000 to $500,000 per client per year for his access and lobbying skills. To give you an idea of the stakes that justify these types of salaries, oil companies stood to gain between $7 billion to $28 billion over a five-year period under an obscure provision in the 2005 energy bill that allows oil companies to avoid paying royalties on oil and gas produced in the Gulf of Mexico ("Big Oil's Big Windfall" 2006).

Lobbying salaries and levels of skills and knowledge have also jumped on the state level. The Center for Public Integrity reported that total spending for lobbying in only forty-two of the fifty states had passed the $1 billion mark in 2005. Here are the numbers on the state level: 40,000 lobbyists, 7,400 legislators, 40,000 new laws, and total state expenditures of $1.3 trillion (Center for Public Integrity 2006).

Many wealthy corporations and some of the richer trade associations retain several of the city's major law firms and perhaps a half-dozen or more lobbying firms as lobbyists to ensure the widest possible representation. Some firms specialize in one type of issue, while others focus on one site of specialization such as the FCC or the Senate Finance Committee. Other firms do public relations (PR), media, or grassroots lobbying. Expertise and access can be very expensive, but it is often worth it to hire experts, given what a change in federal policy may be worth to companies or entire industries.

Lobbyists with especially refined communications skills are frequently based in the public relations industry that began on Madison Avenue in New York City and later established firm foundations in Washington, DC.

Many of these PR-lobbying firms generate extensive billings from their work for foreign governments and interests. A full range of services in PR lobbying can be provided by firms with a mixture of press kits, direct mail, fact-finding trips, traditional lobbying, seminars, and media cultivation activities. Such services can run an interest easily into the seven-figure billing category. Many of the lobbyists who emerged from the Reagan White House come from public relations backgrounds.

The efforts of Hill and Knowlton, a public relations and lobbying firm, in support of the Kuwaiti government during the Gulf War in 1990–1991 represent the most famous PR and lobbying campaign in recent political history. After Iraq invaded Kuwait in 1990, the Kuwaiti government in exile contracted with Hill and Knowlton to increase support in the United States for the liberation of Kuwait. A front group was formed, Citizens for a Free Kuwait, which was financed almost entirely by the Kuwaiti government and paid Hill and Knowlton $11.5 million for its PR lobbying. The agency proved to be a key element in developing U.S. political and military support for Kuwait (Trento 1992).

Just like the law firm that hired Republican Bob Dole to open doors in the Republican-controlled Congress, the Republican-dominated "complete service firm" of Black, Manafort, Stone, and Kelly added a former Democratic party finance chairman in order to enhance its access with Democratic power holders. But the classically successful "Republican-Democratic" lobby is the firm of Wexler and Reynolds. Anne Wexler, a former assistant to President Jimmy Carter, joined with Nancy Clark Reynolds, a vice president and head of Bendix Corporation's Washington office (as well as a personal friend of President Reagan) to establish a lobbying firm that could work both sides of the aisle in Congress or the executive branch. Wexler and Reynolds offers almost every lobbying service a client could require.

Although the full services lobbying giants have dozens of employees, many of the lobbyists listed in the Washington, DC, telephone book (and on the state level) are very small, one- or two-person firms. These "niche firms" tend to specialize in a single industry or around a narrow issue. Specializing in a narrow field, having just a few clients, and having a close, personal, often long-term relationship between clients and lobbyists makes these firms long-term actors and very "service oriented."

When an interest group, a trade association, or a coalition plans a campaign, it often approaches it from a variety of directions. There are many roads to success in Washington, DC, politics. The more voices a cause can produce, the better its chance of success. A corporation engaged in such a campaign may work through its own lobbying team, several lobbying firms, or public relations firms and one or more trade associations. Many may also belong to broad peak associations such as the Chamber of Commerce or the National Association of Small Business. Giant corporations such as Ford and General Electric have double-digit law and consulting firms representing their interests (Soloman 1987). In "emergencies," these corporations go out and buy whatever needs to be bought in order to win a campaign. Broadcast television lobbying with its major trade association, the National Association of Broadcasters, and its ten major constituent groups, including the various television networks, had hired 174 registered lobbyists ranging from stars on the left such as former Texas governor Ann Richards to conservatives including former Republican National Committee chairman Haley Barbour and GOP super-lobbyist Tom Korologos. CBS had retained the services of twenty-nine lobbyists (Safire 1997).

Haley Barbour is an interesting case of a person converting political party experience into lobbying clout and financial compensation. Barbour was a lobbyist before becoming the Republican party head for a four-year period during the first Clinton administration. He quit the party job in 1997 and returned to his old lobbying firm of Barbour, Griffith, and Rogers and brought with him thirteen new clients who had been major Republican money contributors. These new clients nearly doubled the client list of his firm and included such big-spending interests as telecommunications, tobacco, trucking, Mercedes Benz, and Delta Airlines. Barbour, closely identified with the Gingrich-led, Republican-dominated Congress, has been described as one of the best access lobbyists in Washington, DC (Wayne 1997c). He then moved on to become governor of Mississippi, and after Hurricane Katrina devastated the Mississippi Gulf coast, Barbour was noted to be much more effective in getting federal government money for relief and reconstruction than his Democratic party counterpart in Louisiana. Once a lobbyist, always a lobbyist!

Most of the tens of thousands of lobbyists working in Washington and the state capitals are employees of various interests. These are called "in-house" lobbyists. Big, powerful organizations are characterized by large, well-funded governmental relations or legislature liaison staffs. Some of these groups maintain a dozen or more lobbyists and additional staff to support their activities. Weaker organizations do not have permanent lobbying corps, but they often "double hat" their executive directors, who operate as lobbyists when needed and take care of the association the rest of the time. There are thousands of these trade association and interest group in-house lobbyists in Washington, DC.

Amateur lobbyists are both the best and the worst of lobbyists. They can be very useful to grassroots campaigns because of their enthusiasm and dedication, or they can be disastrous because they are often uncontrolled and nonprofessional. Many cause-oriented groups (moral, religious, women's, and environmental issues) choose to use amateur lobbyists because of the nature of the groups or simply because they do not have the money to hire professional lobbyists. Amateur lobbyists can be effective if they possess special talents or resources. An interest group that brings amateur lobbyists from the home district of a member of Congress will probably have its message heard. The message will be communicated even more effectively if it is voiced by several prominent businesspeople who have contributed campaign funds in past elections. The greatest danger with amateur lobbyists is that they can wreck groundwork carefully prepared by the organization with their excessive enthusiasm and perhaps offensive tactics.

Accountants have entered the Washington, DC, lobbying game in recent years. The special contribution of accountants to the lobbying game is their ability to produce data on the tax implications of many types of legislation. Price Waterhouse, with a Washington, DC, staff of 123, did tax law analysis for Hewlett-Packard. The major accounting firms increasingly monitor tax legislation and regulatory actions, help put together coalitions, provide low profile technical advice on lobbying, and even directly lobby Congress and the executive branch. In the early 1990s, Price Waterhouse, for example, had a legislative monitoring service with 150 clients. The service costs each client about $20,000 per year (Stone 1993).

Public relations firms have also been very busy in the lobbying business. It has been estimated that the public relations spending in the United States totaled more than $3.8 billion in 2005. The PR industry has seen a number of mergers of already powerful PR and lobbying firms such as Hill and Knowlton merging with Burson-Marsteller.

Most professions have standards that govern training and ethics, yet traditionally there were no such standards for lobbyists. A lobbyist was anyone who said he was one; but in many cases he was not, or just the reverse. Lobbying has slowly become more professional in its standards and training. In terms of formal educational standards and credentialing, George Washington University's Graduate Program in Political Management (with a lobbying subfield) is the current state-of-the-art program in Washington. The American League of Lobbyists (ALL) was formed, in part, to improve the image of lobbying as a profession. When the Abramoff lobbying scandal exploded in 2005–2006, ALL tried to promote its Code of Ethics for Lobbyists as a solution not requiring new congressional rules or federal government laws. On the state level, books by Hrebenar and Thomas (1987, 1992a, 1992b, 1993) have reported research indicating that lobbying on the state level has also become more professional in recent years as better-trained, better-educated, and higher-paid lobbyists have become more common in many states and the "contract" (i.e., professional, multi-client) lobbyist has emerged in almost all the larger states and in many of the smaller states as well. Another change that has modified the image of lobbying is the increase in the number of women lobbyists in both the nation's capital and many state capitals.

The Lobbyist's Role in Political Issue Campaigns

The job that a lobbyist does in a political issue campaign includes many different types of tasks. A lobbyist may be a contact person who exists to link his or her interest with the appropriate governmental decision-makers, in essence, an access creator. Some lobbyists earn a very fine living based on the people they know and getting their clients' messages to those people. For contact lobbyists, the quality of their contacts is often more valuable than the quantity of their contacts. Interest group campaign strategists are very rare, but they are very valuable. They put together the lobbying campaigns, negotiate the coalitions, and allocate the various group resources to maximize the prospects of success. The most numerous of all are the liaison lobbyists. As their name implies, they act as middlemen between interest groups and government. The liaison lobbyists attend meetings, listen to hearings and debates, and collect information about what is occurring in their assigned territory—be it Congress, the regulatory agencies, or the White House. If something of significance happens or could happen to their clients, the liaison or watchdog lobbyists alert them, may give recommendations for action, and wait for directives. Some may report daily on the broad range of activities they are monitoring; others have a specific list of concerns and just follow those events, such as bills with tax implications for a specific industry such as energy. Finally, the most common type of lobbyist in terms of the public perception of the profession, is the advocate who spends time going from office to office visiting politicians and bureaucrats, presenting data and arguments on their issues, and testifying at committee hearings.

Like the never-ending debate regarding the symbiotic relationship between celebrities and the media, a similar debate exists regarding the relationship between lobbyists on one side and politicians and bureaucrats on the other. Each side uses the other to advance its own political goals. Lester Milbrath (1963) in his classic study of lobbying argues that politicians often use lobbyists in order to gain support for the politician's or bureaucrat's bill. Lobbyists often write major bills; more than one new law has passed the legislature in a form nearly identical to what the lobbyist wrote before the session (Milbrath 1963, 234). Also, many a speech given on the floor of a legislative chamber or in committee hearings was written by supporting lobbyists for the legislator. Like the media and celebrities, lobbyists and legislators have a mutually supportive relationship. Lobbyists provide valuable information of a technical and political nature without which legislators would find lawmaking enormously more difficult.

Lobbyists and Lobbying Campaign Tactics

The art (not yet the science) of lobbying is organized around a wide range of possible tactics that the group strategist or lobbyist can select from to accomplish the group's issue campaign objectives. Some of these tactics are largely external to the everyday activities found in Washington, DC, or the various state capitals.

Before we turn to the tactics of influence, we need to discuss the groundwork that precedes the actual lobbying activities. The most fundamental of these preliminary activities is aimed at creating access for the group, its lobbyists and its messages.

In the world of real estate, the secret of success has been called "location, location, location." In the world of successful lobbying, the secret of success may be "access, access, and access." With tens of thousands of lobbyists seeking to make their case, not all of them will have their chance or their best chance to communicate. Almost every interest group pursues an access-creating strategy to set the stage for future lobbying campaigns. Some of these access-creating activities seek to establishment a personal relationship, if not friendship, between the lobbyists and the governmental officials who can affect the group's fortune. Others involve the utilization of money in the form of campaign contributions from PACs affiliated with interest groups, seeking to reward politicians for past support and entice them to support the group's positions in the future.

One of the interesting outcomes from the 1997 congressional hearings on the Clinton 1996 campaign funding scandals was a series of frank observations from governmental officials and lobbyists about the issue of access. Clinton's attorney general, Janet Reno, sent a letter to the House Judiciary Committee stating that the courts and U.S. law do not regard access (the opportunity to meet with governmental officials) as being the same as a job offer, a government contract, or a policy decision. The Reno conclusion was nicely summarized in a newspaper's headline: "Reno Says It's Legal to Sell Access" (1997). One businessman, Roger Tamraz, admitted giving $300,000 to the Democratic party during the 1996 elections to get access to federal decision makers to seek support for his proposal to build an oil pipeline in the Caspian Sea area. The Clinton administration never gave its permission despite Tamraz's meeting with the president and his staff. Tamraz mentioned at the hearing that he should have given $600,000 instead of $300,000. But doubling the amount would not guarantee success; money can buy access (which he got) but does not guarantee results. The late Nelson Polsby (1997), a prominent political scientist at the University of California at Berkeley, once wrote that "money gains access. So what?" Polsby notes that access is protected by the First Amendment to the Constitution (freedom to petition for the redress of grievances), and the courts have ruled that political contributions are a form of political speech and thus protected by the First Amendment. Access to politicians is granted as a result of many factors, and only some of them are based on money or campaign contributions. Some access is granted on the basis of power or simply residence in the home constituency, old friendships, organizational or issue group affiliations (sometimes being in the same church congregation does not hurt), and many other potential relationships.

It is important to distinguish between access-creating money politics and an old-fashioned bribe. In the late 1800s, a typical pattern of interest group-legislator behavior involved the direct (perhaps under the table in the form of cash-stuffed envelopes) exchange of money for laws. Political bosses, such as William M. Tweed of New York's Tammany Hall political machine, controlled a delegation of New York legislators who were "for sale" for $100 to $5,000, depending on the issue (Thayer 1973, 37). Direct bribery was a standard tactic for many lobbyists a hundred years ago. Relatively few cases of interest group-legislature bribery have occurred in the last fifty years, and the use of direct bribes is considered to be one of the few tactics that lead to nearly certain disaster. For example, the recent conviction of Congressman Randy "Duke" Cunningham (R-California) for accepting more than $2.4 million in bribes from defense contractors illustrates this point—not only did this end Cunningham's congressional career, but he was sentenced to more than eight years in federal prison (Brosnahan 2006).

Today, money flows from interest groups to politicians when a PAC makes a legal contribution to a candidate's campaign. These contributions are not "bribes" for past or future votes, but concrete expressions of an organization's support for past and future efforts and its desire to maintain access established over the years. Lobbyists, and not just the interests they represent, have become a major source of campaign funds for politicians. Between 1998 and 2005, lobbyists' political contributions rose from $17.8 million in the 2000 election cycle to $33.9 million in the 2004 cycle. The 2006 numbers were even higher (Public Citizen 2006).

It has been noted that people in power lust not only for money but for other "vices" as well. It used to be the case that the way to a legislator's heart was through his stomach. Interest groups sponsored very expensive dinners and wined and dined their prospective targets. But in recent years, public and media attention and changing laws and legislative rules have significantly reduced these opportunities. Other groups sponsored golf or tennis tournaments or just played in them in order to meet and befriend political decision-makers. Changing tastes have elevated and reduced the values of these access-creating activities. Golf used to be the preferred sport of lobbyists, since it had several advantages. Golf was expensive and exclusive and thus prestigious. It also had the advantage of being an all-day event, which allowed lobbyists to establish firmer ties with their political counterparts. Yet, the scandal of members of Congress enjoying golf at the famed St. Andrews course in Scotland, paid for by the disgraced lobbyist Jack Abramoff, may have set back the value of golf as an access-creating tool for a while.

Tennis, too, has its place as a preferred sport of lobbyists. Tennis gained in popularity because it was a much shorter game and could be handled over a lunch break or a couple of hours before or after work. One of Washington's most successful lobbyists noted that every PR and lobbying firm had a tennis-playing lobbyist and club memberships. The late Jack Valenti, head of the Motion Picture Association, had a half dozen tennis club memberships. As one Washington tennis pro noted, "Once you get to know people on the court, you can get through on the telephone without going through six or seven intermediaries" (Gamarekian 1983). Other groups use tickets to sporting events (tickets to Washington Redskins football games are especially valuable) and entertainment events such as touring Broadway productions to create their access. The general rule for these access-creating events is that no lobbying business is to be discussed on the course or the courts. That can be done later after the access has been firmly established.

Figure 10.1 displays the increase in total spending on federal lobbying from 1998 to 2006. Even over this short period of time, total spending on lobbying at the federal level has increased by more than $1 billion a year, from just under $1.5 billion in 1998 to more than $2.5 billion in 2006. Table 10.1 presents a list of some of the biggest players in the federal lobbying game during this same period. The top spenders are, not surprisingly, fixtures of the Washington scene. Business interests are well represented here by such entities as the U.S. Chamber of Commerce and the Business Roundtable as well as corporations such as General Electric and Northrop Grumman. The importance of the federal government's actions related to health care over this period is evident from groups such as the American Medical Association, American Hospital Association, and the Pharmaceutical Research and Manufacturers of America all spending more than $100 million on lobbying over the 1998–2006 period.

Table 10.2 shows the amount of money spent on federal lobbying by selected sectors of the economy in just one year. In 2006, spending to lobby the federal government on health care totaled more than $400 million and in both the technology and finance sectors spending in a single year topped $300 million. How is that money being spent? Much of the spending goes to hire lobbying firms that specialize in lobbying Congress or the various agencies of the executive branch. Table 10.3 lists the top lobbying firms in 2006. When ranked by lobbying income, the firm of Patton Boggs was the number one lobbying firm in the nation's capital in that year. Figure 10.2 shows the total lobbying income for the Patton Boggs firm from 1998 to 2006. Although Patton Boggs lobbying income was a staggering $34.7 million in 2006, this total was down slightly from 2005 when the firm was paid $36.3 million for its lobbying services. Who pays a firm like Patton Boggs to lobby on its behalf? According to data compiled from public reports by the Center for Responsive Politics, the list of clients in 2006 for Patton Boggs included large companies such as Mars, Inc. (which spent $2.3 million), Bristol-Myers Squibb ($620,000), and Wal-Mart ($240,000), as well as long-established interest groups such as the Association of Trial Lawyers of America ($920,000) and the American Beverage Association ($200,000). Also included on the long list of clients of Patton Boggs for 2006 were a number of state and local governments including Hawaii ($380,000) and New York ($120,000) as well as the cities of San Antonio ($160,000), San Diego ($200,000), and Baton Rouge ($160,000). Large and successful lobbying firms such as Patton Boggs tend to work for a variety of clients and cover a range of issues.

Lobbyists who are ready to assist legislators when they need help will gain future access. Some lobbyists have sufficient access and influence with existing legislative leaders to be of assistance in helping new legislators gain assignments to desired committees. Because

FIGURE 10.1 Total Spending on Federal Lobbying, 1998–2006

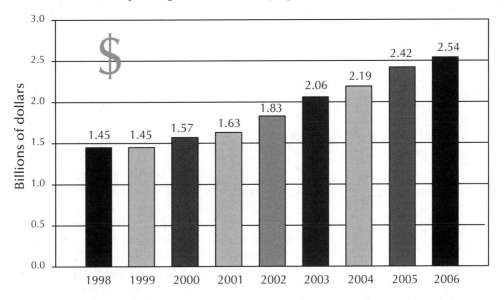

Source: Created by authors using data from Center for Responsive Politics. Available at: www.opensecrets.org.

TABLE 10.1 Top Ten Total Spenders on Federal Lobbying, 1998–2006

Organization	Amount (in millions of dollars)
1. United States Chamber of Commerce	317.2
2. American Medical Association	156.4
3. General Electric	137.8
4. American Hospital Association	129.1
5. Edison Electric Institute	105.6
6. AARP	105.3
7. Pharmaceutical Research and Manufacturers of America	104.3
8. National Association of Realtors	97.5
9. Business Roundtable	97.1
10. Northrop Grumman	95.7

Source: Created by authors using data from Center for Responsive Politics. Available at: www.opensecrets.org.

TABLE 10.2 Spending on Federal Lobbying by Selected Economic Sector, 2006

Economic Sector	Amount (in millions of dollars)
Health Care	412.0
Communication and Technology	345.8
Finance and Insurance	314.6
Retail and Service Business	213.4
Energy and Natural Resources	210.1
Transportation	189.8
Defense	128.4

Note: Sector totals are arrived at by summing the spending on federal lobbying by entities within each sector. For example, the "communication and technology" sector includes spending from corporations such as AT&T, Verizon, Microsoft, and Intel. Categorization by economic sector is only an approximation, as many organizations that report spending may have economic interests in more than one sector. The 2006 yearly totals were calculated by the authors from the January–June and July–December spending reports.

Source: Created by authors using data from PoliticalMoneyLine from Congressional Quarterly. Available at: www.fecinfo.com.

TABLE 10.3 Top Ten Lobbying Firms, 2006

Firm	Lobbying Income (in millions of dollars)
1. Patton Boggs	34.7
2. Van Scoyoc Associates	25.9
3. Akin Gump Strauss Hauer & Feld	25.8
4. Cassidy & Associates	24.0
5. Barbour, Griffith & Rogers	21.6
6. Dutko Worldwide	21.3
7. Hogan & Hartson	17.3
8. Quinn, Gillespie & Associates	16.8
9. DLA Piper Rudnick et al.	16.5
10. PMA Group	16.0

Source: Created by authors using data from Center for Responsive Politics. Available at: www.opensecrets.org.

committees and subcommittees are often the decisive sites for the addition or subtraction of a single critical phrase or even a single word, such tactics can often prove to be invaluable to lobbyists. Such an outcome occurred in the 1998 federal budget bill, which emerged with a well-hidden clause committing the federal government to pay any legal judgments against it arising from continuing litigation on the failed savings and loan companies. Experts estimate that one clause may cost the taxpayers of the United States up to $50 billion. Often these "earmarks" are placed into the bills at the last moment and many of the congressmen and senators voting on the bills do not even know the provisions are there. When the Republicans took control of Congress in 1994, the number of earmarks was 4,155 valued at about $29 billion. In 2004, the earmarks had jumped to 14,211 worth $53 billion (Weisman and Babcock 2006). No wonder some of the most aggressive lobbyists moved to be specialists in inserting earmarks into the various appropriations bills.

Celebrity lobbying also creates access for some interest groups. Groups that have trouble getting a hearing for their political demands may secure a celebrity to gain access to the decision-making system. The Hollywood A-list superstars (and even some of the lesser B-list stars) can be recruited into a cause and brought to Washington, DC, for hearings and media events. Among the stars who have lobbied in recent years have been Richard Gere (Tibet), Sally Fields (farm families), Charlton Heston (gun rights), Morgan Fairchild (environment), Martin Sheen (homeless), Melanie Griffith (arts), Susan Sarandon (arts), the late Christopher Reeve (marine conservation), Quincy Jones (TV production rights), Sting (South American rain forests), Jane Fonda (Nature Conservancy), Billy Joel (Nature Conservancy), Barbara Streisand (women's rights and the environment), Angelina Jolie (the plight of children in Africa), and Michael Keaton (polluted rivers). These "celebrity lobbyists" have great ability to get media attention for a cause.

One environmentalist group, Earth Justice Legal Defense Fund (the former Sierra Club Legal Defense Fund), ran a celebrity ad in the *New York Times Magazine* in 1997 featuring actor Mel Gibson standing under the word "conspiracy," playing on the name of Gibson's 1997 movie. The ad promotes the Earth Justice Fund's recent successes and urges people to contact the group for help in environmentalist issues. Such a celebrity got the organization much more attention than it could have elicited with just a straight advocacy ad. In 2007, groups seeking to aid the people of Dafur in the Sudan used actress Mia Farrow to try to put pressure on the U.S. government and the Chinese government (a major buyer of Sudanese oil and supplier of weapons to the Sudanese military) to force Sudan to allow international peacekeepers into the Dafur region.

When power shifts between political parties in Washington, interest groups often have to turn to coalitions and contract lobbyists to

Figure 10.2 Lobbying Income for the Firm of Patton Boggs, 1998–2006

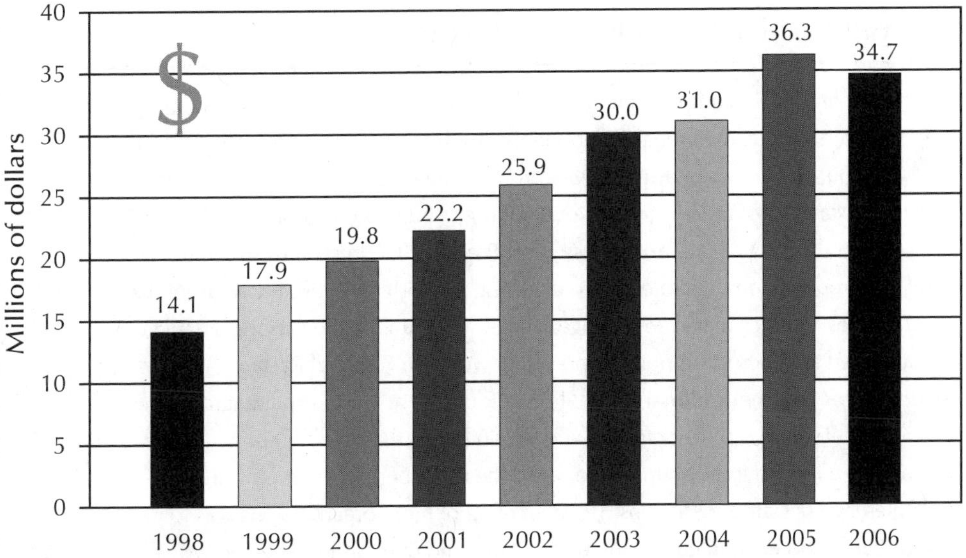

Source: Created by authors using data from Center for Responsive Politics. Available at: www.opensecrets.org.

establish access with the newly powerful members of Congress or the executive branch. Broader coalitions will have many more contacts with a wider range of politicians and bureaucrats than a single interest group. Sometimes even a multigroup coalition has insufficient access and the private sector may have to be hired to generate more access. Some private lobbying firms have added a specialization in coalition building as a way to enhance access. Box 10.3 illustrates the nature of interest group coalitions on two recent issues.

Lobby Campaigns as Information Presentations

A lobbyist has a variety of types of information that can be combined into a presentation in support of his or her organization's campaign. The information a lobbyist uses can be political, emotional, or rational. Statistics generated by the group can be presented to support an argument; political information,

often in the form of public opinion, is frequently summarized in polling data or media commentaries. The lobbyist may also draw on scientific studies. Whatever the nature of the appeal, it must be communicated to the appropriate political decision makers; it is the lobbyist's job to decide which targets are the appropriate ones and how the data is to be communicated.

The first decision is targeting. The conventional wisdom of lobbying suggests that contacts with staff may be as useful as discussions with the politicians themselves. Key staff members often exercise an extraordinary influence over their political masters on certain types of issues. One lobbying study from several decades ago indicated that most lobbyists in Washington, DC, lobbied the politicians' staffs more than they lobbied the politicians themselves (Milbrath 1963, 216). Staff members are involved in every major step in the legislative process—from the initial research to the final vote roundups. However, if a lobbyist is determined to lobby the elected representatives themselves, which ones

BOX 10.3 Tales of Two Coalitions in Washington, DC

Coalition building is a tactic to produce an ad hoc organization stronger than the various individual components. Among the dozens of coalitions active in our nation's capital in 2006 were two organizations that seem to be almost perfect examples of the advantages of deciding to build a coalition.

One coalition was organized to support President George W. Bush's immigration reform proposals on the table before the Congress early in 2006. It was proof that sometimes "politics makes for strange bedfellows." Among the various organizations that joined together to support the president were the National Restaurant Association and the National Council of La Raza, an activist Hispanic group that is seldom allied with the restaurant owners. Two others that seldom cooperated in lobbying efforts, but did so this time, were the Chamber of Commerce and the Conference of Catholic Bishops. The goal of all of these organizations was to pass a law that would expand guest-worker programs and offer undocumented workers already in the United States a chance to become citizens. Also supporting the bill were elements of the labor union confederation, the AFL-CIO, and the Essential Workers Immigration Coalition made up of more than forty business and trade associations seeking a comprehensive immigration law reform.

One would think such a powerful coalition would triumph with little difficulty, but in fact, it lost to a very decentralized and unorganized collection of organizations that demanded strict enforcement of the existing immigration laws. These anti-reform groups deluged members of Congress with a flood of emails, letters, and calls. One of the key groups was Numbers USA, which claimed 135,000 members and an email contact list of more than 1 million names. The anti-reform groups won this battle in part because they better reflected the concerns of conservative Republicans and in part because they had the advantage of needing only to block the proposed reform. Given the nature of the legislative process, it is generally easier to prevent a bill from passing than it is to get it passed. Also, the difficult political circumstances in 2006 for Republican House and Senate candidates meant that most of these candidates were determined not to annoy the conservative base of voters who cared strongly about this issue.

A second coalition operating at about the same time informs us how powerful groups and interests can come together in a different type of lobbying to stop Congress from doing something to undermine their economic interests. Jack Valenti, the former head lobbyist for the Motion Picture Association and one of Washington's legendary lobbyists, was selected to head a coalition designed to communicate to mothers and fathers across the nation on the subject of how to control their children's television- and movie-watching habits. Valenti started the movie rating system back in the 1960s in response to parents' concerns. Now in 2006, he headed a $300 million media effort to teach parents how to use the V-Chips in every new television and mandated by the government in the Telecommunications Act of 1996. The coalition included the Motion Picture Association of America, the National Association of Broadcasters, and the Consumer Electronics Association. The coalition was managed by the Ad Council, a nonprofit organization that distributes public-service ads, and a wave of ads were released to preclude efforts by conservatives to push for strong restrictions on programming and increasing the fines for the broadcasting of indecent content. The Federal Communication Commission had been deluged with complaints after a performance by Janet Jackson and Justin Timberlake at a Super Bowl halftime show. This powerhouse coalition was sufficient to sidetrack meaningful new rules on their industries. Could $300 million in advertising have had an impact?

Sources: Kaplan (2006) and O'Connor (2006).

make the best targets? Experienced lobbyists suggest lobbying friends first; pursue the doubtful and ignore the known opponents. Bypassing opposition members reduces the probability of their becoming involved in the campaign, although not eliminating it.

The successful lobbying visit is pretty individualistic as each lobbyist has a unique style. There is, however, general agreement about the elements of lobbying. The conventional wisdom of lobbying emphasizes the need for a personal presentation set up as a formal appointment if possible, the need to be confident and knowledgeable on the issue, the requirement to be fair and honest in presenting arguments, the need for brevity, the need to request a specific action such as supporting a particular provision in committee, and the importance of leaving a summary fact sheet for later use by the political official. Other useful rules for lobbyists include: (1) never ever lie because being caught reduces your credibility to zero, (2) try to link your issue

either to the politician's home district in a positive manner or to some general political principle that may transcend local-level politics, and (3) never ever threaten politicians, unless your group is able to put such threats into reality (Milbrath 1963, 223–225).

Testifying at hearings and placing your group's arguments in the public record of the debate is a standard means of communication. Hearings on a given bill can be one-sided, since the committee leadership may already have made up its collective mind on a given issue, but these presentations serve a valuable purpose for many interest groups. Participation in formal hearings gives legitimacy to interest groups and allows them to be part of the debate and provide group leadership, even if only for its own membership. Additionally, hearings may be covered by the news media, giving the group much greater dissemination of its arguments.

Washington, DC, is home to dozens of major research organizations called think tanks. One of the early major liberal think tanks was The Brookings Institute; it was joined by the conservative Heritage Foundation in 1973. In an environment in which "information equals power," many think tanks are sponsored by interest groups or work closely with them. During the first half of the Reagan administration, the Heritage Foundation produced hundreds of books, monographs, and analytical papers plus a monthly foreign policy and defense newsletter and a quarterly journal on policymaking. During Reagan's first term, the Heritage Foundation was quite important, as its policy recommendations were used by conservative Republicans in drawing up their action agendas to undo decades of liberal Democratic rule. It also was a significant intellectual influence on the Gingrich Republican revolution's agenda, the "contract with America." Various liberal interest groups such as the Progressive Policy Institute quickly entered the policy debates when the Clinton administration began its transition team policy discussions in late 1992 and early 1993.

Interest groups also seek to dominate staff and committee members when a major study commission is selected to study an emerging policy area. If a group can dominate such a committee, the issue can be framed in a very favorable way to protect the group's political objectives. Sometimes, it is argued, the membership of such study committees is selected to favor a specific policy recommendation. One of the best examples of stacking a study committee was the 1997 federal gambling study commission put together by President Clinton. Opponents of legalized gambling argued that members of the committee were stacked in favor of supporting continued gambling. As more and more political issues have been framed in much more sophisticated analytical forms, research and study committees play more important roles. When the George W. Bush administration sought to develop an energy policy in 2001, Vice President Cheney formed a study group made up largely of energy company representatives,

and the group formed a policy recommendation that became the foundation for the administration's oil and energy policies.

Polling data is another form of information that an interest group can use to frame the political discussion. Few groups can afford to do their own polling, but more groups are contracting out for survey research and focus group analysis. The Health Insurance Association of America's "Harry and Louise" television ads were based on focus groups and research on how people felt about the proposed Clinton health care reforms in 1993–1994. In the same battle, the Pharmaceutical Manufacturers Association hired a pollster to research regularly the public's image of the drug companies. Discovering public ignorance about the role of the drug companies in developing new drugs, the association first ran some unsuccessful ads on the subject of the drug companies' research successes. Later polling encouraged the organization to shift its ad subjects to discussions of specific diseases and related drugs. These ads cost the group more than $32 million during the 1994–1995 period but were cheap when the group considered the financial costs of possible increased governmental regulations and restrictions (Barnes 1995).

Another way interest groups can influence an upcoming debate is to secure membership on a governmental advisory committee. There are well over one thousand different federal advisory committees, commissions, councils, boards, and panels. These committees advise the federal government in virtually every area of policymaking. They span a wide range of subjects. Some multi-interest groups such as the AFL-CIO, and major corporations such as AT&T serve on these boards. Diversity balancing is often a requirement for membership on such advisory committees. The previously mentioned federal advisory committee on gambling was much delayed as President Clinton apparently sought a Native American who had no public positions on legalized gambling but was favorable to continued gambling. A Native American was important, since so much of the nation's gambling is now conducted in reservation casinos.

Advisory committee membership is important to interest groups for a variety of reasons. First, the groups can use them to firm up their relationships with key governmental decision makers. Second, such memberships allow the groups to have a role in "framing the issue" and establishing a foundation of information upon which early recommendations for policies are based. Finally, membership on such committees legitimizes the member groups as "players" in the coming debate and enhances their role in later legislative debates.

Restrictions on Lobbying in the Federal Government

Until the late 1990s, there were no effective federal laws that regulated lobbying. Effective regulation of lobbying has been nearly impossible, given Supreme Court interpretations of the First Amendment as it has applied to the concept of "political speech." The First Amendment guarantees the people the right to freedom of speech and the right "to petition the Government for redress of grievances." Tension between the constitutional rights of freedom of speech and petition and the desire to control or at least bring into the open some of the excesses of the lobbying process has made the implementation of effective lobby laws a very difficult task.

Other than outright bribery, until very recently no lobbying techniques have been prohibited on the federal level. Given First Amendment concerns, almost all reformers have tried to increase public information about lobbying activities rather than prohibit or restrict any specific activities.

Prior to 1935, no laws restricted lobbying. In the 1930s, Congress passed several fragmented and inadequate pieces of legislation in response to specific scandals by public utility holding companies and the maritime industry. The electric power industry, known as the

"Power Trust," was one of the most powerful interests in the 1930s. In an early grassroots campaign aimed at the Congress, it generated more than 5 million letters to members of Congress opposing utility holding company legislation. That piece of legislation, the Public Utilities Holding Company Act of 1935, included within its various provisions a requirement for anyone employed or retained by a registered holding company to file reports with the Securities and Exchange Commission (SEC) before attempting to influence Congress, the SEC, or the Federal Power Commission. This was the first piece of Congressional legislation to restrict lobbying in any manner. A scandal in the shipping industry regarding the lobbying practices of that industry as it attempted to influence a maritime subsidy bill resulted in a lobby registration provision in the Merchant Marine Act of 1936. Shipping companies and shipyards receiving governmental subsidies had to report their income, expenses (including lobbying expenses), and interests on a monthly basis. The information generated by these requirements was considered confidential and was not made public until the passage of the Public Information Act of 1966.

The Foreign Agents Registration Act of 1938, or the McCormack Act, was an attempt to register anyone representing a foreign government or organization in the dangerous period just prior to World War II. The goal was to direct public attention to agents of foreign governments and attempt to neutralize foreign propaganda. The act was not effective to begin with and declined in effectiveness significantly with subsequent amendments over the years. Lawyers, for example, were exempted if they engaged in routine legal activities for their foreign clients. Consequently, many of the lawyer-lobbyists working in Washington, DC, never registered, since they defined themselves as lawyers and not lobbyists.

In 1946, Congress passed as part of a general reorganization act the Federal Regulation of Lobbying Act—a comprehensive piece of legislation to cover lobbying of Congress. It required the registration of any person who was hired by someone else for the principal purpose of lobbying Congress and the submission of quarterly financial reports of lobbying expenditures. The Supreme Court ruled that the act is applicable only to (1) persons or organizations whose principal purpose is to influence legislation and (2) direct communications with congressmen on pending or proposed legislation.

The weaknesses of the 1946 law were legion. Many lobbyists never registered under its provisions, claiming that their principal purpose was not lobbying. Others did not register because they used their own money and did not "receive money for lobbying." Grassroots or indirect lobbying was not mentioned in the act and thus was unregulated. Groups could spend millions of dollars on grassroots campaigns and not report a dime. The law focused on lobbying members of Congress, and thus lobbying their personal staff, the executive branch, or the staff of congressional committees was not covered by the law. The reporting of expenditures was left up to the lobbyists, and many simply reported no lobbying expenses. And, finally, the act had no real investigation or enforcement provisions.

In 1995, Congress finally gave in to demands for reform and passed two provisions that impact lobbying. The first restricts gifts from lobbyists. New rules bar House and Senate members from accepting gifts, meals, and trips except from family members and friends. The Senate allows gifts valued at less than $50, with $100 total limits from a single source in a year. The House allows no gifts of any value from a lobbyist. There are exceptions in the rules, such as allowing trips and attendance at events that are connected to lawmakers' official duties, for example, throwing out the first ball at a baseball game. The exception for trips may be a big loophole in that it allows all-expenses-paid trips that are fact finding or associated with official duties such as "to speak on Congress" before a con-

vention. International trips are limited to seven days and domestic trips to four days, excluding travel time. These changes could be the first steps toward effectively reducing the role of money in creating access. The style of lobbying in Washington has changed dramatically: full-course dinners for members of Congress bought by lobbyists are now illegal, but stand-up buffets are legal (Schmidt 1996).

In 1995, Congress also repealed the 1946 Federal Regulation of Lobbying Act and replaced it with the Lobby Restrictions Act. Many of the 1946 loopholes were closed, but lobbying by religious groups resulted in grassroots lobbying and lobbying by religious groups being exempted from the provisions of the new law. The new law now covers all lobbyists who seek to influence Congress, congressional staff, and policymaking officials of the executive branch including the president, top White House officials, Cabinet secretaries and their deputies, and independent agency administrators and their assistants. Representatives of U.S. subsidies of a foreign owned company and lawyer-lobbyists for foreign entities are required to register. So now we know who the lobbyists are, which interests they represent, and how much money is spent by the interest in their lobbying.

Killing the grassroots reporting requirement and exempting religious groups from the reporting requirement turned out to be fatal flaws in the new lobby law. Another significant provision that was killed would have established an enforcement agency. Attempts were made to ban key U.S. government personnel from ever becoming lobbyists for foreign interests. This failed, but a reform was passed and, for the first time, there were reporting and registration requirements on lobbyists in our nation's capital.

The only other laws that affect lobbying pertain to financial restrictions regarding contributions to federal campaigns. The Federal Election Campaign Act of 1971 banned group donations to general presidential campaigns unless funneled through political action committees, beginning with the 1976 presidential election. Since 1989, House and Senate rules have banned earnings from honoraria usually obtained by speaking before interest groups.

The 1978 Ethics in Government Act limits most ex-federal executive branch officials from lobbying on matters they had worked with in their federal jobs. Another provision banned senior governmental officials from lobbying their former agency or federal department for one year. None of these restrictions applies to former members of Congress. Therefore, when ex-senator Robert Dole joined a major Washington, DC, lobbying firm in 1997, he was careful to say that he was not a lobbyist but merely offered strategic advice to his clients. Dole did not have to be so careful since even as a lobbyist, he would not be in violation of the law as a former senator.

When the Abramoff lobbying scandal hit Washington in 2005–2006, many of the old lobbying reform proposals were dusted off by the reform groups such as Common Cause and Public Citizen, but the Republican-controlled Congress delayed any meaningful reforms as long as they could in 2006. After the Democrats took control of both houses of Congress in January 2007, a variety of reform rules were quickly passed by the two houses. These reforms included the following:

- Bans on gifts from lobbyists.
- Prohibit organizations that hire lobbyists from paying for congressional travel beyond one day in length.
- Prohibit lobbyists from attending congressional trips.
- Require quarterly electronic reporting of all lobbyist activity.
- Impose disclosure of stealth lobbying coalitions.
- Provide online disclosure of earmarks in appropriation and tax bills.
- Restrict spouses of members from lobbying Congress.
- Require lobbyists to report all campaign contributions, fund-raising, and bundling for candidates.

- Slow the revolving door by prohibiting former members from lobbying during a two-year period after leaving office.

Neither house wanted to pass the single most important reform, an independent lobbying enforcement agency (Holman 2007). Common Cause, the governmental reform organization, summarizes the goals of these changes: make governmental ethics laws effective, impose an effective gift and travel ban, reduce the damage of the campaign money chase, slow the revolving door of lobbyists and government political appointees, and shine a light on lobbying activities.

Judicial Lobbying Campaigns

Interest groups have been using the courts and **judicial lobbying** with great success since the 1940s, when the NAACP turned to judicial remedies in the face of legislative refusal to address the issue of segregation in America. Today, hundreds of groups are ready and able to play the "court card" if they lose legislative, bureaucratic, or electoral battles. Judicial lobbying is a strategy available to big and small groups alike, but it requires very specific skills and resources or at least access to such resources. Groups with few resources can follow a minimum-resource strategy and groups with great resources can play the all the cards in the judicial lobbying hand.

Interest groups use indirect judicial lobbying to set the stage for later direct lobbying. Groups try to influence judicial opinion by helping to frame upcoming issues in ways favorable to the group's interest. Tactics useful in legislative and executive branch lobbying do not work well in judicial lobbying (Vose 1958). Picketing a federal courthouse has been illegal since the 1950s. Grassroots campaigns do not seem to be effective either, since judges never acknowledge reading communications on upcoming issues. Letter writing does happen, particularly on the issue of abortion. While many have tried to influence judges by sending letters, such actions do not seem to have influenced any key judicial decisions.

One particularly useful indirect tactic has centered around efforts to influence the selection of federal and state judges. A number of recent presidential elections have had a focus on judicial appointments. For example, in the 1980 election many liberal groups were concerned with possible court appointments by the Republican candidate, Ronald Reagan. By the end of the Reagan administration in 1989, more than half of the 750 federal judges were Reagan appointees. After the Democrats won the White House under Clinton in the 1992 elections, many liberal interest groups were very hopeful of greatly influencing the federal judiciary with Clinton's appointments. Many of these groups were disappointed when President Clinton placed more emphasis on gender and ethnicity than on liberal ideology. Additionally, many liberal groups complained that the Clinton selection process was so slow that many judicial positions remained vacant for far too long. Part of the reason behind dozens of judicial vacancies in the Clinton second term was a Republican strategy that sought to delay and kill as many of the nominations as possible and hope that a Republican president in 2001 could fill the vacancies with judges favorable to conservative interest groups. That is exactly what happened when George W. Bush became president in 2001 and began appointing conservative judges, including two new Supreme Court Justices in 2006.

Federal judges are appointed by the president with the advice and consent of the Senate, producing a selection process that involves legislators, political parties, and pressure groups. Prior to the 1980s, the politics of federal judicial nomination was low-key. However, liberal interest groups mobilizing to kill the Bork nomination in 1989 and to challenge but lose on the Thomas nomination produced a conservative counter reaction and almost guaranteed future conservative opposition to a Democratic president's liberal or moderate judicial nominations. The 1987 nomination of Robert Bork to the Supreme Court came close to the idea of total interest group issue war that we discussed in connection with the health care reform battle in 1993–1994. A large number of groups, 185 of them, opposed the nomination and fought the 53 pro-Bork groups with a range of tactics unseen in previous court nominations. Bell (2002) argues that by this point the traditional confirmation process "fell apart" and interest groups came to dominate it. Indeed, for a time after the Bork nomination, the confirmation process became completely intertwined with the lobbying process in Congress and the electoral process. One issue in presidential and congressional election campaigns was the type of judge a presidential candidate would nominate for the Supreme Court or how a Senate candidate would vote on the issue of confirmation. By the 105th Congress, there were more than four hundred groups taking position on judicial nominees. In the last years of the Clinton administration, interest groups had joined with Republican senators to defeat as many Clinton's judicial nominees as possible with the expectation that a future Republican president would nominate judges more attractive to these groups.

Many observers expected that when President George W. Bush had the opportunity to nominate two justices to the Supreme Court these nominations would generate the same kind of interest group participation evidenced in the Bork hearings. President Bush's nomination of John Roberts to be chief justice and his nomination of Samuel Alito to associate justice on the Supreme Court in 2006, however, did not result in the expected level of interest group participation. Only nine groups (five liberal and four conservative) were present at Roberts's hearings and only three groups (two liberal and one conservative) participated in the hearings for Alito (O'Conner, Yanus, and Patterson 2007). Both justices were confirmed without much political confrontation.

After an issue reaches some form of decision or non-decision in the legislative or executive branches, losing interest groups often try to bring it to the courts for another type of outcome. We have already discussed the idea of shaping the potential debate as a form of indirect lobbying. This can be done by writing articles favoring the group's position on an issue in leading law journals and legal periodicals. Such articles also demonstrate intellectual support for political proposals not yet accepted in legal decisions. Women's groups placed a series of favorable articles in journals prior to significant sex discrimination cases being decided in the 1970s. After 2001, articles in law journals and significant law textbooks have tried to reframe the discussion on the Second Amendment of the Constitution to overturn two hundred years of conventional legal interpretation that the amendment did not apply to individuals but just to the militia. Some of this research was sponsored by the National Rifle Association—an organization that supports the individual's right to have firearms.

Direct judicial lobbying usually involves sponsoring litigation or filing an amicus brief. Litigation sponsorship seeks to obtain court decisions supporting the group's goals. Such litigation requires significant legal resources and can be very expensive, with group costs perhaps running more than $1 million for a case that goes to the Supreme Court. But anyone engaging in judicial lobbying must know that nothing seems to happen quickly in the judicial process. Some cases can take years to reach the Supreme Court. Even if a group can win a case even at the highest levels, it must be prepared to protect its victory in follow-up or compliance cases. Judicial political campaigns require long-term commitment and the resources to stay in the campaign for years and perhaps decades. The NAACP began bringing civil rights and antidiscrimination cases to the courts in the 1940s and is still

bringing such cases to the courts into the twenty-first century.

Group sponsorship of litigation is very expensive and time-consuming. Public interest law firms, such as the National Women's Law Center and the Mountain States Legal Foundation, are designed to litigate their issues in the courts. Sponsoring litigation can produce favorable precedents and maybe even establish constitutional rights such as the right to privacy, as in the abortion cases. Another political goal of sponsoring litigation is to threaten opponents with a long, expensive court case in hopes that they will agree to the group's demands without going to court.

Although a given group may want to initiate a specific interest group legal campaign, the group must have the access to the legal and political expertise needed to be successful in such an environment. Expertise may be found in the group's staff or membership, or perhaps it can be donated to the group from interested outsiders such as law school professors. If the group has sufficient financial resources, it can buy the expertise it needs on the open market. Figure 10.3 shows an advertisement for a group that specializes in undertaking such legal issue campaigns.

In order to bring an issue to the courts, an interest group must have "standing." Whether the party bringing a suit is a person or an interest group, that party must show that there is a real harm or injury resulting from a particular law or policy. Simply being opposed to a law or policy is typically not sufficient for a party to have standing to sue. Another problem with this question of standing is by the time a suit works it way through the court system, the person claiming injury may not be in the same situation and the case may be moot. Prior to the 1960s, rules of standing were quite restrictive; they were liberalized in the 1960s and 1970s but restricted again as the courts became more conservative in the 1980s and 1990s.

For many interest groups, the easiest way to participate in a judicial lobbying campaign is to file an **amicus curiae brief**. Amicus

FIGURE 10.3 Washington Legal Foundation Advertisement

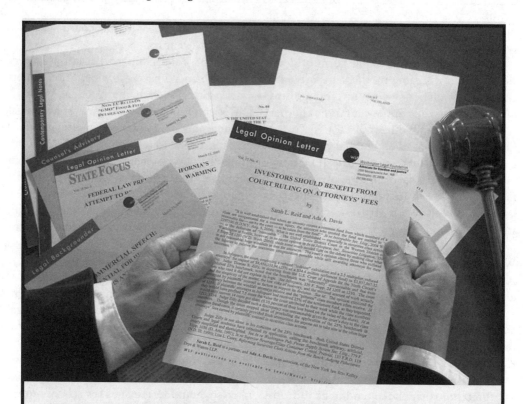

curiae is Latin for "friend of the court." An amicus curiae brief consists of written arguments submitted to the court in support of one of the two sides in a case. A group needs permission from one of the parties or the court in order to file an amicus brief, but, in general, most parties are happy to have additional groups join it in a judicial case, since numbers may show broad-based support for its claims. It has become a commonplace strategy to file amicus curiae briefs. In Supreme Court cases, the percentage of cases in which an amicus curiae brief is filed has risen steadily from around 20 percent to around 90 percent in recent years (Collins 2007, 61). About a third of interest groups appear to sponsor litigation and slightly more file amicus briefs (Walker 1983). Interest group litigation has boomed in recent decades for many reasons; one of the most important seems to be the willingness of foundations to fund such strategies by interest groups on both the left and the right (Berry 1984, 11).

A class action lawsuit allows a large group of "similarly situated" plaintiffs to combine similar suits into a single suit to bring to the courts for action. Among the most significant such suits were *Brown v. Board of Education*, which desegregated public schools and *Roe v. Wade*, which permitted abortion. As David Berger, one of the lawyers who frequently uses class action suits, has noted, "The class action is the greatest, most effective legal engine to remedy mass wrongs" (quoted in Martin 1988). In recent years, the federal courts have made such suits more difficult to file with new requirements that have increased the expense and time needed to qualify such suits. Some courts even require each person in a class (say, consumers who bought a certain product) to be notified and asked for permission to be represented in court. The Reagan administration was particularly hostile to class actions suits, and the number of such cases in federal courts dropped significantly in the late 1980s.

The range of groups that use the courts to advance their political agenda is quite broad.

They have expanded far beyond the traditional sponsors of business and labor and a few civil rights groups to thousands of new groups representing nearly every interest in society in one form or another. Whereas conservatives may complain about activist liberal courts undermining the traditional powers of the legislative and executive branches, liberal groups complain about conservative judicial activism when policy outcomes tend to undermine their political goals. As the third branch of government, the courts are clearly major actors in the policy process. They have always been political actors, as they make political choices that can benefit one group more than another.

A new interest entered the judicial lobbying game in the late 1980s. Led by fundamentalist Christian law firms such as Liberty Counsel, Becket Fund for Religious Liberty, the American Center for Law and Justice (ACLJ), the American Family Association Law Center, the Christian Legal Society Center for Law and Religious Freedom, the Rutherford Institute, and the Western Center for Law and Religious Freedom, Christian views have been presented in a wide variety of suits on issues. Some of these Christian litigating law firms came out of the anti-abortion movement and other moral crusades of our era. Some are sponsored by major political actors such as the ACLJ, which is the legal arm of Pat Robertson's Christian Coalition. Christian law firms began with amicus briefs and later sponsored their own suits, which reached the Supreme Court. Among the victories they have won are decisions on issues of abortion protests, rights of student religious groups to meet on school campuses, and financial aid for students in religious schools. One of the these Christian public law firms largely funded Paula Jones's civil lawsuit against President Clinton, which produced the presidential testimony that formed the basis of many of the impeachment charges against Bill Clinton.

When does it make sense for an interest group to choose judicial lobbying? Almost any group may participate in indirect lobbying (amicus briefs and opinion formation efforts) because the costs are low. Far fewer groups have the resources to do direct judicial lobbying. When judicial lobbying is combined with other traditional forms of lobbying to make a "total issue war campaign," the number of groups that have those resources is smaller still. For years, judicial lobbying was the last resort of groups that had lost in the traditional arenas of politics. Recently, many interest groups think of judicial lobbying as their first tactic in a particular political situations. Thus, judicial lobbying may be the last tactic of the weak; it can also be the first tactic of the strong and powerful.

Conclusion: The Persistence of Lobbying and the Nature of American Politics

Some thought that the change in political power from the Republicans to the Democrats in January 2007 would usher in a new era of honest and transparent lobbying in Washington, DC. Although some Democrats appeared to be sincere in their desire to reform the lobbying process, the actions of many of the senior Democratic congressional leaders indicated that they had learned some techniques of money raising from their Republican counterparts. The lobbying business boomed in 2007. The number of new register lobbyists doubled from 1,222 in the first four months of 2006 to 2,232 in the comparable period in 2007. Hundreds of lobbying firms added Democratic lobbyists to deal with the new Democratic power in the Congress. Major lobbying firms tripled the number of new clients in 2007 compared to 2006. Even major Republican firms like Barbour Griffith and Rogers saw their lobbying business rise as clients needed Republican support in their new minority roles in both houses of Congress (Birnbaum 2007).

The lobbyist is the most visible participant in lobbying campaigns. He or she is the representative of the interest as it contacts elected and appointed representatives with the group's political requests or demands. The strategies and tactics of direct lobbying are many, but they usually begin with the creation of access. After access is established, the key weapon is information in the forms of data or opinion. But no matter how skilled the individual lobbyist, his or her prospects for lobbying success depend on the resources of the group or groups behind the lobbyist.

We have discussed interest groups, organizations, and lobbyists in the context of campaigns and the process of governance. We have defined campaigns very broadly in this book to include the traditional campaigns of parties, candidates, issues, lobbying, and initiative and referendum elections. In terms of their functions, both political parties and interest groups provide communications between the American public and their government. These communications, which may be from the top down or the bottom up, are the essential glue that makes democracy work.

Contemporary American politics may be characterized as an era of the perpetual campaign. Parties and candidates are engaged in the constant fund-raising, organizational staffing, and message testing that characterize modern campaigns. What has changed more recently is the adoption of these strategies, tactics, and techniques from the world of political parties to the world of issue advocacy and issue campaigns. The event that brought the world of issue advocacy to our collective attention was the Clinton health care reform defeat of 1994 and the presidential election campaigns that followed. For the first time in American politics, we can reasonably discuss parties, candidates, and interest groups within the same context of modern political campaigns. What was once a fragmented series of events has become a much more synthesized phenomenon of political campaigning in its various guises.

Campbell and Davidson have described the location of political parties "at the center of extensive and distinctive networks of interest groups" (1998, 135). They noted that the ties between parties and interest groups are complex and symbiotic, based on policy decisions in exchange for money and campaign support. They concluded that when people vote for a political party, they are also selecting a collection of interest groups and their policy preferences as well. When one or another of these party-interest group coalitions triumphs, the policy process can be radically altered. New policies and new laws are written, often by the interest groups for their newly empowered party representatives, and the campaign cycle opens up a new phase as the defeated party and its interest group allies reorganize to recapture power in upcoming issue and election campaigns. It is an unending cycle of parties, interest groups, and campaigns. We invite the reader to follow in the media upcoming episodes in this exciting political process.

Conclusion

The New Style of American Politics

Campaigns of many types have come to dominate American politics as never before. Each year, thousands of interest groups and both major political parties are deeply involved in a never-ending series of issue campaigns in Washington, DC, and in state capitals across the nation. Every two years, and in off years as well, thousands of candidate campaigns are waged in primaries and general elections in each of the fifty states. Increasingly, the major parties are being joined in these campaigns by a growing number of powerful, well-financed interest groups seeking to influence the outcomes of these candidate campaigns. Also, a variety of interest groups are heavily involved in initiative and referendum campaigns in the states that provide for this form of direct democracy. From the process of getting a proposition on the ballot to campaigning for or against, a number of interest groups have attempted to use these initiative items as yet another way to try to influence public policy. In some years, such issue-ratification campaigns have sometimes eclipsed the office-filling campaigns being contested in the same elections.

In this book, we have explored the overlapping worlds of political parties and interest groups in modern political campaigns. Of course, political parties and interest groups have long been a part of our electoral campaigns and our legislatures, attempting to influence the outcome of public policy

debates. Throughout our history, Congress and state legislatures have passed laws, and bureaucracies have filled in the "details" to put these laws into action. Which laws got passed was often the product of how each party had fared in the last election, and which details got filled in has often been influenced by the efforts of interest groups. While that picture is still true of American politics generally, it is also the case that political parties and interest groups are much more visibly engaged in the process of hammering out the nation's political agenda through an ongoing process of public campaigning.

Over the last several decades, there has been an increase in the frequency and the intensity of the overlap between parties and interest group activities in an era of permanent campaigning. Political consultants, who used to work on campaigns only part of the year or just a couple of months every other year, now move from one election campaign to another and fill the rest of the year with lobbying, coalition building, and grassroots campaigns. Interest groups are today more prominently involved in candidate elections and in their own efforts at issue advocacy, with millions of dollars going to issue advocacy and independent expenditures. These permanent campaigns can be terribly expensive. Lobbying in Washington, DC, alone is a $2.5 billion a year activity. Grassroots lobbying costs are unknown because they are unreported on the federal level, but for every dollar spent in traditional lobbying in the nation's capital, another dollar is probably spent on indirect lobbying.

To illustrate the reach of the new style of campaign politics, consider the 2005 off-year elections in California. In November 2005, California voters went to the polls to vote in a special election called by Governor Arnold Schwarzenegger, who prior to becoming governor was perhaps best known as a body builder and action movie star. On the 2005 ballot were eight propositions, three that proposed to amend the California constitution and five to create new laws. Several of these initiative items were part of a "reform agenda" proposed by Governor Schwarzenegger, a Republican, after he was unable to get the state legislature, controlled by Democrats, to pass his proposals. The centerpiece of Schwarzenegger's agenda was a proposal, Proposition 76, to strengthen the governor's control over the state budget and limit future spending growth. The governor also supported an initiative, Proposition 77, to shift the power to draw legislative districts away from the state legislature to a nonpartisan panel of retired judges. The governor also endorsed two other ballot items: Proposition 74 would increase the length of time before newly hired public school teachers could become permanent employees and thus make it easier for teachers to be fired, and Proposition 75 would make it more difficult for public employee unions to use their membership dues for political purposes. In addition to the propositions pushed by the governor, there were four other initiatives on the ballot. One item concerned parental notification for minors seeking an abortion, a proposal to regulate to the state's electricity market, and two proposals to modify the state's prescription drug costs, with one ballot item pushed by consumer groups and the other by the drug industry.

Governor Schwarzenegger began the process with a high approval rating and intended to use his popularity with voters to circumvent what he regarded as an obstructionist legislature and entrenched special interests, but in the end none of his initiatives passed (Weintraub 2006). The reason that the proposals did not pass was largely because they attracted strong opposition from groups that were equally adept as the governor was in battling it out in an election campaign. Each of the governor's proposed reforms was opposed by well-funded interests. More than forty different organizations spent more than $317 million on the eight ballot propositions. More than $220 million was spent on just the four initiatives pushed by Governor Schwarzenegger, with initiative opponents spending nearly $149 million to the $73 million spent by supporters (Furillo 2006). The California Teachers Association and public employee unions were perhaps the most vocal and visible opponents of one or more of the initiatives. But the election was not just about interest groups, as the California Democratic party spent millions opposing Schwarzenegger's initiatives, and the California Republican party spent millions in support (Furillo 2005). Even though the defeat of all his ballot propositions was a serious setback for Governor Schwarzenegger, he was able to reestablish a working relationship with state legislators and was reelected governor in 2006.

The New Nature of American Political Parties

In this book we suggested that it is useful to analyze the parties by examining party organization and how parties have changed over time. We identified four eras of American political party organization and function: (1) parties as elite caucuses (1796–1828), (2) parties as mass organizations (1840–1900), (3) parties as products of state law (1900–1960), and (4) parties as candidate service organizations (1960–present). The era of service organizations is the most important one for understanding the role and function of parties in contemporary American politics and government.

Today's parties have weathered serious challenges from campaign consultants and for-profit campaign service providers to emerge as a resource for candidates seeking public office. We are not saying that parties have defeated their private sector rivals in the field of campaign services. Far from it; parties have learned to coexist with their private sector rivals, provide some of the same services, and be competitive in certain types of political environments. The parties have even survived the recent changes in federal campaign finance laws ending the flow of large soft money contributions to the parties.

Of course, change is inevitable, in politics and in American society more generally. Today's political campaigns, in all the different arenas we have discussed in this book, are a mixture of old styles and new technologies. Candidates, parties, and interest groups have all become quite adept at using new communications technology to get their message out to citizens, voters, and especially to political activists. Yet, the personal touch remains important to politics. Efforts to mobilize voters work best when there is personalized contact. A telephone call intended to get a person out to vote works best when it is made close to election day and in person; "robo-calls" and mass emails simply have less impact. And, the importance of the personal touch is true for candidates, political parties, or interest groups.

Today's parties and their organizations can offer a prospective candidate for public office several tangible benefits or advantages. First, a party has a nomination to offer, and that places the candidate on the general election ballot in a limited, two-person competition. As we noted earlier, the parties have largely lost their monopoly to nominate the candidates the party leadership may prefer. The rise of primary elections in the twentieth century has taken away the selection function of the parties and has given it to the voters and the individual candidates. Parties, however, retain the nomination labels and their access to the ballot. Second, parties have developed a range of campaign services, including media production skills and polling as well as many other services that they can offer their candidates at prices below those charged by the private sector. Third, the most important benefit parties can offer is money. Campaign fundraising is a very tough job. Most candidates hate this part of modern politics, but as campaigns get more and more expensive additional effort has to be put into fund-raising. Even lower-level campaigns are getting expensive. In a state that demands media-intensive campaigning, such as California, the average cost of running for the state assembly is more than $300,000 and more than $450,000 for the state senate. Even in states with less expensive media markets, the cost of campaigning for a state legislative seat can easily be in the $75,000 to $100,000 range.

Party organizations in the United States appear to be hierarchical, powerful structures. They are not. What appears to be a solid pyramid is really a loose collection of relatively independent and often quite weak organizations that periodically come together at election time but often fail to coordinate their various activities effectively. But this is not necessarily bad. This loose structure offers the advantage of maximum flexibility and adaptability, which has allowed parties to change and adapt to different political environments over time. Their most recent adaptation has been the conversion of party organizations into "service organizations," which currently is the most significant function that parties play in political campaigns.

The New Nature of American Interest Group Politics

Interest groups are significant actors in a wide variety of American political campaigns. They have come to exert a greater influence in campaigns because they are better organized and have greater resources than before.

They use these resources to access the skills and techniques of modern political campaigns to try to achieve their policy objectives. Interest group campaigns used to be characterized by the traditional lobbyist and his appeals for support in legislative chambers in the states and in Washington, DC. But in today's politics, interest campaigns are often indistinguishable from those run by political parties or candidates for public office. Interest groups have already demonstrated not only that they will lobby in Washington or the state capitals to try to influence sitting legislators, but that they will spend freely in candidate campaigns to try to influence who gets elected and in advocacy campaigns to try to influence citizens directly on matters of public policy. Interest groups are using all the technology of modern political communications (Internet, fax, direct mail, as well as advertising in all media) and, like the political parties, are increasingly able to pinpoint their message to reach precise segments of the nation's population. Powerful grassroots lobby efforts may cost millions of dollars, but if groups are successful at enacting (or stopping) policy, it might well mean billions of dollars to them.

Interest group politics and campaigns have changed in important ways in the past several decades. As political scientist Allan Cigler (2007, 208) notes,

The pattern of group involvement in elections changed markedly beginning in the late 1960s and early 1970s. . . . By 2000,

there had been an impressive increase in the breadth and intensity of group involvement in electoral politics. This escalation of activity was accompanied by a huge rise in the amount of funds devoted to electoral purposes, often independent of party and candidate campaigns.

During this time, interest groups have formed thousands of political action committees, with the largest and most active of these committees pouring tens of millions of dollars into both candidate and issue campaigns. Loopholes in the political finance laws have given interest groups the legal ability to become "major players" in any campaign they wish to influence. In the 1990s, soft money contributions to the political parties was one path to try to exert additional influence. When that avenue was stopped after the passage of the Bipartisan Campaign Reform Act in 2002, the action shifted to the 527 groups as a preferred way to spend money. Finally, we should note that the range of interest group campaigns is much broader than it was just a few decades ago. Many groups are active on the state and federal levels, in traditional face-to-face lobbying campaigns by professional lobbyists, in grassroots efforts, in media campaigns, in direct democracy efforts in those states which permit initiatives and referenda, and, increasingly, in candidate-centered campaigns. We anticipate new developments in the coming years as parties and interest groups compete to influence our campaigns and our public policies.

Glossary

American National Election Studies: A series of academic surveys conducted in every presidential election year since 1952 as well as in congressional election years since 1954. The National Election Studies provide nationally representative data on individuals for a range of demographic and attitudinal variables related to voting.

Amicus curiae brief: A legal paper submitted to a court by an outside party acting as a "friend of the court." Filing an amicus brief is a common way for an interest group to express its position on a legal case with public policy implications.

Bipartisan Campaign Reform Act of 2002 (BCRA): Federal legislation that banned political parties from accepting soft money contributions as well as making other changes in federal campaign finance laws. BRCA is commonly referred to as "McCain-Feingold" after the chief sponsors of the legislation in the Senate.

Cadre party: A term used to describe a type of political party that lacks a large, popular membership and instead is organized by a relatively small group of activists. Contemporary American political parties are generally considered to be cadre parties.

Candidate image: A term used to describe how individuals evaluate presidential candidates according to the attributes they believe the candidate exhibits such as being a moral person or a caring person. The evaluation of a candidate's image is part of the process of deciding how to vote.

Congressional campaign committee (CCC): An organization created by members of Congress to raise and spend campaign funds to assist candidates for Congress based on party (Democrat or Republican) and legislative body (House or Senate).

Convention bounce: The difference in a presidential candidate's intended vote before and after the party's nominating convention.

Direct primary: The system used in most American states in which the party's nominees for office are selected directly by eligible voters rather than being selected only by party members. In most states, primary elections are conducted as either closed primaries (meaning that voters must be registered as party supporters prior to voting) or open primaries (meaning that any otherwise eligible voter may decide to vote in a party's primary contest).

Electoral college: The constitutional process used to elect the U.S. president. To win election, a presidential candidate needs a majority of electoral college votes (at least 270 of the 538 total electoral votes). Each state has a number of electors equal to its number of

U.S. senators and members of the House of Representatives. The Twenty-third Amendment provides for electors for the District of Columbia.

Elite caucus: A term used to describe political party organizations early in U.S. history. These parties served to organize members of Congress and the executive and other elite political leaders but did not have mass organizations.

Exit poll: A type of election survey that is conducted by interviewing a sample of individual voters as they leave their polling location. National and state exit polls are often conducted by media organizations in presidential elections.

Federal Election Commission (FEC): A federal agency established in 1975 to administer and enforce the Federal Election Campaign Act (FECA). The FEC also collects and disseminates information on federal campaign contributions and spending by candidates, PACs, and political parties.

527 group: A term used to describe political organizations that spend money separately from a political party or a candidate's campaign organization The number 527 is a reference to the section number of federal tax law that defines political organizations. Technically, a large number of political groups fall under the provisions of section 527 but the term is usually used to describe groups that are not subject to the same legal restrictions as PACs so long as they do not advocate the election or defeat of a candidate or coordinate activities with the election campaigns of candidates or parties.

Hard money: Contributions from individuals or PACs to the campaign for a candidate for federal office that are subject to the limits of federal campaign finance laws. (See also soft money.)

Initiative and referendum (I&R) campaign: A term for campaigns conducted by interest groups using either an initiative or a referendum to try to change public policy in a state. Not every state allows for the use of an initiative or referendum.

Issue position: A term used to describe how individuals evaluate the position of presidential candidates on political issues. Along with partisan identification and candidate image, issue positions are an influence on how a person decides to vote.

Judicial lobbying: A term for the efforts of an interest group seeking to influence public policy through the court system. Judicial lobbying may involve the use of law suits as well as efforts to try to influence the selection of judges.

Legislative campaign committee (LCC): An organization created by state legislators to raise and spend campaign funds for candidates of a particular party and legislative body. (See also Congressional campaign committees.)

Lobbying: A term for a wide range of activities by interest groups intended to influence public policy. Most lobbying activities are directed at influencing the actions of legislatures or the executive agencies either directly or indirectly.

Mass party organization: A term used to describe American party organizations after the 1840s when parties adapted to the role of mobilizing the growing number of voters by incorporating individual citizens into the party organization.

National committee: A national party organization led by the party chair and composed of representatives from the states and other constituencies. Each major U.S. political party has a national committee: the Democratic National

Committee (DNC) and the Republican National Committee (RNC).

National nominating convention: National meetings of party delegates held every four years to select a presidential nominee for the party and to establish the party platform. The national convention is also the ultimate authority for each of the major U.S. political parties.

Partisan identification (PID): A term for an individual's affective attachment to a political party. PID is an important factor in vote choice and often influences how an individual regards candidates and issues.

Party activists: People who take part in the activities of one of the political parties on a regular basis. Party activists are often distinguished based on whether they are motivated mostly by tangible benefits ("professional" activists) or by the appeal of a particular candidate or ideology ("amateur" activists).

Party machine: A term used to describe certain local, usually urban, party organizations that sought to win elections in order to provide its supporters with government jobs and other tangible benefits.

Party system: A term used in realignment theory to describe a pattern of competition between the major parties that is stable over the course of several national elections. The history of American political parties is often described as consisting of five party systems.

Plurality system: An electoral system that determines the winner of an election based on which candidate receives the most votes (i.e., a plurality) in the general election.

Political action committee (PAC): An organization defined by federal law that exists to raise money and contribute money to candidates and parties in federal elections. Under federal law, there are two types of PACs: segregated funds and nonconnected committees. Segregated funds are PACs administered by corporations, labor unions, or other interest groups that can solicit contributions only from individuals associated with the sponsoring group. Nonconnected committees are not sponsored by any specific organization and can solicit contributions from members of the general public.

Political consultant: A person who is employed either by a candidate, party, or interest group to work on a campaign. Consultants are often employed to provide specific services such as conducting polls, creating an advertising strategy, organizing fundraising, or conducting issue research.

Presidential primary: An election held in a state to select delegates for each party's national nominating convention. When and how a presidential primary will be conducted in a given state is a result of both state law and the rules of national political parties.

Primary election: An initial election that selects the candidates who will compete in the general election. The function of a primary election may be fulfilled either by a direct primary or by the caucus/convention method.

Proportional representation (PR): An electoral system that attempts to have a political party's level of support among voters reflected in the party's seats in the legislative body.

Realignment: A term used to describe a change in election patterns. The theory of electoral realignments posits that party competition is usually stable over a series of elections but that change may occur in a realigning election that creates a new and enduring pattern of party competition.

Reformed party organization: A term used to describe U.S. political parties after the reforms of the Progressive era increased government regulation of party activities and limited the power of party bosses to control government patronage.

Service party organization: A term for the type of political party in the contemporary period in the United States. The term comes from the fact that the party organization functions largely to provide services for its elected officials and candidates.

Socioeconomic status (SES): A term for the differences in social standing among individuals. In the United States, SES is an important predictor of political participation.

Soft money: Contributions made to political parties for the purposes of conducting "party-building activities." Such contributions were not subject to regulation by federal campaign finance laws prior to 2004. The Bipartisan Campaign Reform Act of 2002 prohibited the political parties from accepting soft money contributions. (See also hard money.)

Vote choice: The decision by an individual citizen about which candidate to vote for.

Voter turnout: A term used to describe both whether or not an individual decides to vote in a particular election as well as the general extent of voting by eligible citizens in an election.

References

Abramowitz, Alan. 2004. "When Good Forecasts Go Bad: The Time-For-Change Model and the 2004 Presidential Election." *PS: Political Science and Politics* 37 (4): 745–746.

Abramowitz, Alan, John McGlennon, and Ronald Rapoport. 1981. "A Note on Strategic Voting in a Primary Election." *Journal of Politics* 43 (3): 899–904.

Abramson, Paul R. 1983. *Political Attitudes in America*. San Francisco: Freeman.

Abramson, Paul R., and John H. Aldrich. 1982. "The Decline of Electoral Participation in America." *American Political Science Review* 76 (3): 502–521.

Abramson, Paul R., John Aldrich, and David W. Rohde. 2007. *Change and Continuity in the 2004 and 2006 Elections*. Washington, DC: CQ Press.

Abramson, Paul R., and William Claggett. 2001. "Recruitment and Political Participation." *Political Research Quarterly* 54 (4): 905–916.

ACIR. 1986. *The Transformation of American Politics*. Washington, DC: Advisory Commission on Intergovernmental Relations.

Adamy, David. 1984. "Political Parties in the 1980s." In Michael J. Malbin, ed. *Money and Politics in the United States*. Washington, DC: American Enterprise Institute.

Aisenbrey, Margaret P. 2006. "Party On: The Right to Voluntary Blanket Primaries." *Michigan Law Review* 105: 603–629.

Aldrich, John H. 1995. *Why Parties? The Origin and Transformation of Political Parties in America*. Chicago: University of Chicago Press.

———. 2000. "Southern Parties in State and Nation." *Journal of Politics* 62 (3): 643–670.

Aldrich, John H., John L. Sullivan, and Eugene Borgida. 1989. "Foreign Affairs and Issue Voting: Do Presidential Candidates 'Waltz Before a Blind Audience.'" *American Political Science Review* 83 (1): 123–141.

Allen, Oliver E. 1993. *The Tiger*. Reading, MA: Addison-Wesley.

Almond, Gabriel, and Sidney Verba. 1963. *The Civic Culture*. Boston: Little, Brown.

Althaus, Scott L. 2007. "Free Falls, High Dives, and the Future of Democratic Accountability." In Doris Graber, Denis McQuail, and Pippa Norris, eds. *The Politics of News*. 2nd ed. Washington, DC: CQ Press.

Anderson, Ed. 2007. "Feds OK Return to Closed Primaries." *Times-Picayune*, January 25.

Anderson, Kristi. 1979. *The Creation of a Democratic Majority, 1928–1936*. Chicago: University of Chicago Press.

Ansolabehere, Stephan, and Shanto Iyengar. 1995. *Going Negative*. New York: Free Press.

Ansolabehere, Stephan, Shanto Iyengar, Adam Simon, and Nicholas Valentino. 1994. "Does Attack Advertising Demobilize the Electorate?" *American Political Science Review* 88 (4): 829–838.

Baer, Denise. 1995. "Contemporary Strategy and Agenda Setting." In James A. Thurber and Candice J. Nelson, eds. *Campaigns and Elections American Style*. Boulder, CO: Westview.

Bai, Matt. 2006. "The Inside Agitator." *New York Times Magazine*, October 1, 54–94.

Balch, George I. 1974. "Multiple Indicators in Survey Research: The Concept 'Sense of Political Efficacy.'" *Political Methodology* 1 (1): 1–43.

Barber, James David. 1965. *The Lawmakers.* New Haven, CT: Yale University Press.

Barnes, James A. 1995. "Privatizing Politics." *National Journal,* August 15, 1330–1334.

Barnes, Robert. 2007. "Justices Reconsider Campaign Finance: Some Are Skeptical of Earlier Ruling." *Washington Post,* April 26.

Barnes, Robert, and Matthew Mosk. 2007. "Justices to Consider Finance Law Limits." *Washington Post,* April 25.

Barone, Michael, and Richard E. Cohen. 2005. *Almanac of American Politics.* Washington, DC: National Journal.

Bartels, Larry M. 1985. "Resource Allocation in Presidential Campaigns." *Journal of Politics* 47 (3): 928–936.

———. 2002. "The Impact of Candidate Traits in American Presidential Elections." In Anthony King, ed. *Leaders' Personalities and the Outcomes of Democratic Elections.* New York: Oxford University Press.

Baumgartner, Jody. 2000. *Modern Presidential Electioneering: An Organizational and Comparative Approach.* Westport, CT: Praeger.

Beck, Paul Allen. 1977. "The Role of Agents in Political Socialization." In Stanley A. Renshon, ed. *Handbook of Political Socialization.* New York: Free Press.

———. 1979. "The Electoral Cycle and the Pattern of American Politics." *British Journal of Political Science* 9 (2): 129–156.

Beck, Paul Allen, and M. Kent Jennings. 1982. "Pathways to Participation." *American Political Science Review* 76 (1): 94–108.

Becker, Lee B., and Sharon Dunwoody. 1982. "Media Use, Public Affairs Knowledge and Voting in a Local Election." *Journalism Quarterly* 59 (2): 212–218.

Beeman, Richard. 1994. "Republicanism and the First Party System." In L. Sandy Maisel and William G. Shade, eds. *Parties and Politics in American History.* New York: Garland.

Bell, Lauren Cohen. 2002. *Warring Factions: Interest Groups, Money, and the New Politics of Senate Confirmation.* Columbus, OH: Ohio State University Press.

Bergan, Daniel E., Alan S. Gerber, Donald P. Green, and Costas Panagopoulos. 2005. "Grassroots Mobilization and Voter Turnout in 2004." *Public Opinion Quarterly* 69 (5): 760–777.

Bennett, Stephan E. 2002. "Americans' Exposure to Political Talk Radio and Their Knowledge of Public Affairs." *Journal of Broadcasting and Electronic Media* 48 (1): 72–86.

Benson, Miles. 2003. "'Demzilla' and 'Voter Vault' Are Watching You." *Newhouse News Service.* Available at: newhouse.live.advance.net.

Bentley, Arthur. 1949. *The Process of Government.* Bloomington, IN: Principia.

Berelson, Bernard, Paul F. Lazarsfeld, and William N. McPhee. 1954. *Voting.* Chicago: University of Chicago Press.

Berke, Richard L. 1995. "The 'Contract' Gets New Ally on the Right." *New York Times,* January 18.

Berns, Walter, ed. 1992. *After the People Vote.* Washington, DC: AEI Press.

Bernstein, Robert, Anita Chadha, and Robert Montjoy. 2004. "Overreporting Voting: Why it Happens and Why it Matters." *Public Opinion Quarterly* 65 (1): 22–44.

Berry, Jeffrey M. 1977. *Lobbying for the People.* Princeton, NJ: Princeton University Press.

———. 1984. *The Interest Group Society.* Boston: Little, Brown.

Bibby, John F. 2002. "State Party Organizations: Strengthened and Adapting to Candidate-Centered Politics and Nationalization." In L. Sandy Maisel, ed. *The Parties Respond.* 4th ed. Boulder, CO: Westview.

"Big Oil's Big Windfall." 2006. *New York Times,* March 28.

Bimber, Bruce. 2003. *Information and American Democracy.* New York: Cambridge University Press.

Bimber, Bruce, and Richard Davis. 2003. *Campaigning Online.* New York: Oxford University Press.

Birnbaum, Jeffrey. 2007. "Seeking Influence: Democratic Lobbying Firms Profit from the Power Shift in Congress, but so do Republicans." *Washington Post National Weekly Edition,* April 30–May 6.

Black, Earl, and Merle Black. 2002. *The Rise of Southern Republicans.* Cambridge, MA: Harvard University Press.

Black, Gordon S. 1972. "A Theory of Political Ambition: Career Choices and the Role of Structural Incentives." *American Political Science Review* 66 (1): 144–159.

Bledsoe, Timothy, and Mary Herring. 1990. "Victims of Circumstances: Women in Pursuit of Political Office." *American Political Science Review* 64 (1): 213–223.

Blum, John Morton. 1991. *Years of Discord: American Politics and Society, 1961–1974.* New York: Norton.

Blumer, Herbert. 1951. "Social Movements." In A. M. Lee, ed. *Principles of Sociology.* New York: Barnes and Noble.

Bowers, Andy. 2007. "Grading Bush's Speech: Our Video Focus Group Rates the Surge." *Slate.* January 11. Available at: slate.com.

Boyce, John R. 2000. "Interest Group Competition Over Policy Outcomes: Dynamics, Strategic Behavior, and Social Costs." *Public Choice* 102 (3–4): 313–339.

Brady, Henry E., Sidney Verba, and Kay Lehman Schlozman. 1995. "Beyond SES: A Resource Model of Political Participation." *American Political Science Review* 89 (2): 271–286.

Briffault, Richard. 2005. "The 527 Problem. . . . And the *Buckley* Problem." *George Washington Law Review* 73: 1701–1758.

Broder, David. 1972. *The Party's Over.* New York: Harper and Row.

———. 1995. "The Big Politics of Small Business." *Washington Post,* November 5.

Brookings Institution. 2001. "Recent Developments in Campaign Finance Regulation: Section 527 Organizations." February 28. Available at: brookings.edu.

Brosnahan, John. 2006. "House to Big House; 4 Members to be Behind Bars." *Roll Call,* September 20.

Brown, Robert D., and Justin Wedeking. 2006. "People Who Have Their Tickets But Do Not Use Them: 'Motor Voter,' Registration, Turnout Revisited." *American Politics Research* 34 (4): 479–504.

Browning, Graeme. 1994. "Zapping the Capital." *National Journal,* October 22, 2446–2450.

Buckley v. Valeo. 1976. 424 US 1.

Burnham, Walter Dean. 1970. *Critical Elections and the Mainsprings of American Politics.* New York: Norton.

———. 1987. "The Turnout Problem." In A. James Reichley, ed. *Elections American Style.* Washington, DC: Brookings.

Burrell, Barbara C. 1994. *A Woman's Place is in the House: Campaigning for Congress in the Feminist Era.* Ann Arbor, MI: University of Michigan.

Burt-Way, Barbara J., and Rita Mae Kelly. 1992. "Gender and Sustaining Political Ambition." *Western Political Quarterly* 45 (1): 11–25.

Butler, David, and Austin Ranney. 1994. *Referendums Around the World.* Washington, DC: AEI Press.

California Democratic Party v. Jones. 2000. 530 US 567.

Campaign Finance Institute. 2003. "Participation, Competition, Engagement: How to Revive and Improve Public Funding for Presidential Nomination Politics." Washington, DC: Campaign Finance Institute. Available at: cfinst.org.

———. 2005. "So the Voters May Choose . . . Reviving the Presidential Matching Fund System." Washington, DC: Campaign Finance Institute. Available at: cfinst.org.

Campbell, Angus, Phillip E. Converse, Warren E. Miller, and Donald E. Stokes. 1960. *The American Voter.* New York: Wiley.

Campbell, Colton C., and Roger H. Davidson. 1998. "Coalition Building in Congress." In Paul S. Herrnson, Ronald G. Shaiko, and Clyde Wilcox, eds., *The Interest Group Connection.* Chatham, NJ: Chatham House.

Campbell, James. 2000. *The American Campaign.* College Station, TX: Texas A & M University Press.

———. 2004. "Introduction—The 2004 Presidential Election Forecasts." *PS: Political Science and Politics* 37 (4): 733–735.

———. 2005. "Introduction—Assessments of the 2004 Presidential Vote Forecasts." *PS: Political Science and Politics* 38 (1): 23–24.

Cardwell, Diane, and Jennifer Steinhauer. 2007. "Bloomberg Severs GOP Ties, Fueling Talk of '08 Bid." *New York Times.* June 20.

Carmines, Edward G., and James A. Stimson. 1980. "The Two Faces of Issue Voting." *American Political Science Review* 74 (1): 78–91.

Carney, Eliza. 1996. "Defending PACs." *National Journal,* July 13, 1518–1523.

Carsey, Thomas M., John C. Green, Richard Herrera, and Geoffrey C. Layman. 2006. "State Party Context and Norms among Delegates to the 2000 National Party Conventions." *State Politics and Policy Quarterly* 6 (3): 247–271.

Caruso, Lisa. 2006. "High Stakes on Web Gambling." *National Journal,* May 13, 54–56.

Carville, James, and Mary Matalin. 1994. *All's Fair: Love, War and Running for President.* New York: Random House.

Center for Media and Democracy. 2007. "Push Poll." Available at: sourcewatch.org.

Center for Public Integrity. 2005. "Checkbook Politics." Press release. July 7.

———. 2006. "State Lobbying Becomes a Billion Dollar Business." Press release. December 20.

Center for Responsive Politics. 2003. "*McConnell v. FEC* Summary of the Supreme Court's Decision." December 10. Available at: fecwatch.org.

———. 2006. "Center Revised Prediction on Midterm Races from $2.6 Billion to $2.8 Billion." November 6. Available at: opensecrets.org.

———. 2007a. "Financiers, Along with Lawyers are Underwriting the Race for the White House." April 18. Available at: opensecrets.org.

———. 2007b. "Top Contributors to 527 Committees, 2006 Election Cycle." May 17. Available at: opensecrets.org.

Chaddock, Gail Russell. 2004. "Money Lessons from a Year on the Campaign." *Christian Science Monitor,* November 9.

———. 2006a. "In Campaigns' Last Hours, a Get-Out-the-Vote Contest." *Christian Science Monitor,* November 6.

———. 2006b. "Pssst. K Street Delivers the Goods—For a Price." *Christian Science Monitor,* August 8.

Chambers, William N. 1967. "Party Development and the American Mainstream." In William Nisbet Chambers and Walter Dean Burnham, eds. *The American Party Systems.* New York: Oxford University Press.

Chaney, Carol Kennedy, R. Michael Alvarez, and Jonathan Nagler. 1998. "Explaining the Gender Gap in U.S. Presidential Elections, 1980–1992." *Political Research Quarterly* 51 (2): 311–339.

Charles, Joseph. 1956. *The Origins of the American Party System.* Williamsburg, VA: Institute of Early American History and Culture.

Cigler, Allan J. 2007. "Interest Groups and Financing the 2004 Elections." In Allan J. Cigler and Burdett A. Loomis, eds. *Interest Group Politics.* Washington, DC: CQ Press.

Ciokajlo, Mickey, and Robert Becker. 2007. "Labor Wasn't Only Big Player in Runoffs." *Chicago Tribune,* April 22.

Clark, Janet, Charles D. Hadley, and R. Darcy. 1989. "Political Ambition Among Men and Women State Party Leaders: Testing the Countersocialization Perspective." *American Politics Quarterly* 17 (1): 194–207.

Clark, John A., John M. Bruce, John H. Kessel, and William Jacoby. 1991. "I'd Rather Switch Than Fight: Lifelong Democrats and Converts to Republicanism among Campaign Activists." *American Journal of Political Science* 35 (3): 577–597.

Clark, Peter B., and James Q. Wilson. 1961. "Incentive Systems: A Theory of Organizations." *Administrative Science Quarterly* 6 (3): 129–166.

Clines, Francis X. 1997. "Turning to State Campaign Overhauls as Models to Stir Up Congress." *New York Times,* April 6.

Clinton, Bill, and Al Gore. 1992. *Putting People First.* New York: Times Books.

"CNN Debunks False Report About Obama." 2007. January 23. Available at: cnn.com.

Cohen, Michael D. 2004. "Polls as the Key to Victory: When to Use Vulnerability, Benchmark and Tracking Polls." *Campaigns and Elections*, July, 35.

Collins, Jr., Paul M. 2007. "Lobbyists Before the US Supreme Court: Investigating the Influence of Amicus Curiae Briefs." *Political Research Quarterly* 60 (1): 55–70.

Colorado Republican Federal Campaign Committee v. Federal Election Commission. 1996. 518 US 604.

Common Cause. 2006. "527 Groups." August. Available at: commoncause.org.

Congressional Quarterly. 1985. *Congressional Quarterly's Guide to US Elections.* 2nd ed. Washington, DC: Congressional Quarterly Press.

Constantini, Edmond. 1990. "Political Women and Political Ambition: Closing the Gender Gap." *American Journal of Political Science* 34 (3): 741–770.

Continetti, Matthew. 2006. *The K Street Gang: The Rise and Fall of the Republican Machine.* New York: Doubleday.

Cooperman, Alan, and Thomas Edsall. 2006. "Christian Coalition Shrinks as Debt Grows." *Washington Post,* April 10.

Corrado, Anthony. 1992. *Creative Campaigning.* Boulder, CO: Westview.

———. 1997. "Financing the 1996 Elections." In Gerald Pomper, et al. *The Election of 1996.* Chatham, NJ: Chatham House.

———. 2006. "Financing the 2004 Presidential General Election." In David Magelby, Anthony Corrado, and Kelly Patterson, eds., *Financing the 2004 Election.* Washington, DC: Brookings Institution Press.

Cotter, Cornelius P., James L. Gibson, John F. Bibby, and Robert J. Huckshorn. 1984. *Party Organizations in American Politics.* New York: Praeger.

Council of State Governments. 2004. *The Book of the States.* Vol. 36. Lexington, KY: Council of State Governments.

Craig, Steven C., and Michael A. Maggiotto. 1992. "Measuring Political Efficacy." *Political Methodology* 8: 85–109.

Crotty, William. 1994. "Urban Political Machines." In L. Sandy Maisel and William G. Shade, eds. *Parties and Politics in American History.* New York: Garland.

Crotty, William, ed. 1986. *Political Parties in Local Areas.* Knoxville, TN: University of Tennessee Press.

Cundy, Donald T. 1986. "Political Commercials and Candidate Image: The Effect Can Be Substantial." In Lynda Lee Kaid, Dan Nimmo, and Keith Sanders, eds. *New Perspectives on Political Advertising.* Carbondale, IL: Southern Illinois University Press.

Dahl, Robert. 1961. *Who Governs?* New Haven, CT: Yale University Press.

Damore, David F. 2004. "The Dynamics of Issue Ownership in Presidential Campaigns." *Political Research Quarterly* 57 (3): 391–397.

Damore, David F., and Thomas G. Hansford. 1999. "The Allocation of Party Controlled Campaign Resources in the House of Representatives, 1986–1996." *Political Research Quarterly* 52 (2): 371–385.

de Tocqueville, Alexis. [1835–1839] 1956. *Democracy in America.* New York: Mentor.

Devlin, Patrick L. 2005a. "Analysis of Presidential Primary Campaign Commercials of 2004." *Communication Quarterly* 53 (4): 451–471.

———. 2005b. "Contrasts in Presidential Campaign Commercials of 2004." *American Behavioral Scientist* 49 (2): 279–313.

Dexter, Lewis. 1969. *How Organizations Are Represented in Washington.* Indianapolis, IN: Bobbs-Merrill.

Dobson, Debra L. 1990. "Socialization of Party Activists: National Convention Delegates, 1972–1981." *American Journal of Political Science* 34 (4): 1119–1141.

Donovan, Beth. 1993. "Much Maligned 'Soft Money' Is Precious to Both Parties." *Congressional Quarterly Weekly Report,* May 15, 1195–1198.

Doppelt, Jack, and Ellen Shearer. 1999. *Nonvoters: America's No-Shows.* Thousand Oaks, CA: Sage.

———. 2001. "America's No-Shows." Available at: yvoteonline.org.

Duverger, Maurice. 1963. *Political Parties.* New York: Wiley.

Dwyre, Diana. 1996. "Spinning Straw into Gold: Soft Money and U.S. House Elections." *Legislative Studies Quarterly* 20 (3): 409–424.

Eckholm, Erik. 1995. "The Dark Science Of Fund-Raising by Mail." *New York Times,* May 28.

Elving, Ronald D. 1996. "Accentuate the Negative: Contemporary Congressional Campaigns." *PS: Political Science and Politics* 29 (3): 440–445.

Encyclopedia of Associations. 1996. Detroit, MI: Gale Research.

Epstein, Leon D. 1986. *Political Parties in the American Mold.* Madison, WI: University of Wisconsin Press.

Erikson, Robert S., and Kent L. Tedin. 1981. "The 1928–1936 Partisan Realignment: The Case for the Conversion Hypothesis." *American Political Science Review* 75 (4): 951–963.

Eu v. San Francisco County Democratic Central Committee. 1989. 489 US 214.

Evans, Diana. 1988. "Oil PACs and Aggressive Contribution Strategies." *Journal of Politics* 50 (4): 1047–1056.

Faucheux, Ron. 1993. "How to Win in '94." *Campaigns and Elections,* September, 21–28.

Federal Election Commission. 2005. "The Federal Election Commission Thirty Year Report." September. Washington, DC: Federal Election Commission. Available at: fec.gov.

———. 2006. "National Party Financial Activity Summarized." Press release, October 30. Washington, DC: Federal Election Commission. Available at: fec.gov.

———. 2007a. "Party Financial Activity Summarized for the 2006 Election Cycle." March 7. Washington, DC: Federal Election Commission. Available at: fec.gov.

———. 2007b. "Presidential Spending Limits If the Elections Were Held in 2007." Washington, DC: Federal Election Commission. Available at: fec.gov.

Federal Election Commission v. Wisconsin Right to Life. 2007. No. 06–609.

Feuer, Benjamin S. 2006. "Between Political Speech and Cold, Hard Cash: Evaluating the FEC's New Regulations for 527 Groups."

Northwestern University Law Review 100 (2): 925–965.

Finkel, Steven E., and John G. Geer. 1998. "A Spot Check: Casting Doubt on the Demobilizing Effect of Attack Advertising." *American Journal of Political Science* 42 (2): 573–595.

Fishkin, James. 1995. *The Voice of the People.* New Haven, CT: Yale University Press.

Fitzgerald, Mary. 2005. "Greater Convenience But Not Greater Turnout: The Impact of Alternative Voting Methods on Electoral Participation in the United States." *American Politics Research* 33 (6): 842–867.

Foster v. Love. 1997. 522 US 67.

Foster, Robin. 1985. "Business PAC Aims for Big Time." *Orlando Sentinel,* September 8.

Fowler, Linda L., and Robert D. McClure. 1989. *Political Ambition: Who Decides to Run for Congress?* New Haven, CT: Yale University Press.

Fowlkes, Diane. 1984. "Ambitious Political Women: Counter Socialization and Political Party Context." *Women and Politics* 4 (1): 5–32.

Fowlkes, Diane, Jerry Perkins, and Sue Tolleson Rinehart. 1979. "Gender Roles and Party Roles." *American Political Science Review* 73 (3): 772–780.

Fox, Richard L., and Jennifer L. Lawless. 2004. "Entering the Arena? Gender and the Decision to Run for Office." *American Journal of Political Science* 48 (2): 264–280.

———. 2005. "To Run or Not to Run: Explaining Nascent Political Ambition." *American Journal of Political Science* 49 (3): 642–659.

Franklin, Mark N. 2004. *Voter Turnout and the Dynamics of Electoral Competition in Established Democracies Since 1945.* New York: Cambridge University Press.

Freeman, Jo. 1983. *Social Movements of the Sixties and Seventies.* New York: Longman.

Frendeis, John P., James L. Gibson, and Laura L. Vertz. 1990. "The Electoral Relevance of Local Party Organizations." *American Political Science Review* 84 (1): 225–235.

Furillo, Andy. 2005. "Parties' Tab: $9 Million." *Sacramento Bee,* November 6.

———. 2006. "For the Ballot, Money Matters." *Sacramento Bee*, February 4.

Gais, Thomas, Mark A. Peterson, and Jack Walker, 1984. "Interest Groups, Iron Triangles, and Representative Institutions in American National Government." *British Journal of Political Science* 14 (1): 161–186.

Gamarekian, Barbara. 1983. "The No. 2 Game: Tennis Everyone?" *New York Times,* May 14.

Gamson, William A. 1974. "Violence and Political Power: The Meek Don't Make It." *Psychology Today*, July, 35–41.

———. 1990. *The Strategy of Social Protest.* Belmont, CA: Wadsworth.

Garfield, Bob. 2004. "Kerry Serves Up Cacophony Of Indecision, Missed Shots." *Advertising Age,* September 13, 53.

Geer, John G. 2006. *In Defense of Negativity: Attack Ads in Presidential Campaigns.* Chicago: University of Chicago Press.

Georgia. 2006. *Official Code of Georgia Annotated.* Section 21-2-111.

Gerber, Alan S., and Donald P. Green. 2000. "The Effects of Personal Canvassing, Telephone Calls, and Direct Mail on Voter Turnout: A Field Experiment." *American Political Science Review* 94 (3): 653–663.

Gerber, Alan S, Donald P. Green, and M. Green. 2003. "Partisan Mail and Voter Turnout: Results From Randomized Field Experiments." *Electoral Studies* 22 (4): 563–597.

Gerber, Alan S., Dean Karlan, and Daniel Bergan. 2007. "Does the Media Matter? A Field Experiment Measuring the Effect of Newspapers on Voting Behavior and Political Opinions." Unpublished paper. Available at: fieldexperiments.com.

Gershtenson, Joseph. 2003. "Mobilization Strategies of the Democrats and Republicans, 1956–2000." *Political Research Quarterly* 56 (3): 293–308.

Gertner, Jon. 2004. "The Very, Very Personal is the Political." *New York Times Magazine.* February 15, 42–47.

Gibson, James L., Cornelius P. Cotter, John F. Bibby, and Robert J. Huckshorn. 1986. "Whither the Local Parties? A Cross-Sectional and Longitudinal Analysis of the Strength of Party Organizations." *American Journal of Political Science* 29 (1): 139–160.

Gibson, James L., John P. Frendeis, and Laura L. Vertz. 1989. "Party Dynamics in the 1980s: Change in County Party Organizational Strength, 1980–1984." *American Journal of Political Science* 33 (1): 67–90.

Gienapp, William E. 1987. *The Origins of the Republican Party, 1852–1856.* New York: Oxford University Press.

———. 1994. "Formation of the Republican Party." In L. Sandy Maisel and William G. Shade, eds. *Parties and Politics in American History.* New York: Garland.

Gierzynski, Anthony. 1992. *Legislative Party Campaign Committees in the American States.* Lexington, KY: University Press of Kentucky.

Gimpel, James G. 1998. "Grassroots Organizations and Equilibrium Cycles in Group Mobilization and Access." In Paul S. Herrnson, Ronald G. Shaiko, and Clyde Wilcox, eds. *The Interest Group Connection.* Chatham, NJ: Chatham House.

Glennon, Michael J. 1992. *When No Majority Rules: The Electoral College and Presidential Succession.* Washington, DC: CQ Press.

Glover, Ronald. 2004. "The Heavyweight on Latin American Airwaves." *Business Week,* August 9.

Goldman, Ralph M. 1990. *The National Party Chairmen and Committees.* Armonk, NY: Sharpe.

Goldstein, Kenneth, and Travis Ridout. 2002. "The Politics of Participation: Mobilization and Turnout over Time." *Political Behavior* 24 (1): 3–29.

Gopoian, J. David. 1993. "Images and Issues in the 1988 Presidential Election." *Journal of Politics* 55 (1): 151–166.

Graber, Doris A. 1989. *The Mass Media and American Politics.* 3d ed. Washington, DC: CQ Press.

Grady, Sandy. 1997. "Chinese Money Buys the Superstars." *Salt Lake Tribune,* March 20.

Green, Donald P., and Alan S. Gerber. 2005. "Recent Advances in the Science of Voter

Mobilization." *Annals of the American Academy of Political and Social Science* 601 (September): 6–9.

Green, Donald P., Bradley Palmquist, and Eric Schickler. 2002. *Partisan Hearts and Minds*. New Haven, CT: Yale University Press.

Greenhouse, Linda. 2007. "Justices Raise Doubts on Campaign Finance." *New York Times*, April 26.

Greenhouse, Steven. 2007. "Sharp Decline in Union Membership in '06." *New York Times*, January 26.

Grimaldi, James V. and Thomas B. Edsall. 2004. "Super Rich Step into Political Vacuum; McCain-Feingold Paved Way for 527s." *Washington Post*, October 17.

Gronbeck, Bruce E. 1987. "Functions of Presidential Campaigns." In L. Patrick Devlin, ed. *Political Persuasion in Presidential Campaigns*. New Brunswick, N.J.: Transaction.

Hall, Donald. 1969. *Cooperative Lobbying*. Tucson, AZ: University of Arizona Press.

Hansen, John Mark. 1985. "The Political Economy of Group Membership." *American Political Science Review* 79 (1): 79–96.

Hardy, Bruce W., and Dietram A. Scheufele. 2005. "Examining Differential Gains from Internet Use: Comparing the Moderating Role of Talk and Online Interactions." *Journal of Communication* 55 (1) March. 71–84.

Hayes, Danny. 2005. "Candidate Qualities through a Partisan Lens: A Theory of Trait Ownership." *American Journal of Political Science* 49 (4): 908–923.

Hayward, Allison R., and Bradley A. Smith. 2005. "Don't Shoot the Messenger: The FEC, 527 Groups, and the Scope of Administrative Authority." *Election Law Journal* 4 (2): 82–104.

Hedlun, Ronald D., and Meredith W. Watts. 1986. "The Wisconsin Open Primary, 1968 to 1984." *American Politics Quarterly* 14 (2): 55–73.

Herrera, Richard. 1995. "The Crosswinds of Change: Sources of Change in the Democratic and Republican Parties." *Political Research Quarterly* 48 (2): 291–312.

Herrnson, Paul S. 1988. *Party Campaigning in the 1980s*. Cambridge, MA: Harvard University Press.

———. 1990. "Reemergent National Party Organizations." In L. Sandy Maisel, ed. *The Parties Respond*. Boulder, CO: Westview.

———. 2000. 3rd ed. *Congressional Elections*. Washington, DC: CQ Press.

Hertzgaard, Mark. 1988. *On Bended Knee*. New York: Farrar, Strauss, and Giroux.

Hertzke, Allen D. 1993. *Echoes of Discontent*. Washington, DC: CQ Press.

Hill, David, and Seth C. McKee. 2005. "The Electoral College, Mobilization, and Turnout in the 2000 Presidential Election." *American Politics Research* 33 (5): 700–725.

Hill, Kevin A., and John E. Huges, 1998. *Cyberpolitics*. Lanham, MD: Rowman and Littlefield.

"Hillary's Team Has Questions About Obama's Muslim Background." 2007. *Insight*, January 16–22. Available at: insightmag.com .

Hillygus, D. Sunshine, and Simon Jackman. 2003. "Voter Decision Making in Election 2000: Campaign Effects, Partisan Activation, and the Clinton Legacy." *American Journal of Political Science* 47 (4): 583–596.

Hindman, Matthew. 2005. "The Real Lessons of Howard Dean: Reflections on the First Digital Campaign." *Perspectives on Politics* 3 (1): 121–128.

Hoadley, John F. 1986. *Origins of American Political Parties, 1789–1803*. Lexington, KY: University Press of Kentucky.

Hofstadter, Richard. 1969. *The Idea of a Party System*. Berkeley, CA: University of California Press.

Hofstetter, C. Richard. 1998. "Political Talk Radio, Situational Involvement, and Political Mobilization." *Social Science Quarterly* 79 (2): 273–286.

Hofstetter, C. Richard, David Barker, James T. Smith, Gina M. Zari and Thomas A. Ingrassia. 1999. "Information, Misinformation, and Political Talk Radio." *Political Research Quarterly* 52 (2): 353–369.

Hogan, Robert E. 2002. "Candidate Perceptions of Political Party Campaign Activity in State

Legislative Elections." *State Politics and Policy Quarterly* 2 (1): 66–85.

———. 2005. "State Campaign Finance Laws and Interest Group Electioneering Activities." *Journal of Politics* 67 (3): 887–906.

Holbrook, Thomas M., and Scott D. McClurg. 2005. "The Mobilization of Core Supporters: Campaigns, Turnout, and Electoral Composition in the United States Presidential Elections." *American Journal of Political Science* 49 (4): 689–703.

Holder, Kelly. 2006. "Voting and Registration in the Election of November 2004." Current Population Reports P20–556. Washington, DC: U.S. Census Bureau.

Holian, David B. 2004. "He's Stealing my Issues! Clinton's Crime Rhetoric and the Dynamics of Issue Ownership." *Political Behavior* 26 (2): 95–124.

Holman, Craig. 2007. "The Cleanest Congress in History?" May 7. Available at: tompaine.com.

Hrebenar, Ronald J., Kirk L. Jowers, and Audrey Perry. 2006. "The Struggle to Regulate the 527s: Through the FEC, Congress, and the Courts." *Nexus* 12: 97–117.

Hrebenar, Ronald J., and Clive S. Thomas, eds. 1987. *Interest Group Politics in the American West.* Salt Lake City, UT: University of Utah Press.

———. 1992a. *Interest Group Politics in the Northeastern States.* College Park, PA: Pennsylvania State University Press.

———. 1992b. *Interest Group Politics in the South.* Tuscaloosa, AL: University of Alabama Press.

———. 1993. *Interest Group Politics in the Midwest.* Ames, IA: Iowa State University Press.

Huckshorn, Robert J. 1976. *Party Leadership in the States.* Amherst, MA: University of Massachusetts Press.

———. 1991. "State Party Leaders." In L. Sandy Maisel, ed. *Political Parties and Elections in the United States.* New York: Garland.

Hudson, William E. 2006. *American Democracy in Peril.* 5th ed. Washington, DC: CQ Press.

Huff, Nathan. 2003. "*Landell v. Sorrell*: Lessons Learned From Vermont's Pending Challenge to *Buckley v. Valeo*." *Catholic University Law Review* 53: 239–265.

Huffington, Ariana. 2007. "I Made the 'Vote Different' Ad." *The Huffington Post.* March 21. Available at: huffingtonpost.com.

Jackson, Brooks. 1997. "Financing the 1996 Campaign: The Law of the Jungle." In Larry Sabato, ed. *Toward the Millennium.* Boston: Allyn and Bacon.

Jennings, M. Kent, and Richard G. Niemi. 1981. *Generations and Politics.* Princeton, NJ: Princeton University Press.

Johnson, Glen. 2000. "'Push Poll' Angers McCain; Bush Denies Backing Negative Tactic." *Chicago Sun-Times,* February 11.

Johnson, Haynes, and David Broder. 1996. *The System.* Boston: Little, Brown.

Johnson, Peter. 2007. "Web Becomes Source—Not Outlet—for News." *USA Today,* March 26.

Johnson, Victoria K. 1984. "Good Letters from Public Find Their Capitol Hill Targets." *Salt Lake Tribune,* February 12.

Johnson-Cartee, Karen S., and Gary A. Copeland. 1991. *Negative Political Advertising.* Hillsdale, NJ: Erlbaum.

Kahn, Kim Fridkin, and Patrick J. Kenny. 1999. "Do Negative Campaigns Mobilize or Suppress Turnout? Clarifying the Relationship between Negativity and Participation." *American Political Science Review* 93 (4): 877–889.

Kaiser, Robert G. 2007a. "Inventing the Earmark." *Washington Post,* April 5.

———. 2007b. "The Power Player: How the Rise of One Lobbying Firm Helped Transform the Way Washington Works." *Washington Post,* March 4.

Kamarck, Elaine C. 2006. "Assessing Howard Dean's Fifty State Strategy and the 2006 Midterm Elections." *The Forum* 4 (3): Article 5. Available at: bepress.com/forum/vol4/iss3/art5.

Kaplan, Jonathon E. 2006. "Jack is Back $300M with Ad Campaign." *The Hill,* February 28.

Kaufmann, Karen M., James G. Gimpel, and Adam H. Hoffman. 2003. "A Promise Fulfilled? Open Primaries and Representation." *Journal of Politics* 65 (2): 457–476.

Kaufmann, Karen M., and John R. Petrocik. 1999. "The Changing Politics of American Men: Understanding the Sources of the Gender Gap." *American Journal of Political Science* 43 (3): 864–887.

Keeter, Scott. 1987. "The Illusion of Intimacy: Television and the Role of Candidate Personal Qualities in Voter Choice." *Public Opinion Quarterly* 51 (3): 344–358.

Keleher, Alison G. 1996. "Political Parties, Interest Groups, and Soft Money: Does the Money Flow Both Ways?" Paper presented at the Western Political Science Association Meeting, San Francisco.

Kern, Montague. 1989. *Thirty-Second Politics.* New York: Praeger.

Key, V. O. 1955. "A Theory of Critical Elections." *Journal of Politics* 17 (1): 3–18.

———. 1959. "Secular Realignment and the Party System." *Journal of Politics* 21 (2): 198–210.

Kirkpatick, David G. 2006. "Trading Votes For Pork Across the House Aisle." *New York Times*, October 2.

Kleppner, Paul. 1987. *Continuity and Change in Electoral Politics, 1893–1928.* Westport, CT: Greenwood.

Kolbert, Elizabeth. 1992. "Low Tolerance for Political Commercials? Just Count to 10." *New York Times,* May 30.

Kolodny, Robin. 1998. *Pursuing Majorities: Congressional Campaign Committees in American Politics.* Norman, OK: University of Oklahoma Press.

Ladd, Everett Carll. 1970. *American Political Parties.* New York: Norton.

———. 1991. "Like Waiting for Godot: The Uselessness of 'Realignment' for Understanding Change in Contemporary American Politics." In Byron E. Shafer, ed. *The End of Realignment? Interpreting American Electoral Eras.* Madison, WI: University of Wisconsin Press.

Larson, Bruce. 2004. "Incumbent Contributions to the Congressional Campaign Committees, 1990–2000." *Political Research Quarterly* 57 (1): 155–161.

Latham, Earl. 1952. *The Group Basis of Politics.* Ithaca, NY: Cornell University Press.

Lau, Richard R., Lee Sigelman, Caroline Heldman, and Paul Babbitt. 1999. "The Effects of Negative Political Advertisements: A Meta-Analytic Assessment." *American Political Science Review* 93 (4): 851–875.

Laurence, Robert P. 1996. "TV Viewers, Koppel Bored with GOP's Infomercial." *San Diego Union-Tribune*, 14 August, Republican Convention Supplement.

Lawless, Jennifer L., and Richard L. Fox. 2005. *It Takes a Candidate: Why Women Don't Run for Office.* New York: Cambridge University Press.

Lazarsfeld, Paul F., Bernard Berelson, and Hazel Gaudet. 1948. *The People's Choice.* New York: Columbia University Press.

Lefkowitz, Joel. 2004. "Mobilization Matters: The Changing Impact of Mobilization on Vote Choice in Congressional Elections, 1978–2002." *Congress and the Presidency* 31 (2): 119–131.

Lieberman, David. 2006. "Elections Rake in Big Bucks for Media Outlets." *USA Today* November 2.

Lijphart, Arend. 1990. "The Political Consequences of Electoral Laws, 1945–85." *American Political Science Review* 84 (2): 481–496.

———. 1994. *Electoral Systems and Party Systems.* New York: Oxford University Press.

Lockard, Duane, and Walter F. Murphy. 1980. *Basic Cases in Constitutional Law.* New York: Macmillan.

Lublin, David, and Sarah E. Brewer. 2003. "The Continuing Dominance of Traditional Gender Roles in Southern Elections." *Social Science Quarterly* 84 (2)379–396.

Luntz, Frank. 1988. *Candidates, Consultants and Campaigns.* Oxford: Blackwell.

McCarthy, Aoife. 2007."D'Amato Hits the Jackpot." *Politico*, March 5. Available at: politico.com.

McConnell v. Federal Elections Commission. 2003. 540 US 93.

McDonald, Michael P. 2007. United States Election Project. Available at: elections.gmu.edu/.

McDonald, Michael P., and Samuel L. Popkin. 2001. "The Myth of the Vanishing Voter." *American Political Science Review* 95 (4): 963–974.

McKitrick, Eric L. 1967. "Party Politics and the Union and Confederate War Efforts." In William Nisbet Chambers and Walter Dean Burnham, eds. *The American Party Systems.* New York: Oxford University Press.

Madison, James. 1948. In Charles A. Beard, ed. *The Enduring Federalist.* New York: Garden City Book.

Magleby, David B. 1998. "Ballot Initiatives and Intergovernmental Relations." Paper presented at the Western Political Science Association Meeting, Los Angeles.

Malbin, Michael J. 2004. "Political Parties Under the Post-McConnell Bipartisan Campaign Reform Act." *Election Law Journal* 3 (2), 177–191.

———. 2006. "A Public Funding System in Jeopardy: Lessons from the Presidential Nomination Contest of 2004." In Michael Malbin ed., *The Election After Reform: Money, Politics, and the Bipartisan Campaign Reform Act.* Lanham, MD: Rowman and Littlefield.

Malbin, Michael J., and Sean A. Cain. 2007. "The Ups and Downs of Small and Large Donors: An Analysis of Pre- and Post BCRA Contributions to Federal Parties and Candidates, 1999–2006." Washington, DC: Campaign Finance Institute. Available at: cfinst.org.

Marcus, Ruth. 1998. "The Advocates Pare Down the Ads." *Washington Post,* October 23.

Marinucci, Carla. 2007. "'Hillary 1984': Unauthorized Internet Ad for Obama Converts Apple Computer's '84 Super Bowl Spot Into a Generational Howl Against Clinton's Presidential Bid." *San Francisco Chronicle.* March 18.

Markus, Gregory B., and Philip E. Converse. 1979. "A Dynamic Simultaneous Equation Model of Electoral Choice." *American Political Science Review* 73 (4): 1055–1070.

Martin, Douglas. 1988. "The Rise and Fall of Class-action Lawsuits." *New York Times,* January 8.

Martinez, Michael D., and Tad Delegal. 1990. "The Irrelevance of Negative Campaigns to Political Trust: Experimental and Survey Results." *Political Communication and Persuasion* 7 (1): 25–40.

Matthews, Donald R. 1960. *US Senators and Their World.* Chapel Hill, NC: University of North Carolina Press.

Mayhew, David R. 1986. *Placing Parties in American Politics.* Princeton, NJ: Princeton University Press.

———. 2002. *Electoral Realignments.* New Haven, CT: Yale University Press.

Mead, Walter B. 1987. *The United States Constitution.* Columbia, SC: University of South Carolina Press.

Medvic, Stephen K., and Silvo Lenart. 1997. "The Influence of Political Consultants in Congressional Campaigns." *Legislative Studies Quarterly* 22 (1): 61–77.

Merkle, Daniel M. 1996. "The National Issues Convention Deliberative Poll." *Public Opinion Quarterly* 60 (4): 588–619.

Mesrobian, Shant. 2004. "Covering the Bases." *Campaigns and Elections,* February, 18.

Michel, Robert. 1962. *Political Parties.* New York: Free Press.

Mihalopoulos, Dan. 2007. "16th Ward a Battlefield in Labor's Fight For City." *Chicago Tribune,* April 14.

Mihalopoulos, Dan, and Rick Pearson. 2007. "Unions Score Key Victories in Council." *Chicago Tribune,* April 18.

Milbrath, Lester. 1963. *The Washington Lobbyists.* Chicago: Rand McNally.

Miller, Warren E. 1992. "The Puzzle Transformed: Explaining Declining Turnout." *Political Behavior* 14 (1): 1–40.

Miller, Warren E., and M. Kent Jennings. 1986. *Parties in Transition.* New York: Russell Sage Foundation.

Miller, Warren E., and J. Merrill Shanks. 1996. *The New American Voter.* Cambridge, MA: Harvard University Press.

Milligan, Susan. 2007. "States May Force Megaprimary, Winnow the 2008 Field Early." *Boston Globe,* March 6.

Mills, C. Wright. 1956. *The Power Elite*. New York: Oxford University Press.

Mitchell, Alison. 1997. "Clinton Pressed Plan to Reward Donors." *New York Times,* February 26.

Morin, Richard. 1996. "Bouncing Along with the Bounce." *Washington Post National Weekly Edition,* August 26.

Morison, Samuel Eliot. 1965. *The Oxford History of the American People: 1789 Through Reconstruction*. Vol. 2. New York: Mentor.

Mushkat, Jerome. 1971. *Tammany*. Syracuse, NY: Syracuse University Press.

Mutch, Robert E. 1988. *Campaigns, Congress, and the Courts: The Making of Federal Campaign Finance Law*. New York: Praeger.

Nagler, Jonathan. 1991. "The Effect of Registration Laws and Education on U.S. Voter Turnout." *American Political Science Review* 85 (4): 1393–1405.

Napolitan, Joseph. 1971. "Zeroing in on the Voter." In Ray Hiebert, Robert Jones, John Lorenz, and Ernest Lotito, eds. *The Political Image Merchants*. Washington, DC: Acropolis.

"A Nation." 1995. *Washington Post National Weekly Edition,* July 7.

Nickerson, David W. 2006. "Volunteer Phone Calls Can Increase Turnout: Evidence from Eight Field Experiments." *American Politics Research* 34 (3): 271–292.

———. 2007. "Quality is Job One: Professional and Volunteer Voter Mobilization Calls." *American Journal of Political Science* 51 (2): 269–282.

Nimmo, Dan. 1970. *The Political Persuaders*. Englewood Cliffs, N.J.: Prentice-Hall.

Nimmo, Dan, and Robert L. Savage. 1976. *Candidates and Their Images*. Pacific Palisades, CA: Goodyear.

Nokken, Timothy P. 2003. "Ideological Congruence versus Electoral Success: Distribution of Party Organization Contributions in Senate Elections, 1990–2000." *American Politics Research* 31 (1): 3–26.

Norris, Pippa. 2004. *Electoral Engineering: Voting Rules and Political Behavior*. New York: Cambridge University Press.

O'Conner, Karen, Alicandra Yanus, and Linda Mancillas Patterson. 2007. "Where Have All the Interest Groups Gone? An Analysis of Interest Group Participation in Presidential Nominations to the Supreme Court of the United States." In Allan J. Cigler and Burdett A. Loomis, eds. *Interest Group Politics*. Washington, DC: CQ Press.

O'Connor, Patrick. 2006. "Anti-Immigration Groups Up Against Unusual Coalition." *The Hill,* February 28.

Ohio. 2006. *Ohio Revised Code*. Title 35, Elections.

O'Leary, Brad. 1994. "Fire Power." *Campaigns and Elections,* December, 32–35.

Olson, Mancur. 1965. *The Logic of Collective Action*. Cambridge, MA: Harvard University Press.

"Opponents of Health-Care Reform Spent $60 Million on Lobbying." 1998. *Salt Lake Tribune,* November 28.

Ornstein, Norman J. 2007. "The House That Jack Built." *New York Times,* January 14.

Owens, Diana. 1997. "The Press' Performance." In Larry J. Sabato, ed. *Toward the Millennium*. Boston: Allyn and Bacon.

Patterson, Kelly D. 2006. "Spending in the 2004 Election." In David B. Magleby, Anthony Corrado, and Kelly D. Patterson, eds. *Financing the 2004 Election*. Washington, DC: Brookings Institution Press.

Paulson, Arthur. 2000. *Realignment and Party Revival*. Westport, CT: Praeger.

Pelling, Henry, and Alastair J. Reid. 1996. *A Short History of the Labour Party*. 11th ed. London: St. Martin's.

Petrocik, John R. 1996. "Issue Ownership in Presidential Elections, with a 1980 Case Study." *American Journal of Political Science* 40 (3): 825–850.

Petrocik, John R., William L. Benoit, Glenn J. Hansen. 2003. "Issue Ownership and Presidential Campaigning, 1952–2000." *Political Science Quarterly* 118 (4): 599–626.

Pew Research Center for the People and the Press. 2004. "News Audiences Increasingly Polarized." June 8. Available at: people-press.org.

———. 2006a. "Early October Turnout Survey." October 18. Available at: people-press.org.

———. 2006b. "Online Papers Modestly Boost Newspaper Readership." July 30. Available at: people-press.org.

———. 2006c. "Public Cheers Democratic Victory." November 16. Available at: people-press.org.

———. 2006d. "Public to '08 Contenders—It's Too Early." December 14. Available at: people-press.org.

———. 2007a. "Election 2006 Online." January 17. Available at: pewinternet.org.

———. 2007b. "Public Knowledge of Current Affairs Little Changed by News and Information Revolutions." April 15. Available at: people-press.org.

Pfau, Michael, and Henry C. Kenski. 1990. *Attack Politics.* New York: Praeger.

Phillips, Kate. 2007. "Group Reaches Settlement with FEC Over 2004 Campaign Advertising." *New York Times,* March 1.

Piven, Francis Fox, and Richard A. Cloward. 1977. *Political Power in Poor Neighborhoods.* New York: Pantheon.

Polsby, Nelson W. 1997. "Money Gains Access. So What?" *New York Times,* August 13.

Powell, G. Bingham. 1986. "American Voter Turnout in Comparative Perspective." *American Political Science Review* 80 (1): 17–43.

"President's Remarks on Rewards for Donors." 1997. *New York Times,* February 27.

"The Public Relations Industry: Do We Have a Story for You." 2006. *Economist,* January 21.

Public Citizen. 2002. "Déjà vu Soft Money: Outlawed Contributions Likely to Flow to Shadowy 527 Groups that Skirt Flawed Disclosure Law." April 9. Available at: citizen.org.

———. 2006. "The Bankrollers: Lobbyists' Payments to the Lawmakers They Court, 1998–2006." May 22. Available at: citizen.org.

Putnam, Robert B. 2000. *Bowling Alone: The Collapse and Revival of American Community.* New York: Simon and Schuster.

Rae, Douglas W. 1967. *The Political Consequences of Electoral Laws.* New Haven, CT: Yale University Press.

Randall v. Sorrell. 2006. 126 S Ct 2479.

Reichley, A. James. 1992. *The Life of the Parties.* New York: Free Press.

———. 1996. "The Future of the American Two-Party System after 1994." In John C. Green and Daniel M. Shea, eds. *The State of the Parties.* 2d ed. Lanham, MD: Rowman and Littlefield.

"Reno Says It's Legal to Sell Access." 1997. *Salt Lake Tribune,* October 8.

RePass, David E. 1971. "Issue Salience and Party Choice." *American Political Science Review* 65 (2): 389–400.

Republican National Committee. 2007. "2004 Proved It's All About the Grassroots." Available at: gop.com.

"Rights vs. Revenues." 1997. *Salt Lake Tribune,* November 1.

Romano, Lois. 2007. "Gatekeepers of Hillaryland." *Washington Post,* June 21.

Rosenbloom, David Lee. 1973. *The Election Men.* New York: Quadrangle Books.

Rosenof, Theodore. 2003. *Realignment.* Lanham, MD: Rowman and Littlefield.

Rosenstone, Steven J., and John Mark Hansen. 2003. *Mobilization, Participation and Democracy in America.* New York: Longman.

Rosenstone, Steven J., Roy L. Behr, and Edward Lazarus. 1996. *Third Parties in America.* 2d ed. Princeton, NJ: Princeton University Press.

Rosenthal, Cindy Simon. 1994. "Where's the Party?" *State Legislatures* 20 (6): 31–37.

———. 1995. "New Party or Campaign Bank Account? Explaining the Rise of State Legislative Campaign Committees." *Legislative Studies Quarterly* 20 (2): 249–268.

Rothmeyer, Karen. 1981. "Money in Politics." *Common Cause,* August 13–15.

Rusk, Jerrold G. 2001. *A Statistical History of the American Electorate.* Washington, DC: CQ Press.

Saad, Lydia. 1996. "Average Convention 'Bounce' Since 1964 Is Five Points." *Gallup Poll Monthly,* August, 8–9.

———. 2007. "Americans Prefer Presidential Candidates to Forgo Public Funding." *Gallup Poll News Service.* April 27.

Sabato, Larry J. 1981. *The Rise of the Political Consultants.* New York: Basic.

———. 1988. *The Party's Just Begun.* Glenview, IL: Scott, Foresman.

Safire, William. 1997. "Broadcast Lobby Triumphs." *New York Times,* July 23.

Salisbury, Robert. 1969. "An Exchange Theory of Interest Groups." *Midwest Journal of Political Science* 13 (1): 1–32.

———. 1986. "Washington Lobbyists: A Collective Portrait." In Allan J. Cigler and Burdette A. Loomis, eds. *Interest Group Politics.* Washington, DC: CQ Press.

Sapiro, Virginia. 1983. *The Political Integration of Women.* Urbana, IL: University of Illinois Press.

Sapiro, Virginia, and Barbara Farah. 1980. "New Pride and Old Prejudice: Political Ambitions and Role Orientations Among Female Partisan Elites." *Women and Politics* 1 (1): 13–36.

Schattschneider, E. E. 1942. *Party Government.* New York: Holt, Rinehart, and Winston.

———. 1975. *The Semi-Sovereign People.* Hinsdale, IL: Dryden.

Schlesinger, Joseph A. 1966. *Ambition and Politics.* Chicago: Rand McNally.

Schlozman, Kay Lehman, and John T. Tierney. 1986. *Organized Interests and American Democracy.* New York: Harper and Row.

Schmidt, Eric. 1996. "New Lobbying Rules, From Bagels to Caviar." *New York Times,* February 11.

Schmidt, Susan, and James V. Grimaldi. 2005. "The Fast Rise and Steep Fall of Jack Abramoff." *Washington Post,* December 29.

Schneider, Deborah E. 1999. "As Goes Maine? The 1996 Maine Clean Elections Act: Innovations and Implications for Future Campaign Finance Reforms at the State and National Level." *Journal of Urban and Contemporary Law* 55: 235–273.

Schwartz, Mildred A. 1990. *The Party Network.* Madison, WI: University of Wisconsin Press.

Schwartz, Tony. 1973. *The Responsive Chord.* Garden City, NY: Anchor.

———. 1985. *The Thirty Second President.* Alexandria, VA: PBS video.

Sciolino, Elaine. 1996. "China, Vying with Taiwan, Explores Public Relations." *New York Times,* February 2.

Shade, William G. 1994. "The Jacksonian Party System." In L. Sandy Maisel and William G.

Shade, eds. *Parties and Politics in American History.* New York: Garland.

Shah, Dhavan V., Jaeho Cho, William P. Eveland, and Nojin Kwak. 2005. "Information and Expression in a Digital Age: Modeling Internet Effects on Civic Participation." *Communication Research* 32 (5) 531–565.

Shays v. Federal Election Commission. 2004. 337 Federal Supplement 2nd 28.

———. 2005. 367 US Appellate DC 185.

Shea, Daniel M. 1995. *Transforming Democracy: Legislative Campaign Committees and Political Parties.* Albany, NY: State University of New York Press.

Shepard, Scott. 2007. "Democrats Praise Dean's Much-Criticized 50-State Strategy." *Austin American Statesman.* February 4.

Shouten, Fredreka. 2007. "Taxpayers Elect Not to Pay For Campaigns." *USA Today* April 18.

Shulte, Brigid, and Jodi Enda. 1997. "Cash Severs Ties as It Cuts Deals in DC." *Salt Lake Tribune,* January 13.

Shultz, David. 2006. "*Buckley v. Valeo, Randall v. Sorrell,* and the Future of Campaign Finance on the Roberts Court." *Nexus* 12: 153–176.

Sides, John, Jonathan Cohen, and Jack Citrin. 2002. "The Causes and Consequences of Crossover Voting in the 1998 California Elections." In Bruce E. Cain and Elisabeth R. Gerber, eds. *Voting at the Political Fault Line.* Berkeley, CA: University of California Press.

Sigelman, Lee, and Emmett H. Buell, Jr. 2004. "Avoidance or Engagement? Issue Coverage in U.S. Presidential Campaigns, 1960–2000." *American Journal of Political Science* 48 (4): 650–661.

Silbey, Joel H. 1991a. "Beyond Realignment and Realignment Theory: American Political Eras, 1789–1989." In Byron E. Shafer, ed. *The End of Realignment? Interpreting American Electoral Eras.* Madison, WI: University of Wisconsin Press.

Silbey, Joel H. 1991b. *The American Political Nation, 1838–1893.* Stanford, CA: Stanford University Press.

Silver, Brian, Barbara Anderson, and Paul Abramson. 1986. "Who Overreports Voting?"

American Political Science Review 80 (2): 613–624.

Simon, Stephanie. 2006. "Unregulated 527 Groups Put Millions in Election." *Los Angeles Times*, October 31.

Simpson, Dick W. 1996. *Winning Elections*. New York: HarperCollins.

Sorauf, Frank. 1992. *Inside Campaign Finance*. New Haven, CT: Yale University Press.

Squire, Peverill, Raymond E. Wolfinger, and David P. Glass. 1987. "Residential Mobility and Voter Turnout." *American Political Science Review* 81 (1): 45–65.

Stern, Philip. 1988. *The Best Congress Money Can Buy*. New York: Pantheon.

Stone, Peter H. 1993. "Called to Account." *National Journal,* July 17, 1810–1813.

———. 2006. *Heist: Superlobbyist Jack Abramoff, His Republican Allies, and the Buying of Washington*. New York: Farrar, Straus & Giroux.

Stone, Walter J., and Alan I. Abramowitz. 1983. "Winning May Not Be Everything, But It's More Than We Thought: Presidential Activists in 1980." *American Political Science Review* 77 (4): 945–956.

Stonecash, Jeffrey M. 2006. *Political Parties Matter: Realignment and the Return of Partisan Voting*. Boulder, CO: Lynne Rienner.

Strattman, Thomas. 1998. "The Market for Congressional Votes: Is Timing of Contributions Everything?" *Journal of Law and Economics* 41 (1): 85–113.

Sullivan, Ronald, and Eddie Glaude, Jr. 2007. "Rethinking the NAACP." *Washington Post National Weekly Edition,* March 26–April 1.

Sundquist, James L. 1983. *Dynamics of the Party System*. Rev. ed. Washington, DC: Brookings Institution.

Swinyard, William R., and Kenneth A. Coney. 1978. "Promotional Effects on a High Versus Low-involvement Electorate." *Journal of Consumer Research* 5 (2): 41–48.

Taagepera, Rein, and Matthew Soberg Shugart. 1989. *Seats and Votes*. New Haven, CT: Yale University Press.

Taibbi, Matt. 2006. "Meet Mr. Republican: Jack Abramoff." *Rolling Stone Magazine,* March 24.

Tashjian v. Republican Party of Connecticut. 1986. 479 US 208.

Tate, Katherine. 1991. "Black Political Participation in the 1984 and 1988 Presidential Elections." *American Political Science Review* 85 (4): 1159–1176.

Teixeira, Ruy A. 1992. *The Disappearing American Voter*. Washington, DC: Brookings Institution.

———. 1987. *Why Americans Don't Vote*. New York: Greenwood.

Thayer, George. 1973. *Who Shakes the Money Tree?* New York: Simon and Schuster.

Times Mirror Center for the People and the Press. 1992. "The People, the Press, and Politics in Campaign 92: The Generations Divide." Los Angeles: Times Mirror Center.

Toner, Michael, and Melissa Laurenza. 2007. "Emerging Campaign Finance Trends and Their Impact on the 2006 Midterm Elections." In Larry Sabato, ed. *The Six Year Itch: The Rise and Fall of the George W. Bush Presidency*. New York: Pearson-Longman.

Traugott, Michael W., and Paul J. Lavrakas. 2004. *The Voter's Guide to Election Polls*. 3rd ed. Lanham, MD: Rowman and Littlefield.

Truman, David. 1971. *The Governmental Process*. New York: Knopf.

Tynan, Daniel. 2004. "GOP Voter Vault Shipped Overseas." *PC World*. September 24. Available at: pcworld.com.

U.S. Census Bureau. 2005. *The Statistical Abstract of the United States, 2006*. Washington, DC: U.S. Government Printing Office.

Vaida, Bara. 2006. "Pots of Gold." *National Journal,* February 11, 24–32.

Varoga, Craig. 2001. "Benchmark Polls Direct Mail Color, Acquiring Campaign Finance Reports." *Campaigns and Elections*, July, 61.

Verba, Sidney, and Norman H. Nie. 1972. *Participation in America*. Chicago: University of Chicago Press.

Verba, Sidney, Norman H. Nie, and Jae-on Kim. 1978. *Participation and Political Equality*. New York: Cambridge University Press.

Verba, Sidney, Kay Lehman Schlozman, and Henry Brady. 1995. *Voice and Equality: Civic Voluntarism in American Politics*. Cambridge, MA: Harvard University Press.

Verba, Sidney, Kay Lehman Schlozman, Henry Brady, and Norman H. Nie. 1993. "Citizen Activity: Who Participates? What Do They Say?" *American Political Science Review* 87 (2): 303–318.

Victor, Kirk. 1995. "Labor's New Look." *National Journal,* October 14, 2522–2527.

Vogel, Kenneth. 2007a. "Gambling Industry Dealt a Good Hand in New Congress." *Politico,* January 30. Available at: politico.com.

———. 2007b. "Poker Players Put Chips on Entertainment Value." *Politico,* January 30. Available at: politico.com.

Vose, Clement. 1958. "Litigation as a Form of Pressure Group Activity." *Annals of the American Academy of Political and Social Science* 319 (1): 20–31.

Walker, Jack. 1983. "The Origins and Maintenance of Interest Groups in America." *American Political Science Review* 77 (2): 390–406.

Wallsten, Peter, and Tom Hamburger. 2006. "The GOP Knows You Don't Like Anchovies." *Los Angeles Times.* June 25.

Ware, Alan. 1996. *Political Parties and Party Systems.* New York: Oxford University Press.

Wattenberg, Martin. 1991. *The Rise of Candidate-Centered Elections.* Cambridge: Harvard University Press.

Wattenberg, Martin, and Craig Leonard Brians. 1999. "Negative Campaign Advertising: Demoblizer or Mobilizer?" *American Political Science Review* 93 (4): 891–899.

Wayne, Leslie. 1997a. "Congress Uses Leadership PACs to Wield Power." *New York Times,* March 13.

———. 1997b. "Gingrich in 98: Money Gushing Both In and Out." *New York Times,* August 13.

———. 1997c. "With GOP Chief a Lobbyist, Donors Are Clients." *New York Times,* June 8.

Weintraub, Daniel. 2006. "Schwarzenegger Rebuffed." *State Legislatures* 32 (1): 27–28.

Weisman, Jonathon, and Charles E. Babcock. 2006. "K Street's New Ways Spawn More Pork." *Washington Post,* January 27.

Wekkin, Gary D. 1991. "Why Crossover Voters Are Not 'Mischievous' Voters: The Segmented Partisanship Hypothesis." *American Politics Quarterly* 19 (2): 229–247.

West, Darrell M. 1997. *Air Wars.* Washington, DC: CQ Press.

Wielhouwer, Peter W. 2003. "In Search of Lincoln's Perfect List: Targeting in Grassroots Campaigns." *American Politics Research* 31 (6): 632–669.

Wielhouwer, Peter W., and Brad Lockerbie. 1994. "Party Contacting and Political Participation, 1952–1990." *American Journal of Political Science* 38 (1): 211–229.

Wildavsky, Aaron. 1965. "The Goldwater Phenomenon: Purists, Politicians, and the Two-Party System." *Review of Politics* 27 (3): 386–413.

Wilson, James Q. 1962. *The Amateur Democrat.* Chicago: University of Chicago Press.

———. 1995. *Political Organizations.* Princeton, NJ: Princeton University Press.

Wines, Michael. 1992. "Bush's Campaign Tries Madison Avenue." *New York Times,* May 27.

Wines, Michael, and Robert Pear. 1996. "President Finds Benefits In Defeat on Health Care." *New York Times,* July 30.

Wolff, Michael. 1989. "Say It Ain't So, Joe! Is Political Radio Dead?" *Campaigns and Elections,* October, 34.

Wolfinger, Raymond E., and Steven J. Rosenstone. 1980. *Who Votes?* New Haven, CT: Yale University Press.

Zuckman, Jill. 2007. "Clinton's Campaign Boss a Pioneer Too." *Chicago Tribune,* June 14.

Index